Is Academic Feminism Dead?

Theory in Practice

EDITED BY

*The Social Justice Group at The Center
for Advanced Feminist Studies,
University of Minnesota*

New York University Press

NEW YORK AND LONDON

NEW YORK UNIVERSITY PRESS
New York and London

Chapter 5 has been reprinted from Akhil Gupta and James Ferguson, eds., *Anthropological Locations: Boundaries and Grounds of a Field Science,* courtesy of the University of California Press. © 1997 The Regents of the University of California.

Chapter 13 has been reprinted from Joanna Kadi, *Thinking Class: Sketches from a Cultural Worker,* by permission of South End Press. © 1996.

Library of Congress Cataloging-in-Publication Data
Is academic feminism dead? : theory in practice / edited by
The Social Justice Group at The Center for Advanced
Feminist Studies, University of Minnesota.
      p.   cm.
Includes bibliographical references and index.
ISBN 0-8147-2705-0 (pbk. : alk. paper) —
ISBN 0-8147-2704-2 (cloth : alk. paper)
1. Feminist theory. 2. Feminism and education.
3. Women's studies.   I. University of Minnesota.
Social Justice Group. II. Title.
HQ1190 .I76 2000
305.42'01—dc21   00-009147

New York University Press books are printed on acid-free paper, and their binding materials are chosen for strength and durability.

Manufactured in the United States of America
10 9 8 7 6 5 4 3 2 1

Is Academic Feminism Dead?

Contents

Acknowledgments   *vii*

Introduction   *1*

PART I   Theory Binds: The Perils of Retrofit   5

1   Retrofit: Gender, Cultural, and Class Exclusions in
     American Studies   8
     VèVè A. Clark

2   Ethnocentrism/Essentialism: The Failure of the
     Ontological Cure   47
     Marilyn Frye

3   Maternal Presumption: The Personal Politics of
     Reproductive Rights   61
     Alice Adams

4   Sex, Gender, and Same-Sex Marriage   86
     Peggy Pascoe

PART II   Storytelling: Sites of Empowerment, Sites
          of Exploitation   131

5   The Virtual Anthropologist   137
     Kath Weston

6   How History Matters: Complicating the Categories
     of "Western" and "Non-Western" Feminisms   168
     Mrinalini Sinha

7   Bringing It All Home to the Bacon: A Ph.D.
     (Packinghouse Daughter) Examines Her Legacy   187
     Cheri Register

8   Blood Ties and Blasphemy: American Indian
    Women and the Problem of History   204
        Kathryn Shanley

9   Ella Que Tiene Jefes y No Los Ve, Se Queda en Cueros:
    Chicana Intellectuals (Re)Creating Revolution   233
        Edén E. Torres

PART III   Starting Here, Starting Now: Challenges
           to Academic Practices   261

10 Being Queer, Being Black: Living Out in
    Afro-American Studies   266
        Rhonda M. Williams

11 Learning to Think and Teach about Race and
    Gender despite Graduate School: Obstacles
    Women of Color Graduate Students Face
    in Sociology   283
        Mary Romero

12 Anger, Resentment, and the Place of Mind
    in Academia   311
        Diana L. Vélez

13 Stupidity "Deconstructed"   327
        Joanna Kadi

14 To Challenge Academic Individualism   347
        Sharon Doherty

    Editors and Contributors   375
    Index   ·381

Acknowledgments

This anthology was made possible by the generous support of the Rockefeller Foundation, which allowed us to bring many of the contributors to this collection to the University of Minnesota campus as visiting scholars and to hold the conference, Thinking, Writing, Teaching, and Creating Social Justice. We also are grateful for the support of the Center for Advanced Feminist Studies at the University of Minnesota. We further thank those individuals who contributed to this project at various stages in its development, including Asha Vaharajadan, Brit Abel, Melissa Buchard, Lisa Disch, David Zopfi-Jordan, and Lou Huckbody. A special thanks goes to Shannon Olson, who demonstrated in uncountable ways her dedication to this project as well as her editorial skills. We especially appreciate the many long hours she spent preparing the manuscript for publication. Finally, we thank the editorial staff at New York University Press, Despina Gimbel, Rosalie Morales Kearns, and Niko Pfund. We are grateful not only for their insights and extraordinary efforts, but also the kindness they showed us throughout the editing process.

Introduction

Feminist struggles for social justice—against inequality, exclusionary practices, political disenfranchisement, and economic exploitation—are struggles of theory and practice. So when activists took feminism into the university in the 1970s, our aim was to transform all three: theory, practice, and the university. Feminists challenged the tendency of those privileged by and in academia to claim knowledge while remaining indifferent to those they ignored or objectified. Today such willed ignorance is constantly challenged by feminists and others both inside and outside the university who refuse to place uncritical faith in conventional figures of authority, even (or especially) when we slide back into those old practices ourselves.

Scholars who do transgressive work look outside the university for new sources of knowledge and experience, but we need to do more than mine those sources for what they can contribute to our work. More than new "material," transgressive scholarship demands a widened community of knowers and knowledge producers and democratic critical engagement among them. This collection of essays is an effort to build such an exchange, in which, as María Lugones says, a crucial aspect of respectful engagement is regarding the other as a faithful mirror of the self—as giving back an image of oneself one has to take seriously—but also as someone with projects and engagements of her own.[1]

The collection includes authors who are differently located in their relationships to the university, not just "inside" or "outside." These writers highlight the ways the university perpetuates exclusionary practices: alienating working-class people and promoting a middle-class ethic, demanding too much of its faculty of color, and blocking attempts at learning social justice or at changing the system from within. These writers demonstrate the ways a commitment to social justice demands critical consciousness regarding one's location; the use of the personal voice demonstrates further the inseparability of the act of theorizing and the location of the theorizer. The different styles of thinking and writing in this collection—some essayistic and others more formal and what we think of as theoretical—reflect both the personal styles and the different locations of their authors.

Despite the fact that we are aware of the willingness of antifeminists to seize on moments of self-criticism and hurl them in our faces, we have included many essays that criticize aspects of feminism. To stifle criticism out of fear of antifeminist appropriation would be to confirm our critics' picture of feminism as monolithic. More important, especially when criticism comes from less privileged women, stifling criticism would be a profound abuse of privilege—as though a trapeze artist with the protection of a net (especially one acquired at others' expense) were to be no more ready to take risks than when she performed over the bare circus floor.

But these essays also question the naturalness of this image of the theorist as trapeze artist—high up and dazzling to those below, a picture of theory as providing an overview of our lives, more accurate and fuller because distanced and removed from the supposedly distorting details of the messy and mundane. Rather than taking us over the tangled complexities of our locations and connections, our theorizing needs to engage with them. Those of us in the academy need to learn how to theorize *with* those we have been trained to theorize *about*.

The essays here are an argument that theory needs to be neither grand nor totalizing. Criticism of universal claims about women are well taken, as are criticisms of the idea that theory develops according to its own logic and then gets applied in practice. The need for globally explanatory theories arises materially from the increasingly global interconnectedness of the structures of inequality. As Mrinalini Sinha's essay argues most directly, but nearly all the others do implicitly, it is not our *theories* that need to be articulated into a grand synthesis called global feminism: it is our *theorizing* that needs to be shaped by practices of responsibility for the effects of our actions, however far they radiate, as well as for our relationships to those on whom, because of our privilege, we are dependent. The challenge this book poses for feminists is to practice and develop different feminisms out of theories that are both locally, contextually articulated and globally responsible.

Our editorial work with each other and with the authors in this book has changed our relation to all the other work we do and altered its future directions. The aim of the collection has become not to settle the issues it raises, but rather to *unsettle,* to set up the lines of tension in energizing ways for readers, to be an intervention in this place and time. Some sort of intervention is clearly called for, since, if you believe what you read in the papers, feminism is either dead or deadly—or, confusingly, both: we are, apparently, the vampires of the political and intellectual scenes. Feminists are charged with the death of the family as a site of social stability, and with the death of the university as a site of objective knowledge production. At the same time, we are alleged to have succumbed to irrelevance: feminism is proclaimed dead with almost comical regularity. The essayists whose work you are about to read demonstrate amply that feminist critical engagement with the university and the rest of society, far from being either dead or deadly, is both vital and vitalizing.

NOTE

1. See María C. Lugones, "On the Logic of Pluralist Feminism," in *Feminist Ethics,* ed. Claudia Card (Lawrence: University Press of Kansas, 1991), 35–44.

Part I

Theory Binds
The Perils of Retrofit

Feminist change means reimagining and transforming institutions, and envisioning fuller and richer possibilities for social justice. Historically, feminists have sought equality, but our ultimate aims take us beyond it. We hope to change the culture of inequality, to create something different from the institutions out of which inequality grew. Any effort in this direction necessarily grows out of and engages with existing structures and social institutions. But it is not enough to patch up these faulty institutions and hope they will be strong and flexible enough to bear the weight of genuine social justice.

To achieve transformation in feminist theory and practice, VèVè A. Clark tells us, we must go beyond "retrofitting," a term *Webster's New Collegiate Dictionary* defines as the industrial practice whereby a faulty structure is "furnish[ed] with new parts or equipment not available at [the] time of construction." Going beyond retrofitting means not simply incorporating "new" ideas into existing theories and feminist practice, but fundamentally changing the very practices and theories themselves. In her discussion of pedagogy, Clark argues against a retrofitted multiculturalism that sets up parallel historical tracks of different groups, leaving intact a fundamentally Eurocentric educational structure. Instead, she advocates bringing these groups and their histories into conversation with each other—a process she calls creolization. In its acknowledgment that these histories are relational, such a pedagogy challenges the very construction of traditional history—going beyond a jury-rigged multiculturalism to acknowledge the complex ways different groups are always already implicated in each other's histories.

Specifically addressing feminist theory, Marilyn Frye criticizes the recent framing of differences among women. Like Clark, she points out that the theoretical "problem of difference" presumes the absence of some women's voices, as though what we needed to do was to incorporate the voices of lesbians and women of color into problematically white and heterosexual feminist theory. In the language of retrofit, we can understand Frye's essay as interrogating what constitutes "new parts" and what constitutes "availability" within feminist theory. She analyzes Linda Nicholson and Nancy Fraser's influential article, "Social Criticism without Philosophy," which argues that feminist scholarship of the 1970s was essentialist. As Frye demonstrates, Nicholson and Fraser's failure to use "available parts" in building their thesis renders invisible the existing work of poor and working-class women, women of color, and lesbians. Frye shows that the theorists of the 1970s whom Nicholson and Fraser discuss were actively ethnocentric rather than theoretically essentialist. She shows further that by not including in their own analysis lesbians and women of color who were writing feminist theory in the 1970s, Nicholson and Fraser reproduce their own ethnocentrism.

Peggy Pascoe's look at the particular institution of marriage reveals the contextual specificity of what is and is not retrofitting. Contrary to many advocates of same-sex marriage—and in agreement with those who oppose it—Pascoe argues that gay and lesbian marriage cannot be retrofitted into the institution as it exists. Her essay allows us to see "defense of marriage" statutes as accurately named, not simply as hyperbolic, homophobic hysteria. The institution of marriage decidedly needs defending even though individual marital relationships might not crumble if the gay or lesbian couple next door got married. For Pascoe traditional marriage functions largely to reinforce binary gender categories and "appropriate" expressions of sexuality, so that gays and lesbians are not simply absent from the institution of marriage; their absence defines the institution as it has existed. Same-sex marriage does not mimic traditional marriage, as Pascoe argues, but rather is "a bomb that will blow the traditional family to pieces."

Alice Adams's essay speaks to the impossibility feminists face in trying to retrofit the discourse of rights to women's decisions about reproductive freedom. As Adams observes, when feminists claim rights to reproductive freedom—specifically abortion—they are met with challenges by others, typically the right wing, about the rights of the unborn. "As long as the discourse feminists use to defend endlessly women's rights to custody and abortion is the same discourse antifeminist lawyers, judges, obstetricians, social workers, and psychologists use to argue against women's reproductive rights, feminists will accomplish no more than a defense of the limited and contingent privileges now held by a few women." Adams's answer is to jettison the discourse of rights, leaving open the question of what to do instead.

There is no way to decide in the abstract whether struggles for social justice require or would have the effect of jettisoning, modifying, or buttressing traditional institutions. These essays remind us that responsibility in the face of these uncertainties requires us to pay at least as much attention to our practices as the academy has trained us to pay to our theories.

Chapter 1

Retrofit

Gender, Cultural, and Class Exclusions in American Studies

VèVè A. Clark

As I began to revise the outline for this essay, the January 17, 1994, earthquake in Northridge outside Los Angeles had already occurred. Aftershocks erupted unmercifully while construction crews worked briskly to shore up shaky passages along Los Angeles's interminable freeways. In northern California the media trotted out file tapes from the 1989 Loma-Prieta disaster, supposedly to highlight by comparison just how destructive the recent quake had been. That bit of comparative calamity discourse was intended, as ever, to increase the ratings, to keep us watching someone else's loss. And watch I did. But it was not until the work crews arrived to control the damage that I revived from my voyeuristic stupor and the pain I was feeling for the Angelenos. Throughout the week media commentary reported calmly and repeatedly on the process of *retrofitting*. Somehow the term seemed offensive. I became angry, because the word itself reminded me of my disgust five years earlier as I watched the news from Boston—where I then resided—describing the collapse of the Nimitz Freeway of West Oakland in a predominantly working-class, ethnic neighborhood. The collapse, which killed forty individuals of various ethnicities driving home in supposed safety, was caused by faulty construction.[1] In Los Angeles, the earthquake capital of our country, the same phenomenon was occurring once again. Engineers and construction workers had designed and erected highways, homes, and campuses as though city dwellers would be living free of tremors in Kansas, in the land of Oz—not in California. More important, these technicians set up systems of transport and habitation that functioned environmentally as mere blueprints come alive, ever more tangible than the human beings who would drive on, live in, and learn in these badly conceived structures. *No Humans Involved.*[2]

The retrofit practice in America has troubled me since 1989 and has become more real because I am now living in Berkeley and teaching a course that fulfills the American cultures requirement at the University of California.[3] The place and the pedagogy are not disconnected. In this essay I am using retrofit as a metaphor for two contentious processes of development in education, namely, Anglo-conformity and multiculturalisms. Throughout American cultural history and to this day, the two approaches are linked ironically by *conscious practices of exclusion and inclusion,* reflecting, on one hand, status quo representations, and on the other, dissident revisions. The older construction of an American democratic model, its political, social, and cultural identity, was established by exclusion according to blueprints that were unsound even in the eighteenth century because they were based on the synecdoche of white Anglo-Saxon male Protestant desires represented in the Constitution, which required two centuries of amendments to bring the whole into the part. Reconstructions of American political life through radical social action and curriculum development erupted in the mid-twentieth century among those citizens whose ideologies had been previously excluded from legislative and educational practices on a broad level. African Americans began the charge in the 1950s and 1960s; feminists and other ethnic groups followed in the 1960s and 1970s. All these efforts to be included represent retrofit. Our current, multicultural mandates for the inclusion of the formerly excluded shore up and disguise a flawed but highly touted system of citizen representation—known as democracy throughout the world.

Take as examples the struggles for the right to vote among women and emancipated African Americans from Reconstruction through the 1960s. Those gendered and racially based confrontations over the definition of inclusion, although different in character, have helped us see more clearly the parameters of exclusion. Civil rights, as they are inscribed in U.S. foundational narratives, replicate European feudal privileges accorded to white male landowners alone. The incorporation of diverse ethnic/immigrant backgrounds into notions of superiority and acceptance in the United States remained biased toward northern European cultures well into the nineteenth and twentieth centuries, as reflected in immigration, legal, and public education standards. From the perspective of women and undervalued ethnicities—Native American, African American, Jewish, and southern European—our "home of the free" rhetoric, notwithstanding the malleable structures of representation built into the Constitution, contains a history of colonization that American studies continues to unmask. The problem of interpretation rests with the word *colonial* itself. As a scholar and teacher of African and Caribbean studies, I was surprised to realize how differently my students in New England, enrolled at Tufts University, understood the term when I addressed movements of decolonization throughout the twentieth century. For many of them, *colonial* was equated with liberation—the thirteen colonies, Paul Revere's ride, and the history of American independence that they had learned to digest without question in high school. Serving as "translator," I provided texts that set the term and process in global perspectives, beginning in the fifteenth century with European explorations, trafficking, colonization, and settling throughout the African continent. Essentially, we engaged in a dialogue about resistance to imposed overseas governance that set their definitions of colonization against mine and within a broader perspective continuing beyond the founding eighteenth-century American histories well into the 1960s. Readings on the Harlem Renaissance, *Négritude, Negrismo, Insularismo,* and African and Caribbean independence movements brought the older U.S. republican dissent closer to 1960s versions of decolonization in our hemisphere and elsewhere.[4] More important, students gathered, read, and critiqued primary texts written by colonized subjects outside this country that led from the 1930s and 1940s into the 1960s era of resistance among my generation.

Together, we examined how in any colonized culture, the status quo supports the agendas of a privileged settler class that maintains its dominance by colonizing the minds of its minions. Mastery imposed from top to bottom controls and distorts collective memories by consistently erasing oppositional stances from the stories of discovery and resettlement.[5] No better place to do so than in the schools, as the writings of a number of immigrant or colonized subjects have demonstrated both in America and in the Third World.[6] Radical responses to foundational narratives have retrieved ethnic differences and public dissent from the record by challenging the fixed logics of colonization. The colonizing mind and desire redefine as settlement *collective appropriation* of already occupied lands, socialized space, and indigenous or—as in the American case—enslaved cultures. Over the centuries, political control wielded by colonial or neocolonial administrations attempts to suppress methodically all but the founding/occupying fathers' narratives of origin.[7] When previously silenced stories do enter into public or academic discourses, they upset the so-called truths embedded in rote and uncritical teachings of the past. "Fugitive," "outlawed," "maroon," "radical," or feminist interventions insist that their ancestors, their gender, their political advocacy, their selves be included in the nation's history well into the postcolonial 1990s. The contemporary conservative agenda that attempts to limit the parameters of cultural literacy opposes beauty against beast in a dubious formula: to conform = the beauty of belonging; to contest = the bestiality of upsetting preestablished definitions of who is, in fact, American. Laws, social policies, and lay beliefs regarding citizenship and cultural literacy have been focused myopically on exclusion and inclusion, as though significant transformations in the definition of who is American have not occurred throughout U.S. history. Consequently, theories and practices promoting Anglo-conformity or multiculturalism in education are both retrofitted, in my opinion, because in each case—separated even as these theories are by centuries—they shift emphasis from systems of knowledge to the more obvious hierarchies of cultural production and memory. Since its inception, American culture has consistently struggled to guarantee a melting pot philosophy of inclusion when, in fact, most communities are characterized these days by separatism, and their histories represented in terms of cultural pluralism.

In my interactions with American studies programs in the Northeast and the Northwest, but specifically in team-teaching the course "Cultural Identity in American History: Theory and Experience" with Professor Lawrence Levine of the History Department at Berkeley during the fall of 1993, I have learned the need to expand our American diaspora literacy.[8] The opening of the American mind in contemporary education would include a variety of subjectivities, including the founding fathers' agendas, the resettlement of Native Americans and Chicanos, the enslavement of African Americans, histories of immigration other than that of northwestern European ethnicities, the subcultures of illegal aliens, and the emergence of first-generation mixed-race families in the United States whose children we now teach.[9] When we do engage in multicultural education across the country, are we holding on to undigested ideologies of diversity created in the 1970s? To replicate these noble yet flawed approaches to cultural inclusion twenty years later amounts to acts of containment rather than intellectual dialogues with generations born after some of us engaged in our one good fight. As I will attempt to demonstrate later, our students represent a *not yet/always already* consciousness emboldened to critique erasure from the curriculum by efforts initiated during the Civil Rights Movement, by the radical Left, and by Black studies as of 1968, followed by ethnic, feminist, and gay and lesbian studies.[10] However, undergrads and grads working with us have surpassed and transformed the learning environment. Access to new technologies has charted another sphere of intellectual theory, practice, and pedagogy that has no name beyond the inevitable *post* depictions of the century's latter years. Our students do not read and gather information in the ways we once did; the pace of learning is not only more rapid, but global. Modems allow them to scan library sources without ever leaving the dorms or journey across the country and the world through the Internet and Web. More important, students of Generation X connected through e-mail have taken the notion of study groups and affiliations beyond the classroom, beyond those strategies of intragenerational communication established by their professors two decades ago. In most cases, our theories of teaching practice and pedagogy are evolving along with the computer literacy and networking expertise of our students; however, in some areas we are clearly behind the times.

Standing on the Points of One's Origins

The relationship of the kind of ethnicity I'm talking about to the past is not a simple, essential one—it is a constructed one. It is constructed in history, it is constructed politically in part. It is part of narrative. We tell ourselves the stories of the parts of our roots in order to come into contact, creatively, with it. So this new kind of ethnicity—the emergent ethnicities—has a relationship to the past, but it is a relationship that is partly through memory, partly through narrative, one that has to be recovered. It is an act of cultural recovery.
—Stuart Hall, "Ethnicity: Identity and Difference"

Feminism has taught me the value of standpoint as a means of analyzing and revealing the subjectivity of my position as a scholar, teacher, activist, and African American woman. To continue to work for social justice, I must evaluate my performance in the sites where these theoretical and ideological practices emerge most frequently—the classroom. In addition, I must ask myself how my critical pedagogy relates to my upbringing. Did I suddenly in the 1950s through 1970s join social justice movements as a lemming seeking to become a sorority member of the radical Left, as many detractors claim, although we have never met?[11] No! My path to this place of criticism and teaching, like that of other African Americans of my generation—the babies born during the Second World War—was prefigured by a number of sociocultural barriers to personal development. My generation responded to the constant narrative of prejudice and racism—the necessity and ugliness of the confrontations in 1950s and 1960s America—by promoting cultural, class, and gender inclusions within public institutions designed by law to recognize us after the fact, but structured not to hear our voices.

In the 1970s and 1980s, persons of color and women played the game of altering their subjectivities for the prospects of gaining acceptance in the workplace. We did so during job interviews by copying the privileged, white male model to which generations of men from various classes have long succumbed: blue-striped suits, starched shirts, (yellow-checkered) ties sometimes replaced by colorful scarves or neckwear showing off indigenous designs as though that difference really mattered. The re-dress effect was a sign of assimilation, of potential belonging in corporate or congressional clubs. Or, in the academy, we often complied with concepts of discipline as we imitated without question military styles of learning—the captain at the helm of the class, chairs lined up strictly in rows, unquestioned adoption of the curriculum. When many of us later became tenured professors, we did not often recognize that we were imitating the pedagogical styles of certain rigid professors who had guided us into graduate work and beyond. Moreover, I believe that we failed to situate the ethos of military-style patriarchy played out before us. Undoubtedly, many professors and male corporate leaders of the 1950s were veterans from world and regional wars who were imposing on us modes of dominance they had internalized during the War. The clash of worldviews in terms of gender, culture, and class was formidable; our minds were being colonized in these situations, even as we thought we were moving into the elite. Those of us raised in working-class homes—unaccustomed to sanctioning elitism of any kind—were transformed into *been-to's* not unlike those well-educated individuals in Third World societies who returned home to rule or supervise their peers denied exposure to the metropole or elite universities.

I am deeply concerned with the behavior of U.S. working-class *been-to's* whose disconnections from homeplace are more disturbing in that most never return physically to their sources. Having paid the dues of inclusion into America's cultural mainstream, too many of us have preferred to settle and work isolated from the very communities that nurtured us, those neighborhoods where relatives currently live a dead-bolt existence, equating grillwork on every window with safety. As offspring, we have become a *virtual working class*—often at our parents' behest—talking the appropriate talk in public, dressing the part, "doing the upper-class do" for the sake of assimilation.[12] More often we practice resistance through social or cultural work or our writings, but all these activities are *virtual realities* representing a disconnected double-consciousness. In the post-integration generation, the "beam me up and away" phenomenon has too easily eroded the economic stability and tranquility of working-class neighborhoods when children do not come home or work directly with similar communities elsewhere. Using my personal history as an example, I will attempt to demonstrate ways the virtual can be consciously transformed, especially when one's gender, culture, and class remain positive counternarratives to the very systems that include but surreptitiously seek to exclude from positions of leadership a "too tall, too strong" African American woman.[13]

I come from a family of slave ancestry located originally in the American South and in the Caribbean. When these two clans immigrated to New York (Brooklyn and Jamaica, Queens) during the 1910s and 1920s, they became part of an African Diaspora moving after Emancipation from North Carolina and Trinidad/Barbados into one of the world's most culturally diverse metropolises. My father and mother, born respectively in 1915 and 1918, were children of the Depression and lived through a period of high unemployment and economic disarray not unlike the era we are experiencing now. One was an only child, the other the eldest female in a family of eight. When they met at Jamaica High School in the 1930s and were later married in the 1940s, they found their cross-cultural union assailed by competing narratives perpetuated by the elders of the North Carolinian tarheel heritage (my great-grand-mother and grandmother on my father's side) and the parents from the Caribbean who had disassociated themselves from elders left behind in the islands. Discord in my extended family taught me early on that Diaspora differences are a subject that we have not fully addressed in African American studies, and remain a central but overlooked issue in the very construction of American identity based generally on theory rather than experiences.[14]

Despite memories of enslavement, of the need to seek mobility beyond homeplace, my family has retained a gentleness in the midst of overt and subtle racism. The only times that I remember any of my relatives expressing anger, the outbursts concerned economic disparity or disrespect of the self. In public, whites and the Jewish merchant class of Queens offended us; in private West Indians demeaned homegrown Blacks or the reverse. There were always the predictable, unresolved arguments among my great-aunts and uncles from North Carolina. Every year of my childhood, Thanksgiving became a sanctioned *communitas* where encrusted disputes were revisited and aired under the influence of my father's homemade eggnog spiced with white lightnin'. These concoctions allowed his elders the space to speak out. The kinds of battering commonly associated these days with African American working-class behavior did not occur in my family beyond the codes of verbal sparring that unsilenced pain—memories shared collectively among individuals who would never consider revealing their leftover injuries to a therapist. At the dinner table, as my cousin Gwendolyn and I giggled over these acrimonious mini-dramas, we were learning to hear and contextualize old-time stories trailing after these "immigrants" who rarely returned South.

In the 1960s the paternal side of my family—with which I lived when my parents divorced—became devoted to confronting broader issues of social injustice in the society at large. My church, Lemuel Haynes Congregational, provided the place for me to comprehend my grandmother Swannora's disturbing behavior in public. Before I enrolled at Queens College in 1962, my Sunday school teacher, Andrea Rushing née Benton, and our minister, the late Channing Phillips, revealed the workings of American racism through biblical references to the oppression of the Jews. In addition, their local activism inspired and defined our responsibility as youth to join the

Civil Rights demonstrations nationally during the March on Washington in 1963.

These two individuals gave me an education in discerning public policies and practices of racism that helped me accept the fact that a woman so loving as my grandmother had the right to *go off* in public. Church schooling did not assuage, however, the embarrassment I felt as the confrontations evolved on site. The setting and the behaviors were always the same: we would go shopping at Gertz in Jamaica rather than Macy's because my grandmother maintained an eye for quality in merchandise and an impeccable credit record with the department store. Inevitably, after we had chosen a particular item to purchase, the salesperson—perceived by us as Jewish—would look past our position first in line to serve a *white* individual. My grandmother would become furious, totally out of her home character, and berate the salesperson for rendering us invisible. Her temper changed, her face, her body, on so many occasions over the years that I began to fear rather than relish a shopping excursion to downtown Jamaica under the el. At the time I did not realize how she was revisiting similar acts of dismissal that had forced the family to leave North Carolina. Migration of Blacks to the North was not simply an issue of economic opportunity; it was clearly an escape from the South's apartheid system, so that another human being would not disrespect you *in your face.* Geographic displacement did not subsequently prevent public disgrace because the racism was systemic—replicated by stand-in, Anglo-conformed individuals, no matter the ethnicity. Memories and acts of discrimination persist even in regions and countries proclaiming equality based on merit, despite your abilities to pay cash, maintain good credit, buy a house, and pay off the mortgage.

Like other "immigrants" before and after them, my paternal family worked to develop my literacy about *home* through stories retold at the dinner table. My father—a math wizard and four-letter man—dropped out of high school in his senior year because he had no long pants to wear. Too tall to count on family hand-me-downs when knickers were no longer fashionable, Alonzo Thomas Clark left school to work as a Redcap at Pennsylvania Station in Manhattan for the rest of his life. Failing to fulfill first-generation migrant expectations, he continued his studies in local Masonic lodges and at home through his daughter by purchasing historical and literary works on

African American life and lore at Henry's Bookstore in Harlem. His bibliophile efforts to teach me our culture were not confined to books; a prized collection of some three hundred 78 rpm records still sits in our basement. They were part of his after-school or *schul*-man curriculum (not unlike the *schuls* many of my Jewish classmates attended) that introduced me to Billie Holiday, Eric Dolphy, and Katherine Dunham—the latter by way of my father's associations with one of her dancers, Lawaune Ingram. As Daphne Muse, a dear friend and contemporary, demonstrated in a recent presentation for the St. Clair Drake Graduate Cultural Forum at UC Berkeley, our working-class parents kept us connected to African Diaspora culture through their own participation as supporters of the arts and scholarship produced during the 1930s and afterward.[15]

I have often wondered why I was drawn to foreign languages in junior high school. Beyond talents for learning languages and reading music, I believe that my interests in French- and Spanish-language literatures and cultures responded subconsciously to the latent xenophobia among my paternal family members, who, like so many other homegrown African Americans, resented West Indians—their accents, their style, their accomplishments as what we now call *model minorities.* The resentment was both economic and cultural. According to my North Carolinian family members, West Indians were depriving African Americans of their rightful low-level jobs and at the same time practicing *obeah* (or witchcraft) on them. I resisted these representations of Diaspora differences because they impugned my mother, her likewise "immigrant" upbringing in New York, and her dedication to working for the family, which literally consumed her identity in her second marriage. Despite paternal rhetoric to the contrary, my mother also spent her life after high school graduation laboring in working-class sites—a Pullman Porter laundry, a defense industry riveting factory, a pharmaceutical laboratory at Pfizer's in Brooklyn. Disproving the myth of West Indians' occupying positions that might have gone to African Americans is a complex issue. Rather than rely on statistical evidence to argue the point, I cite as testimony my mother's work history to demonstrate how access to economic opportunities can so easily become distorted when gender and cultural differences are ignored in tabulations.

In the case of my mother, Pauline Kirton Clark Moore, the three positions that she held during and after the War were clearly gender-specific. Popular belief in African American urban communities would have us assume that Pauline was hired and retained because of her cultural background. Her status as a light-skinned West Indian, rather than job performance, suggests why she did not follow the domestic trail into Jewish homes like so many of the dark-skinned southern women in my extended paternal family. Skin color may have indeed allowed my mother to integrate easily into workplaces where working-class southern Europeans, mostly Italians, were hired by Pfizer's. Nonetheless, phrases such as "they takin' our jobs" remain uninformed reactions to economic usury, those employment injustices promoted by business elites when their workforce is comprised mainly of skilled but not higher-degree–holding citizens. Identifying the "they" in power relationships requires a shift in consciousness upward toward those dominant minorities constantly re-creating systems of control. In that regard, the current backlash against affirmative action, initiated across class lines by *angry white males,* sounds like an old story. I heard it first through interclass grapevines. Now I recognize this knee-jerk paranoia as classic American "divide and control" market practices setting ethnicities against each other at the lowest levels of production. The difference in the 1990s is that working- and middle-class white males overlook the insidious behavior known as "downsizing" in corporate culture. As a result, they agree to deflect their unemployed status onto affirmative action policies supposedly benefiting people of color at their expense. The old saw about "last hired/first fired" describing the unstable grounds of employment for African Americans has been reversed. Now white males see themselves as victims—first fired/last hired—refusing to analyze how their white male counterparts among corporate executives have exported labor abroad for profit to everyone's detriment. Not unlike the chronic complaining within African Diaspora immigrant communities, these troubling situations shift our focus systemically toward hiring away from firing and to easy targets, such as women joining the workplace and "minorities" of all colors. I was exposed early on to economic and psychological dismissals, and inclusion through revisions of epistemes defines my activist mission in the 1990s. With other *been-to's* who have not sacrificed their origins, their locations to mainstream definitions of social justice, I have chosen to redefine parameters of belongings in American society through the medium of education.

The triptych of this essay—gender, cultural, and class exclusions—examines the consequences of displacement using as case studies the West Indian Pauline Kirton, born into an adopted mother country, and the uprooted Alonzo Thomas Clark, whose North Carolinian identity was resettled into a northern suburban environment. The academic choices that I made, that my father left me free to assume, were probably subliminal efforts on my part to understand the diasporas from which my parents and their ancestors came. My response at the time was to become a xenophile from junior high school through a master's degree at the Université de Nancy, France, and Queens College, where I continued to major/minor in French and Spanish. Throughout my entire public education in New York, ending in 1966, I was never required to read a work by a Black author, but did so on my own through extracurricular learning promoted by both my father and mother. In 1968 my home schooling and public education merged for the first time. In the S.E.E.K. Program (Search for Education and Elevation through Knowledge) we were teaching students drawn to the university through open admissions, later known as affirmative action. Using Lilyan Kesteloot's newly published *Anthologie Négro-Africaine* (1967), I was encouraged by the Frenchwoman directing the program to include writings by Francophone African and Caribbean authors in a lower-division French language course. At the same time, I was completing a master's thesis in French on characterizations of women in Sartre's theatre, and found myself already engaged in the intellectual practice that has sustained me since, namely, the study of Francophone African and Caribbean literatures. Thirty-one years later, I recite this history in order to reveal the nonviolent ways many of us changed the curriculum following Martin Luther King, Jr., later switching over to Malcolm X's ideology for systemic change once he returned from Mecca. During my undergraduate years at Queens College, I did not join contemporaries such as Andrew Goodman, who actually participated in and/or lost their lives during the Freedom Rides and Schools. My family would not let me go back south. In solidarity with the commitments of my peers, I supported their efforts at a distance through church and family-sanctioned activities.

Social justice per se did not motivate my teaching in 1968. I was concerned with chasms in the literary record that had to be addressed by an African Diaspora history that ventured beyond the confines of authors writing in English. My commitment to African American studies was clear in the 1960s, although for too long I have not been in a departmental position to teach the broad range of new subjectivities emerging in indigenous and colonial languages. At Berkeley I am able to do so now, and that perspective allows for a reassessment of the Civil Rights road (1962–68) that led me here and the postmodern discourse of diversity at once sustaining and troubling to the current generation of students.

Eurocentricity and Afrocentricity in Context

The debate ignited in 1987 by Allan Bloom, E. D. Hirsch, Jr., and to a lesser public extent by Molefi K. Asante resurrected what Gayatri Spivak might call "a dying discourse."[16] Eurocentricity and Afrocentricity in American education were no longer compelling ideological positions at the time because cultural theory and practice had moved on to embrace multicultural learning in the United States. Although numerous scholars have critiqued multiculturalism in opposition to these older *centricities,* most have not examined the historical frames out of which Eurocentricity and Afrocentricity emerged, nor have they addressed scholarly participation in one or both. In separate writings J. M. Blaut and Sylvia Wynter remind us that these ideologies must be understood in the context of their creation during the mid-nineteenth century and in 1968.[17] These are nostalgic standpoints for lost time and places defining American identity from abroad in purist, puritanical terms based on Western or African origins.

As many of us do, I define my intellectual position in dialogue with worldviews and values that reflect my experience. As a result, I find particularly disturbing two remarks by Allan Bloom and Henry Louis Gates, Jr., because they misrepresent the work of a generation of activist scholars to change the curriculum in African Diaspora studies during the 1960s and afterward. Let me begin with an excerpt from Bloom's chapter "The Sixties" in *The Closing of the American Mind* (1987).

> The American university in the sixties was experiencing the same dismantling of the structure of rational inquiry as had the German universities in the thirties. No longer believing in their higher vocation, both gave way to a highly ideologized student populace. And the content of

the ideology was the same—value commitment. The university had abandoned all claim to study or inform about value—undermining the sense of the value of what it taught, while turning over the *decision* about values to the folk, the *Zeitgeist,* the relevant. Whether it be Nuremberg or Woodstock, the principle is the same. As Hegel was said to have died in Germany in 1933, Enlightenment in America came close to breathing its last during the sixties. (Bloom 313–14)

The consistent analogies to fascism in 1930s Europe in this passage and the remaining chapter are overstated for several reasons that Bloom was unable to tease out. First of all, he lumps together radical and African American methods as though they were struggling together for curriculum change in 1969. Paul Lauter with Louis Kampf in *The Politics of Literature* (1970) reminds us of the split between the radical Left and Black Nationalists in political action and in writing. In the introduction to their text Lauter and Kampf note the absence of African American scholars among the contributors, which they attribute to the ongoing conflict between the two camps.[18] Bloom's second fallacy is to equate the rough and tough weapon-wielding call for Black studies at Cornell University in April 1969 with other less violent confrontations based on legislated curriculum change occurring elsewhere on campuses that traditionally served the working and middle classes. Cornell was not Queens or City College, where the student constituencies differed radically. Clearly the student response at Cornell and recently at Stanford took on an "in your face" posture—justifiable or not—because universities serving the wealthy and elite make change more slowly. The conflict between Afrocentricity and Eurocentricity was, I would argue, a class conflict that Bloom remembered as purely ideological.

The more disturbing issue here is how student demands for inclusion of Black studies in the curriculum are treated as childlike, compared throughout the chapter to parent/child relationships (Bloom 313–35). Although that stance is shocking to me as an instructor who has always used an interactive method, I recognize the persistence of parent/child models in pedagogy throughout the nation. When we assume that position in our students' lives, ultimately we serve as surrogates or foster guardians, treating them as orphans. Certainly there are other modes of interaction from mentoring to coaching that we might consider. Moreover, this model allows university systems of knowledge to reproduce dependency vertically. Students "raised" in authoritarian classroom climates often become professors who fear to challenge their administrative "parents"—deans, provosts, chancellors, and presidents. Feminist practice in teaching—established well before Bloom's publication—provides another more open means of listening and learning at the university level, as Frances Maher and Mary Kay Thompson Tetreault document in *The Feminist Classroom* (1994). In *Engaging Feminism: Students Speak Up and Speak Out* (1992), the editors Jean O'Barr and Mary Wyer call for student-centered teaching:

> We are presenting the ideas, insights, and (yes) critiques of students as if they are of central importance to the educational enterprise, as if we could learn from each other—that a book like *Engaging Feminism* could be a self-help guide for students to learn about women's studies. It is even acceptable to say that women's studies has something to teach all faculty, that we should learn with students, cooperating with them in a common classroom activity. It is another issue altogether to suggest that those teaching in American higher education today, including those in women's studies, *would be enriched by a shift in our perspectives on students, to suggest that we might be more effective teachers if our approach was grounded in an appreciation for the knowledge, diversity, and intellectual strengths of those who take our classes.* (O'Barr and Wyer 1, emphasis added)

Inevitably, instructors will continue to debate over structures of authority in classrooms, during campus demonstrations and among colleagues and administrators. We may be missing the essential point. The cross-generational team approach described above represents an *opening* that Bloom's retrospective text is not prepared to consider. Bloom sees closing culturally; I see pedagogical closure as endemic within the one institution where most of us have spent our lives.

The charges of jingoism leveled against Afrocentricity by Bloom (although the term was not used during the 1960s) and by Henry Louis Gates, Jr., are serious accusations. Gates is clearly one of our most prodigious African American scholars, whose views on and participation in the renaissance of scholarship I value and support. In *Loose Canons: Notes on the Culture Wars* (1992) and in other essays, Gates navigates us through the landscapes of intellectual and scholarly development awaiting African American studies in the twenty-first century.[19] Consistently, the theoretical and political consequences of a retreat into ethnocentrism are displayed and illuminated. While I agree with Gates's willingness to uncover the leftover dirty laundry in some African American studies programs, I am particularly displeased with the distillation of his thoughtful essays published elsewhere into a one-page piece for *Essence* magazine (February 1994) during Black History Month to be consumed by an implied readership of working- and middle-class folk.

My displeasure concerns an apparent insensitivity toward the ways our words influence constituencies beyond the academy. Anyone who has taught for a period of time in African American studies knows that the choice to major in the field remains problematic. Many parents and some advisors wonder how beneficial a bachelor's degree in African American studies could possibly be in the future. Consequently, demonstrating the benefits of majoring in this interdisciplinary field is a constant negotiation. Thousands have chosen African American studies, not by default, but through conscious commitment to the field; others, however, elect to double-major in a more traditional department. That difference has shaped the structures of two Ph.D. programs in African American studies in this country at Temple and Yale Universities. Speaking directly to past and future constituencies—no matter their ethnicity—Gates has framed his argument in terms of good news (recent scholarship) and bad news (old programs):

> We are in the midst of a renaissance of solid scholarship about African-American social and cultural forms. Scholars are writing fascinating monographs and editing anthologies. Biographers are addressing the tensions and ambiguities of Black life in America with a freer hand than ever before. Sociologists and economists are researching the tragic connections between race and poverty without regard for the ideological correctness of their conclusions.

> That's the good news.

> The bad news is that too many Black Studies programs—where this new knowledge ought to be created and disseminated—have become segregated, ghettoized amen corners of quasireligious feeling, propagating old racial fantasies and even inventing new ones. One of the greater ironies of this situation is that the racial ideologies of many Afrocentrists are simply inverted versions of the White racisms of the past few centuries. (Gates, "Black Studies" 138)

As in Bloom's assessment cited above, Gates has portrayed the state of the field in binary terms that omit other long-standing efforts, such as the thirty-year-old tradition at the University of California, Berkeley. Here African American Studies and Ethnic Studies have continued to work programmatically and pedagogically against "the scapegoating of other ethnic groups" (138). To attack Afrocentricity is easy because, like Eurocentricity, it is bound to stasis, consumed by romantic representations of exploits centuries and decades old. The more flagrant examples might be classified as separatism, where all-white or all-Black superior accomplishments leave out important cross-cultural influences or the process of acculturation known as Creolization. Although systemically different in terms of power dynamics separating the dominating from the dominated, both stances champion race pride, the elite, heroic males, and nostalgia for a return to better days.

While I agree with Gates's remarks about some Black studies programs, it might be more useful to critique Afrocentricity in the contexts of disciplinary, pedagogical, and institutional practice. Too often we forget that Afrocentric ideologies were created in the 1960s as by-products, like Kwanzaa, of Black nationalism in America. In other words, the movement was and still is an attempt to forge a ritual and intellectual bridge between African American identity and African histories and cultures. Most of our students think that Afrocentricity is of recent vintage, promoted by Molefi K. Asante's 1987 work *The Afrocentric Idea* or his earlier writings of the 1980s.[20] Moreover, the majority learn to embrace the ideology through lecturers who come to campuses extolling the psychological benefits of replacing a Eurocentric paradigm with an Afrocentric one. The trickle-down effect of this kind of preaching comes back to haunt us in the classroom, particularly if one is a scholar well-trained in African studies. The students generally have not read Asante, and even if they have, the Afrocentric paradigm confines itself to two issues: that Egypt was a Black civilization; and that African explorers sailed to and settled in an old world before Columbus declared the new. Despite the rich data amassed and examined by scholars such as Ivan van Sertima, Asa Hilliard, Martin Bernal, and others, the field itself has its own limitations. Afrocentric scholars attempting to engage in the history of science rely primarily on archival rather than applied archaeological research; few, if any, are trained in the sciences. Among U.S. scholars, laudable work has revealed African inclusions in the rise of civilization and exploration, African preeminence in science and technology, and cross-cultural contacts as early as the medieval period. We must admit, however, that the majority of Afrocentric scholarship on which our students rely was conducted by nonscientists. Such was not the case with the Leakey clan working in East Africa or the activist scholar Cheikh Anta Diop of Sénégal, whose renowned career as a practicing scientist and scholar Afrocentrists champion and cite repeatedly. The work of his lesser-known student, Théophile Obenga— an Egyptologist and linguist from the Congo—continued Diop's combined training in hands-on scientific research and historiography that is sorely missing these days from the Afrocentric idea. Obenga's *L'Afrique dans l'Antiquité* (1973) remained untranslated for far too long. As a result, the serious dialogue that many Afrocentric students were seeking to derive from the evidence failed to emerge because Black studies as a discipline has not required proficiency in a language other than English.

In some instances, the "quasireligious feeling" among our students harks back to the 1960s and the participation of their parents in working-class uplift promoted by the separatist theology known as the Nation of Islam. We are now teaching students who were raised in that critical environment, as well as other immigrants from the Islamic world who perceive critique of their fundamental family values as an attack on their subjectivities. As we turn our attention increasingly to providing reference works and anthologies for the benefit of teachers and students alike, we must simultaneously address the ideologies of closure persisting among our Black Nationalist implied readers along with Eurocentrists still stuck in the 1950s intellectual climate romanticized by Bloom. How do we break through these totalizing cultural walls/wars politically and intellectually? I suggest that we begin by defining stasis in learning as a disease afflicting both sides of the *centricity* conflicts. Locating innovative means of healing beyond the binaries will require major shifts in theory, practice, and pedagogy. As several scholars in American studies have suggested, we need to focus on epistemes—the ways universities and American education in general compartmentalize the consumption of knowledge as a system of human containment. Packaged and replicated in separate departments, the systems of knowledge inherited from Eurocentric and Afrocentric universities in medieval Paris and Mali have more in common than we accept as our legacy. Those scholars who challenge us to break out of preestablished epistemes are describing *not yet/always already* visions of potential transformations suggested in the title of Ayi Kwei Armah's

1968 novel *The Beautyful Ones Are Not Yet Born,* Frantz Fanon's writings on the psychology of alienation and revolution, and the deconstructionist agendas initiated by Jacques Derrida, Mikhail Bakhtin, Michel Foucault, and Julia Kristeva among others. In 1968 when Armah's novel was published, the field of African American studies was *not yet* integrated into elite universities, as Bloom's recall of confrontations at Cornell indicates; however, practice of serious scholarship had been continued since the nineteenth century and *always already* institutionalized at Black colleges, such as Howard University during the 1940s. In the process of breaking through to a new consciousness of knowledge production and dialogue, the construction of African American studies in the 1960s served as a model and means of practicing interdisciplinary research, writing, and teaching for the ultimate purposes of restructuring epistemes.

African American studies programs throughout the United States have persisted, but few have lasted long enough to become departments granting doctoral degrees, with notable exceptions, for instance, at Temple, Yale, and at Berkeley in 1997. In the 1980s and 1990s graduate students who wish to commit their work to African Diaspora studies have become peripatetic researchers stretching well beyond the departmental disciplines in which their professors were trained. These new scholars in American studies, anthropology, comparative literature, ethnic studies, or women's studies are on the cusp of the new discourses and research for which Gates argues. To return for a moment to those already existing African American studies programs, I suggest that they rework the infrastructures that force undergraduates to choose between a social science or humanities concentration. Moreover, there is a great deal of retraining toward cross-disciplinary research and teaching to be promoted among faculty. At Tufts University in the 1980s, the American Studies Program inaugurated by Jesper Rosenmeier of English did exactly that through NEH sponsorship. Yearly summer workshops drew together faculty seeking to revise an old course or create new ones based on previous research; my approach to "Caribbean Literature by Women" emerged from that type of interdisciplinary exchange.[21] African American studies departments and programs would benefit from such an enterprise. In the midst of shrinking budgetary support, we might continue to seek outside funding through venues such as the Ford Foundation, business cosponsorships, or, falling back on the self-help associations of the nineteenth century, fund the "good news" in African Diaspora studies through appeals to citizens supporting our efforts here and abroad.

Teaching for the Human

As social theories and practices, Anglo-conformity and multiculturalism represent the antipodes of learning systems operating in American public and private education. Anglo-conformity has promoted exclusion and assimilation among America's native, slave, and immigrant populaces; multiculturalism has facilitated inclusion and diversity in the curriculum and the classroom.[22] Emerging a century apart, they do share one common denominator, *deliberate* exclusion, *deliberate* inclusion. Both strategies are protecting endangered structures of knowledge. Both amount to retrofit, however differently, because the gender/cultural/class exclusions and inclusions in each of these influences on the curriculum are the same. Ultimately, neither exposes students to the human history of their exclusion from or inclusion within a changing mainstream.

In *Ethnicity and American Social Theory: Toward Critical Pluralism* (1983), Gerard Postiglione sets the rise of Anglo-conformity in context, arguing that the nineteenth-century version supported Darwin's evolutionary theories: "therefore, reasoned many of its supporters, one race must represent the most highly evolved race, and, as the argument went, presumably this was the race of northwestern Europe" (14–15). According to Postiglione, Anglo-conformity

> originated in 17th century America wherein the English settlers dominated all others and succeeded in establishing their ways as the norm for all. However, it became strengthened and popularized in the late 19th and early 20th century. It asserted that the culture of the Aryan and Nordic races of northern and western Europe was superior to those of the peoples of southern and eastern Europe. It was commonly believed that the inferior cultural groups posed a serious threat to the structure of American society during this historical period. The Anglo-conformity social doctrine was later used as a justification for changes in immigration policies which, in effect, further restricted the entrance of eastern and southern Europeans into the country. (14)

Anglo-conformity has defined the intellectual borders in education from the nineteenth century through the 1988 conflicts at Stanford

University over the Western civilizations required courses. In private institutions Western Civ replicated the synecdoche on which the United States was founded by extolling as normative the evolved state of democratic achievements among transplanted northwestern Europeans. That same curriculum was imposed on generations of immigrants, Native Americans, and African Americans in the public schools as a means of guaranteeing assimilation into an already established narrative of Anglo-Saxon cultural superiority.

When the narrative begins to open toward inclusion of the broad spectrum of ethnicities defining American culture (the concept we now call multiculturalism), the ship of governance, historiography, and learning has not been sufficiently restructured—it has only been retrofitted to make the unsound systems more safe to travel on until the next national crisis erupts. As elsewhere in the world, demonstrative, often violent reactions to unemployment, poverty, and other social injustices stem from the paradox of inclusion, which translates as exclusion of all but the fully conformed. The geographer J. M. Blaut refers to this inside/outside conception of world civilizations as "tunnel history": "The walls of this tunnel are, figuratively, the spatial boundaries of Greater Europe. History is a matter of looking back or down in this European tunnel of time and trying to decide what happened where, when, and why. . . . Outside its walls everything seems to be rockbound, timeless, changeless tradition" (Blaut 5).

In *The Colonizer's Model of the World: Geographical Diffusionism and Eurocentric History* (1993), Blaut reviews the narratives of world history and geography as they have appeared in textbooks and other writings in America since the nineteenth century. Moving beyond the cultural pluralism theories of the 1920s, Blaut describes the postmodern era in terms of containment rather than the multicultural opening that we expected it to be.

> After World War II . . . history textbooks began to exhibit another, more subtle, form of tunnel history. The non-European world was now beginning to insert itself very firmly in European consciousness, in the aftermath of the war with Japan and in the midst of the intensified decolonization struggles, the Civil Rights movement in the United States, and the like. Most newer textbooks enlarged the discussion of non-European history, and said something about the historical achievements of non-European cultures. Most textbooks gave a flavor of historicity, of evolutionary progress, to non-European history, thus departing from

the older pattern, which dismissed these societies as stagnant and nonevolving. . . .

And tunnel history dominated most textbooks in the most important matter of all, the question of "why," of *explanation*. Historical progress still came about because Europeans invented or initiated most of the crucial innovations, which only later spread out to the rest of the world. So the textbooks depicted a world in which historical causes were to be found basically inside the European tunnel of time, although historical effects were to be seen basically everywhere. (Blaut 5–6)

Lest we think that Blaut's assessments have little to do with the ongoing struggle for gender, cultural, and class inclusions in American education, Joyce King's 1992 article "Diaspora Literacy and Consciousness in the Struggle against Miseducation in the Black Community" proves the opposite. Even among California educators devoted to multicultural representations in textbooks, distortions of ethnic (read Black) history were maintained despite repeated objections and efforts to raise the literacy among members of the California Curriculum Development and Supplemental Materials Commission from 1986 to 1990, when King was a member of the advisory board (King 317–40). Retrofit may indeed perpetuate multicultural illiteracy, because administrators running the show were not schooled themselves in multiple systems of American cultural production. To confront the prospects of cultural exclusions in the American story, these gatekeepers would have to question the limitations of their own educational backgrounds and their right to judge a curriculum to which they were never exposed—K through 12 and beyond.

To shift the metaphor for a moment, not all the liberal and radical calls for gendered, cultural, and class inclusions since the 1970s have reformed the curriculum at the core; most represent the *farce* introduced into the caverns of an already valued episteme. "Diversity" is no more than a buzzword these days, amounting to retrofit, when teachers do not do their homework. As such the tasty multicultural stuffing spices up the blandness of our systems of knowledge and satisfies desires to ingest and eliminate the Other, and the burp of fulfillment loudly proclaims the end of exclusion in Rabelesian terms. What could possibly be wrongheaded in the multicultural scheme?

Teaching African and Caribbean literatures at Berkeley in the 1990s, I see the effects of our myopia primarily in the laudable areas of feminist studies, ethnic studies, and multicultural agency. Many of my students have read Chinua Achebe, Frantz Fanon, or Jamaica Kincaid in social science and humanities courses where these texts are meant to represent diverse cultural narratives, but serve instead as tokens. The texts become displaced, included as illustrations without the benefit of historical or literary contexts. They represent a particular theme, political stance, genre, or example of narrative technique. In 1992, as I was teaching my upper-division theory course devoted to Caribbean literature by women authors, I had to take time out when I realized that the students from the English department, in particular, were reading a work by Jean Rhys in the wind. Eager to apply feminist ideologies and theories to their interpretations, too many of the undergraduates and graduates were unable at the outset to place *Wide Sargasso Sea* in the historical era of the novel's setting. When I asked them to keep one foot in slavery as we evaluated the eight required novels, I told them that such a request was new for me. Consumed with issues of madness affecting female subjectivities, prepared to approach *Wide Sargasso Sea* from feminist perspectives, these same students had no idea what *seasoning* as a process of acculturation meant in the slave, indentured, and landowning narratives of exploration addressed by Rhys.

Those of us committed to multicultural education have failed our students in other ways. We have invented an ethnic canon inserted into established European discourses by calling repeatedly on the writings of Zora Neale Hurston, Paula Gunn Allen, Gerald Vizenor, Cherríe Moraga, Richard Rodríguez, and Maxine Hong Kingston without providing the contexts out of which their narratives derive. Would any of us dare to teach Diderot, Mark Twain, or Virginia Woolf in such a deculturalized fashion? Where are the origins of these texts? Where do these diasporas end and begin again? We cannot locate intertexts unless we know the sources, unless we follow the Native, Chicano, African American, and Asian American trails of forced resettlement, the immigrant routes of displacement to America from elsewhere.

Ronald Takaki's book *A Different Mirror: A History of Multicultural America* (1993) contests the stasis in our literacy by uncovering a rich, multiethnic counternarrative challenging homogenized representations of American history. The story begins before Columbus, during fourteenth-century skirmishes between Native Americans and Vikings in the settlement known as Vinland (present-day Newfoundland), and concludes with reflections on the subtexts of discord erupting among ethnic groups in contemporary America.

> Do the televised images of racial hatred and violence that riveted us in 1992 during the days of rage in Los Angeles frame a future of divisive race relations—what Arthur Schlesinger, Jr., has fearfully denounced as the "disuniting of America"? Or will Americans of diverse races and ethnicities be able to connect themselves to a larger narrative? Whatever happens, we can be certain that much of our society's future will be influenced by which "mirror" we choose to see ourselves. America does not belong to one race or one group, the people in this study remind us, and Americans have been constantly redefining their national identity from the moment of first contact on the Virginia shore. By sharing their stories, they invite us to see ourselves in a different mirror. (Takaki 17)

Takaki's work attempts to break free from previous systems of knowledge production in a number of enlightened ways. The study is interdisciplinary, based on the researcher's training in American history with specializations in African American and Asian history and culture; a broad range of data derived from archival research and cross-cultural linguistic etymologies; the recovery of forgotten testimonies collected as oral histories. The focus on working-class contributions to the establishment of infrastructures was particularly pleasing to me because, as in Alice Walker's novel *The Color Purple,* I heard familiar voices in the documents and variations on the paradoxical themes of usury and uplift embedded in the American Dream. Memories of my grandmother's and great-grandmother's southern teachings transplanted northward with our extended family of four generations living together in Queens came alive for me in Takaki's study. For the first time I realized how deeply distrust combined with trust had shaped their thinking and mine; how double-consciousness in Du Bois's theory of cultural exclusion/inclusion was experienced differently by former slaves, independent farmers, sharecroppers, and domestic workers—none of whom belonged to the elite talented tenth.

Responding to a reviewer who challenged his methodology in a previous work, Takaki has presented *A Different Mirror* as a history of multidimensional ethnic interaction (Takaki, author's note). Although these intentions are not fully fulfilled, Takaki's research is indeed culturally diverse. *Ethnic interaction,* however, is restricted to two arenas: (1) cultural baiting among the Irish, African Americans, and Chinese working in northeastern companies owned by European immigrants of the power elite; (2) coalitions between African Americans and Jews during the Civil Rights era. Each historical example of what multiculturalism might become in America dissolves back into ethnic pluralism. The very structure of the study, presenting cultures in contained chapters or subchapters, demonstrates balkanized, ethnic reactions to public policies initiated by elites from above. Consequently, the interstices that the middle and working classes have filled together remain short-lived spaces of insurgency, nothing more. When their revolt against WASP authority is stated and perhaps overcome, folk speaking from the borders and margins return inevitably to an uneasy alliance with Anglo-conformed members of their own culture who participate fully in the master's version of history. Despite these reservations, Takaki's invaluable study is written for the human in American history rather than any particular ideology of exclusion.

We are all looking for models, as was Takaki, for representing the mosaic of American cultural production and social interactions across ethnic lines. The two projects at Tufts in which I participated—American Studies and World Civilizations—shared common structures of support similar to the American cultures requirement here at UC Berkeley. All were team-taught and benefited from external grant monies. In these recessionary times, to suggest such a model for changing the curriculum remains idealistic. Nonetheless, it is conceivable that mini-versions of these courses might be offered on other campuses, that published course readers will be generated in the future, or simply that other instructors will be inspired to broaden existing courses by our examples.

The American Studies Program at Tufts University was unique in the 1980s because faculty participated fully in interdisciplinary research and teaching. Our introductory course, "Work in America," was team-taught by tenured faculty from English, Sociology and Biology and one assistant professor from Romance Languages. From that experience I learned above all the importance of including the history of science and the disciplinary outlook of a practicing scientist in multicultural courses. The biologist Saul Slapikoff added to our discussions of gender discrimination in the workplace the research on women's brains used to deny the capacity for certain intellectual pursuits among women, particularly in the computer industry. Jesper Rosenmeier's extensive research on interactions between the Puritans and Wampanoack helped our students reread foundational texts by Benjamin Franklin, Ralph Waldo Emerson, and Henry Thoreau. The sociologist Saul Bellin deconstructed the analysis of work as satisfying or deleterious in a variety of professions. Principally my contribution was to broaden our definitions of "America" by including peasant and *favelado* representations of laboring in plantation America through analyses of two texts, Jacques Roumain's *Masters of the Dew* (1944) and Carolina de Jesus's *Child of the Dark* (1960). Using the theme of work, we taught the course twice to forty to fifty students each year, many of whom decided afterward to major in American studies. This effort was my first attempt to cross over cultural and disciplinary borders beyond my previous training in African/Caribbean literatures and cultures.

The second experiment in multicultural education was a global *tour de force*. Five professors at Tufts followed the lead of Lynda Shaffer of History, who had succeeded in organizing a world history course. Avoiding rigid notions of diffusionism, she had worked out an elaborate "bare bones" chronology of cultural interactions on which the World Civilizations Program and courses at Tufts depended. We saw ourselves as a "Mighty Handful" creating the bases for three interrelated but different courses offered as of 1988. This particular cross-disciplinary collective coalesced because of our previous work in the world history course or American studies. We had already expanded the borders of our disciplinary training and did not fear to further seek out ethnic interactions across time and the globe. The team included Lynda Shaffer (History), Howard Solomon (History), Steven Hirsch (Classics), Jesper Rosenmeier (English), and me (Romance Languages). Without entering into the details here, we convinced our fellow faculty members that one of the series of courses should be required of all lower-division students, and attracted to the World Civilizations Program committed faculty members, from Eurocentric to multicultural, willing to work through their intellectual terrains of difference. Although I left Tufts for Berkeley before I actually taught a course in the program, my work with the "Mighty Handful" clearly changed the ways I conceive of presenting regional or global topics. Those pedagogical experiences traveled with me to UC Berkeley, and were called on a year after my arrival.

Cultural Identity in American History:
Theories and Experiences

In 1992 and 1993 I worked with Professor Lawrence Levine to create a new course that would fulfill the American cultures requirement at Berkeley. Originally the conception was Levine's, based on Alexis de Tocqueville's musings about American identity from the perspective of a European traveler to the United States in 1831:

> Imagine, my dear friend, if you can, a society formed of all the nations of the world . . . people having different languages, beliefs, opinions: in a word, a society without roots, without memories, without prejudices, without routines, without common ideas, without a national character, yet a hundred times happier than our own; more virtuous? I doubt it. That is the starting point: *What serves as the link among such diverse elements? What makes all of this into one people?* (de Tocqueville 38, emphasis added)

In our quest to respond to de Tocqueville's queries, working with two graduate students in history and ethnic studies, Burton Peretti and Claudia May, we chose to include writings from 1755 to 1993—Benjamin Franklin's "Observations concerning the Increase of Mankind, Peopling of Countries" to Takaki's *Different Mirror*. The course was organized around five major themes: (1) Anglo-conformity; (2) the melting pot; (3) cultural pluralism; (4) multiculturalism; (5) Creolization. The latter was drawn from Caribbean theories of socialization defined in 1971 by Edward Kamau Brathwaite in *The Development of Creole Society in Jamaica, 1770–1820* and recently applied to the United States by the anthropologist Ulf Hannerz in "American Culture: Creolized, Creolizing" (1987). We tested these theories of American cultural identity against the experiences recorded in writing, oral histories, and films among five ethnic designations, namely, Native American, European American, African American, Chicano/Latino, and Asian American. In the summer of 1992 as we worked on the course reader, the experiences of our chosen documentors demanded space for discussions of separatism and bilingualism as well. Issues of educational policies, immigration laws, and gender exclusions preoccupied our deliberations as the draft of the reader was revised and assembled. Claudia May's background in ethnic, feminist, and diaspora studies radically altered the first drafts of the reader, which we all felt did not provide sufficient examples of literary texts published by contemporary writers of color. In the final draft we opened with sections on theory followed by experiential documents gathered in ethnic clusters. That approach would prove to be no different from Takaki's, a latter-day form of cultural pluralism, where each one researches and teaches contestations or brief alliances between the centers and borders rather than cultural mixing.

By the summer of 1993 the course had been accepted as a team-taught, cross-departmental freshman seminar listed as History 17A and African American Studies 17AC. The university's infrastructure was not quite prepared for such an interdisciplinary offering, but we were. Most of the newly devised American cultures classes had been taught by a single individual. With support from departmental funds and his endowed chair, Levine hired three graduate assistants, Michael Thompson, Sara Nickel, and Valerie Mendoza, to teach two sections of the course while we offered one apiece. The lectures to the hundred enrolled students were led by Levine and me once a week. The three graduate student instructors attended each lecture and consistently advised us on how we might elicit discussions in the eight sections, limited to fifteen to eighteen students. Beyond the structural dynamics, Michael Thompson—who served as head graduate student instructor—reorganized the course reader into an integrated syllabus by introducing students to the theories and experiences together across ethnic lines. For instance, during the three weeks devoted to Anglo-conformity, theory and experience ranged from writings by and about the founding fathers to Polish, Russian, Jewish, Native American, Latino, Italian, and Chinese responses to the assimilative role that education has assumed in the process of creating American identity.

Crossing the theoretical, cultural, disciplinary, and pedagogical borders defining American identity and American studies was clearly the intent of the course, as the readings, films, and discussions reflected. The most difficult barrier still left to theorize and represent is multiculturalism. Not unlike Creolization, multiculturalism is an old practice and recent theory that looks back on cross-cultural interactions documented historically among monocultural groups. Edward Kamau Brathwaite's and Ulf Hannerz's research on Creolization in Jamaica and the United States and Ronald Takaki's pioneering approaches to ethnic American historiography provide bases for conceptualizing truly multicultural and interdisciplinary approaches to American cultural identity. Valuable as these sources were for us at the time, they are not nearly as probing as the essays published by David Theo Goldberg in 1994, *Multiculturalism: A Critical Reader*. In the future, scholars committed to multicultural research and education in the United States might wish to reflect on and situate their standpoints within three distinct areas of practice defined by Goldberg in his introduction, "Multicultural Conditions."

Goldberg's provocative opening uncovers silenced areas of discourse and collective fixations. He argues that the political economy of location has been overlooked by a majority of scholars, while much of the writing on multicultural societies has focused on cultural identity and difference. Seeking to draw readers beyond "prevailing concerns and considerations, principles and practices, concepts and categories that fall under the rubric of 'multiculturalism'" (ix), Goldberg begins by contextualizing the nineteen essays in a brilliant overview of the fields of American and cultural studies. In that effort, he pluralizes the theory of intra-ethnic relations and identifies three intellectual and political bases out of which *multiculturalisms* emerge: (1) managed multiculturalism; (2) transgressive multiculturalism; (3) critical multiculturalism. The managed practice has been developed by multinational corporate executives primed to avoid discrimination suits and centrist academics devoted to promoting diversity. The transgressive (i.e., incorporative of the "hybrid") approach represents the counter-response from the 1960s among ethnic groups and feminists whose insurgency led to the very notion of multicultural education within the academy. As I have argued above, these types of interventions are important; however, they amount to nothing better than retrofit. By contrast, critical multiculturalism or heterogeneity reconfigures cultural inclusion as an insurgent, polyvalent system of analysis working toward discovering the *fit* rather than retrofit. Responding to disturbing portrayals of these United States as a monocultural union, critical multiculturalism reveals the shaky normative building blocks on which our systems of cultural identity and pedagogy were and still are erected. These blocks have become architectonic barriers preventing us from seeing and acknowledging the degrees to which American cultural identity has been a Creolized, mixed marriage from the outset.

Explaining that "irrepressible traces of heterogeneity, however tenuous, dot any mapping of human histories" (28), Goldberg provides useful agendas for researching multiculturalism beyond pluralist theories:

> I project (self-) critical multicultural conditions as ways of cultivating those improvisational expressions that have survived the repressive thrust of homogeneous and unicultural impositions. Even within the parameters of a culture . . . heterogeneity is the norm, and homogeneity (as in fundamentalisms) is achieved only at the cost of censorious restriction. Even in the face of the most extremely repressive forms of imposed homogeneity, the inevitable cultural hybridity that heterogeneity licenses promotes the renewable possibilities of playing novel expression. Witness jazz and gospel blues and rap in the United States, kwela music and sculpture parks in South Africa, religious animism throughout Africa, reggae in the Caribbean and beyond, cubism in Europe, tea drinking in England, pasta in Italy, and so on. (28)

> The aims of (self-) critical multiculturalisms, of promoting multicultural conditions, are to undo the effects of repressive and constraining power. Polyvocal and insurgent multiculturalisms undertake to transform power and its values to commonly emancipatory ends and effects. So the point of instituting renewable multicultural conditions is to facilitate and promote incorporative heterogeneity through hybrid interaction and the production of hybrid effect. (30)

As I look back on the pedagogical principles that we developed as a team during the organization and teaching of the "Cultural Identity in American History" course, I see that our engagements with theories and experiences were not directed to "postcolonial" articulations, as the majority of essays in the Goldberg reader are. We never used the fashionable terms "hybrid" or "subaltern," nor did we focus primarily on current ideologies. Awaiting another collective revision of this course, I would agree with Goldberg's call for scholars to deal with heterogeneity and the politics of location.[23]

Building on some of our previous lectures and discussions of films, I would like to focus on Creolization and multiculturalism together by addressing the still sore issue of influences in American cultural production. Homi Bhabha's insights in *The Location of Culture* (1994) are particularly relevant:

> Cultural diversity is the recognition of pre-given cultural contents and customs; held in a time-frame of relativism it gives rise to liberal notions of multiculturalism, cultural exchange or the culture of humanity. Cultural diversity is also the representation of a radical rhetoric of the separation of totalized cultures that live unsullied by the intertextuality of their historical locations, safe in the Utopianism of a mythic memory of a unique collective identity. (Bhabha 30)

A critical approach would revisit historical moments of ethnic interactions among Irish, African American, and Chinese workers, or between African Americans and Jewish Americans, as researched by Ronald Takaki in *A Different Mirror*. A section of the course devoted to work sites and activist alliances might well generate other hidden sources in the historical record. In addition, we might explore influence and intertexts intraracially and intraculturally by examining cross-cultural developments in performance—such as gospel, tap dancing, jazz, modern dance, and popular music. Initially, the multicultural texts and relationships that I would propose to use as indicators of the politics of location, economies of appropriation, and gendered performance idioms would include "Amazing Grace," Bill Robinson/Shirley Temple, Fred Astaire/Ginger Rogers, Martha Graham/George Balanchine/Katherine Dunham, Carole King in rock and roll, the distortions of American musical history where jazz loses its African American origins for the sake of promoting an American "original." Locating historically the stories, the sources of creolization in the United States—those areas of cross-cultural fertilization persisting beyond monocultural migrations, residencies, and cultural production—redefine the *multi-* both historically and critically. Similar cross-cultural, interdisciplinary exchanges leading to critical multiculturalism will likely occur in the classroom, depending on the student body, the instructors, and their collective views on multicultural conditions, in Goldberg's terms.

Standing on the Practice of Critical Pedagogy

The value of having a Jewish American man and an African American woman of different generations lead the course was not lost on our students. Differences of opinion or interpretation and the ways we dealt with classroom authority were less divisive than one might expect them to be in a mixed gender, mixed ethnic, and multicultural classroom. The initial sessions were perhaps more impressive to us than they were for the students. Looking superficially at the faces of those hundred students, Lawrence Levine and I were pleased to see the broad range of ethnic diversity among them. Such is Berkeley! The undergraduates perceived over time that Levine and I were in sync, not only in our teaching praxis, but in our belonging to immigrant working classes. They did not know that our intellectual bond and rather ludic approach to each other had developed over twenty years, from the time that I was a graduate student at Berkeley.

Our cultural identities as professors and the ethnic diversity among our graduate assistants were not nearly as central to the students, given their perceptions recorded in student evaluations after the fact. Cross-disciplinary approaches to texts distinguished us. Students appreciated the discipline-focused ways a historian and a literary historian examined evidence; interdisciplinary inquiry in the field of cultural studies that we shared with and elicited from them; differences in pedagogical style to which they were exposed in weekly meetings. Each instructor created methods of engaging the students in theory and the experiences of diversity that had drawn many of them to Berkeley; these interactions were played out in each section, where multiculturalism was not a theory but a reality.

In my section, I initiated a practice of having groups of students lead discussions by arguing for a particular theory derived from the readings and their own experiences. In other words, responses to the published texts extended outward to daily interactions elsewhere on campus—some supportive, others painful. In addition to the intellectual challenge of reading and interpreting more than eight hundred pages in the reader, there were curative benefits that developed during the fifteen weeks and afterward. An exercise created by Michael Thompson led to startling revelations. Beginning with identifications of our own cultural standpoints as instructors, students were asked to reply to a series of questions: (1) identify yourself ethnically; (2) relate the time span of that identification within the family and among ancestors; (3) indicate the moment in life when your ethnicity was defined negatively outside the family. A Latina born on the East Coast was particularly outspoken and angry about Berkeley's practice of separating students according to strict ethnic backgrounds. Coming from a mixed cultural background over several generations—so common in the Caribbean—she checked off a number of "ethnic" boxes on her application, and was overwhelmed before she arrived at Berkeley with a barrage of information about specific campus groups and activities targeted to the five or more ethnicities that she claimed. The enticements of ethnic diversity turned sour once she arrived and found that cultural balkanization was the norm on campus. Among other frustrations, she learned that in California Chicano and Latino experiences are regional, that command of the Spanish language does not guarantee inclusion. Throughout the course and a semester later, confronting issues of cultural identity and parental expectations allowed this student to finally feel at home at Cal.

Clearly, we had not anticipated the fact that large numbers of our students live multicultural lives, particularly in those ports of call (Miami, Texas, Washington D.C., New York, Los Angeles, San Francisco) where exiles and immigrants flow into our systems at a rapid pace. In such environments, new citizens are exposed to many of the older theories and experiences at close quarters in time and space. Reflecting on that situation, another student invented *combo practice* as a response to the historical evidence; others challenged the need to establish a unifying theory as hopelessly flawed, because none of the five themes represented the experiences of various ethnicities, nor did they apply uniformly to gender, class, or regional differences.

The final writing assignment in this course provided several options: new theories of cultural identity in America; theories to describe America in 2013, over the twenty years from 1993; an oral history describing family definitions of ethnicity; interviews with fellow students of a different cultural grouping or the history of a student-based ethnic organization on campus. Most students chose the oral history proposal, leading inevitably back to the first days of the section when we asked them to portray their ethnicity according to both endogamous and exogamous definitions. Those vignettes generally led to descriptions of ethnic dismissal: the first time you were called "nigger" or some other derogatory term in public. These latter discussions were often painful to hear; they also provided a *telling field* that students could use as a base for interviewing their parents or other family members.

Oral histories conducted with parents served a function of incorporation that Professor Joyce King had experienced when she brought the parents directly into the textbook controversy here in

California. I would like to suggest that for the purposes of changing public policy we need to broaden our teaching outward into the legislative bodies, to those persons whose diaspora literacy is dormant, but who wield enormous power over immigration policies and funding for education in this country. How to do so is a matter that we must address as we reform multicultural learning at every level in our schools. The last words on "Cultural Identity in American History: Theory and Experience" rest with two anonymous evaluations from students:

> It really opened my mind to the other cultures in America; although I realized the diversity of America, I was never really aware of the impact of the cultures on each other or how/why they exist in America. This was the best class I took this semester.

> Of the American cultures courses I've taken, this has been by far the best. It considers the broadest range of ethnicities' experience and women's experiences, and also theoretical and experiential perspectives.[24]

Perhaps someday on the floors of Congress, our legislators will argue likewise for radical changes in the curriculum by supporting the work of those who have questioned the construction of American identity by exclusion and inclusion. If reform of the curriculum remains retrofitted rather than true to human experience, we will always be working to shore up shaky systems of learning in the final years of the twentieth century.

NOTES

I wish to acknowledge my profound debt to Professors Jesper Rosenmeier (Tufts University), Sylvia Wynter (Stanford University), and Lawrence Levine (UC Berkeley) for their visionary approaches to American studies grounded in systemic learning and interdisciplinary studies. To the editorial collective at the University of Minnesota, my deep appreciation for leading me to rethink several points in this essay.

1. For critiques of the design and construction of the Nimitz Freeway on shaky ground, see various articles in the *New York Times*, October 21, 1989, 1.2; October 22, 1989, 26.1; and November 5, 1989, 28.1.

2. I am referring here to Sylvia Wynter, "'No Humans Involved': An Open Letter to My Colleagues."

3. The American cultures requirement was first instituted at the Univer-

sity of California, Berkeley in the spring of 1989 based on faculty recommendations and administrative and student support. The Center for the Teaching and Study of American Cultures, chaired originally by Professor William Simmons of Anthropology, has supported some two hundred new or revised courses since the fall of 1991 through 1995. Each course approved for inclusion in the program must examine the cultures of at least three ethnic groups: Native American, European American, African American, Chicano/Latino, or Asian American. California's broad array of ethnic populations and Berkeley's commitment to representing that diversity in its enrollment policies are perhaps unique; however, the educational principles might well be replicated in other urban areas, particularly cities and towns where newer immigrant populaces have arisen. For the problems concerned with balkanization among ethnically diverse student groups on campus, see Troy Duster, *The Diversity Project*. Although she does not use the term "retrofit," Hazel Carby reaches similar conclusions in "The Multicultural Wars."

4. This summary describes several of my courses in African American studies devoted to investigations of colonialism as a system of appropriation and resistance strategies as counter-response. Most were designed to be taught in French and English in Romance Languages at Tufts University. The versions offered at UC Berkeley include colonial and neocolonial representations from the anglophone, creolophone, francophone, hispanophone, and lusophone areas of Africa and the Caribbean.

5. See, for example, the anticolonial writings of Ngugi wa Thiong'o, *Decolonising the Mind*, and *Moving the Centre*.

6. To display the process of forced assimilation and Americanization among Native Americans, European Americans, African Americans, and Asian Americans in public education, we included reports and testimonies from 1912 onward in debates over bilingual education among Chicanos/Latinos. We are indebted to the graduate assistants Burton Peretti, Claudia May, and Cecilia O'Leary for locating these sources. See also Paul Gilroy, *The Black Atlantic: Modernity and Double Consciousness*, and Sandra Adell, *Double-Consciousness/Double Bind*.

7. Two novels published in 1956 by the Cameroonian novelist Ferdinand Oyono demonstrate the extent to which mind control of subjects across the generations benefits overseas colonial administrations. In addition, Oyono portrays women characters collaborating with or resisting occupying colonial forces. See the English translations, *Houseboy* and *The Old Man and the Medal*.

8. "Diaspora literacy" was a term that I originally used in critiques of Caribbean works by women authors in order to motivate explorations of cultural differences within African Diaspora studies. Beyond the specificities of Jewish migrations over the centuries, the term "diaspora" has also described

the locations of diverse populaces within immigrant nation-states, such as the United States, Canada, and Australia. Development of diaspora literacy in American studies seems to be a central process in our work toward critical multiculturalism. See VèVè A. Clark, "Developing Diaspora Literacy," "Developing Diaspora Literacy and *Marasa* Consciousness," and "Talking Shop."

9. On issues of "new ethnicities" or "emergent ethnicities," see Stuart Hall, "Ethnicity: Identity and Difference."

10. "Not yet/always already" represents those oppositional stances that exist below the surface of mainstream policies awaiting a team of activists or a movement prepared to organize radical change in society. Obviously, the references are to Ayi Kwei Armah's novel from 1968, *The Beautyful Ones Are Not Yet Born* and the discourse of deconstruction.

11. The competing narratives from the Left and Right describing the struggles of African Americans to be included in the curriculum appear in Louis Kampf and Paul Lauter, eds., *The Politics of Literature: Dissenting Essays on the Teaching of English,* and Allan Bloom, *The Closing of the American Mind.*

12. I am deeply indebted to Kath Weston for her provocative title and arguments in "The Virtual Anthropologist," included in this volume. Her presentation and our subsequent conversations during the conference in Minnesota awakened memories of the virtual working class operating in America, known also as *been-to's* in African and Caribbean literatures.

13. "Too tall, too strong" was a phrase used "under the table" during the tenure process to describe my service record at Tufts. Although personalized, the remark sought ultimately to diminish collective efforts to reform the curriculum in Romance Languages and across the campus. The ubiquitous *too* suggests that adding courses rather than reforming systems is a more comfortable area of engagement among some colleagues. Older faculty who had participated in curriculum revisions long before I arrived portrayed my endeavors as a "force of nature." Surely, neither represents the ways I see myself in the academy; I am still teaching the "neighborhood children" how to overcome barriers obstructing their inclusion in systems of learning.

14. Harold Cruse in *The Crisis of the Negro Intellectual* (1967) examined undigested Diaspora differences among African, Afro-American, and Afro–West Indian scholars working together in Black studies. See chapter 5, "Ideology in Black," 420–48.

15. The presentation by Daphne Muse, a consultant for the New Press Multicultural Project, examined working-class progress in the essay "Collecting Our Intellectual and Cultural Power."

16. See Sara Danius and Stefan Jonsson, "An Interview with Gayatri Chakravorty Spivak."

17. J. M. Blaut, *The Colonizer's Model of the World,* and Sylvia Wynter, "The Ceremony Must Be Found: After Humanism."

18. Kampf and Lauter, 8.

19. See Henry Louis Gates, Jr., *Loose Canons: Notes on the Culture Wars,* and "Beyond the Culture Wars: Identities in Dialogue."

20. See Molefi K. Asante, *Afrocentricity: The Theory of Social Change* for earlier statements on Afrocentric praxis.

21. For broader issues relating to activism cum pedagogy in this course, see Clark, "Talking Shop."

22. See, for example, Peter McLaren, "Multiculturalism and the Post-Modern Critique: Toward a Pedagogy of Resistance and Transformation."

23. See the fine work on the politics of location by Carole Boyce Davies, *Black Women, Writing and Identity: Migrations of the Subject.*

24. Excerpts from student evaluations for "Cultural Identity in American History," fall 1993.

WORKS CITED

Adell, Sandra. *Double-Consciousness/Double Bind: Theoretical Issues in Twentieth-Century Black Literature.* Urbana: University of Illinois Press, 1994.

Armah, Ayi Kwei. *The Beautyful Ones Are Not Yet Born.* Boston: Houghton Mifflin, 1968.

Asante, Molefi Kete. *The Afrocentric Idea.* Philadelphia: Temple University Press, 1987.

——. *Afrocentricity: The Theory of Social Change.* Buffalo: Amulefi, 1980.

Bernal, Martin. *Black Athena: The Afroasiatic Roots of Classical Civilization.* Vol. 1, *The Fabrication of Ancient Greece.* London: Free Association Press, 1987.

——. *Black Athena: The Afroasiatic Roots of Classical Civilization.* Vol. 2, *The Archaeological and Documentary Evidence.* London: Free Association Press, 1991.

Bhabha, Homi K. *The Location of Culture.* New York: Routledge, 1994.

Blaut, J. M. *The Colonizer's Model of the World: Geographical Diffusionism and Eurocentric History.* New York: Guilford Press, 1993.

Bloom, Allan. *The Closing of the American Mind.* New York: Simon and Schuster, 1987.

Brathwaite, Edward Kamau. *The Development of Creole Society in Jamaica, 1770–1820.* Oxford: Clarendon Press, 1971.

Carby, Hazel. "The Multicultural Wars." *Radical History Review* 54 (1992): 7–18.

Clark, VèVè A. "Developing Diaspora Literacy: Allusion in Maryse Condé's *Heremakhonon.*" In *Out of the Kumbla: Womanist Perspectives on Caribbean Literature,* ed. Carole Boyce Davies and Elaine Savory Fido, 315–31. Trenton, NJ: Africa World Press, 1989.

———. "Developing Diaspora Literacy and *Marasa* Consciousness." In *Comparative American Identities: Race, Sex, and Nationality in the Modern Text,* ed. Hortense Spillers. New York: Routledge, 1991.

———. "Talking Shop: A Comparative Feminist Approach to Caribbean Literature by Women." In *Borderwork: Feminist Engagements with Comparative Literature,* Ed. Margaret Higonnet. Ithaca: Cornell University Press, 1994.

Cruse, Harold. *The Crisis of the Negro Intellectual.* New York: Morrow, 1967.

Danius, Sara, and Stefan Jonsson. "An Interview with Gayatri Chakravorty Spivak." *Boundary 2,* 20.2 (summer 1993): 24–50.

Davies, Carole Boyce. *Black Women, Writing and Identity: Migrations of the Subject.* New York: Routledge, 1994.

De Tocqueville, Alexis. *Selected Letters on Politics and Society,* ed. and trans. Roger Boesche. Berkeley: University of California Press, 1985.

Duster, Troy, ed. *The Diversity Project.* Berkeley: Institute for the Study of Social Change, 1991.

Gates, Henry Louis, Jr. "Beyond the Culture Wars: Identities in Dialogue." In *Profession 93,* 6–11. New York: Modern Language Association of America, 1993.

———. "Black Studies: Myths or Realities?" *Essence,* February 1994, 138.

———. *Loose Canons: Notes on the Culture Wars.* New York: Oxford University Press, 1992.

Gilroy, Paul. *The Black Atlantic: Modernity and Double Consciousness.* Cambridge: Harvard University Press, 1993.

Goldberg, David Theo. *Multiculturalism: A Critical Reader.* Oxford: Blackwell, 1994.

Hall, Stuart. "Ethnicity: Identity and Difference." *Radical America* 23.4 (1991): 9–20.

Hannerz, Ulf. "American Culture: Creolized, Creolizing." Keynote address at the Nordic Association for American Studies, Uppsala, May 28, 1987.

———. *Cultural Complexity: Studies in the Organization of Social Meaning.* New York: Columbia University Press, 1992.

Hilliard, Asa. *Free Your Mind, Return to the Source: The African Origin of Civilization.* San Francisco: Urban Institute for Human Services, 1978.

Hirsch, E. D., Jr. *Cultural Literacy: What Every American Needs to Know.* Boston: Houghton Mifflin, 1987.

Kampf, Louis, and Paul Lauter, eds. *The Politics of Literature: Dissenting Essays on the Teaching of English.* New York: Pantheon, 1970.

King, Joyce Elaine. "Diaspora Literacy and Consciousness in the Struggle against Miseducation in the Black Community." *Journal of Negro Education* 61.3 (1992): 317–40.

Maher, Frances, and Mary Kay Thompson Tetreault. *The Feminist Classroom.* New York: Basic Books, 1994.

McLaren, Peter. "Multiculturalism and the Post-Modern Critique: Toward a Pedagogy of Resistance and Transformation." In *Between Borders: Pedagogy and the Politics of Cultural Studies*, ed. Henry A. Giroux and Peter McLaren. New York: Routledge, 1994.

Muse, Daphne. "Collecting Our Intellectual and Cultural Power." *Proceedings*, "Reading between the Black and White Keys," ed. Vèvè A. Clark, 161–64. Series 2 of the St. Clair Drake Cultural Studies Forum. Berkeley: African American Studies, 1994.

Ngugi wa Thiong'o. *Decolonising the Mind: The Politics of Language in African Literature*. London: James Currey, 1993.

———. *Moving the Centre: The Struggle for Cultural Freedom*. London: James Currey, 1993.

O'Barr, Jean, and Mary Wyer, eds. *Engaging Feminism: Students Speak Up and Speak Out*. Charlottesville: University Press of Virginia, 1992.

Obenga, Théophile. *L'Afrique dans l'Antiquité: Egypte Pharaonique/Afrique Noire*. Paris: Présence Africaine, 1973.

———. *Ancient Egypt and Black Africa*, ed. Amon Saba Saakana. London: Karnak House, 1992.

Oyono, Ferdinand. *Houseboy*. 1956; New Hampshire: Heinemann, 1966.

———. *The Old Man and the Medal*. 1956; New Hampshire: Heinemann, 1969.

Postiglione, Gerard A. *Ethnicity and American Social Theory: Toward Critical Pluralism*. Lanham, MD: University Press of America, 1983.

Takaki, Ronald. *A Different Mirror: A History of Multicultural America*. Boston: Little, Brown, 1993.

Van Sertima, Ivan. *They Came before Columbus*. New York: Random House, 1976.

Weston, Kath. "The Virtual Anthropologist." In *Anthropological Locations: Boundaries and Grounds of a Field Science*, ed. Akhil Gupta and James Ferguson. Berkeley: University of California Press, 1997. Reprinted in this volume.

Williams, Patrick, and Laura Chrisman, eds. *Colonial Discourse and Post-Colonial Theory: A Reader*. New York: Columbia University Press, 1994.

Wynter, Sylvia. "The Ceremony Must Be Found: After Humanism." *Boundary 2*, 12.3-13.1 (spring–fall 1984): 19–70.

———. "'No Humans Involved': An Open Letter to My Colleagues." *Aesthetics, Vision and Urban American Voices of the African Diaspora. African American Studies Research Review* (University of Michigan) 8.2 (fall 1992): 13–16.

Chapter 2

Ethnocentrism/Essentialism
The Failure of the Ontological Cure

Marilyn Frye

Introduction

This essay is located within a larger project in which I am exploring categories and categorization with a view to building an understanding of pluralism in theories and plurality in identity. Feminists have some grip on the workings of monologic; I am trying to get a grip on polylogic. One thing I hope to do eventually is create and/or demonstrate the possibility of politics that are committed to certain kinds of identities and their positive political value, but not to ethnocentrism (of an obnoxious sort) or to essentialism (of an obnoxious sort). But essentialism and ethnocentrism are not the same thing, and feminist critiques of essentialism that fail to distinguish between them have contributed to confusion about the issues involved here. Also, because they make it easy to substitute a theoretical anxiety about essence for a political concern about domination and injury, such critiques tend to detour or obscure political and moral problems that need to be very directly confronted if pluralist theories are to be concretely realized and plural identities wholesomely actualized in real women's lives and social relations.[1]

I single out one article here for analysis and criticism, "Social Criticism without Philosophy: An Encounter between Feminism and Postmodernism," by Linda Nicholson and Nancy Fraser (1990).[2] It is not uniquely deserving of criticism, but it has been quite widely read and cited,[3] and it presents in revealing cameo a dynamic of theory and practice that I believe is commonly manifest in the 1980s and 1990s among U.S. academic feminists, a dynamic in which theory and ethnocentrism play tricks on the theorist—catch her up in precisely the positions she is trying to avoid.

I

One thing that is bothersome about "anti-essentialism" as recently articulated in academic feminist writing is that it is common for theories to be declared essentialist, condemned, and dismissed, with no intermediate or prior step of explaining what essentialism is or what is wrong with it. In order not to be complicit with this practice of talking about essentialism without saying what it is or what may be wrong with it, I will state the dogma I would call "essentialism":

> The world is ultimately constituted of entities each of which exists independently of all others: for example, Plato's Forms, Aristotle's individual substances (tables, men, etc.), Descartes's ego (the thing that thinks), and atoms or subatomic particles. Each such entity has a distinctive identity: it is something . . . it is Justice, or it is Descartes's self, or it is a man, or it is a cesium atom . . . and it is what it is in virtue of one or more intrinsic, innate, structured-in or inborn properties (like rationality and animality), which are its Essence. A thing's essential properties are those intrinsic properties without which it would not be what it is. Definitions of things specify what the things are, by giving their essences. The classic Aristotelian example: Man is a rational animal; all men, and only men, have this essence.

This is quite simplified. The notion of essence and related ideas have a long and complicated history to which I am not trying to do justice here (and to which recent feminist discussions of essentialism do not generally do justice). What is central in this context is the idea that things, and whatever makes them *what* they are, exist independently of each other and of human cognition, categories, and cultures. The opposing general picture of reality, which most academic feminists now embrace, is the picture according to which everything *is,* and *is what it is,* by virtue of its place and relations in structures of human cognition, categorization, language, and cultural organization. This is the view I take it the terms "constructionism" or "social constructionism" refer to.

Saying what is wrong with essentialism is a bit problematic, which may be why the matter is seldom directly addressed. One might wish to say just that essentialism is *false*: one might say that things and kinds of things do not have essences and do not have identities that are determined by essences; there just are no essences. But this is a *metaphysical* statement, if there ever was one, and feminist anti-essentialists have not been inclined to provide metaphysical arguments to support it, nor would most of them approve of "doing metaphysics."[4] For the nonce, I will just say that I do not believe in essences, and I assume that the reader doesn't either.

II

Nicholson and Fraser present several examples of feminist theories in which they claim to find essentialist assumptions. One is Shulamith Firestone's (1970) theory. Seeking a materialist analysis of the oppression of women, Firestone suggested that the physiological burden of childbearing, combined with human infant nutritional dependency, is the material base of male domination. They also object to Michelle Rosaldo's early theory of the universality of a "public/private" distinction, and to Carol Gilligan's theory of a "woman's voice," and Nancy Chodorow's theory of the reproduction of masculine and feminine gender identities. Nicholson and Fraser's criticism of these theories is that they "project onto all women and men qualities which develop under historically specific social conditions" (28) and "falsely generalize to all societies an historically specific conjunction of properties" (29). Summing up in each case, they name the flaws in the theories "essentialism," and "the use of essentialist categories."[5]

The notion of *erroneously projecting onto all x's qualities observed in some x's* indiscriminately covers a number of different things it is useful to sort out.

After my first ride on a Minneapolis city bus, I wrote home in amazement, "They have poetry posted in the buses in this city!" But thereafter, I rode many buses that had no poetry posted in them, alas. I had drawn a mistaken general conclusion. I had assumed that the transit authority imposed a great degree of uniformity in what would be posted in buses: a mistaken though sensible assumption; an erroneous generalization. Ordinary overgeneralizing in a scientific or quasi-scientific mode may be just careless, and it may be mediated by mistaken assumptions about structures or conditions that would impose a certain regularity on things (like my assumptions about the policies of the transit authority). Such mistakes are to be found in feminist theorizing, and they need to be corrected. But they are mundane, discoverable, correctable; they are not profound, and usually do not merit passionate or paranoid denunciation.[6]

However, there may be something more unsavory going on in some theorizing. To get at it, I will use Lawrence Kohlberg's theory of moral development, as presented in Gilligan's critique of it.

Kohlberg studies some people who are demographically just like himself and discovers that they go through certain stages of moral development. He then concludes that these are *the* stages of *human* moral development. He takes it that if something is characteristic of this very small sample of human individuals, this is adequate indication of what we may assume to be characteristic of the species.

It probably is not the case that Kohlberg simply, and mistakenly, thought that his sample was large enough and representative enough in statistical terms to ground universal conclusions about all humans. But his approach is sufficiently empirical that one also cannot reasonably imagine that he thought of himself as engaged in the sort of speculative psychology of earlier folk like David Hume or perhaps William James. So how is he thinking; why does he draw such huge conclusions from such a small observed sample? One suggestion is that he was taking himself and a few other males of his culture (narrowly drawn) as paradigm cases within what might be called a paradigm-case category.[7]

Categories of this kind are common, and from my present point of view, quite interesting. The category *book* is an example. A perfect-bound volume of printed paper pages about an inch thick in hardcover, about nine inches high and seven inches wide, is a paradigm book. All other books approximately match this paradigm, deviating from it in some degree along one or more quality-vector(s). Anything too far away, or distant on too many vectors, is a questionable case of a book. There's nothing wrong with the category *book* being that sort of category. One interesting thing, though, about categories of this sort is that people's judgments of similarities and differences among things in such categories are asymmetrical.[8] For instance, for most North American non-ornithologists, robins are the paradigm case of the category of birds. In the cognitive frame of these folk, ducks are also indisputably birds, but are not paradigm cases of birds. In similarity-rating tests, folks tend to rate ducks as being more similar to robins than robins are to ducks. And new information about robins is more likely to be generalized to ducks than new information about ducks is to be generalized to robins.

I am suggesting that what Kohlberg did was to take himself as a paradigm case and construct the rest of humanity as a paradigm-case sort of category around himself. This is a pretty familiar cognitive operation; listen to how it sounds when we substitute for 'robin' and 'duck' the words 'man' and 'woman', or 'whites' and 'Blacks'.

> Women are judged more similar to men than men are to women; new information about men is more likely to be generalized to women than new information about women is to be generalized to men.

> White people (the nice ones anyway) tend to proclaim that Blacks are "just like us," but not that "we" are "just like them."[9]

What this suggests to me is that what is wrong in some of the cases of problematic generalization to be found in some feminist theorizing is that the theorist has situated herself, or her family, or her culture as a paradigm case that structures a paradigm-case type of category. I am inclined to think that this kind of construction is central to much of the thought and perception that we call "ethnocentric."[10] Such construction is an act of arrogance, and it is one of the kinds of exercise of power by which individuals participate in socially constructing domination. But it is *not* essentialism. The asymmetries of similarity judgments and the asymmetrical extensions of generalization across a paradigm-case category are due precisely to the fact that what has been constructed is *not* an internally homogeneous category defined by a set of necessary and sufficient conditions (an essence) that are satisfied equally and decisively by all its members; it is an internally structured, nonhomogeneous category organized by a paradigm and its aura. Making oneself a paradigm case of human beings, or one's culture a paradigm case of human culture is not commitment to an essence.

It seems plausible to me that there is an element of self-as-paradigm cognition in Firestone's, Rosaldo's, Gilligan's, and Chodorow's early theories. Condemning these theories as essentialist seems to me to misdirect our attention, to obscure rather than illuminate, and to leave unanalyzed the active constructive ethnocentrism implicit in such theories.[11]

III

There is a very significant passage in which Nicholson and Fraser reveal that they themselves have engaged in this kind of self-as-paradigm category construction that, by my reckoning, they have criticized without analyzing or correctly naming. I would suspect that the failure to analyze and correctly name it made it that much easier unknowingly to repeat it.

They say that although feminist theory kept being "plagued" by "vestiges of essentialism," the practice of feminist politics in the 1980s generated "a new set of pressures" against the metanarratives associated with essentialism. They say that "poor and working-class women, women of color, and lesbians" have objected to feminist theories that fail to illuminate their lives and address their problems. They list as examples Bell Hooks (*sic*), Gloria Joseph, Audre Lord (*sic*), Maria Lugones (*sic*) and Elizabeth Spelman, Adrienne Rich, and Marilyn Frye (33). Anyone familiar with the works of these women knows that this is a strikingly heterogeneous list. In the Nicholson and Fraser article, these very diverse theorists are lumped together as all, alike, having significance and entering into the story told by the essay *only* as "critics" of other women's feminist theories, and all with the same criticism: you have failed to illuminate my life and address my problems. This is also the *only* reference in the article to Black, Latina, explicitly antiracist, or explicitly Lesbian feminist theory. And these women are not referred to here either as "feminists" or as "theorists"—we are "writers."

It appears to me that Nicholson and Fraser constructed the category of feminist theorists with white, middle-class, heterosexual theorists as its paradigm case. I think that to make their own general statements about feminist theorists and theories plausible, they *had* to set aside many volumes of feminist theory as nonparadigmatic. To create the appearance of a *general* tendency in feminist theory to overgeneralization in ways that make it unilluminating for poor women, working-class women, women of color, and lesbians, they had to exclude theory *by* and from the perspectives of poor women, working-class women, women of color, and lesbians from the paradigm of "feminist theory." Consider the alternative. bell hooks's *Ain't I Woman?* (1981), Maxine Hong Kingston's *The Woman Warrior* (1975), Jill Johnston's *Lesbian Nation* (1973), Mary Daly's *Gyn/Ecology* (1978), Sidney Abbott and Barbara Love's *Sappho Was a Right-On Woman* (1972), Barbara Smith's "Toward a Black Feminist Criticism" (1977), Toni Cade (Bambara)'s anthology *The Black Woman* (1970), Tillie Olsen's *Silences* (1978) could all be considered paradigmatic of feminist theory.[12] And if you stir these into the mix of theories that will serve as paradigms structuring the category of feminist theory, you will not make the generalizations about feminist theory that Nicholson and Fraser made.

In their article Nicholson and Fraser are spinning a yarn that has become something of an official "family history" of second-wave feminism, as it is told by a certain set of academically influential feminists. "We" theorized along, essentializing the experience of middle-class heterosexual white U.S. women, and then one day "they" brought our attention to the fact that "we" had left them out of the theories. But all along, there have been theorists theorizing from experience that is not "middle-class heterosexual white U.S." This theory (and with respect to the sexuality dimension of this situation I can say "our" theory) has been original, and only some of it is reactive to other feminisms that leave many women out. A historical narrative of "feminist theory" or of "feminism" that leaves out theorists who theorize as women of color, poor and working-class women, and/or lesbians until they can be bunched together solely as critics of the "main" stream is an ethnocentric narrative.

(I have suggested that situating one*self* or one's family, group, or culture as a paradigm case that structures a paradigm-case type of category is central to much of the thought and perception that we call "ethnocentric." Nicholson and Fraser author in the voice of the detached neutral narrator, distancing themselves from these theories and theorists they criticize as "essentialist." I do not know Nicholson's or Fraser's own real-life demographic locations, but reading this article, one cannot avoid taking its authors to be white, middle-class, and heterosexual. The way they package and marginalize the "poor and working-class women, women of color, and lesbians" who have objected to those feminist theories defeats a reader's attempt to imagine that either of them *is* poor or working-class, a woman of color, or a lesbian. Practicing a certain group's ethnocentrism is a way of announcing one's membership in that group; and if one is not in fact a member, it may be a way of passing.)[13]

IV

In assessing the damage done by reading all errors of scope as consisting of or rooted in essentialism, we should note that the texts subjected by Nicholson and Fraser to this buckshot denunciation were composed by authors who were innocent of the canonical writings of what is being called postmodernism. These feminist texts were written before, or anyway outside, the era and the intellectual circles in which it is fashionable to claim that there is nothing but systems of signifiers that signify either nothing or nothing but themselves, outside the era and the social circles in which the terms 'ahistorical', 'universal', 'essence', and others became "terms of infallible critique" (Fuss 1989). They were not written by authors working self-consciously in the shadow of an inquisition that inspects every sentence for suspect ontology—suspect according to a philosophical stance that pretends it is not one and that claims not to engage in metaphysics. This supposedly postmodern critique of these supposedly pre-postmodern texts seems to me to impose an interpretive scheme and philosophical agenda on them that are both foreign and suffocating.

Though there is language in these writings that smacks of essentialism to the latter-day tastes of Nicholson and Fraser (and I can hear it that way too), the general drift of all this thinking that is now being rejected as essentialist is markedly and creatively "social constructionist." In fact, it is heir(ess) quite directly to Beauvoir's constructionism ("woman is made, not born"). Much of it can easily be read as very practical projects of tracking the concrete processes and mechanisms of the social construction of women and men and the structure of male domination, even if what those theorists perceived of those social constructions and constructs was more local and specific than they realized.

Chodorow, for example, does not seem to me to think that a masculine or feminine "deep self" is innate or determined by chromosomes. She seems to me to be trying to give an account of the social construction of gendered selves and to suggest interventions that would change that construction. Gilligan, too, is plotting the trajectory of social processes that construct orientations to morality, and types of orientations to morality. She does not think that aptitude for one type or another is innate or fixed by anybody's essence; on the contrary, she thinks anyone can and everyone to some extent does learn to operate with more than one kind of moral deliberation process. Firestone did not imagine as later theorists have that even the fact that there are two sexes is socially constructed, but her whole point in making the case of the causal explanation of male dominance by reproductive asymmetry was to say that different ways of socially organizing and technically intervening in the anatomical mechanics of reproduction could break that causal link. She did not see "biology" as irresistibly and irremediably dictating our social structures. She thought that the social meanings of biological asymmetry were quite definitely amenable to social reconstruction.

These theories may err in oversimplifying things—in suggesting that this or that thing is everywhere *the* most significant construct, the one that, if dismantled, would lead to the collapse of patriarchy. And this oversimplification may well have roots in ethnocentrism and related bad attitudes. (It almost certainly has roots in Marxist styles of thought and explanation, which also generally reject ideas of given natures.) But the spirit of the inquiry is, I believe, constructionist and politically progressive, not essentialist and regressive.

Misconstruing these theories as essentialist (in the late 1980s, early 1990s usage) seems to me almost perverse. It retroactively figures some of the most recognized, widely read, groundbreaking creators of feminist theory as philosophically unsophisticated, politically retrograde, and "immature" (32). I see no positive point in doing this. Historically, in many cultures, men have forced women over and over to invent anew without a genealogy, without a history of intellectual "mothers" whose existence, and brilliance, and production of schools of thought legitimate our own ambitions even as we critique and abandon some of their beliefs and ways of thinking (perhaps, eventually, all of them). Feminist theorists need not help bury our intellectual foremothers again, here and now.

V

The naturalistic developmental narrative that features the theories of Firestone, Rosaldo, Chodorow, Hartsock, MacKinnon, and Gilligan (among others) as "youthful" (32) takes an interesting turn after the part where the motley of "marginalized" women has been featured as arriving with their criticisms of the theories that the narrative has featured as paradigmatic feminist theories. According to this story, what "the critics" object to is essentialism, and to generate theory that is not essentialist, feminist theory should become, in Nicholson and Fraser's words, "more consistently postmodern" (34). The tale is brought into the present (and feminist theory into "maturity" [32]) with a rush to postmodernism, which is claimed to be motivated and justified as a conscientious response to, and called for by, these "critics," especially by women of color and Third World women.[14] But interestingly enough, the women of color theorists actually cited by Nicholson and Fraser did not themselves, in their own theorizing, join the rush to postmodernism, at least not to any intense engagement with the texts and projects of the European and American male philosophers and literary critics commonly given that name. Some, for example, María Lugones, have scrupulously avoided adopting the vocabulary characteristic of those texts.

Anti-essentialism is promoted as a cure or preventative of racism and ethnocentrism in feminist theorizing.[15] What I am suggesting here is that reading racist and/or ethnocentrist overgeneralization as essentialism and rushing to a mode of theorizing that is thought to be immune to essentialism is not a conscientious, positive response to the problems of racism and ethnocentrism in some feminist theory and among feminists. This response forecloses the patient investigation and analysis of modes of generalization and associated kinds of error or mistake—analysis that can reveal some of the ways ethnocentrism and racism may be practiced in the process of doing theory; the self-understanding involved in this response includes a narrative that repeats the pattern of ethnocentrism present in some earlier theories—a pattern not adequately appreciated partly because it is misnamed "essentialism"; and this response is not really very finely attuned to the work and writing of the critics who supposedly demand it, since many of those critics in fact neither call for nor join the headlong and heady rush to postmodernism, and while most of them would or do reject essentialism, they do not generally make anti-essentialism their primary battle cry. Without attributing any conscious or articulate intention here, I think it may be wondered whether white academic feminists' "postmodern turn" is in part a flight from direct, interactive, responsible engagement with women of color.[16]

Of course many women of color, both as feminist theorists and as theorists of colonialism and race, do take up the frameworks and languages originating with the privileged male postmodernists of the metropole, and brilliantly adapt them to their own purposes. For these women of color this holds a variety of promises and risks. For white and privileged women who have thought postmodernism to be politically "safer" (with respect to racial/ethnic politics) than other intellectual terrains, the appropriation by women of color of some postmodern language and strategies holds the promise that wherever feminist theory is taking place, that place is a site of engagement and interaction between women of dominating and women of subaltern groups. White theorists take whiteness there like a shadow; and women of color are there, with resources, critiques, and just demands. Engagement cannot be endlessly deferred—it cannot be deferred, in fact, at all.

Theories of political power and action that give key significance to identity run some risk of constructing overly simple or falsely unitary pictures of group, cultural, or personal identities or sexual, class, or racial identities—or of being (mis)interpreted as doing so. A politics of active construction of identity runs some risk of creating real social categories that operate, politically, as coercively normative constructs—or of being (mis)interpreted as doing so. Such a politics runs the risk of constructing social categories structured to give some politically dominant group paradigmatic status—or of being (mis)interpreted as doing so. I think it is far from clear, yet, whether these things are after all merely risks attendant to working and being interpreted within a wider context of domination and monologic, or are unavoidable disasters somehow built in to the logic of identity—even in to the polylogic of plural identity. But sorting this out requires both analytical and moral clarity about generalization, categories, identity, ethnocentrism, and racism that we will not achieve by using "essentialism" as an all-purpose term of criticism or assuming that if our theory is postmodern it is not ethnocentric.

NOTES

1. The substitution of theoretical concern for political and moral concern is well described and analyzed by María Lugones in "On the Logic of Pluralist Feminism" (1991: 41). The critique I develop in this chapter is directly indebted to that essay.

2. Parenthetical page references in the rest of this essay are to this text.

3. Prior to its publication in the Nicholson anthology, this essay was published in four journals and anthologies in 1988 and 1989 (Nicholson and Fraser 1990: 19).

4. There probably is a Wittgensteinian argument available, roughly to the effect that the language of essences arises through grammatical mistakes and theoretical muddles and can be, and should be, dispensed with once those muddles are cleared up and the grammatical mistakes are corrected. But this is not the sort of argument one finds among anti-essentialist feminists. An exception to the rule that anti-essentialist feminists eschew metaphysics is Linda Alcoff (1988: 428–29). Alcoff also discusses essentialism in a way that comes close to actually explaining what it is and what is wrong with it.

5. Another criticism Nicholson and Fraser make of several of these theories is that they are monocausal in spirit—they seem to offer "the one key factor which would explain sexism cross-culturally and illuminate all of social life" (29). I agree with them that several of the theories they discuss have this character, and that such theorizing surely oversimplifies and suggests political strategies that would be ineffective or self-defeating; but this tendency and a commitment to essentialism are distinct.

6. Jane Roland Martin makes this point, at more length, in "Methodological Essentialism, False Difference, and Other Dangerous Traps" (1994: 645).

7. I am indebted here to discussions with María Lugones.

8. I am referring here to some of what are called "prototype effects" in the empirical study of categories (Lakoff 1987: 41–46).

9. "In the United States white children like me . . . were told by well-meaning white adults that Black people were just like us—never, however, that we were just like Blacks" (Spelman 1988: 12).

10. A good deal of discussion about sexist, racist, or ethnocentric constructions of human and of woman uses the vocabulary of "center" and "margin." I am suggesting here that it is useful at least for some purposes to think of this "centering" and "marginalizing" as someone constructing the category of humans or persons as a paradigm-case category, with him- or herself and a small number of folk s/he identifies with located as the paradigm case governing the category.

11. There is also a rhetorical reason not to misname this constructive ethnocentrism. In some cases, if an ethnocentric generalizer is told that she has

"defined" a category "by an essence," this simply will not ring true to her—she knows in her bones that she is not committed to the category of women being internally homogeneous, that she has *not* said or implied that all women are, as women, exactly alike; and then the critic has lost the persuasive authority that comes with dead-on accuracy.

12. The works Nicholson and Fraser cite as the "feminism" that encounters "postmodernism" are dated from 1970 through 1983.

13. I am indebted to Naomi Scheman for bringing my attention to these implications of the term "self-as-paradigm," and in particular to its connection with this last point.

14. Lesbians criticizing heterosexualism in some feminist theory are not particularly taken into account at this juncture, for reasons that I will not try to explain in this essay.

15. It is supposed to be a nostrum also against *both* a heterosexualism that makes female heterosexuality normative/natural *and* a lesbian "naturalism" that makes lesbianism normative/natural, but in the writings denouncing essentialism what is most likely to be problematized is lesbian "naturalism"—heterosexualism is rarely noted.

16. I need to say again that the tendencies of thought I have been analyzing here are by no means those of Nicholson and Fraser alone. Their views are shared and similar arguments endorsed by a great many feminist theorists of the same decade. I have not, myself, been entirely innocent of "fleeing direct, interactive, responsible engagement with women of color." My course led, though, by its own logic, back to engagement and interaction. For the tracks of my flight and re-entry, see Frye "The Possibility of Feminist Theory" and "White Woman Feminist," in *Willful Virgin* (1991).

WORKS CITED AND CONSULTED

Abbott, Sidney, and Barbara Love. *Sappho Was a Right-On Woman*. New York: Stein and Day, 1972.

Alcoff, Linda. "Cultural Feminism versus Post-Structuralism: The Identity Crisis in Feminist Theory." *Signs* 13.3 (1988): 405–38.

Cade (Bambara), Toni. *The Black Woman*. New York: New American Library, 1970.

Chodorow, Nancy. *The Reproduction of Mothering: Psychoanalysis and the Sociology of Gender*. Berkeley: University of California Press, 1978.

Daly, Mary. *Gyn/Ecology: The Metaethics of Radical Feminism*. Boston: Beacon Press, 1978.

Firestone, Shulamith. *The Dialectic of Sex*. New York: Bantam, 1970.

Frye, Marilyn. *Willful Virgin: Essays in Feminism*. Freedom, CA: Crossing Press, 1991.

Fuss, Diana. *Essentially Speaking: Feminism, Nature and Difference.* New York: Routledge, 1989.

Gilligan, Carol. *In a Different Voice: Psychological Theory and Women's Development.* Cambridge: Harvard University Press, 1983.

hooks, bell. *Ain't I a Woman?* Boston: South End Press, 1981.

Johnston, Jill. *Lesbian Nation: The Feminist Solution.* New York: Simon and Schuster, 1973.

Kingston, Maxine Hong. *The Woman Warrior.* New York: Vintage Books, 1975.

Lakoff, George. *Women, Fire and Dangerous Things: What Categories Reveal about the Mind.* Chicago: University of Chicago Press, 1987.

Lugones, María C. "On the Logic of Pluralist Feminism." In *Feminist Ethics,* ed. Claudia Card, 35–44. Lawrence: University Press of Kansas, 1991.

Martin, Jane Roland. "Methodological Essentialism, False Difference, and Other Dangerous Traps." *Signs* 19.3 (1994): 630–57.

Nicholson, Linda J., and Nancy Fraser. "Social Criticism without Philosophy: An Encounter between Feminism and Postmodernism." In *Feminism/Postmodernism,* ed. Linda J. Nicholson, 19–38. New York: Routledge, 1990.

Olsen, Tillie. *Silences.* New York: Delacorte Press/St. Lawrence, 1978.

Rosaldo, Michelle Zimbalist. "Woman, Culture, and Society: A Theoretical Overview." In *Woman, Culture, and Society,* ed. Michelle Zimbalist Rosaldo and Louise Lamphere, 17–42. Stanford: Stanford University Press, 1974.

Smith, Barbara. "Toward a Black Feminist Criticism." Brooklyn: Out and Out Books, 1977; Freedom, CA: distributed by Crossing Press, 1980.

Spelman, Elizabeth V. *Inessential Woman: Problems of Exclusion in Feminist Thought.* Boston: Beacon Press, 1988.

Chapter 3

Maternal Presumption
The Personal Politics of Reproductive Rights

Alice Adams

> "If a pregnant woman is attacked by a bull, may she run for her life even though running may cause her to abort?"
>
> —quoted by Adrienne Rich, *Of Woman Born*

Abortion politics in the United States epitomizes what Elizabeth Kingdom describes as the phenomenon of "the attraction of opposite rights," in which any appeal to rights invites the opposition to mount its argument in terms of an equal and opposing right (2, 62). The debate trudges on without hope of resolution, with every blow for women's reproductive rights met by an equally battering blow from the opposition. To date, the questions we can pose are largely determined by the discourses of systems markedly hostile to women and mothers. The media are interested in lesbian custody cases, mothers on crack, surrogate motherhood, the latest repro-technological miracle (the recent success of a human cloning experiment drew plenty of attention, for instance), and the pyrotechnics of the pro-life movement. At the time of writing, pro-life terrorists have seized the discursive field—and made headlines across the continent—by shooting five people and killing two women in two abortion clinics in Brookline, Massachusetts.[1] A thousand supporters of abortion rights marched following the killings in Brookline, but any message such a march manages to communicate—about women's refusal to be intimidated, about the persistence of pro-choice activism—must be overshadowed in most people's minds by the explicit threat from the other side: if you seek an abortion, or accompany a woman to an abortion clinic, or work in a clinic, you may be shot. The main players in these dramas are not the women whose lives are at risk. The protagonists are the doctors, researchers, lawyers, ethical "experts," and representatives of the religious right, all of whom have access to channels for discursive power, in the sense that they have the attention of the media, and in the sense that they can directly impact on, or interfere with, women's reproductive lives.

It is clear enough that the violence of the pro-life movement impedes women's ability to exercise their right to choose an abortion. Such violence is just the other face of legislative and judicial efforts to deprive women of the right to abortion. What seems to get lost in the argument is the realization that even if the pro-life movement decided to give up bombing clinics and killing clinic workers, and even if abortion was a federally guaranteed right, many women would still not be able to afford abortions. Most important, most women's reproductive needs would not be met by a greater availability of abortion.

The question that preoccupies abortion clinics and pro-choice supporters following the killings in Brookline is, "How can we defend ourselves?" The media focuses on the manhunt and responses to the violence from government officials. Pro-lifers may be concerned about how to deal with the public relations difficulties that arise as their movement becomes identified with terrorism. Legislators, depending on their sympathies, may respond by devising new laws to punish violent pro-lifers or to further restrict women's access to abortion. One of the most widely felt effects of pro-life violence will be the new energy it injects into the old abortion rights debate, a debate that, for many people, provides the most powerful and most familiar forum for a discussion of women's reproductive lives. One of the attractions of the abortion debate is that the questions it pursues are construed as fundamental to our humanity: maternal responsibility, personhood, sexual morality, and family values all seem to be met head-on in the abortion debate, and complex questions seem to be resolvable by a simple decision either for or against women's right to abortion. Part of my intention in this essay is to show how the discourse of individual reproductive rights and responsibilities has been used to direct attention away from the responsibilities of communities to women—women whose economic, racial, and sexual differences defy the universalism of the generic, abstract "individual" whose rights and responsibilities attract so much discursive attention.

A comprehensive account of rights discourse, which has a particularly thick history in legal theory, is beyond the scope of this essay. I will focus on more commonly encountered examples of the rights discourse at work in the popular media, in feminism, and in nonfeminist analyses of maternal rights and responsibilities. From my perspective in the mid-1990s, I find no feminist advocacy of reproductive rights that improves on one drawn up in 1969 by Lucina Cisler. Her essay "Unfinished Business: Birth Control and Women's Liberation" appeared in the popular anthology *Sisterhood Is Powerful*. Cisler's proposal takes into account the overlapping legal, medical, economic, and social mazes set up to prevent women from exercising the few reproductive rights they had at the time she was writing. According to Cisler, a woman's reproductive rights should not be contingent on any forces outside herself. *"Woman's rights to limit her own reproduction"* should be relative to nothing (309). Cisler compares the reproductive rights movement to the suffrage movement, which lost its "original breadth of force" when it appealed to expediency rather than justice (310).

Angela Davis spells out the problem more precisely: "If the suffragists acquiesced to arguments invoking the extension of the ballot to women as the saving grace of white supremacy, then birth control advocates either acquiesced to or supported the new arguments invoking birth control as a means of preventing the proliferation of the 'lower classes' and as an antidote against race suicide" (210). Appealing to expediency rather than to all women's absolute rights to suffrage and reproductive choice, feminist reformers allowed their movement to be exploited for racist and classist ends. To ensure that rights are dealt out equally according to race and class, and to prevent the government from reducing or abolishing women's rights when governments find it expedient to do so, Cisler proposes that all laws designed to obstruct or regulate women's access to reproductive technologies should be repealed, and laws to ensure free access should be passed. The right to choose has never been granted to more than the minority of women who already enjoy a degree of privilege based on their race, sexuality, and class. In practice, the discourse of women's rights is always vulnerable to the demands of "expediency."

"Rights" and "responsibilities" are ideas that can no longer help us to change the miserable conditions under which most women must make their reproductive "choices." In order to defend the few reproductive privileges some women have for now, we must *also* continue to argue in the old way. But at best it is a conservative approach.

Apart from its inability to address inequalities in women's ability to exercise their rights, the evocation of women's rights inevitably leads to an evocation of a mother's responsibility. Article 16 of the 1992 United Nations Convention on the Elimination of All Forms of Discrimination against Women stated that women should have "the right to decide freely and *responsibly* on the number and spacing of their children and to have access to the information, education and means to enable them to exercise these rights" (my emphasis). The statement implies that if women all over the world are given their reproductive rights, they must and will act responsibly to plan their families. The paired terms "rights and responsibilities" seem to imply a careful and even elegant balance between an individual woman's rights and her responsibilities to family and community, but I think they hold us deadlocked—the apparently weightless freedom of "rights" forever shackled to the leaden weight of "responsibilities." This deadlock is simultaneously rhetorical and material. The terms themselves block out the possibility of any other logical system through which to think about women and their reproductive lives. In the wedding of "rights" and "responsibilities," the former agrees to honor and obey the latter. In a society that typically blames the mother for every possible physical or emotional problem suffered by her children, the logic that backs up the argument that women are individuals with human rights is too easily appropriated to construct each woman as a culpable individual who can and should be held solely responsible for the care of her children and for all their ills.

Robert H. Blank's 1992 book *Mother and Fetus: Changing Notions of Maternal Responsibility* represents a conservative view of women's moral obligations to fetuses. Considered within the logical framework he presents, Cisler's feminist advocacy of the principle of women's absolute reproductive rights is not radical—it's just impossible. Blank asserts that "Although some rights are more fundamental than others, not even those highest in the hierarchy are absolute." Rights are contingent on the absence of a "compelling state interest" (7). The "state" as Blank represents it has the potential to operate logically and predictably even when faced with the daunting complexities of women's reproductive lives. But if human rights are not absolute, neither is the ability of the state to divine what is most just. It is not a monolith, coordinating all its powers to grant rights and impose responsibilities on human subjects so that everyone has a fair shake at economic, social, and reproductive equality. It is, rather, a diverse collection of institutions with shifting aims, each suffering from bureaucratic myopia about the lives and needs of certain citizens. As such, the "state" cannot have a "compelling interest" in granting all women certain rights and imposing on all women certain responsibilities. The state's interests will shift depending on the historical moment, what institution is representing the state, and whose rights and responsibilities are under consideration. For instance, Davis writes that slave owners found it "unnatural" that slave women often aborted their pregnancies on their own and sometimes killed newborns. This form of "population control" was not in the economic interests of the slave owners, who consulted each other about how to stop the practice. But after slavery was abolished, campaigns were launched to sterilize or impose birth control on African American women, whose children no longer represented an economic asset to whites. At one historical moment the institution of slavery held that African American women did not have the right to abort their fetuses; a few years later, after slavery was abolished, institutions of law and medicine held that African American women did not have the right to bear children at all.

Elizabeth Kingdom attacks the notion of "absolute rights" from a direction different from Blank's and with a feminist aim. She argues that absolute rights cannot be exercised under any known (i.e., real) social conditions, and that the effect of asserting absolute rights is to negate efforts to improve social conditions (57). "Simply to assert a woman's right to choose is to skate over the complex business of working out specific proposals and strategies for improving abortion and related provision" (59). I will add that, however attractive the idea of absolute rights may be as a defense against the inequitable distribution of rights, the idea of an "absolute right" implies a universality of conditions and interests among women. As a rhetorical gesture, arguing for an "absolute right" masks the diversity of women's cultures and the social hierarchies of class, race, and sexuality that affect our various cultures.

The universality implied in the idea of "absolute rights" masks other important differences among people. Rights that, in feminist proposals belong only to women are extended in conservative proposals to men and fetuses. This is accomplished rhetorically by an elision of the differences in how women and men parent, biologically and socially. For instance, Blank writes that America has a "tradition of individual autonomy and privacy in parenting" (21). Blank's discussion of the Western "tradition" asserting the individual's "right to have progeny" opens the door—ironically enough—to considering male and female parents not as separate individuals, but as a unit. The same "tradition" that supports "privacy in parenting" also supports male hegemony in male-female couples. Even when "woman" is posited as an individual in her own right, the principle of "absolute rights" can readily be taken to mean that whatever rights women have, men have as well. Kingdom notes that an appeal to a woman's "right to reproduce" is liable to be translated into a *human* right to reproduce, a right that a man can exercise only by means of a woman's body (72).

A related problem, evident in Blank's analysis, is the failure to consider gendered differences in how subjective "autonomy" is constructed in our society. The concept of autonomy depends on a generic (i.e., masculine) definition of the individual as isolated in body. Viewing a pregnant woman as autonomous depends on being able to separate her, conceptually although not yet literally, from the fetus she carries. Only when this gesture is accomplished can she achieve the same legal status as a man. At the moment the pregnant woman is figured as an autonomous individual, another apparent individual emerges from obscurity: the fetus. According to pro-life discourse, this other conceptually autonomous individual, however intricately merged into the flesh of its mother, must have rights of its own, potentially opposed to those of its mother. From this point, it is an easy leap to the conclusion that the fetus, which is physically and mentally incapable of recognizing or exercising rights, must be protected when its mother attempts to exercise her rights to self-determination.

According to Blank, two of the questions we must address in "a balanced and reasoned" dialogue about "regulating maternal behavior" are these: (1) "What degree of intrusion into a pregnant woman's privacy and autonomy is justified—from education and counseling to forced *in utero* surgery?"; and (2) "If society has a responsibility to intervene in maternal life style, what means are appropriate for maximizing maternal compliance, and what means are inappropriate?" (19). The "if" in the second question is belied by the first question. Within Blank's framework, society does indeed have the "responsibility" to intrude, intervene, educate, counsel, and ensure compliance as long as there is a "compelling state interest" in doing so. The state's interest can then be defined in terms of ensuring the health of its fetal citizens so that they can become healthy babies who pose no financial burden to the state. The state can best protect its interests in that event by invoking the right of the fetus to gestate in a healthy *in utero* environment and pitting that right against the right of a woman to determine her own "life style."

Joseph Fletcher, an eminent ethicist, refers to rights as "egocentric" (quoted in Blank 11). Self-centeredness is excusable in an unborn human being whose egocentricity is being asserted and defended by a self-appointed guardian of the "right to life," but according to mainstream mothering ideology, it is unforgivable in a potential mother. At this point the logic of the right-to-life argument suffers, because in the same moment that the discourse of "rights and responsibilities" produces an autonomous and therefore culpable maternal subject, the right-to-life argument, which of course is based on rights discourse, denies her autonomy and rights and figures her as an "environment." Her worth is measured by the degree to which her body and "lifestyle" serve the needs of the fetal individual. The argument pushes ahead in spite of this contradiction. If women are guilty individuals (but not really individuals, only environments), the fetus is a truly innocent, and therefore truly deserving, individual.

Discursive Paralysis

As I discuss these issues with students in my women's studies courses, I find that, for many of my students, confronting the entwined intricacies of the emotional, physical, legal, familial, ethical, medical, economic, racial, and sexual aspects of women's reproductive lives does not necessarily—or at least not immediately—lead them to find a feminist voice that might bespeak the revolution. The questions at the center of the traditional debate lead us in circles: When does life begin? Is a fetus a part of a woman's body, or an individual in its own right? Is it more important to have reproductive choice (having lots of options about when and how to have babies), or is it more important to be able to resist unwanted interventions? When should a woman be held responsible for the health of her fetus if she uses drugs or alcohol, and when should we blame society for failing her? No matter how one responds to these questions, and even when the participants are in agreement, the result is dialectical paralysis.

The only decisive conclusion that my students and I have reached about these questions is that they lead to confusion, conflicting allegiances, frustration, and anger. To give an idea of the way such questions eat up valuable intellectual energy, I have sometimes assigned students essays about "fetal child abuse." Joseph Losco, in "Fetal Abuse," suggests that mothers should be held responsible if they do things that doctors believe may cause debilitating and untreatable disabilities in the fetus (271). By contrast, in "Prenatal Harm as Child Abuse?" Joan C. Callahan and James W. Wright argue that "a woman whose behavior is believed to cause prenatal harm" should not be "a candidate for forcible interference or criminal prosecution" (149). Although they come to different conclusions about women's culpability, Losco on the one hand and Callahan and Wright on the other agree on the terms of the debate. They all offer peripheral arguments that hostile social and economic circumstances make it difficult for some women, especially those who are poor, black, and young, to receive adequate prenatal care, and both articles assert that something needs to be done about the social causes of "fetal abuse." However, most of the analytical space in both articles is taken up with asserting or refuting the responsibility of mothers, and explaining in detail the legal precedents and ethical assumptions that back up the argument.

The plight of women who are coerced and punished through the legal and medical institutions is urgent and must be addressed. But so much intellectual energy is spent on delving into the philosophical grounds for either condemning or aiding mothers that there remains little energy for even considering the revolutionary social and economic changes that would make the philosophizing unnecessary.

After the first few weeks of a course I taught entitled "Reproductive Futures," women from the class began to visit me during office hours to talk about how the class was affecting their thinking about infertility treatments, sex selection, midwifery, surrogacy, and abortion. One student, whose concerns were eventually echoed by most of the women in the class, told me that she used to think she had her views worked out—she had firm ideas about what women's reproductive rights and responsibilities should be. Now, after a few weeks of reading what "ordinary" women, feminist theorists, physicians, researchers, and right-to-lifers had to say about reproduction in the age of technology, her old views seemed simplistic. Eventually, many of us had to realize that the questions made available to us through the mainstream debate seemed designed to divert our attention from women's lives and women's problems.

Feminist responses to the 1989 *Webster* decision were framed in familiar terms: women's personhood, privacy, and ownership of self were suddenly in greater danger.[2] Some argued that the decision should serve as a warning that women were about to lose their reproductive rights—not only access to abortion services, but the right to determine if, when, and by what means we would reproduce. What is left out in the analysis, besides a clear statement that most women have never been able to exercise these rights anyway, is an exploration of the practical limits imposed by the discourse of rights—and an exploration of what lies beyond those limits. Is the Supreme Court the only power that can extend or contract the boundaries of a woman's private space? To what degree are the boundaries of privacy dependent on a woman's ability or willingness to consider her body and needs as abstract principles, isolated from the influence of lovers, children, parents, friends, physicians, priests, commercial slogans ("It's a Baby, Not a Choice"), and economic exigencies? Evoking a woman's right to privacy may be read as staking a claim to an inviolate space in which a woman can mull over her choices. But at the same time, it reproduces the conventional public/private divide, marking out the private as a black box that is immune to analysis because it is filled with the messy, inchoate details of particular lives.

Personal Differences

In the example that follows, I violate the boundary between public and private by recounting personal experience. I do this in order to map out another kind of boundary, a self-consciously local boundary, on the discourse of reproductive rights. Such a strategy doesn't produce revolutions, but it suggests how difficult it is for a real person to

occupy the blank space of the "autonomous individual" who is invoked in so much rights rhetoric. By the time I was sixteen, I already
had reason to doubt the practical adequacy of claims to personhood,
privacy, and ownership of one's own body. My best friend, Linda,
then eighteen years old, decided to marry. A number of my friends
and I, members of the underclass in an otherwise affluent community,
were schooled to see ourselves as disqualified from a college education and a career, or even a respectable working-class job. For us,
marriage or dereliction seemed the only imaginable futures. Although Linda's plan did not include children, she got pregnant almost immediately. She had planned to use contraceptives, but she
could not find a Planned Parenthood clinic anywhere near her new
home in Nevada, and she did not own a car. She could not afford a
private doctor. Her new husband preferred intercourse condomless,
and she had banked on the hope she would escape pregnancy in spite
of it all.

As soon as she suspected she was pregnant, even her lack of access
to clinic services was not enough to keep her down. She called
Planned Parenthood in San Jose and got a referral to an abortion
clinic in San Francisco. She had to wait a month—a month of scraping
together money by borrowing and working extra hours, trying not to
internalize her parents' assertion that she had made her bed etc.,
dealing with morning sickness, arguing with her husband about the
abortion (he liked the idea of her pregnancy), and trying to avoid his
abuse, before she could borrow a car, insist that her husband drive
her to San Francisco, face the physical and emotional trauma of her
abortion, and drive immediately back to Nevada because she could
not afford a motel room for the night. It was 1973, and the Supreme
Court had just endowed her with the legal right to abortion.

I learned about Linda's abortion after the fact. She had been afraid
to tell me about her pregnancy. She was afraid I would think her stupid for failing to get birth control (with sixteen-year-old arrogance, I
had been critical of girls who failed either to use something or say no)
and immoral for seeking an abortion (I had once claimed I would
never have one even though I thought abortion should be legal).
Nothing in the way I had learned to talk about abortion could begin
to account for what Linda had gone through. I was not then prepared
to face the proposition that personal choice, guaranteed by law, was
not the answer to it all. But she taught me to see that a woman seek-

ing an abortion would need, at the barest minimum, a way to get to the clinic, money to pay, a cooperative and sympathetic family, and a friend to support her.

This happened in a decade when "women's liberation" seemed to be coming about, tantalizingly, somewhere just beyond the range of our reality. We saw only the Helen Reddy and *Ms.* magazine surface of the movement, and did not know that feminism had already put into question the terms of our reproductive lives. Linda, convinced that pregnancy was barbaric and unnecessary, would have felt herself vindicated by Shulamith Firestone's *Dialectic of Sex* (1970) and might have welcomed the idea that we could be liberated by giving up pregnancy and opting for artificial wombs. I became pregnant in 1977 and, at that moment, would have felt my own experience validated by Adrienne Rich's assertion in *Of Woman Born* (1986) that "female biology—the diffuse, intense sensuality radiating out from clitoris, breasts, uterus, vagina; the lunar cycles of menstruation, the gestation and fruition of life which can take place in the female body—has far more radical implications that we have yet come to appreciate" (39–40). In the middle of pregnancy, when my awareness of my own body magnified day by day, I would have welcomed any discourse that could have helped me explain the dissonance between the private pleasures and pains of pregnancy and my encounters with the alienated woman I seemed to become whenever I ventured into the "public" space of pregnancy. This public space was defined mostly by obstetrics. I recognized my obstetrician as an authority to whom I was accountable. Each so-called choice, each conflict—about what blood tests to have, where to give birth, who should be present, whether to use drugs—was negotiated against a background of the discourses of rights-and-responsibilities, obstetric tradition, the hospital regulations, and state law. Each time my obstetrician wielded his power to override my choices, I tripped over the threshold between public and private.

The answer to the question, "Who has the right to choose?" was answered for me repeatedly: the obstetrician. Rights discourse renders invisible the unequal relations of power between mother and physician, in which the physician's choices are backed up by obstetric tradition, hospital routine, ownership of birth technology, and the support of nursing personnel; the mother's choices are backed up by sheer will and, if she is lucky, the support of a sympathetic partner. If the mother is a mature, pleasant, middle-class woman with whom the physician has something in common, she may find that her physician is willing to cooperate to a degree; if she is an underclass teenager with a chip on her shoulder, she may find that her choices count for little.

Both women, however, must sign a delivery consent form that gives away the right to choose. From the moment a woman is admitted to the hospital, the obstetrician has the legal right to override her stated choices about fetal monitoring, whether to have a vaginal or cesarean delivery, whether to augment labor with hormones, or to have or not to have an episiotomy. Using rights discourse, we might be able to construct an argument that a woman in labor should have the right to make decisions about procedures. However, as long as the decision about whether or not a woman should be allowed to exercise that right is in the hands of physicians, women whose social, economic, educational, institutional, sexual, and/or racial identities alienate them from their physicians will not be allowed to make such decisions. When I asked an obstetrician how she stood on the question of a woman's right to make decisions during childbirth, she replied diplomatically that she liked to involve both parents in decision making (one of the effects of having fathers present during childbirth is that the couple can be considered a unit). I pressed her, asking who had ultimate decision-making power when there was a conflict between patient and physician. She replied that the physician does.

I recounted this exchange in a recent introductory women's studies class. The silence that followed my comments was broken by a young woman who finally protested, "But why would you want to argue with the doctor?" Immediately other students jumped in to argue with each other, punctuating their opinions by accounts of personal experiences and the experiences of friends or relatives. One of the effects of allowing the private and subjective language of women's reproductive lives to erupt into public discourse is that it quickly becomes clear that there are few truths held in common. Although Linda's experience and mine had much in common (youth, financial instability, social isolation, unhappy marriages), our decisions were different. The result was a conversation, complex, conflicted, and uncomfortable, in which I began to recognize the constraints on her (although I only became conscious of the constraints of my own situation much later) and learned how to show respect for the choices she made. Such ongoing conversations can create a clearer space for women to support each other. Getting to that point means overcoming pressures to conform to the comfortable, if illusory, objectivity of rights discourse.

This pressure need not be exerted by an immediately identifiable outside source. It is (also) internal. When I began to do background research for this essay, I took Phyllis Chesler's *Mothers on Trial: The Battle for Children and Custody* down from my bookshelf. I bought it in 1992 but had never been able to read past the preface without stumbling over my own intensely emotional reactions to Chesler's accounts of abusive fathers who got custody and "good-enough" mothers who lost custody. On this occasion, I finally gave up, too upset to read another word, when I reached Chesler's account of her testimony as an expert witness at the custody trial of a lesbian mother who was not permitted to keep her child. Anyone would think that I had lost custody of my own child. But I hadn't. My daughter, Nicole, has been continuously in my custody since her birth. My reaction is based only on an equally continuous fear that my ex-husband would *try* to get custody of our daughter. Nicole is now seventeen, slightly less than a year from her eighteenth birthday, only ten months away from the final exemption of our relationship from any question of custody. So I feel almost safe now, safe enough to live as an out lesbian.

My reaction to Phyllis Chesler's book is not rational, and it will seem beside the point to some readers. But I cannot dissipate my fear and anger by giving a rational turn to my thoughts (*if* it is accurate to say that rights discourse is the product of rational thought—a point I'm not yet willing to concede). As long as the discourse feminists use to defend endlessly women's rights to custody and abortion is the same discourse antifeminist lawyers, judges, obstetricians, social workers, and psychologists use to argue against women's reproductive rights, feminists will accomplish no more than a defense of the limited and contingent privileges now held by a few women.

When Is a Choice Not a Choice?

The established limits of rights discourse are more than strict. A public confession of personal griefs may, in fact, be grounds for disqualification from the debate. There is no room, within the discourse of reproductive rights, to account for the fear, love, inertia, and shame that would keep a lesbian closeted for the duration of her child's minority, even though that experience is determined within social and judicial systems that regularly use the discourse of rights to nullify or affirm mother-child relationships. The relationship a mother has with her child, created amidst the day-to-day matters of feeding and diapering and nursing to sleep, may have a huge impact on the choices she makes about how to live. But that relationship has no more real authority in the courtroom than do a mother's choices in the delivery room. In a custody battle the mother-child relationship may be permitted to continue or it may not; a mother may be judged fit or unfit according to criteria formulated on the spot with respect to the linguistic facility of lawyers, the crankiness or sympathy of judges, and the vindictiveness or fair-mindedness of fathers. In *Mothers on Trial*, Chesler demonstrates that fathers who seek custody win 70 percent of the time, and that this inequity holds even if the father is abusive or absent and the mother has proven herself, by living a traditional, nuclear-family–centered life, "fit" to mother. It can happen even if the mother is highly privileged by race and class, as Chesler shows by the case of Dr. Elizabeth Morgan, who was jailed for more than two years because she refused to reveal the hiding place of her daughter (xiv). It is reasonable to argue that Morgan's rights to raise her child were violated when she was imprisoned, but this understanding of her experience cannot begin to analyze the forces that determined her "choice" to sacrifice her own freedom for the sake of her daughter, or the motives of the judge who ordered Morgan's imprisonment. The fear of being discounted as a participant in the debate about maternal rights is a pallid version of the fear of being disqualified as a mother—of having your child snatched from you. Fear alone has been enough to keep me from doing what Elizabeth Morgan did: confronting the system head-on.

Within a year of Nicole's birth, my husband left me to marry another woman who he thought would be a fine mother to Nicole. He told me that if I tried to get more child support or showed myself in any way to be a bad mother, he would go back to court to get custody. I was on the brink of deciding to listen to my desire to be with a woman, but I read his threat as an authoritative command and rededicated myself to heterosexual life. I consciously decided to find someone who would be a good father, from whom I could borrow enough respectability to qualify as a fit mother. I told myself that it was a reasonable bargain: I would provide a "normal" family life for my daughter in exchange for my right to raise her.

Can I explain a decade and a half of compromise as an expression of my right to choose? Other women, facing similar threats and similar opportunities, might have chosen differently: chosen to live as a lesbian, or fight an ex-husband in court for custody, or give custody to the father without a court battle, or fight for adequate child support, or flee the state with the child to live incognito. Many people, even those sympathetic to the right to choose, would not even recognize these as *reproductive* choices. How, then, can rights discourse be used to explain how social, financial, and familial pressures affect the different choices women make? Poverty may keep one woman from being able to pay for an abortion even when it is legal, while a wealthier woman will be able to find safe abortion services even when abortion is illegal. The different values and expectations of families and communities may keep one woman from seeking the abortion of a Down's syndrome fetus when she knows that would be best for her, while another woman may be pressured to seek an abortion of a Down's syndrome fetus even though she wants to continue the pregnancy. Combined racism and poverty may make it hard for a woman of color to find prenatal care unless she "consents" to postnatal sterilization, while a white woman, even when she can afford the surgery and has already had several children, may have to endure humiliating interrogations and delays before a surgeon will sterilize her.

Right-to-life activists construct a discourse that directs attention away from women's differences. "Woman" as potential reproducer figures as the idealized container of new life, or as the victim of a lesbian feminist plot to kill babies and destroy the family, or as a profligate, selfish offender who cares only for her own pleasure and comfort. Those who are interested in real women don't feel at home with the dogmas a pro-life stance encourages, but neither, usually, do they find much inspiration in the grim necessity of asserting a woman's right to choose. On the campus of Miami University, where I teach, the faculty advisor for the student group for choice has found that the campus pro-lifers are so well organized that leaflets advertising pro-choice meetings don't stay up for even a few hours (leaflets advertising meetings of the gay and lesbian student group and African American student group also have short lives).

Pro-choice activism can be daunting because it brings students face-to-face with single-minded, potentially violent zealots whose most potent gesture is to fling a fetus (or, perhaps just as effectively, an image of a fetus) at clinic defenders. The gesture speaks a language of rights and responsibilities anyone can understand. The extra uterine fetus represents an individual whose right to life has been monstrously violated. The right-to-life movement depends on being able to structure the debate in terms of "rights and responsibilities," terms that insistently construct the mother-fetus relationship as one of opposition.

The fetus in this discourse is also generic; that is, its prototype is white, genetically perfect, and about to be aborted, it is, therefore, worthy of protection. The fate of fetuses who do not match the prototype—those who have African blood, those who die not through abortion but because of malnutrition, exposure to toxins, or inadequate medical care—is of no concern. Davis cites the case of an African American woman who gave birth to a stillborn baby after being refused treatment at three hospitals. Calling attention to the malnutrition that causes anemia and toxemia in pregnant women, Davis focuses not on rights but on the poverty and racism that make African American women's reproductive lives especially hazardous. The rhetoric of individual rights cannot accommodate the needs or experience of a mother whose fetus dies because she is refused treatment; it cannot account for or remedy the racism and class oppression that create such a disaster.

Mother-the-Caregiver

According to Carol Gilligan's study of women and ethics, women are likely to view their own assertions of individual interest or need as a form of selfishness. Ellen, a woman considering an abortion, is quoted in *In a Different Voice* as suggesting that her married lover's idea that she should raise their child without his presence or financial help was "better thought-out and more logical and more correct" than her decision to abort (89). If she carried the fetus to term and then raised the child, she would be demonstrating her nurturing, generous nature. By having an abortion, she denies the essential qualities of womanhood that require her to negate herself and her needs.

In either case, however, her feminine culpability persists. Constructed as an autonomous individual, she will be responsible for the death of the (conceptually autonomous) fetus. Constructed as a mother whose interests are the same as, and yet subordinate to, those of the child, she will be held responsible for the unhappy, afflicted life of the child, who would suffer because she has neither the financial means nor the emotional strength to raise it. In both cases, she fails to make good on the "logical and correct" expectation that she demonstrate her ability to nurture a child.

My students and I mused over the issues implied in Gilligan's example and realized that the discourse of rights, even modified by a discourse of care, cannot resolve the emotional and intellectual stalemate Ellen faces. One version of right-to-life rhetoric plays on the supposedly feminist notion that women are essentially superior to men because they are more caring. A pamphlet put out by the organization Feminists for Life of America insists that "truly liberated women reject abortion" because they refuse "the right to contribute equally [with men] to the evil of the world." Women should "strive instead to create a world that recognizes the moral superiority of maternal thinking and is, therefore, gentle, loving, nurturing, and pro-life." Pro-choice rhetoric sometimes uses a similarly warped idealization of woman-as-caregiver to argue that women *should* have the right to abortion. One of the arguments advanced in favor of abortion rights, for instance, is that women sometimes have to have an abortion in order to be able to continue caring for the children they have already. Although I know women who have been in this position, and I understand their need to have access to abortion services, it is a poor argument to advance on the field of abortion politics because it promotes the notion that morally superior maternal thinking must guide women's decisions about their sexual and reproductive lives. The serpentine logic evident in the right-to-life pamphlet cited above twists this already distorted reasoning further, implying that only those women who are morally superior (i.e., "Feminists for Life" who have transcended the evils of patriarchy) should have the right to make any decision about their reproductive lives, and the only "decision" they can make and still retain their status as gentle, nurturing maternal thinkers is to not have abortions. Left blank in their argument is the space within which this nondecision would be made: Does the woman get to reject abortion herself, in the privacy of her own heart, or does she need a constitutional amendment criminalizing abortion to make sure that official representatives of patriarchy have the power to ensure that she continues to adhere to her (supposedly antipatriarchal) stance?

The "woman-as-caregiver" ideal, whether it is invoked to argue for or against reproductive rights for women, can only oppress us further. However, women who don't demonstrate properly "maternal thinking" are in an especially vulnerable position; compared with the ideal, they can only be thought of as victims of patriarchy or as betrayers of their sex. Insisting that women *are* naturally gentle, loving, and maternal leaves us with no way to argue for the reproductive rights of women whose behavior suggests to physicians, lawyers, and judges that they are not gentle, loving, and maternal.

Anna Lowenhaupt Tsing addresses this problem in her examination of recent cases in which women were charged with perinatal endangerment in the United States. In many instances, women were prosecuted for the crime of giving birth precipitously and without medical intervention to infants who died; the cases were often complicated because the women failed to report to officials the birth and the death of the infant. Tsing cites the responses of law enforcement officials and prosecutors, who described the women as unnatural, bizarre, "without basic human emotions," and "very cold" (283, 287). In particular, the women's apparent lack of caring, demonstrated in their refusal to grieve or show remorse, influenced opinion against them. However, Tsing documented the fact that the severity of the judgment depended on the race and class of the women accused. A white college student who gave birth on the toilet in her dormitory bathroom and disposed of the body in a trash can received five years' probation, whereas a black woman on welfare who gave birth on a toilet at home to an infant who died received a twenty-five-year prison sentence (even though a relative had called 911), and a white woman on welfare who gave birth in the same way received a twenty-year sentence. Similarly, the severity of the punishment of women who use drugs or refuse medical interventions in the form of fetal surgery, fetal blood transfusions, months of bed rest, or cesarean sections depends on race and class. Women who, from the perspective of any of the main players in the current reproductive rights debate, are not eligible to exercise their rights will not fare any better when their access to reproductive services depends on their perceived ability to make "caring" decisions about their reproductive lives.

The second major objection to using a discourse of care is that when women are considered recipients of care, rather than as care-givers, they are often figured as infants themselves, incapable of making their own decisions. This becomes most apparent when women try to refuse medical interventions. Tsing comments that when poor women and women of color refuse medical care, they are seen not as "educable products of a defective maturation," as are middle-class white women, but as "unfamiliar, alien beings" who "can be controlled but not changed" (294–95). The fact that women who refuse medical interventions when pregnant are liable to be thrown in jail and forcibly "cared for" against their will suggests the unreconcilable contradiction at the center of this discourse: Even as the discourse of care is being used to cast women in the role of social dependents who (along with their potential or living children) must be saved from the effects of their own incompetence, woman-as-caregiver is considered solely responsible for the lives of her offspring. Tsing cites the case of a working-class white woman who gave birth in a motel room. The infant died and the woman was given a ten-year sentence; Tsing notes that the woman, who worked as a maid, did not have medical insurance or access to state medical assistance (294). The idealized figure of the autonomous woman-as-caregiver is used to justify the nearly total lack of services and support for mothers, who receive almost no material care in the form of friendly, affordable, and noncoercive reproductive services, adequate child care, and good job opportunities. The figure of the autonomous caregiver is called up to deemphasize, or nullify, the responsibility of everyone else (father, family, doctors, the community, social service agencies) to mothers and children.

Incorporating a discourse of care into hierarchical systems of government tends only to perpetuate their hegemony. For instance, Nafis Sadik, executive director of the United Nations Population Fund and secretary general of the Cairo conference, asserted, "If we wish for a wider range of choice," communities must take responsibility for their "weaker and most vulnerable members."[3] This version of the discourse of care implies that those who are currently disempowered would remain so, but that those who have power over them would learn to be more kindly. Any discourse—the discourse of rights or the discourse of care and protection—can be used to reinforce the power and material advantages of those who are already in positions of power, while failing to address the ongoing problems of members who, because of their sex and class, are already shut out of making decisions about their own reproductive lives.

Unlocking the Deadlock

The inadequacy of a discourse of care as a substitute for a discourse of rights is not unique. Any substitute discourse powerful enough to enter the mainstream would present the same problems because it would do everything that rights discourse does currently for politicians, lawmakers, physicians, and lawyers: displace lengthy, subjective, and personal expressions of women's complex experiences and needs with a readily, if speciously, intelligible set of oppositions.

Patricia Williams sets forth a principle that I will use to describe the basic structure of any mainstream discourse about reproduction in our time. She describes a "tit for tat" discursive economy in which "words like 'freedom' and 'choice' are forms of currency. They function as the mediators by which we make all things equal, interchangeable" (31). Rights discourse facilitates a zero-sum mathematics of entitlement in which the "rights" of the fetus and the "rights" of the mother compete only to cancel each other out, but the discourse of care can fit into the same oppositional structure. The fetus's need for care and protection can be set against the mother's.

The structure of the debate is set up to prevent people from resolving their differences. Players etch their X's and O's on a tic-tac-toe grid of potentially infinite proportions. The secret of tic-tac-toe is that equally advantaged players always end up in a deadlock. I have witnessed this frustration again and again in the classroom when students open up a debate about reproductive rights and responsibilities. Even when the debaters are on the same side, their discussions stall. I witness this every time one of my students tries to explain just *why* every woman should have the right to abortion, or why every fetus has the right to be carried to term, or why every man should have an equal right to decide whether his female lover should continue a pregnancy. The source of my students' frustration, and my own, is the dual realization that (1) unless we are willing to play the rhetorical game as it has always been played, we are virtually silenced in the legal or medical arenas, where vital decisions about our reproductive health are made; and (2) playing the game means staying within a discursive field where it is not possible to make progress toward solving problems that affect women and children. Perhaps most frustrating of all, we cannot abandon the field. If a pro-choicer places her X's strategically, she may at least be able to prevent the opposition from taking over the field entirely. This is more than a matter of words, as any woman who has held her ground and claimed her right to an abortion can attest.

Patricia Williams, in a suggestively titled chapter, "The Pain of Word Bondage," asserts that although "blacks never fully believed in rights," they also "believed in them so much and so hard that we gave them life where there was none before, mothered them and got the notion of them" (163). Thus Williams's impatience with the "rights mythology" that conceals "a universalism of need and oppression" in the United States is tempered by the realization that the concept of rights is empty only when there is no humanity, and no human energy, to give it meaning and direction. Society, Williams writes, must give rights away: "Give to all of society's objects and untouchables the rights of privacy, integrity, and self assertion; give them distance and respect. Flood them with the animating spirit that rights mythology fires in this country's most oppressed psyches" (165). I feel the urgency of Williams's call, and I suspect that here, in the evocation of rights as a living form, is the beginning of an answer to the frustration so many of my women's studies students express. They want to know, and want to know *now*, not just how "society's objects and untouchables" have been oppressed, but what we can do about it. But when Williams says society must give away rights, what specific people will do that? I'm inclined to think that rights will not be given away; that our society has no collective will to do so. Then which individuals and groups have the power to mother rights, to give them life and then give them away until every person is imbued with their spirit?

It may be that rights can find new life only outside the institutions that govern their distribution. If feminists have little to gain, and something to lose, by battling with the opposition to occupy the discursive field of reproductive rights, it may be that an extralegal focus would yield better results. A mother gave her prescription for action in Chesler's book, describing how her custody battle had made her lose respect for the law: "If the child is yours, take that child and go! . . . Forget about the law. There is none" (343). With similar pragmatism, an activist for reproductive rights commented in an informal gathering of students and faculty that we shouldn't despair if we lose the legal right to abortion because abortion could easily go underground; the technology for surgical abortions is easy to produce and master, and many women have learned how to do safe first-trimester abortions through their training in abortion clinics. Although I think she overestimates women's knowledge and the reach of underground networking, her basic point is well taken: the laws that determine women's reproductive rights and obligations decide not what is morally right or wrong (how can abortion be wrong in many states in the 1960s, right for the entire country for part of the 1970s and 1980s, and wrong again in many states in the late 1980s and 1990s?) but only what is legal and illegal.

The women in my class spent some time thinking and writing about how women might seize the means of (re)production, especially reproductive technologies, and use them to further the interests of women. After mulling over the practical difficulties of getting knowledge, money, and laboratories, we confronted a question regarding the material expression of the discursive problem of rights and responsibilities: is it ever possible to divorce reproductive technologies from their patriarchal origins? If women use technologies created in systems that are organized to conform to the language of rights and responsibilities, will they abort their own revolution? Some thought that the only technology potentially recoupable for feminist aims is what Joanna Russ called "egg merging," a sister of cloning that would enable lesbian partners to have a daughter who was the genetic descendent of both. At present, the right of lesbians to even so simple a technology as clinical artificial insemination is hotly contested; in this climate, of course, no researcher could find the funding to perfect reproductive technologies that would benefit lesbians. Most fertility clinics will serve only heterosexual *couples,* a fact that makes it difficult to argue that reproductive technologies work to promote the interests of heterosexual women. It is not as individual heterosexual women, but as mates of men, that they are admitted to the clinics.

However, other more or less underground efforts, using simpler technologies, might begin to remove women's reproductive lives from public scrutiny and place them beyond the reach of the law. When women learn how to do safe abortions in their homes; when RU486 is available in the United States; when lesbians can find a way to access safe, anonymous sperm without having to apply to clinics; when women who are custodially embattled escape the law and keep their children; when women who cannot seek prenatal care without becoming experimental or teaching material can find skilled and loving care in noninstitutional settings; when women who reject or cannot afford hospital birth can locate midwives who will perform home births (which are still illegal in many states); when we take all measures to circumvent the processes of the medical and legal systems that at present determine women's reproductive lives, then we may be able to create a space in which to construct another discourse that takes into account the diverse experiences and needs of women.

In spite of the difficulties and logical obstacles, I think we are beginning to ask the right questions when we bypass the question of whether we, as women, have the right to determine our lives and the lives of our children and begin more vigorously to ask *how* we gain the power to formulate a future—almost unimaginable from our current position—in which women's reproductive lives will no longer be an expression of women's oppression, in which the needs of women, needs which differ from woman to woman and culture to culture, and which change over time, will be met as a matter of course.

NOTES

1. See, for instance, Kifner. This latest act of "domestic terrorism," as President Clinton and others termed it, follows almost two years of similarly brutal attacks, resulting in the deaths of two doctors who performed abortions, and also resulting in injuries to others. It may not be a coincidence that one of the clinics involved was participating in a national trial of the abortion drug RU486, which has the potential of obviating the need for most surgical abortions and therefore making abortion more accessible to many women. RU486 also may eventually deprive pro-life protesters of the abortion clinics that are their favorite targets.

2. For instance, in their spring 1990 issue, the editors of *Affilia* confronted the issue. Miriam Dinerman wrote that women would "be reduced from the status of persons to that of walking wombs" (99). Beatrice Saunders

described the ruling as "an invasion of privacy" (101). Carol Meyer defined as "central" the idea that "a woman's body belongs only to herself" (100).

3. *A Citizen's Guide to the International Conference on Population and Development 6.*

WORKS CITED AND CONSULTED

Blank, Robert H. *Mother and Fetus: Changing Notions of Maternal Responsibility.* New York: Greenwood, 1992.

Callahan, Joan C., and James W. Wright. "Prenatal Harm as Child Abuse?" In *The Criminalization of a Woman's Body,* ed. Clarice Feinman, 128–49. New York: Haworth Press, 1992.

Chesler, Phyllis. *Mothers on Trial: The Battle for Children and Custody.* New York: McGraw Hill, 1986.

Cisler, Lucina. "Unfinished Business: Birth Control and Women's Liberation." In *Sisterhood Is Powerful: An Anthology of Writings from the Women's Liberation Movement,* ed. Robin Morgan, 274–323. New York: Random House, 1970.

A Citizen's Guide to the International Conference on Population and Development. Washington, DC: Population Reference Bureau. (No year available.)

Davis, Angela. "Racism, Birth Control, and Reproductive Rights." In *Women, Race, and Class.* New York: Random House, 1981.

Dinerman, Miriam, Carol Meyer and Beatrice Saunders, eds. Introduction to *Affilia* 5.1 (1990).

Feminists for Life of America. *Abortion Does Not Liberate Women.* Kansas City: MO: Feminists for Life Education Project, [late 1980s?].

Firestone, Shulamith. *Dialectic of Sex: The Case for Feminist Revolution.* New York: Morrow, 1970.

Gilligan, Carol. *In a Different Voice: Psychological Theory and Women's Development.* Cambridge: Harvard University Press, 1982.

Kifner, John. "Gunman Kills 2 at Abortion Clinics in Boston Suburb." *New York Times,* Dec. 31, 1994, 1.8.

Kingdom, Elizabeth. *What's Wrong with Rights: Problems for Feminist Politics of Law.* Edinburgh: Edinburgh University Press, 1991.

Losco, Joseph. "Fetal Abuse: An Exploration of Emerging Philosophic, Legal, and Policy Issues." *Western Political Quarterly* 42.2 (June 1989): 265–88.

Nsiah-Jefferson, Laurie, and Elaine J. Hall. "Reproductive Technology: Perspectives and Implications for Low-Income Women and Women of Color." In *Healing Technology: Feminist Perspectives,* ed. K. S. Ratcliff. Ann Arbor: University of Michigan Press, 1990.

Rich, Adrienne. *Of Woman Born: Motherhood as Experience and Institution.* New York: W. W. Norton, 1986.

Tsing, Anna Lowenhaupt. "Monster Stories: Women Charged with Perinatal Endangerment." In *Uncertain Terms: Negotiating Gender in American Culture,* ed. Faye Ginsberg and Anna Lowenhaupt Tsing, 282–99. Boston: Beacon Press, 1990.

Williams, Patricia. *The Alchemy of Race and Rights: Diary of a Law Professor.* Cambridge: Harvard University Press, 1991.

Chapter 4

Sex, Gender, and Same-Sex Marriage

Peggy Pascoe

In 1973 the Maryland state legislature passed "an act to . . . require that a marriage must be between a man and a woman in order to be valid."[1] Perhaps the lawmakers regarded the act as an exercise in stating the obvious. From the beginning of American history, the major institutions—legislatures, courts, churches, even social custom—had agreed that marriage was the union of a man and a woman. So deeply ingrained was this assumption that the legal system, often a stickler for precise definitions, had simply taken it for granted. Only half the states had even bothered to place a formal definition of marriage in their legal codes; nearly all of those defined marriage as "a civil contract, to which the consent of the parties capable in law of contracting is essential."[2]

Not until 1970 did anyone argue that sex-neutral terms such as "parties" or "persons" might be open to interpretation. But when several gay male couples pressed the issue by applying to Los Angeles county clerk William Sharp for marriage licenses, Sharp was forced to admit that under California law, only "custom and propriety" stood in their way.[3] Although Sharp told a reporter that he found the idea of same-sex marriage "so revolting" that he would not issue such a license "under any circumstances," he recognized the legal vulnerability of his position.[4] He urged the state legislature to solve the problem by adopting a sex-specific marriage law and, further, to "require [marriage license] applicants to swear to their sex and furnish a medical declaration of sex in addition to the blood-test certificates."[5]

Neither California nor any other state has yet followed Sharp's final suggestion, but many, including California, followed Maryland's example and "clarified" their marriage laws. They chose a variety of methods—passing opposite-sex definitions of marriage, re-placing sex-neutral terminology with sex-specific terminology, or passing absolute prohibitions on same-sex marriage—but the result was the same. Between 1973, when Maryland changed its law, and 1993, eighteen American states added formal sex-specific prerequi-sites to their marriage laws.[6] These sex-specific definitions laid the basis for the most recent (and continuing) wave of laws against same-sex marriage, which includes federal as well as state action. In Sep-tember 1996 the federal government passed the so-called Defense of Marriage Act (DOMA), which established the first truly national defi-nition of marriage by proclaiming that "the word 'marriage' means only a legal union between one man and one woman as husband and wife, and the word 'spouse' refers only to a person of the opposite sex who is a husband or wife."[7] Between 1994 and 1999, thirty-one state legislatures enacted similar laws, many of which, like DOMA, in-clude provisions for refusing recognition to same-sex marriages per-formed in other states.[8] In 1998 voters in two states, Alaska and Hawaii, went so far as to pass state constitutional amendments limit-ing marriage to opposite-sex couples.[9]

Sex, Gender, and Same-Sex Marriage

I started thinking about the issue of same-sex marriage nearly a decade ago, but delayed writing about it as long as possible, wonder-ing why I, a lesbian feminist, had decided to study, of all things, mar-riage. My initial attitude toward same-sex marriage, which tended to-ward dismissing the subject out of hand, had been conditioned—per-haps overdetermined is a better word—by two decades of brilliant feminist critiques of marriage as the core institution of patriarchy.[10]

In assuming that these critiques made same-sex marriage unthink-able, I had plenty of company. Consider, for example, the distress oc-casioned by the recent emergence of lesbian weddings. In the circles I moved in, lesbian weddings engendered a whole new debate about connections between the personal and political; merely receiving an invitation to such an event could throw a longtime lesbian feminist into a crisis of conscience.[11]

For lesbian feminists, the question of how to weigh feminist cri-tiques of (heterosexual) marriage against demands for the complete recognition of our own intimate relations has been—and continues to be—a central challenge. Two responses to this challenge are by now so commonplace that many of us can recite them by rote. The first is a kind of political purist argument that marriage is such an oppressive institution that it must be critiqued rather than expanded. Purists see lesbian relationships as alternatives to heterosexual marriage; they consider same-sex marriage political anathema. The second is a kind of "of course, but" argument. Its adherents grant that "of course" prohibiting same-sex couples from marriage is unfair and wrong and should be changed, "but" insist that we have much better uses for our limited political energies than same-sex marriage.[12] In this formulation, same-sex marriage may be a right, but it is a right not worth defending. More recently a third argument, the one I have come to believe and want to make here, has taken shape. Its proponents turn familiar patterns upside down to argue that supporting same-sex marriage may be a better way to honor feminist critiques of sexual inequality in marriage than continuing to see marriage as an unchanging and unchangeably oppressive institution.[13]

A look at the rise of sex-specific marriage laws and the recent history of attempts to legalize same-sex marriage can illuminate this argument. It can also provide us with a new window on an old issue in feminist theory: the changing political salience of the distinction between sex and gender.[14] In the 1970s, feminists fit their critiques of marriage conveniently within the politically powerful distinction they had begun to draw between supposedly biological "sex" and supposedly social "gender." It is in large part because of their efforts that the concept of social construction, as applied to "gender," has since grown strong enough to be extended back to "sex"—and on to "sexuality"—as well.[15] As a result, we now stand at a point where it is possible to recognize that the dividing line between sex and gender is much murkier—and feminist politics needs to reach deeper—than any simple split between sex and gender would allow.[16]

"So Unsupportable a Basis"

Although the first public demands for same-sex marriage came as early as the 1950s, it was not until the 1970s that they were able to emerge from the cultural shadow of the defensive cold war marital ideology Elaine Tyler May has so aptly labeled "domestic containment."[17] By the 1970s, domestic containment was under siege. Census takers reported that the traditional family no longer formed the majority of American households; popular magazines featured the "decline of the family" and the rise of the "sexual revolution." Examples were easy to find. Defiant youth of the "counterculture" took pride in casting off their parents' suburban married stability to experiment with new "lifestyles." Radical feminists argued that the family was the core institution of patriarchy. Gay liberationists ridiculed monogamy as old-fashioned, describing marriage and the family as something they had escaped, often at great personal cost.

The first lesbian and gay couples who decided to fight for the right to marry swam both with and against this social tide. On the one hand, the swell of social critiques allowed them the very opportunity to argue for same-sex marriage, an idea considered abhorrent by conservatives and bizarre by the general public. The sheer audacity of the demand won support from emerging gay liberation groups that considered its "in your face" political style something of a dividing line between old and new gay politics.[18] But even in this early period, the demand for same-sex marriage was controversial within both lesbian feminism and the (largely male) gay liberation movement, and it would become even more so as organized gay politics coalesced around demands for the right to sexual experimentation, an end to job discrimination, and the repeal of sodomy laws.[19]

Controversy among gay activists should not, however, prevent us from understanding that in the 1970s, demands for same-sex marriage were one of several attempts to question the naturalness of social categories—like "sex" and "race"—that had long been taken for granted. In this period before the widespread adoption of the term "gender," challenges to the naturalness of "sex" were at the heart of feminist analysis, visible in everything from radical feminist theories to campaigns for "nonsexist" language.

The central symbolic expression of this challenge was the Equal Rights Amendment, designed to prohibit inequality on the basis of "sex." In 1970, when the Congress dusted off the long-neglected amendment and began to hold hearings on it, its potential to sweep away sexual categories seemed almost unlimited. As the lawyer Rita Hauser explained, speaking to the American Bar Association, "Legal distinction on the basis of sex is no longer reasonable. . . . And I am willing to apply that view to any and all sets of circumstances the mind may conceive." To make her point, Hauser, a Republican who served as U.S. representative to the United Nations Human Rights Commission during the Nixon administration, added that even "the right to marry, a right guaranteed by law, cannot be premised on sex distinctions which serve to deny equal protection of the law to all persons."[20]

Feminist challenges to legal distinctions on the basis of "sex" owed a great deal to civil rights activists, who had for decades challenged legal categories based on "race." By the mid-twentieth century, African American protests combined with NAACP lawsuits had forced American judges to recognize that, because legal racial categories long justified as benign natural "distinctions" were actually "discriminations" that denied racialized Americans "equal protection" under the law, they should be excised from the statute books. Beginning with now-famous cases on the internment of Japanese Americans and school segregation, courts dismantled the structures of formal racial segregation.[21] Judges declared racial categories legally "suspect," and held that they should be subjected to such "strict scrutiny" that they must be abandoned unless the state could offer "compelling" (not just "reasonable") justification for their existence.

These challenges to racial categories in the law had reached their height by 1967, when the U.S. Supreme Court struck down American laws against interracial marriage in the case of *Loving v. Virginia*.[22] Laws against so-called miscegenation had been among the strongest and most enduring of American legal traditions.[23] Dating all the way back to the 1660s, they had eventually been enacted by forty-one American states.[24] Justified by white supremacists as natural biological restrictions on marriage, the laws formed the ground floor of American racial segregation.

In declaring these laws unconstitutional, Supreme Court justices pinpointed the connection between legal racial categories and the maintenance of white supremacy. The justices were well aware that for more than a century, courts had upheld laws against interracial marriage, deeming them compatible with the Fourteenth Amendment guarantee of equal protection because they applied "equally" to both whites and blacks.[25] But in the *Loving* case, a unanimous Supreme Court overruled these precedents and struck down the laws. Labeling the freedom to marry "one of the vital personal rights essential to the orderly pursuit of happiness" and also one of the "basic civil rights of man," the Court declared that "to deny this fundamental freedom on so unsupportable a basis as the racial classifications embodied in [these] statutes, classifications so directly subversive of the principle of equality at the heart of the Fourteenth Amendment, is surely to deprive all the State's citizens of liberty without due process of law."[26] Thus, the *Loving* case was an indictment of racial categories in the law and more; it was also an indication that the justices had come to think of marriage, which had earlier been conceptualized as both a civil contract and a privileged social status, as a fundamental civil right.

The Supreme Court's position in the *Loving* case also reflected the challenges to marriage common in the late 1960s and early 1970s. With the number of couples who fit the traditional definition of marriage in precipitous decline and the number who rejected marriage altogether on the rise, the legal system had come under considerable pressure to stretch the moral and legal boundaries that made marriage an exclusive, privileged status. In the *Loving* case, for example, the U.S. Supreme Court allowed interracial couples to redefine as legitimate marriages relationships that courts had long stigmatized as "illicit sex." State courts moved in a similar direction, diminishing legal distinctions between "legitimate" and "illegitimate" children and offering limited but significant legal recognition to the partnership claims of cohabiting heterosexual couples.[27]

A small but determined group of lesbian and gay couples saw in these developments reason to hope that they might win the right to same-sex marriage. They made connections everywhere. They used feminist insistence on the use of nonsexist language to support their claim that laws that defined marriage as a contract between "parties" could be interpreted to include same-sex couples. They thought it logical that a Supreme Court that found "race" an "unsupportable" basis on which to deny entrance to the civil right of marriage could be persuaded to say the same about "sex." And they believed that, as they put it, allowing George to marry Sally, but forbidding Linda to do the same thing, was sex discrimination, and so a violation of both the constitutional guarantee of equal protection and the proposed Equal Rights Amendment.

Armed with these arguments, a number of lesbian and gay couples went to county clerks to demand marriage licenses.[28] After their applications were summarily rejected, some couples took even bolder steps. In the name of gay liberation, two men in Minnesota and two women in Kentucky filed lawsuits against the county officials who had refused them licenses.

Sex, Gender, and "Homosexual Marriage"

The Minnesota and Kentucky cases brought the issue of same-sex marriage before American courts for the first time. The cases served as litmus tests for three groups—judges, feminists, and conservatives—whose reactions to demands for "homosexual" marriage, fired in the crucible of the campaign to ratify the ERA, would set the terms for debates about same-sex marriage.

Let's begin with the judges, who had a hard time tempering their incredulity at what they regarded as the nonsensical contention that same-sex couples had a right to marry. Exasperated by the need to provide explicit justification for assumptions they and so many others had long taken for granted, judges fumbled to find legal authority for their belief that marriage always had been—and always must be—an opposite-sex institution. They couldn't find this justification in the language of the laws, for although every state placed explicit restrictions on bigamy, consanguinity, and the age of marriage partners, no state explicitly forbade same-sex marriage.

Yet in both cases, judges rejected the couples' arguments that they had the right to marry. In Minnesota, where one observer noted that the nine judges listened to the arguments of James Baker and Michael McConnell in "stony silence," the court wasted no time issuing its opinion.[29] Unconcerned that the Minnesota code did not expressly prohibit same-sex marriage, judges refused to see any room for interpretation in the language of the state marriage law. They flatly rejected Baker and McConnell's argument that the *Loving* decision made restrictions on gay marriage comparable to restrictions on interracial marriage. "In commonsense and in a constitutional sense," the judges declared, "there is a clear distinction between a marital restriction based *merely* upon race and one based upon the *fundamental* difference in sex."[30]

In Kentucky the case of Marjorie Jones and Tracy Knight was handled with similar dispatch. The court admitted that Kentucky laws neither offered a definition of marriage nor prohibited same-sex marriage, but the judge bypassed these difficulties by maintaining that "[Jones and Knight] are prevented from marrying, not by the statutes of Kentucky or the refusal of the County Court Clerk . . . to issue them a license, but rather by their own incapability of entering into a marriage as that term is defined.[31] "What they propose," the court insisted, "is not a marriage."[32]

In drawing these lines, judges professed to hold the view that marriage must be what marriage always had been. When stripped to its essentials, marriage could be reduced to the biological imperative to procreate. In the *Baker* case, for example, Minnesota judges proclaimed that "The institution of marriage as a union of man and woman, uniquely involving the procreation and rearing of children within a family, is as old as the book of Genesis. . . . This historic institution manifestly is more deeply founded than the asserted contemporary concept of marriage and societal interests for which petitioners contend.[33] In so doing, judges made it clear that, when considering cases involving "homosexual" marriage, they had no difficulty falling back on tradition, even while courts all around them were enforcing new—and dramatically different—definitions of (heterosexual) marriage.[34]

There was more. In same-sex marriage cases, judges and state officials went out of their way to fortify the traditional (and also rapidly eroding) dividing line between legitimate marriage and illicit sex. The Kentucky county attorney held that the Jones-Knight relationship did not have "the requisites of a happy home, the love and affection desired by society, with the proper concern for the children involved" because it was formed for the "pure pursuit of hedonistic and sexual pleasure."[35] The judge who heard the case in the circuit court agreed. "We see no reason," he was quoted as saying, "why we should condone and abet a spirit of what is accepted as perverted lust anymore than we should condone and abet a spirit of thievery or chicanery."[36]

At first glance, feminists approached these early same-sex marriage cases from a much different direction than judges. In 1970s radical feminism, the argument that marriage was the core institution of patriarchy was an article of faith; the challenge was to connect theoretical critiques to practical political agendas. Among radical feminists, the belief that marriage was irredeemably patriarchal tended to lead to rejection of marriage and the promotion of a variety of alternatives, ranging from communal living to partnership contracts to lesbian feminist households.[37] Radicals' incisive critiques drove feminist theory, but radicals' dismissal of marriage—and the legal system that stood behind it—made them peripheral players in institutional settings. As a result, it was liberal feminist theorists and their activist counterparts (I'll call them feminist family reformers) who developed practical feminist political stances on the issue of same-sex marriage.

Feminist family reformers took their cue from a handful of well-publicized panels of women leaders. Beginning with the United Nations Commission on the Status of Women in 1958, these groups included the U.S. President's Commission on the Status of Women, appointed by John Kennedy in 1963, and the U.S. President's Task Force on Women's Rights and Responsibilities, appointed by Richard Nixon in 1972. All three groups considered marriage law a central example of the persistence of sexual inequality, issued reports in which they tried to replace traditional notions of marriage with a "partnership" theory, and recommended dramatic changes in existing marriage laws. They insisted, for example, that sexist language—and such sex differentials as separate ages of consent for men and women—should be excised from the laws. They protested married women's loss of control over their national citizenship, their domicile, and their own names. They opposed limitations on married women's right to contract, inherit property, and control their own income, and they set out to study the impact of sex differentials in alimony and child custody awards. Their lists of sexual inequalities in marriage law served liberal feminists of the 1970s not only as critiques of marriage law but also, and increasingly, as arguments for the passage of the Equal Rights Amendment.[38]

Feminist family reformers took their lists to state legislatures and pressured them to reform state marriage laws. Working in combination with family legal experts who sought to "modernize" anachronistic state codes, they persuaded lawmakers to remove most formal sexual classifications from marriage law. Men and women should, they argued, be able to marry at the same age; "husbands" and "wives" should henceforth be considered "spouses"; both partners should be expected to contribute to the family's economic maintenance. In this vein, they set in motion what were undoubtedly the most significant marriage law reforms in American history; the results ranged all the way from no-fault divorce to joint custody to sex-neutral support awards.[39]

Yet there was a clear exception to the range of these concerns, for feminist family reformers did not question the assumption that marriage should be an opposite-sex institution. To judge from their published accounts, the argument lesbian and gay plaintiffs made—that denying same-sex couples marriage licenses was a form of sex discrimination—does not seem to have even occurred to them.[40] And because it did not, their marriage law reforms were often packaged in terms that transformed what had been an implicit—if pervasive—legal assumption that marriage was an opposite-sex union into a formal legal definition of marriage as an opposite-sex institution.

Take Colorado and Virginia, for example. Ever since the 1860s, Colorado had defined marriage as a contract between "parties." In 1973 the state legislature replaced this technically sex-neutral definition with a new provision that "a marriage between a man and a woman, licensed, solemnized, and registered . . . is valid in this state."[41] The new law was designed to bring Colorado into compliance with federal and state equal rights amendments. It was modeled on the proposed Uniform Marriage and Divorce Act, a statute touted by feminist family reformers and ERA advocates.[42] Virginia never ratified the federal Equal Rights Amendment, but its 1971 state constitution included a provision prohibiting sex discrimination.[43] To comply with it, the legislature revised several aspects of state marriage law, abolishing sex differences in age requirements for marriage and replacing every mention of "male and female" or "husband and wife" with "persons" or "spouses." The very same bill added the provision that "a marriage between persons of the same sex is prohibited."[44]

I have found no evidence to suggest that feminist family reformers consciously intended their actions to exclude actual same-sex couples from marriage. What they do seem to have been doing is drawing a line between supposedly benign sexual "distinctions" (man/woman) and supposedly pernicious sexual "discriminations" (that men could marry at age x but women must wait till age y, or that men were called "husbands" and women called "wives"). This line had the strategic advantage of reassuring conservatives that while sexual discrimination was subject to question, sexual distinctions were beyond challenge. It also reflected—and, in significant ways, shaped—the growing distinction in feminist thought between supposedly biological "sex" and supposedly social "gender."

If neither judges nor feminist family reformers fully registered the argument that denying lesbians and gays the right to marry might be a form of sex discrimination, a third group, conservatives, did. So certain were conservatives that same-sex marriage would spell disaster for the traditional family that when same-sex marriage cases reached U.S. courts, they rushed to barricade heterosexual privilege and opposite-sex marriage. Acting as if the same-sex couples whose arguments judges had dismissed out of hand were harbingers of the imminent collapse of the family as an institution of Western culture, they turned the specter of "homosexual marriage" into a call to arms against the feminist movement in general and the Equal Rights Amendment in particular.

At the core of the conservative position was the old, familiar belief that sex-based laws were practical recognitions of supposedly natural distinctions. If feminists had begun to draw the line between sex and gender so that everything except the man/woman distinction fell in the realm of socially constructed (and therefore malleable) "gender," conservatives drew the line so that every legal distinction between men and women remained rooted in biologically necessary (and therefore immutable) "sex."

One of the key players in advancing the conservative position was Sam Ervin, a Democratic senator from South Carolina who would, only a few years later, become the hero of the Watergate hearings. Ervin's seat on the Senate Judiciary Committee put him in a position to translate grassroots conservative antifeminism into legal and political resistance to the proposed Equal Rights Amendment. In congressional hearings on the amendment, Ervin explained what he considered to be obvious. "The physiological and functional differences between men and women constitute earth's important reality," Ervin said. "Without them human life could not exist." His thinking on the subject connected sexual difference directly to "the protection of women and the existence and development of the race" through "marriage, the home, and the family."[45]

However naturally secure Ervin might have believed the link between physiological sex and legal sexual categories to be, he sensed that his feminist challengers had something else in mind. Fearful that ERA proponents intended to annul "every existing Federal and State law making any distinction between men and women," he was led, almost in spite of himself, to the conclusion that the problem with an amendment designed to stop discrimination on the basis of sex was that "the word 'sex' is imprecise in exact meaning."[46]

The irony of hearing what is now a postmodern feminist assertion from a conservative antifeminist should not stop us from pinpointing Ervin's political agenda. In these hearings, Ervin was trying out arguments he hoped would stop feminism and the ERA dead in their tracks. He did his best to prevent congressional passage of the amendment. When the theoretical issues he raised failed to move his colleagues, he reached for more concrete examples. Ervin told Congress that the passage of the ERA would mandate unisex toilets, force women into the military, and make laws against same-sex marriage as untenable as those against interracial marriage.[47] He offered a raft of amendments to the amendment, asking Congress to change its language to read that "neither the United States nor any State shall make any law treating men and women differently unless the difference in treatment is based on physiological or functional differences between them" or that the ERA "shall not apply to any law prohibiting sexual activity between persons of the same sex or the marriage of persons of the same sex."[48]

In the short run, Ervin failed. In 1972 his congressional colleagues voted the ERA out of committee, passed it through Congress, and sent it on to the states for ratification. For a while, the amendment's future looked bright. But in the long run, it would become only too clear that Ervin had succeeded in making "homosexual marriage" a potent conservative battle cry.[49]

Sexual Distinctions and Sex Discrimination

Once these political battle lines had been drawn, the stage was set for repeated encounters between lesbian and gay couples, judges, feminists, and antifeminists. Three of these encounters—the 1974 *Singer* case, the 1977 political elections, and the 1993 *Baehr* case—offered potential turning points for the future of same-sex marriage.

The first incident, the *Singer* case, took place in Washington state. On September 20, 1971, John Singer, a twenty-six-year-old typist at the Federal Equal Opportunity Commission, and twenty-four-year-old Paul

Barwick, manager of Seattle's Gay Community Center, applied to King County clerk Neil Pearson for a marriage license.[50] The two men, who had tipped local news media to their intentions, came prepared to make a political statement. Barwick wore a T-shirt that said "Gay" on the front; Singer told a reporter from a gay newspaper that, although both men considered marriage "wrong" and "rather oppressive," they felt that "as long as the marriage laws do exist, and do create benefits like the tax break, we will apply for it."[51] This position, which merged the disdain for marriage common in the gay male community with firm insistence on equal rights, won them kudos from both the Seattle Gay Alliance and the local Gay Liberation Front, but it cut no ice with Pearson, who refused them a license. The couple promptly brought suit in the King County Superior Court. When they lost the case, they appealed to the Washington State Court of Appeals.[52]

The *Singer* case might have unfolded along the lines of earlier same-sex marriage cases (that is, been summarily dismissed) were it not for the fact that by the time it reached the appeals court in 1974, Washington had passed a state equal rights amendment. Singer and Barwick made the ERA, and the claim that denying same-sex marriage was a form of sex discrimination, central to their case.[53]

For national ERA strategists, the *Singer* case could not have come at a worse time. By 1974 the high hopes that had surrounded Congressional passage of the national amendment had evaporated. Twenty-two of the necessary thirty-eight states had ratified the amendment in 1972; eight more had added their approval in 1973. But by 1974, momentum had slowed to a trickle; only three states would ratify in that year.[54] And although some supporters predicted that the 1975 elections would put the amendment over the top, others feared that victory was beginning to slip from their grasp. They were having more and more trouble rejecting conservative claims that the ERA would lead to unisex toilets, the drafting of women, and homosexual marriage.

Thus, ERA supporters found themselves at the mercy of the three-judge panel of the Washington State Court of Appeals. If the court held that a state equal rights amendment did in fact protect same-sex marriage, conservatives would have gained a formidable weapon in the ERA propaganda wars. As it turned out, though, neither ERA strategists nor feminist family reformers had anything to fear from the court. In the *Singer* case, judges found a way to explain how it was that refusing to grant two men a marriage license that would have been granted to a man and a woman might have been a sexual distinction, but was not sex discrimination.

To do so, judges had to rely on exceedingly convoluted logic. Their first step was to invalidate the comparison Singer and Barwick tried to make between race discrimination, as outlawed in the *Loving* case, and sex discrimination. There was, the court insisted, no analogy between the two. Discrimination on the basis of race might be unconstitutional, but Singer and Barwick "[were] not being denied a marriage license because of their sex; rather, they [were] being denied entry into the marriage relationship because of the recognized definition of that relationship as one which may be entered into only by two persons who are members of the opposite sex."[55] Having rendered the analogy to race legally inoperative, the court then felt able to use language eerily reminiscent of "miscegenation" cases to uphold the state's claim that "there is no violation of the ERA as long as marriage licenses are denied equally to both male and female pairs."[56]

The court's second step was to make sexual categorizations seem to be a necessary part of marriage. Here they were in muddy waters, for one of the justifications they resorted to, defining marriage as intimately related to the "procreation and rearing of children," was increasingly threadbare.[57] No state actually required opposite-sex couples to prove their fitness for procreation as a requirement of marriage. Given the growing popularity of campaigns for birth and population control and the rise of single-parent and "blended" families, no state could realistically have done so.

But if procreation could not serve to clinch the argument, it seemed that biological sexual distinctions might. Under the Washington state ERA, the judges opined in a key sentence of the decision, "laws which differentiate between the sexes are permissible so long as they are based upon the unique physical characteristics of a particular sex, rather than upon a person's membership in a particular sex per se."[58] This statement is so perplexing (what kind of distinction could you draw between the "unique physical characteristics of a particular sex" and "membership in a particular sex"?) that it is tempting to believe that judges chose it just to obfuscate the issue.

There is, however, more to this story than just judicial determination to bolster heterosexual privilege, for, in defense of their position, judges pointed to the writings of prominent ERA supporters.[59] In so doing, they had fastened on a significant feminist predicament. Feminist theorists, by then convinced that it was all but impossible to strip the word "sex" of its biological connotations, had begun to place central emphasis—and nearly all their theoretical energy—on developing the concept of "gender," which signaled a socially constructed phenomenon seemingly distinct from "sex." Both the legal system and the language of the ERA, however, remained firmly grounded in the terminology of "sex," which was rapidly becoming the unexamined residue of feminist thinking.

Accordingly, ERA strategists had to negotiate between their own belief that most of what the legal system labeled "sex" was really "gender" and their conservative opponents' belief that most of what feminists labeled "gender" was really "sex." What they arrived at was a general position that "classification by sex . . . ought *always* to be regarded as unreasonable" with one qualification: "except where the law pertains to a unique physical characteristic of one sex."[60] In legal journals and congressional hearings they elaborated on their meaning. As ERA advocates saw it, laws involving unique physical characteristics were "relatively rare"; they might include laws covering wet nurses or sperm banks, but did not include laws protecting women workers from fertility hazards on the job.[61] Until Sam Ervin's grandstanding and the *Singer* case forced their hand, same-sex marriage was all but absent from their discussions.

When, however, the issue could no longer be avoided, liberal feminists joined politicians and judges in separating "homosexual marriage," which they regarded as little more than a conservative red herring, from the issue of sex discrimination. Building on this budding liberal consensus, Birch Bayh, the congressional sponsor of the ERA, responded to Sam Ervin's baiting by insisting that under the ERA, prohibitions on same-sex marriage could stand because they affected males and females equally.[62] And thus, the judges in the *Singer* case fastened on the exception feminists would have granted to "unique physical characteristics of a sex" and made it the basis for exempting same-sex marriage from coverage of the Washington state equal rights amendment.

Feminists likely would have preferred to avoid raising the issue of same-sex marriage at all, but it nonetheless must be said that the *Singer* case solved a strategic problem for them. The precedent it set offered legal sanction for the view that there was no connection between the ERA and the issue of "homosexual" marriage.[63] And as legal precedent, the *Singer* decision held firm. Between its issuance in 1974 and 1993, judges rejected every attempt same-sex couples made to demand the right to marry, frequently relying on the *Singer* case as what one judge called the "best reasoned" legal example for doing so.[64]

But if liberal feminists imagined that separating the ERA from "homosexual marriage" would disarm conservative opposition to the amendment, they couldn't have been more wrong. The patterns set in the *Singer* case were, in fact, only further entrenched in the second encounter between these groups, the elections of 1977. Both sides of the ERA debate regarded the 1977 elections, which took place under the shadow of the 1978 deadline for ratification of the ERA, as crucial ones. The scene was set in Florida, one of the key unratified states, and the home of Anita Bryant's now infamous campaign to "Save Our Children" from homosexuality.[65] While Bryant stirred up antigay publicity and linked lesbian and gay rights issues to the ERA campaign, Florida state legislators showed that they, too, knew how to connect these dots. The 1977 Florida legislature not only refused to ratify the ERA but also passed bills that denied "homosexuals" the right to adopt children and that provided that "a marriage license shall not be issued unless one party is a male and the other party is a female."[66]

And in 1977 the popularity of antigay measures, including bills prohibiting same-sex marriage, was by no means limited to states still battling over the ERA. Bryant herself went to Minnesota, where she helped persuade St. Paul voters to repeal their gay rights ordinance. That same year the Minnesota legislature adopted a new definition of marriage as a contract between a "man and a woman."[67] In California, too, the legislature changed its marriage law to read that marriage was "a contract between a man and a woman."[68] The California law was proposed by Assembly Republican Bruce Nestande, who said it would reaffirm "that the family is the essence of western civilization"; it was supported by Senate Republican John V. Briggs (later to become the sponsor of the rabidly homophobic Briggs amendment), who said it "would restore some sense of morality to the state of California."[69]

In Colorado, which had, as we have seen, already adopted a sex-specific marriage validity clause, conservatives no longer considered it enough to do the job. Incensed by the actions of a Boulder county clerk who in 1975 had issued marriage licenses to six same-sex couples ("I don't profess to be knowledgeable about homosexuality or even understand it," she said, ". . . [but] no minority should be discriminated against"), the state house of representatives passed a bill that would have added an additional ban on same-sex marriage.[70]

The outcome of the 1977 elections revealed that, whatever judges and courts might say, conservatives were convinced that, as one delegate to the 1977 National Women's Conference in Houston explained,

> ERA says you cannot discriminate on the basis of sex, and if you want to deny a marriage to a man and a man or to deny a homosexual the right to teach in the schools or to adopt children, it would be on account of sex that you would deny it. And under the ERA, that would be unconstitutional.[71]

The result was the passage of a second wave of sex-specific marriage laws that, unlike the first, was specifically intended to stop same-sex couples from marrying by lodging the notion that marriages must be opposite-sex so firmly in law that it could never again be questioned.[72]

"A Bomb That Will Blow the Traditional Family to Pieces"

For nearly a decade after these conservative triumphs in the elections of 1977, the issue of same-sex marriage was all but dormant. Liberal feminists did eventually come to support some lesbian and gay political demands (beginning with the resolution to "eliminate discrimination on the basis of sexual and affectional preference" adopted at the 1977 National Women's Conference in Houston), but they continued to avoid the issue of same-sex marriage.[73] Meanwhile, gay activists found that downplaying the issue of same-sex marriage allowed them to build a political bridge between the gay male valorization of nonmonogamous sexual experimentation and lesbian adherence to feminist critiques of marriage.

In these years, every attempt to raise the issue of same-sex marriage had to contend not only with conservative opposition but also with the political, strategic, and theoretical "lessons" activists drew from the 1970s.[74] The sheer force of the conservative backlash seemed to dictate new legal tactics. After the defeat of the ERA,

American courts felt free to stop what progress they had been making toward excising legal categories based on sex; the result was that, when considering laws rooted in sexual distinctions, courts subjected them to "intermediate" rather than "strict" scrutiny and did not require states to offer "compelling" justification for their existence.[75] Chastened by these developments, lesbian and gay plaintiffs abandoned the argument that discrimination against lesbians and gays was discrimination on the basis of "sex." Attaching themselves to emerging theories that distinguished sexuality from both sex and gender, they began to argue that "homosexuality" itself should be seen as a "suspect" legal category and/or protected as part of a constitutional right to privacy.[76]

Meanwhile, lesbian and gay activists' attempts to challenge the economic and social privileges that accrued to (heterosexual) marriage increasingly took the form of demands for domestic partnership laws. These laws sought to minimize the economic disadvantages cohabiting couples suffered by extending to them such benefits as family health insurance plans and sickness or bereavement leave.[77] Partnership laws offered the beleaguered lesbian and gay activists of the 1980s significant strategic advantages. Because they stopped short of demanding marriage, they raised less ire among conservatives and less discomfort among gay critics of marriage; because many of them covered opposite-sex as well as same-sex couples, they allowed for the building of political coalitions with straight activists.[78] Domestic partnership laws offer only a few of the economic and legal benefits of marital status (and they offer none of the social legitimacy that accompanies marriage), but they were politically feasible: by 1999 they had been adopted by 66 cities and counties, 6 state governments, 128 colleges and universities, and hundreds of private employers.[79]

Yet even as lesbian and gay activists avoided the issue of same-sex marriage to focus on domestic partnership proposals, an increasing number of lesbian and gay couples concluded that only marriage could provide them with the social legitimacy heterosexual married couples had long enjoyed.[80] They gathered support from liberal church leaders, many of whom came to endorse same-sex "union" ceremonies, and the ACLU, which endorsed the principle of same-sex marriage in 1986.[81] Still, those who considered filing lawsuits faced the likelihood that their cases might only add to the growing list of court precedents against same-sex marriage.[82]

Here the situation stood when, in 1990, two lesbian couples and one gay male couple in Hawaii once again demanded the legal right to marry. The prospects for their case, *Baehr v. Lewin,* seemed so dim that the lesbian and gay activists they approached for support warned them against the action and refused to help them.[83] One of the plaintiffs, Ninia Baehr, a feminist and historian who reevaluated her own critiques of marriage in order to take part in the case, recounted the objections she heard from other lesbians and gays. "They had valid concerns that we were never going to win, so why waste resources?" she remembered. "Then there was the whole debate that maybe we shouldn't ape heterosexuals. Then there was another argument that maybe we shouldn't win because it would make the right wing angry and there would be a terrible backlash."[84]

The lawyer the couples finally convinced to take the case, Dan Foley, was a straight, married man associated with the ACLU. Foley remembers that the case struck him as unwinnable, but he was willing to give it a try.[85] Building his briefs on arguments about the need to declare homosexuality a suspect classification and protect the right to privacy, Foley and his clients went to court.[86] When a lower court dismissed their claims, Foley appealed to the Hawaii Supreme Court.

To nearly everyone's surprise, the Hawaii Supreme Court took the opportunity to embark on a serious reexamination of all the previous court cases involving same-sex marriage. Concluding that the *Jones* and *Singer* cases were little more than exercises in "tortured and conclusory sophistry," the Hawaii court dismissed Foley's arguments about privacy protections for homosexuality and turned the focus firmly back to issues of sex (and race) discrimination.[87]

When it came to marriage, the court said, the language of the law did indeed matter, and the classification set by Hawaii marriage law was not homosexuality (straight/gay) but sex (man/woman). Pointing out that opposite-sex marriages might conceivably be entered into by individuals whose sexual orientation was heterosexual or homosexual, the court refused to believe that the same might not be true of same-sex marriages.[88] Holding that the issue must therefore be discrimination on the basis of "sex" rather than on the basis of "homosexuality," the court went on to offer an analysis of how sex discrimination should be analyzed under Hawaiian law.

Hawaiian law is unusual in that the state constitution includes an equal rights provision that explicitly forbids discrimination (and the denial of equal protection) on the basis of "race, religion, *sex* or ancestry."[89] In interpreting it, the Hawaii Supreme Court went further than any American court had ever gone toward declaring "sex" a fully suspect legal category. Extending the logic by then routine in race discrimination cases to sex discrimination cases, the court explained that sex distinctions in the law should be considered automatically "suspect," and must therefore be scrutinized strictly by the courts; they could not stand unless the state could provide a "compelling" justification for their existence. Having gone this far, the court then turned the case back to a lower court for reconsideration.[90]

After the Hawaii Supreme Court gave this preliminary indication that it would uphold same-sex marriages, the stage was set for the enactment of the latest round of anti–gay marriage laws. The Hawaii legislature immediately scrambled to "clarify" its law so as to justify continuing to ban same-sex marriage.[91] One proposal was to enact a bill offering the kind of "compelling" justification for sexual classifications the court had hinted it might consider accepting. Representative Terrance Tom, a Democrat, put forth such a bill, which would have limited marriage to couples who "appear to present the biological possibility of producing offspring," thus serving the supposedly compelling state interest in "the propagation, health and well-being of future generations."[92]

In proposing this bill, Tom inadvertently exposed the basic illogic of this widely held but irrational argument. There are, of course, many heterosexual couples who marry but, due to health, age, or inclination, cannot or do not have children, and the state neither inquires into their ability to procreate nor prevents them from marrying. And, although Tom showed no awareness of this fact, many lesbians and gays are themselves parents, whether from previous marriages or through adoption or artificial insemination. So many people were offended by the bill that Tom tried to appease some of them by adding a proviso that "the state does not, and should not, inquire into whether the male-female couples apply[ing] for a marriage license presently intend to have children, or test opposite-sex couples to determine whether they may be presently fertile."[93]

As it seemed likely that the Tom bill would not fly, logically or politically, attention soon centered on a second proposal, to adopt a state constitutional amendment that would read, "Marriage is the legal union of one man and one woman as husband and wife."[94] This strategy, which raised the trend of legal sex-specific marriage definitions from statutory to state constitutional heights, was unusual indeed. There was, in fact, only one obvious precedent in American legal history. After the Civil War, a number of southern states had passed state constitutional bans on interracial marriages.[95]

In the months after these two proposals were offered, Hawaii newspapers printed numerous letters to the editor and the Hawaii legislature held a series of emotional public hearings, at which hundreds of people expressed their opinions. Conservatives kept up a steady attack, associating same-sex marriage with everything from generic "immorality" and the breakdown of the traditional family to bigamy, polygamy, and, perhaps strangest of all, teenage pregnancy.[96] The evangelist Gerald Wright called same-sex marriage an "odious oxymoron that destroys the whole concept of marriage." Mike Gabbard, leader of a group designed to "Stop Promoting Homosexuality [in] Hawaii," called same-sex marriage "a bomb that will blow the traditional family to pieces."[97]

In 1994 the state legislature tried to satisfy both sides of the debate by appointing a commission to study domestic partnership laws on the one hand, and passing a law declaring that "the marriage contract—shall be only between a man and a woman" on the other.[98] It succeeded in satisfying neither. A year later, the legislature's Commission on Sexual Orientation and the Law issued a report recommending that the state allow same-sex marriage, placing its proposal for a "universal comprehensive domestic partnership act" as only a second priority.[99] Meanwhile, conservatives continued to push for a constitutional amendment. Hoping that if they could avoid a legislative vote, they might also be able to avoid accepting any kind of domestic partnership bill, they began gathering the signatures necessary to hold a new state constitutional convention.[100]

On the mainland, reaction to the *Baehr* decision was similarly extreme. The possibility that the Hawaii Supreme Court might allow same-sex couples the right to a marriage license spurred state legislators to pass a wave of laws against same-sex marriage. After Hawaii changed its marriage law in 1994, thirty other states followed suit.[101] Many of the new bills refused interstate recognition to (potential) same-sex marriages; most established or reiterated an opposite-sex definition of marriage. In Indiana the state legislature added a section of marriage law called "Gender requirements," which reads, "Only a female may marry a male. Only a male may marry a female—a marriage between persons of the same gender is void in Indiana even if the marriage is lawful in the place where it is solemnized."[102] In Michigan the law states that

> Marriage is inherently a unique relationship between a man and a woman. As a matter of public policy, this state has a special interest in encouraging, supporting, and protecting that unique relationship in order to promote, among other goals, the stability and welfare of society and its children. A marriage contracted between individuals of the same sex is invalid in this state.[103]

Meanwhile, back in Hawaii, Circuit Court Judge Kevin Chang began hearing the new lower court case. Most of the testimony focused on a single issue: the state's contention that it could and should limit marriage to opposite-sex couples because the state had "a compelling interest" in "promoting the optimal development of children." (Although the state also charged that "legalized prostitution, incest and polygamy will occur if same-sex marriage is allowed," its lawyers presented little evidence on this or other possible state interests in promoting marriage.) On December 3, 1996, Judge Chang issued the ruling that by then nearly everyone expected, holding that the state had failed to make its case and that the sex-based classification of Hawaii's marriage law violated the state constitution's guarantee of equal protection. Chang ordered the State Department of Health to stop refusing to give marriage licenses to same-sex couples, but the next day he stayed that order, pending an appeal to the Hawaii Supreme Court.[104]

Judge Chang's decision reinvigorated the conservative campaign for an amendment to the state constitution, which continued to gain strength until 1997, when the Hawaii legislature hammered out another "compromise."[105] To the distress of conservatives, the legislature passed the most comprehensive domestic partnership act now in force in any American state, a bill that extends benefits to "reciprocal beneficiaries," including relatives (such as sisters) as well as same-sex couples.[106] But to the distress of lesbian and gay activists, it also passed a constitutional amendment declaring that "the legislature shall have the power to reserve marriage to opposite-sex couples."[107] On November 3, 1998, the amendment came before Hawaii's voters, who passed it by a vote of 285,381 (69.2 percent) to 117,827 (28.6 percent).[108]

In the wake of the *Baehr* decisions, same-sex marriage has become a hotly contested issue all across the nation. Proponents and opponents are choosing sides, girding themselves for legislative action, and making hopeful predictions about the future.[109] The initial victory in Hawaii, along with pending cases in Alaska and Vermont, has raised the possibility that some courts may come to recognize same-sex marriage. As Arnoldo Ramirez, a gay activist in Florida, explains, "Hawaii has given people hope that the civil right of marriage is within our grasp, that it's a matter of time."[110] Yet the rush by state legislatures to enshrine sex-specific definitions of marriage in the law continues. As I write the final version of this essay, the legislature in my own state, Oregon, is considering its own "Defense of Marriage" bill; in November 2000, California voters are scheduled to vote on a "definition of marriage" initiative that would limit marriage to opposite-sex couples and deny recognition to same-sex marriages celebrated in other states.

From its beginnings in the 1970s, activists had carried on a great deal of the campaign for same-sex marriage by making analogies between the denial of same-sex marriage and the denial of interracial marriage, between lesbian and gay activism and civil rights, between "homosexuality" and "race" as suspect categories.[111] The ACLU, which has participated in both kinds of cases, has been quick to make the connection. One of its lawyers, Carl M. Varady, who participated in the *Baehr* case, explained that same-sex marriage cases "are really the miscegenation cases of the '90s. . . . The same type of religious and natural-law arguments were put forth against interracial marriage."[112] Lesbian and gay activists themselves have offered so many comparisons between gay rights and the civil rights campaign that they sometimes provoke angry reactions from racially oppressed groups.[113]

What is even more striking than the consistency with which lesbian and gay activists have resorted to comparisons to discrimination on the basis of race was the reluctance they initially showed to connecting gay rights issues to categorization by sex.[114] One of the reasons the *Baehr* case came as a surprise is that over the past decade, lesbian and gay legal strategists have concentrated so much energy on trying to have "homosexuality" declared a suspect category that they paid less and less attention to categories of "sex" itself. Only after the Hawaii court made its preliminary decision did most gay rights activists recognize the utility of seeing the denial of same-sex marriage as sex discrimination. Once they did, though, arguments about sex discrimination began appearing regularly in the writings of gay male scholars; they range from the utilitarian (hopeful comments that the sex discrimination argument might be effective with courts or that it might make feminists allies of lesbian and gay rights campaigns) or the critical (complaints that *Baehr* is a sex discrimination victory *rather* than a victory for lesbian and gay rights) to serious attempts to connect the denial of same-sex marriage to the reproduction of male supremacy and traditional gender roles.[115]

But while lesbian feminist theorists have by now gone well beyond their earlier focus on socially constructed "gender" to probe the socially constructed nature of "sex," they have held so tightly to 1970s critiques of traditional marriage that they have not, by and large, connected their challenges to sexual categories to the issue of same-sex marriage. At the end of the 1990s, conservatives are more likely than lesbian feminists to argue that same-sex marriage is a "time bomb that will blow the traditional family apart," and gay male activists are more likely than lesbian feminists to argue that the denial of same-sex marriage is sex discrimination.

It is time, I think, to rethink these habits of feminist inattention—and lesbian feminist resistance—to the issue of same-sex marriage. The *Baehr* decisions offer the most significant potential turning point yet for the legalization of same-sex marriage. And because the court's logic so clearly identifies the issue as one of sex discrimination, the *Baehr* case also offers the possibility that feminists could put aside two decades of hesitation about the issue and finally join with lesbian and gay activists to challenge sex-based limitations on marriage. For both lesbian and gay rights and sex discrimination law, the potential is unprecedented, and the stakes are high.

For more than two decades feminists have looked for ways to dismantle the production of patriarchy in marriage. Radical feminists, who identified marriage as the core institution of patriarchy, tried to bypass the institution altogether. Feminist family reformers relied on the newly emerging distinction between biological sex and socially constructed gender to focus their attack on the aspects of marriage that could most easily be defined as arbitrary gender privileges, establishing gender-neutral provisions for age of marriage, child custody, and economic support obligations. But as I've tried to show in this essay, the liberal feminist reform of marriage laws purchased seeming gender neutrality at the cost of embedding sex difference even more deeply in marriage law than ever before.

It is time we recognized something that conservatives have known all along—that same-sex marriage has real potential to short-circuit the process by which the institution of marriage links legal sexual categories (men and women) to social power differentials, translating ostensibly equal men and women into advantaged husbands and disadvantaged wives. Precisely because it stands at the junction between the legal, social, and economic world and the private and personal one, marriage holds considerable power to naturalize social relationships, to turn men into "husbands" and women into "wives."[116] As feminist legal activists of today note, even in the absence of the wide variety of gender differentials that used to be built into marriage law, this process—and the social subordination of women it produces—continues. Same-sex marriage strikes at its heart by depriving the institution of marriage of the dividing lines that allow for the connection of supposedly natural "sex" to supposedly social "gender." There is a reason that it seems nonsensical to conceive of a marriage between two women as one between two "wives": in the absence of a man/husband to define it against, the social role of "wife" is exposed for the gendered creation it is.

Same-sex marriage is not, of course, a panacea. As lesbian feminists have long recognized, same-sex relationships are by no means free of power differentials. Within same-sex relationships, however, the power imbalances that exist between partners cannot reliably be associated with either sex *or* gender difference. It is for this reason that Nan Hunter has argued, in a brilliant article on the subject, that when the issue of same-sex marriage is seen "as one of gender systems, rather than of minority rights," it may well be that "legalizing lesbian and gay marriage would have enormous potential to destabilize the gendered definition of marriage for everyone.[117] In the meantime, it seems clearer and clearer that as long as marriage continues to be defined as a union between "a man and a woman," it will prove impossible to establish sex *or* gender equality.

NOTES

I would like to express my deep gratitude to Karen Engle, Estelle Freedman, Dorothee Kocks, Andrew Koppelman, Valerie Matsumoto, Joanne Meyerowitz, Ann Mussey, Barbara Pope, Kathryn Stockton, Nancy Tuana, and Barbara Welke for the suggestions and support they offered while I was writing this article; Nick Rosenthal and Taro Iwata for superb research assistance; and Marc Scruggs for his generosity in sharing crucial source materials.

1. Maryland *Laws*, 1973, ch. 213.

2. In 1970, for example, twenty-four states used contract definitions of marriage. Twenty-two of these were expressed in sex-neutral terms of "parties" or "persons" (AZ, AR, CA, CO, GA, ID, KS, LA, MI, MN, MO, MT, NE, NV, NM, NY, ND, OK, OR, SD, WI, WY). Only two states (AK and WA) used the sex-specific terms "male and female."

3. "Upsurge in Men Who Want to Marry Men," *San Francisco Chronicle*, May 29, 1970, 1; "The Boom in 'Gay' Marriages," *San Francisco Chronicle*, July 14, 1970, 1, 16.

4. "Clerk Wants Tighter Law Against Gay Marriages," *Advocate*, June 24–July 7, 1970, 4.

5. "Upsurge in Men Who Want to Marry Men," 1; "Clerk Wants Tighter Law," 4.

6. The states are MD (1973); TX (1973); CO (1973, 1977); VA (1975); NV (1975); OK (1975); ND (1975); MT (1975); LA (1975, 1987); FL (1977); UT (1977); CA (1977); IL (1977); MN (1977); WY (1977); AZ (1980); KS (1980); IN (1986).

7. Defense of Marriage Act, Pub. L. no. 104–199, 110 *U.S. Stat.* 2419 (1996). Although the federal government routinely determines the validity of marriages as part of its various functions (including collecting income taxes and distributing Social Security), it relies on individual state definitions to do so. There is considerable debate about whether or not DOMA is constitutional. See, for example, Jon-Peter Kelley, "Note: Act of Infidelity: Why the Defense of Marriage Act Is Unfaithful to the Constitution," *Cornell Journal of Law and Public Policy* 7 (fall 1977); 203–53.

8. The states are HI (1994); UT (1995); OK (1996); LA (1996); IL (1996); AZ (1996); KS (1996); TN (1996); ID (1995, 1996); GA (1996); AK (1996); SC (1996); NC (1996); DE (1996); MI (1996); SD (1996); MO (1996); PA (1996); ME (1997); AR (1997); IN (1997); MN (1997); MT (1997); FL (1997); MS (1997); ND (1997); VA (1997); IA (1998); KY (1998); WA (1998); AL (1998). On this latest wave, see Barbara J. Cox, "Are Same-Sex Marriage Statutes the New Anti-Gay Initiatives?" *National Journal of Sexual Orientation Law* 2, (no. 2 (1996), 194–208.

9. Alaska *Constitution*, art. 1, sec. 25 (1999), which states that "To be valid or recognized in this state, a marriage may exist only between one man and

one woman"; Hawaii *Constitution*, art. 1, sec. 23 (1999), which states that "The legislature shall have the power to reserve marriage to opposite-sex couples."

10. Classic examples include Kate Millett, *Sexual Politics* (New York: Ballantine Books, 1969); Shulamith Firestone, *The Dialectic of Sex: The Case for Feminist Revolution* (New York: Morrow, 1970); and Germaine Greer, *The Female Eunuch* (New York: McGraw-Hill, 1971). See also Vivian Gornick and Barbara K. Moran's introduction to their edited collection, *Woman in Sexist Society: Studies in Power and Powerlessness* (New York: Basic Books, 1971); and the manifestos collected in Anne Koedt, Ellen Levine, and Anita Rapone, eds., *Radical Feminism* (New York: Quadrangle Books, 1973), 365–87.

11. For reviews of changing attitudes, see Becky Butler, ed., *Ceremonies of the Heart: Celebrating Lesbian Unions* (Seattle: Seal Press, 1990), 35–41; Andrew Sullivan, ed., *Same-Sex Marriage: Pro and Con* (New York: Vintage Books, 1997); and Robert M. Baird and Stuart E. Rosenbaum, eds., *Same-Sex Marriage: The Moral and Legal Debate* (New York: Prometheus Books, 1997). For an intriguing exploration of the (also changing) meanings of family among lesbians and gay men, see Kath Weston, *Families We Choose: Lesbians, Gays, Kinship* (New York: Columbia University Press, 1991).

12. For the first two arguments, see Paula L. Ettelbrick, "Since When Is Marriage a Path to Liberation?" *Outlook* 2, no. 9 (fall 1989): 14–17; Nitya Duclos, "Some Complicating Thoughts on Same-Sex Marriage," *Law and Sexuality* 1 (summer 1991): 31–61; Nancy D. Polikoff, "We Will Get What We Ask For: Why Legalizing Gay and Lesbian Marriage Will Not 'Dismantle the Legal Structure of Gender in Every Marriage,'" *Virginia Law Review* 79 (October 1993): 1535–52; and Ettelbrick, "Wedlock Alert: A Comment on Lesbian and Gay Family Recognition," *Journal of Law and Policy* 5, no. 1 (1996): 107–66.

13. Nan D. Hunter, "Marriage, Law, and Gender: A Feminist Inquiry," *Law and Sexuality* 1 (summer 1991): 9–30; Barbara J. Cox, "The Lesbian Wife: Same-Sex Marriage as an Expression of Radical and Plural Democracy," *California Western Law Review* 33 (spring 1997): 155–67; Cox, "A (Personal) Essay on Same-Sex Marriage," in Baird and Rosenbaum, *Same-Sex Marriage*, 27–29; and E. J. Graff, "Retying the Knot," in Sullivan, *Same-Sex Marriage*, 134–38.

14. There is, of course, a voluminous literature on this distinction. Key arguments include Gayle Rubin, "The Traffic in Women: Notes on the 'Political Economy' of Sex," in Rayna R. Reiter, ed., *Toward an Anthropology of Women* (New York: Monthly Review Press, 1975), 157–210; Joan Wallach Scott, "Gender: A Useful Category of Historical Analysis," *American Historical Review* 91 (December 1986): 1053–75; and Donna J. Haraway, "'Gender' for a Marxist Dictionary: The Sexual Politics of a Word," in *Simians, Cyborgs, and Women: The Reinvention of Nature* (New York: Routledge, 1991), 127–48. For a short summary, see my discussion, Peggy Pascoe, "Gender," in Richard Fox and James Kloppenberg, eds., *A Companion to American Thought* (Oxford: Blackwell, 1995).

15. On these points, see Gayle Rubin, "Thinking Sex: Notes for a Radical Theory of the Politics of Sexuality," in Carol S. Vance, ed., *Pleasure and Danger: Exploring Female Sexuality* (Boston: Routledge and Kegan Paul, 1984), 267–319; Judith Butler, *Gender Trouble: Feminism and the Subversion of Identity* (New York: Routledge, 1990); and Eve Kosofsky Sedgwick, *Epistemology of the Closet* (Berkeley: University of California Press, 1990), 1–63.

16. For a parallel argument about sex discrimination law more broadly, see Katherine M. Franke, "The Central Mistake of Sex Discrimination Law: The Disaggregation of Sex from Gender," *University of Pennsylvania Law Review* 144 (November 1995): 1–99. For a pathbreaking argument about the connections between legal discrimination against lesbians and gays and the reproduction of sexism and heterosexism, see Sylvia A. Law, "Homosexuality and the Social Meaning of Gender," *Wisconsin Law Review* (1988): 187–235.

17. Elaine Tyler May, *Homeward Bound: American Families in the Cold War Era* (New York: Basic Books, 1988), 14–15 and passim; Eric Marcus, *Making History: The Struggle for Gay and Lesbian Equal Rights, 1945–1990: An Oral History* (New York: HarperCollins, 1992), 51–53; William N. Eskridge, Jr., *The Case for Same-Sex Marriage: From Sexual Liberty to Civilized Commitment* (New York: Free Press, 1996), 42–50. For an important challenge to the domestic containment thesis, see Joanne Meyerowitz, ed., *Not June Cleaver: Women and Gender in Postwar America, 1945–1960* (Philadelphia: Temple University Press, 1994).

18. For example, Marjorie Jones and Tracy Knight held a "Gay Liberation marriage ceremony" in a Lexington, Kentucky, cocktail lounge before going to the county clerk's office to demand a legal marriage license; the clerk's refusal sparked the formation of the Louisville Gay Liberation Front. See "Women to Fight for Kentucky License," *Advocate*, August 5–18, 1970, 6–7; "Louisville GLF Pickets Bar, Backs Suit," *Advocate*, August 19–September 1, 1970, 2.

19. On the controversies, see "Gay Marriage 'Boom': Suddenly, It's News," *Advocate*, August 5–18, 1970, 6–7; "Marriage Suit Shunned by Tribunal," *Advocate*, November 8, 1972, 3, 7; Suzanne Sherman, ed., *Lesbian and Gay Marriage: Private Commitments, Public Ceremonies* (Philadelphia: Temple University Press, 1992); and Butler, *Ceremonies of the Heart*. For accounts of the development of lesbian and gay politics, see Marcus, *Making History*; Barry D. Adam, *The Rise of a Gay and Lesbian Movement* (Boston: Twayne, 1986); John D'Emilio and Estelle B. Freedman, *Intimate Matters: A History of Sexuality in America* (New York: Harper and Row, 1988), 318–25, 354–60; Margaret Cruikshank, *The Gay and Lesbian Liberation Movement* (New York: Routledge, 1992); and Lillian Faderman, *Odd Girls and Twilight Lovers: A History of Lesbian Life in Twentieth-Century America* (New York: Columbia University Press, 1991). For accounts of contemporary lesbian/gay debates on same-sex marriage, see

Evan Wolfson, "Crossing the Threshold: Equal Marriage Rights for Lesbians and Gay Men and the Intra-Community Critique," *New York University Review of Law and Social Change* 21 (1994–95): 567–615; and Eskridge, *Case for Same-Sex Marriage,* 58–85.

20. "Nixon Nixes Same-Sex Marriages," *Advocate,* September 2–15, 1970, 1, 22; "Homosexual Marriages Defended by U.N. Aide," *New York Times,* August 11, 1970, 23. In making this comment, Hauser became one of the first of many lightning rods through which opposition to the campaign for same-sex marriage would strike. When the press reported her speech with heavy emphasis on her supposed advocacy of "homosexual marriage," Nixon quickly repudiated her comments. Hauser herself backtracked, insisting that she had no intention of promoting same-sex marriage as official policy and that she had meant to be "humorous." For an argument that early ERA proponents sought to make sex a "prohibited" legal classification, see Jane Mansbridge, *Why We Lost the ERA* (Chicago: University of Chicago Press, 1986), 51, 128–29.

21. The key cases in this development are Hirabayashi v. U.S., 320 U.S. 81 (U.S. Supreme Court, 1943); Korematsu v. U.S., 323 U.S. 214 (U.S. Supreme Court, 1944); and Brown v. Board of Education, 347 U.S. 483 (U.S. Supreme Court, 1954).

22. Loving v. Virginia, 388 U.S. 11 (U.S. Supreme Court, 1967).

23. The term "miscegenation," which means "race mixture," came into common usage in the 1860s, at precisely the time that laws against interracial marriage, which had formed only one part of the system of racial control under slavery, became crucial to post–Civil War racial hierarchies. See Eva Saks, "Representing Miscegenation Law," *Raritan* 8 (fall 1988): 39–69; Peggy Pascoe, "Race, Gender, and the Privileges of Property: On the Significance of Miscegenation Law in the U.S. West," in Valerie Matsumoto and Blake Allmendinger, eds., *Over the Edge: Remapping the American West* (Berkeley: University of California Press, 1998), 215–30; and Pascoe, "Miscegenation Law, Court Cases, and Ideologies of 'Race' in Twentieth-Century America," *Journal of American History* 83 (June 1996): 44–69.

24. The most complete list of these laws now available is the lengthy appendix to David H. Fowler, *Northern Attitudes towards Interracial Marriage: Legislation and Public Opinion in the Middle Atlantic and the States of the Old Northwest, 1780–1930* (1963; New York: Garland, 1987).

25. The key case is Pace v. Alabama, 106 U.S. 583 (U.S. Supreme Court, 1882); for an example of similar reasoning extended to racialized groups other than African Americans (in this case American Indians), see In re Paquet's Estate, 200 P. 911 (Oregon, 1921).

26. Loving at 12.

27. On these developments, see Mary Ann Glendon, *The Transformation of*

Family Law: State, Law, and Family in the United States and Western Europe (Chicago: University of Chicago Press, 1989); and Phyllis W. Beck, "Nontraditional Lifestyles and the Law," *Journal of Family Law* 17 (1978–79): 685–702.

28. In addition to the cases discussed in the text, see "Judge Blocks 2 Marriages," *Advocate,* January 6–19, 1971, 6 [Tampa, FL]; "Welfare Thinks They're Couple, but License Bureau Won't Agree," *Advocate,* September 29–October 12, 1971, 4 [Hartford, CT]; "Women Ask License," *Advocate,* October 17, 1971, 30, and "Black Lesbians' Wedding Crowded," *Advocate,* February 2, 1972 [Milwaukee]; "Socialite Son Sues," *Advocate,* February 2, 1972, 7 [Chicago].

29. "License Fight Reaches Minnesota High Court," *Advocate,* October 13, 1971, 3, 32; "Jack, Mike Lose on Job, Marriage," *Advocate,* November 10, 1971, 1, 8, 30.

30. Baker v. Nelson, 191 N.W.2d 185 (Minnesota, 1971) at 187; emphasis mine. To anyone who knows anything about the history of race discrimination in American law, this can only be described as an incredible statement. Marital restrictions based on race had been "fundamental" parts of American law from the 1660s through the 1960s; by prohibiting interracial couples from marrying, they served, as legal prohibitions on same-sex marriage do, to stigmatize such relationships as illicit sex rather than legitimate marriage.

31. Jones v. Hallahan, 501 S.W.2d 588 (Kentucky, 1973) at 589.

32. Jones at 590.

33. Baker at 186. The upper and lower court judges in the Kentucky case agreed; both cited *Webster's Dictionary* to the effect that marriage was "the institution whereby men and women are joined in a special kind of social and legal dependence, for the purpose of founding and maintaining a family." Jones at 589; "Marriage Bid Rejected; Pair Appeal," *Advocate,* April 14–27, 1971, 4.

34. Beck, "Nontraditional Lifestyles"; Hannah Schwarzchild, "Same-Sex Marriage and Constitutional Privacy: Moral Threat and Legal Anomaly," *Berkeley Women's Law Journal* 4 (1988–89): 94–122; Harvard Law Review, *Sexual Orientation and the Law* (Cambridge: Harvard University Press, 1990), 93–101. The presumed opposition between gay relationships and marriage has proven so enduring that right up to the present day, legal advocates of same-sex marriage put a good deal of effort into arguing either that popular conceptions of marriage have changed enough to encompass gay relationships or that the assumption that same-sex marriages never before existed is factually inaccurate. For examples, see Alissa Friedman, "The Necessity for State Recognition of Same-Sex Marriage: Constitutional Requirements and Evolving Notions of Family," *Berkeley Women's Law Journal* 3 (1987–88): 134–70; Jennifer Heeb, "Homosexual Marriage, the Changing American Family, and the Heterosexual Right to Privacy," *Seton Hall Law Review* 24 (1993): 347–93; William N. Eskridge, Jr., "A History of Same-Sex Marriage," *Virginia*

Law Review 79 (October 1993): 1419–1511; and Eskridge, *Case for Same-Sex Marriage*, 15–50.

35. "Women to Fight for Kentucky License," 6. He then suggested that local officials investigate whether by attempting to marry Tracy Knight, Marjorie Jones was guilty of contributing to the delinquency of a minor, her fourteen-year-old son.

36. "Marriage Bid Rejected," 4.

37. See, for example, Firestone, *Dialectic of Sex*, 227–42; Koedt et al., *Radical Feminism*, 240–45, 365–87, and Jill Johnston, *Lesbian Nation: The Feminist Solution* (New York: Touchstone, 1973).

38. United Nations Commission on the Status of Women, *Legal Status of Married Women* (New York: United Nations, 1958); U.S. President's Commission on the Status of Women, *Report of the Committee on Civil and Political Rights* (Washington: Government Printing Office, 1963); U.S. President's Commission on the Status of Women, *American Women: The Report of the President's Commission on the Status of Women and Other Publications of the Commission* (New York: Scribner's, 1965); Citizens' Advisory Council on the Status of Women, *Report of the Task Force on Family Law and Policy* (Washington: Government Printing Office, 1968); Citizens' Advisory Council on the Status of Women, *The Proposed Equal Rights Amendment to the United States Constitution: A Memorandum* (Washington: Citizens' Advisory Council, 1970); U.S. President's Task Force on Women's Rights and Responsibilities, *A Matter of Simple Justice* (April 1970), reprinted in Catharine Stimpson, ed., *Women and the "Equal Rights" Amendment: Senate Subcommittee Hearings on the Constitutional Amendment, 91st Congress* (New York: R. R. Bowker, 1972).

39. Glendon, *Transformation of Family Law*, passim.

40. Rita Hauser's ill-fated comments on the connection between sex discrimination and same-sex marriage (cited above) are a rare example in which a liberal feminist raised this issue. For a more representative—and extremely influential—example of the general pattern, in which critics pinpoint and critique patterns of sex discrimination throughout marriage law without even mentioning opposite-sex definitions of marriage, see Barbara A. Brown, Thomas I. Emerson, Gail Falk, and Ann E. Freedman, "The Equal Rights Amendment: A Constitutional Basis for Equal Rights for Women," *Yale Law Journal* 80 (April 1971): 871–985.

41. Colorado *Laws*, 1973, ch. 290.

42. The Uniform Marriage and Divorce Act was proposed by the National Conference of Commissioners on Uniform State Laws in 1970. States that adopted sex-specific marriage laws based on the uniform model or along with legislation designed to eliminate sexist language or sex differentials in marriage age include Montana, Nevada, North Dakota, and Oklahoma (all in 1975), and Illinois, Utah, and Wyoming (in 1977).

43. Virginia *Constitution,* art. 1, sec. 11, (1971). For commentary, see "Twentieth Annual Survey of Developments in Virginia Law, 1974–75," *Virginia Law Review* 61 (December 1975): 1732–51; and Mary Frances Berry, *Why ERA Failed: Politics, Women's Rights, and the Amending Process of the Constitution* (Bloomington: Indiana University Press, 1986), 95–96.

44. Virginia *Acts,* 1975, ch. 644.

45. The hearings can be followed in U.S. Senate, Committee on the Judiciary, Hearings before the Subcommittee on Constitutional Amendments, *The "Equal Rights" Amendment,* 91st Cong., 2d sess., S.J. Res. 61, May 5–7, 1970; U.S. Senate, Committee on the Judiciary, Hearings on S.J. Res. 61 and S.J. Res. 231, *Equal Rights 1970,* 91st Cong., 2d sess., September 9–15, 1970; U.S. House of Representatives, Committee on the Judiciary, Subcommittee No. 4, Hearings on H.J. Res. 35, 208, and Related Bills and H.R. 916 and Related Bills, *Equal Rights for Men and Women 1971,* 92d Cong., 1st sess., March 24, 25, 31 and April 1, 2, 5, 1971. The Ervin quotes are from *Equal Rights 1970,* 4. Ervin elaborates on his opposition to the ERA in Sam J. Ervin, Jr., *Preserving the Constitution: The Autobiography of Senator Sam J. Ervin, Jr.* (Charlottesville: Michie, 1984), 249–74.

46. *Equal Rights 1970,* 5.

47. *Equal Rights for Men and Women 1971,* 73.

48. Ervin, *Preserving the Constitution,* 266; *Congressional Record,* v. 118, pt. 7, March 21, 1972, 9314.

49. Historical analyses of the ERA campaign include Donald G. Mathews and Jane Sherron De Hart, *Sex, Gender, and the Politics of ERA* (New York: Oxford University Press, 1990); Berry, *Why ERA Failed;* and Mansbridge, *Why We Lost the ERA.*

50. Accounts include "Two Men Refused License to Marry," *Seattle Post-Intelligencer,* September 21, 1971, A14; and "'Non-Believers' Seek License to Wed," *Advocate,* November 10, 1971, 12.

51. "'Non-Believers,'" 12.

52. "Judge Upholds Denial of Marriage," *Seattle Post-Intelligencer,* April 28, 1972, A4.

53. This was an argument that had been getting some attention in legal circles. See "The Legality of Homosexual Marriage," *Yale Law Journal* 82 (January 1973): 573–89.

54. A useful chart of state ratifications is provided in Janet K. Boles, *The Politics of the Equal Rights Amendment: Conflict and the Decision Process* (New York: Longman, 1977), 2–3.

55. Singer v. Hara, 522 P.2d 1187 (Washington, 1974) at 1192.

56. Singer at 1191.

57. Singer at 1195.

58. Singer at 1194.

59. Specifically, the Court cited Brown et al., "The Equal Rights Amendment." This account, written by legal analysts and supporters of the ERA, was considered authoritative by both feminists and conservatives.

60. Thomas Emerson, "In Support of the Equal Rights Amendment," in "Equal Rights for Women: A Symposium on the Proposed Constitutional Amendment," *Harvard Civil Rights–Civil Liberties Law Review* 6 (March 1971): 229; Brown et al., "The Equal Rights Amendment"; and Mathews and De Hart, *Sex, Gender, and the Politics of ERA,* 47. For accounts of the development of this phrasing, which initially emerged from disputes in the 1920s between women reformers who disagreed over the value of the then newly proposed ERA, see Cynthia Harrison, *On Account of Sex: The Politics of Women's Issues, 1945–1968* (Berkeley: University of California Press, 1988), esp. 26–38, 130–31; and Jo Freeman, "How 'Sex' Got into Title VII: Persistent Opportunism as a Maker of Public Policy," *Law and Inequality* 9 (March 1991): 163–84.

61. Brown et al., "The Equal Rights Amendment," 894–96.

62. *Congressional Record,* v. 188, pt. 7, March 21, 1972, 9331. As Bayh put it, under the ERA, "if a State legislature makes a judgment that it is wrong for a man to marry a man, then it must say it is wrong for a woman to marry a woman."

63. See, for example, the use of the *Singer* case as the last word on this subject in Barbara A. Brown, Ann E. Freedman, Harriet N. Katz, and Alice M. Price, *Women's Rights and the Law: The Impact of the ERA on State Laws* (New York: Praeger, 1977), 29–30.

64. The quote is from Adams v. Howerton, 486 F. Supp. 1119 (California, 1980) at 1122; see also references to the *Singer* case in Dean v. District of Columbia, 18 F.L.R. 1141 and 1387 (Washington, D.C., 1991 and 1992) at 1141 and 1387; and De Santo v. Barnsley, 476 A.2d 952 (Pennsylvania, 1984) at 953–54.

65. For Bryant's view, see Anita Bryant, *The Anita Bryant Story: The Survival of Our Nation's Families and the Threat of Militant Homosexuality* (Old Tappan, NJ: Fleming H. Revell, 1977).

66. Florida *Laws,* 1977, ch. 77–139, 77–140.

67. Minnesota *Laws,* 1977, ch. 441, sec. 1.

68. California *Stats.,* 1977, ch. 339.

69. "A Vote to Ban Gay Marriages," *San Francisco Chronicle,* April 22, 1977, 9; "Senate Approves Measure Banning Gay Marriages," *Los Angeles Times,* August 12, 1977, I, 33. The Briggs initiative, proposed in 1978, would have allowed school systems to fire employees who were gay or who advocated or encouraged homosexuality. In what turned out to be a landmark gay rights campaign, it was defeated at the polls.

70. "Homosexual Weddings Stir Controversy in Colorado," *New York Times,* April 27, 1975. The clerk in question, Clela Rorex, was immediately threatened with recall; her decision to grant the licenses was overturned by

the state attorney general in Colorado *Atty. Gen. Op.,* April 24, 1975. Although the proposed ban on same-sex marriages passed the Colorado House by a vote of fifty-four to four, it did not make it into the state law codes; perhaps it did not pass the Colorado Senate. For coverage of the measure, see "Dispatch," *Advocate,* March 9, 1977, 18; March 23, 1977, 10; and April 6, 1977, 12. For commentary, see "Colorado Waits for a 'Messiah,'" *Advocate,* May 4, 1977, 14.

71. "Breakthrough in Houston: Women's Movement Throws Support behind Gay Rights," *Advocate,* January 11, 1978, 10.

72. In addition to Florida, Minnesota, California, and Colorado, examples include Louisiana (1975 and 1986), Arizona (1980), Kansas (1980), Indiana (1986), and, as we will see below, Hawaii (1994).

73. For the text of the Houston resolution, see Caroline Bird, *What Women Want* (New York: Simon and Schuster, 1978), 167.

74. See, for example, Eskridge, *Case for Same-Sex Marriage,* 57–58.

75. Under this intermediate standard, the question of what kind of justification states need to offer for sexual classifications in the law varies from "reasonable" to "important" to "substantial."

76. For examples of the legal arguments, see Friedman, "Necessity for State Recognition"; Heeb, "Homosexual Marriage"; and Janet E. Halley, "The Politics of the Closet: Towards Equal Protection for Gay, Lesbian, and Bisexual Identity," *UCLA Law Review* 36 (June 1989): 915–76.

77. For a pathbreaking introduction to the very complex economic issues involving lesbians and gays, see M. V. Lee Badgett and Rhonda M. Williams, "The Economics of Sexual Orientation: Establishing a Research Agenda," *Feminist Studies* 18 (fall 1992): 649–57.

78. According to Steven K. Wisensale and Kathlyn E. Heckart, most domestic partnership ordinances in the United States apply to both opposite-sex and same-sex couples; "Domestic Partnerships: A Concept Paper and Policy Discussion," *Family Relations* 42 (April 1993): 199–204. There has, however, been a recent trend toward limiting them to same-sex couples only; in these cases, the exclusion of opposite-sex couples is usually justified on the grounds that opposite-sex couples, unlike same-sex couples, have the legal option of marriage available to them.

79. These figures are from the Partners Task Force for Gay and Lesbian Couples (Box 9685, Seattle, WA 98109-0685), "Governments Offering Benefits," <http://eskimo.com/~demian/d-p-gov.html>, July 14, 1999; "Colleges and Private Schools Recognizing Partners," <http://www.eskimo.com/~demian/d-p-col.html>, July 14, 1999; and "Private Employment Benefits," <http://www.eskimo.com/~demian/d-p-pri.html>, July 14, 1999. For more information on the development and provisions of domestic partnership agreements, see Wisensale and Heckart, "Domestic Partnerships"; and Craig

A. Bowman and Blake M. Cornish, "A More Perfect Union: A Legal and Social Analysis of Domestic Partnership Ordinances," *Columbia Law Review* 92 (June 1992): 1164–1211. For a recent example of the argument that domestic partnership laws and other alternatives are preferable to the campaign for same-sex marriage, see Ettelbrick, "Wedlock Alert," 142–45; for the opposite opinion, see Wolfson, "Crossing the Threshold," 604–8.

80. See, for example, Marcus, *Making History,* 419, 517–18; and the interviews in Sherman, *Lesbian and Gay Marriage,* and Butler, *Ceremonies of the Heart.*

81. Sherman, *Lesbian and Gay Marriage,* 5–6, 241–79; Butler, *Ceremonies of the Heart,* 41; "Rights Group Backs Homosexual Marriages," *New York Times,* October 28, 1986, A20.

82. See, for example, "D.C. Couple Files Gay Marriage Suit; Outlook Called Dim," *Advocate,* January 1, 1991, 24. By 1991, this list included the cases cited in note 64 above and Jacobson v. Jacobson, 314 N.W.2d 78 (North Dakota, 1981); Slayton v. State, 633 S.W.2d 934 (Texas, 1982); Succession of Bacot, 502 S.2d 1118 (Louisiana, 1987); Cuevas v. Mills, 1986 U.S. Dist. LEXIS 18503 (Kansas, 1986); In Re Cooper, 564 N.Y.S.2d (New York, 1990); Williams v. Williams, 1991 U.S. App. LEXIS 23525 (North Carolina, 1991); and Gajovski v. Gajovski, 610 N.E.2d 431 (Ohio, 1991).

83. "Till Death Do Us Part: A Hawaii Court Upholds a Challenge to the Denial of Same-Sex Marriages," *Advocate,* June 15, 1993, 26-27. My discussion of the *Baehr* case is deeply indebted to Marc Scruggs, who generously shared with me his remarkable clippings file on the same-sex marriage issue in Hawaii.

84. Baehr, quoted in John Gallagher, "Marriage, Hawaiian Style," *Advocate,* February 4, 1997, 23; Eskridge, *Case for Same-Sex Marriage,* 3.

85. "Till Death Do Us Part," 27; "Hawaii Could Be First State to OK Same-Sex Marriage," *San Francisco Examiner,* February 20, 1994, A–11; John Gallagher, "Marriage, Hawaiian Style," 22–23.

86. "Till Death Do Us Part," 24.

87. Baehr v. Lewin, 852 P.2d 44 (Hawaii, 1993) at 63.

88. Baehr at 51.

89. Hawaii *Constitution,* art. 1, sec. 5 (1978) provides that "No person shall be deprived of life, liberty or property without due process of law, nor be denied the equal protection of the laws, nor be denied the enjoyment of the person's civil rights or be discriminated against in the exercise thereof because of race, religion, sex or ancestry." Cited in Baehr at 50.

90. For a fascinating account of the judicial politicking behind the *Baehr* decision, see Robert Stouffer, "Another View of Same-Gender Marriage," *Island Lifestyle,* January 1994, 15–17.

91. "Request on Marriages," *Honolulu Advertiser,* January 8, 1994; "Same-Sex Marriage Ban on Track," *Honolulu Advertiser,* February 4, 1994, A10.

92. The quote is from "Hawaii Could Be First State," A–1, A–11; "Gay-Wed Bill: Can It Be Upheld?" *Honolulu Advertiser,* February 1994, A1. On Tom's intentions, see "Terrance Tom Answers Questions from the Honolulu Gay Support Group," *Gay Community News,* January 1994, 5.

93. "Alex Santiago, State Representative," *North Shore News,* March 2, 1994, 16; "Same-Sex Marriage: Don't Get Bogged Down on It," *Honolulu Advertiser,* February 2, 1994. The quotation, from proposed House Bill 2312, is given in "Gay-Wed Bill," A2.

94. Advertisement, *Honolulu Star-Bulletin,* January 26, 1994.

95. The following states placed bans on interracial marriage directly in their state constitutions: Alabama (1865), Georgia (1866), Tennessee (1870), North Carolina (1875), Florida (1885), Mississippi (1890), and South Carolina (1895). Hawaii was one of a relative handful of American states that never enacted a law against interracial marriage. The state has higher rates of interracial marriage and lower rates of opposition to same-sex marriage than the United States as a whole.

96. See, for example, "Wants Gay-Marriage Ban," *Honolulu Advertiser,* February 14, 1994; "No More Social Experiments," *Honolulu Advertiser,* February 7, 1994; and "Gay-Wed Bill."

97. Both are quoted in "Hawaii Could Be First State," A–11.

98. Hawaii *Laws,* 1994, ch. 217. On this bill, and for intelligent commentary on the compromise issue in general, see Stouffer, "Another View," 15–17; Derek Ferrar, "Sleeping with the Legislature," *Honolulu Weekly,* February 23, 1994, 3; "Move to Kill Bill on Same-Sex Unions Greeted with Cheers," *Honolulu Advertiser,* circa March 30, 1994; "Same-Sex Ban is Approved," *Honolulu Advertiser,* April 13, 1994; "The Wedding is off," *Advocate,* May 17, 1994, 24–26.

99. See "Report of the Hawaii Commission on Sexual Orientation and the Law," in Baird and Rosenbaum, *Same-Sex Marriage,* 211–26.

100. Gallagher, "Marriage, Hawaiian Style," 24.

101. See note 8 above.

102. Indiana *Stat. Ann.,* 1997, ch. 31-11-1-1.

103. Michigan *Comp. Laws Ann.,* 1999, ch. 551, sec. 1.

104. Chang's ruling is Baehr v. Miike, Civil No. 92-1394 (Hawaii, December 3, 1996).

105. John Gallagher, "Marriage Compromised," *Advocate,* May 27, 1997, 71.

106. Hawaii, HB 118 CD1 (1997); Gallagher, "Marriage Compromised," 71; Bettina Boxall, "A New Era Set to Begin in Benefits for Gay Couples," *Los Angeles Times,* A3.

107. Hawaii, HB 117 CD 1 (1997).

108. After the passage of the amendment, the Hawaii Supreme Court asked both sides of the Baehr case to submit briefs addressing the question of

how the amendment would affect the outcome of the case; while this article was in press, the Court issued its final decision. Declaring that "the marriage amendment has rendered the plaintiff's complaint moot," the court reversed its earlier judgment its earlier judgment that denying marriage to same-sex couples was unconstitutional. Baehr v. Miike, Supreme Court of Hawaii No. 20371, Civ. No. 91-1394-95, December 9, 1999.

109. See, for example, Steven K. Homer, "Against Marriage," *Harvard Civil Rights–Civil Liberties Law Review* 29 (summer 1994): 506–30; Andrew Koppelman, "Why Discrimination against Lesbians and Gays Is Sex Discrimination," *New York University Law Review* 69 (May 1994): 197–287; Wolfson, "Crossing the Threshold," 567–615; Mark Strasser, *Legally Wed: Same-Sex Marriage and the Constitution* (Ithaca: Cornell University Press, 1997); Sullivan, *Same-Sex Marriage*; and Baird and Rosenbaum, *Same-Sex Marriage*.

110. Ramirez, quoted in Gallagher, "Marriage, Hawaiian Style," 25. In the Vermont case, Superior Court Judge Linda Levitt relied on language from the *Singer* case to reject the argument of "members of Vermont's homosexual population" that they were entitled to the right to marry. On December 20, 1999, the Vermont Supreme Court reversed Judge Levitt's decision and declared that under the Common Benefits Clause of the Vermont state constitution, "the State is constitutionally required to extend to same-sex couples the common benefits and protections that flow from marriage under Vermont law." Having gone this far, however, the judges then noted that "[w]hether this ultimately takes the form of inclusion within the marriage laws themselves or a parallel 'domestic partnership' system or some equivalent statutory alternative, rests with the Legislature. Baker v. State, Supreme Court of Vermont, Docket No. 98-032, December 20, 1999. In Alaska, however, Superior Court Judge Peter A. Michalski used arguments about sex discrimination and the right to privacy to declare Alaska's state marriage law an unconstitutional violation of the right of a gay male couple of marry. This case is on appeal. Brause v. Bureau of Vital Statistics, 1998 W.L. 88743 (Alaska, February 27, 1998).

111. Andrew Koppelman, "The Miscegenation Analogy: Sodomy Law as Sex Discrimination," *Yale Law Journal* 98 (November 1988): 145–64; Mark Strasser, "Family, Definitions, and the Constitution: On the Antimiscegenation Analogy," *Suffolk University Law Review* 25 (1991): 981–1034; James Trosino, "American Wedding: Same-Sex Marriage and the Miscegenation Analogy," *Boston University Law Review* 73 (January 1993): 93–120; Strasser, *Legally Wed,* 66–67, 114–18; Wolfson, "Crossing the Threshold"; Eskridge, *Case for Same-Sex Marriage,* 153–62. I make a version of this argument myself in Pascoe, "Race, Gender, and the Privileges of Property."

112. "Hawaii Court Revives Suit on Gay Marriages," *Los Angeles Times,* May 7, 1993, A27.

113. See, for example, "Blacks Reject Gay Rights Fight as Equal to Theirs," *New York Times,* June 28, 1993, A1. For an especially thoughtful critique of these analogies as they function within the campaign for same-sex marriage, see Darren Lenard Hutchinson, "Out Yet Unseen: A Racial Critique of Gay and Lesbian Legal Theory and Political Discourse," *Connecticut Law Review* 29 (winter 1997), esp. 585–602.

114. See, for example, Eskridge, "A History of Same-Sex Marriage," 1507–10.

115. See, for example, Homer, "Against Marriage"; Eskridge, *Case for Same-Sex Marriage,* 172–75; Koppelman, "Discrimination Against Lesbians and Gays."

116. Nancy F. Cott, "Giving Character to Our Whole Civil Polity: Marriage and the Public Order in the Late Nineteenth Century," in Linda K. Kerber, Alice Kessler-Harris, and Kathryn Kish Sklar, eds., *U.S. History as Feminist History: New Feminist Essays* (Chapel Hill: University of North Carolina Press, 1995), 107–21.

117. Hunter, "Marriage, Law, and Gender," 12.

WORKS CITED AND CONSULTED

Complete citations for the legal documents referenced in this essay can be found in the endnotes.

Adam, Barry D. *The Rise of a Gay and Lesbian Movement.* Boston: Twayne, 1986.

"Alex Santiago, State Representative." *North Shore News,* 2 Mar. 1994.

Badgett, M. V. Lee, and Rhonda M. Williams. "The Economics of Sexual Orientation: Establishing a Research Agenda." *Feminist Studies* 18 (Fall 1992): 649–57.

Baird, Robert M., and Stuart E. Rosenbaum, eds. *Same-Sex Marriage: The Moral and Legal Debate.* New York: Prometheus Books, 1997.

Beck, Phyllis W. "Nontraditional Lifestyles and the Law," *Journal of Family Law* 17 (1978–79): 685–702.

Berry, Mary Frances. *Why ERA Failed: Politics, Women's Rights, and the Amending Process of the Constitution.* Bloomington: Indiana University Press, 1986.

Bird, Caroline. *What Women Want.* New York: Simon and Schuster, 1978.

"Black Lesbians' Wedding Crowded." *Advocate,* 2 Feb. 1972.

"Blacks Reject Gay Rights Fight as Equal to Theirs." *New York Times,* 28 June 1993.

Boles, Janet K. *The Politics of the Equal Rights Amendment: Conflict and the Decision Process.* New York: Longman, 1977.

"The Boom in 'Gay' Marriages." *San Francisco Chronicle,* 14 July 1970.

Bowman, Craig A., and Blake M. Cornish. "A More Perfect Union: A Legal and Social Analysis of Domestic Partnership Ordinances." *Columbia Law Review* 92 (June 1992): 1164–1211.

Boxall, Bettina. "A New Era Set to Begin in Benefits for Gay Couples." *Los Angeles Times,* 7 July 1997.

"Breakthrough in Houston: Women's Movement Throws Support behind Gay Rights." *Advocate,* 11 Jan. 1978.

Brown, Barbara A., Thomas I. Emerson, Gail Falk, and Ann E. Freedman. "The Equal Rights Amendment: A Constitutional Basis for Equal Rights for Women." *Yale Law Journal* 80 (Apr. 1971): 871–985.

Brown, Barbara A., Ann E. Freedman, Harriet N. Katz, and Alice M. Price. *Women's Rights and the Law: The Impact of the ERA on State Laws.* New York: Praeger, 1977.

Bryant, Anita. *The Anita Bryant Story: The Survival of Our Nation's Families and the Threat of Militant Homosexuality.* Old Tappan, NJ: Fleming H. Revell, 1977.

Butler, Becky, ed. *Ceremonies of the Heart: Celebrating Lesbian Unions.* Seattle: Seal Press, 1990.

Butler, Judith. *Gender Trouble: Feminism and the Subversion of Identity.* New York: Routledge, 1990.

Citizens' Advisory Council on the Status of Women. *The Proposed Equal Rights Amendment to the United States Constitution: A Memorandum.* Washington: Citizens' Advisory Council, 1970.

————. *Report of the Task Force on Family Law and Policy.* Washington: Government Printing Office, 1968.

"Clerk Wants Tighter Law against Gay Marriages." *Advocate,* 24 June–7 July 1970.

"Colorado Waits for a 'Messiah.'" *Advocate,* 4 May 1977.

Cott, Nancy F. "Giving Character to Our Whole Civil Polity: Marriage and the Public Order in the Late Nineteenth Century." In *U.S. History as Feminist History: New Feminist Essays,* ed. Linda K. Kerber, Alice Kessler-Harris, and Kathryn Kish Sklar, 107–21. Chapel Hill: University of North Carolina Press, 1995.

Cox, Barbara J. "Are Same-Sex Marriage Statutes the New Anti-Gay Initiatives?" *National Journal of Sexual Orientation Law* 2, no. 2 (1996): 194–208.

————. "The Lesbian Wife: Same-Sex Marriage as an Expression of Radical and Plural Democracy." *California Western Law Review* 33 (spring 1997): 155–67.

Cruikshank, Margaret. *The Gay and Lesbian Liberation Movement.* New York: Routledge, 1992.

"D.C. Couple Files Gay Marriage Suit; Outlook Called Dim." *Advocate,* 1 Jan. 1991.

D'Emilio, John, and Estelle B. Freedman. *Intimate Matters: A History of Sexuality in America.* New York: Harper and Row, 1988.

Duclos, Nitya. "Some Complicating Thoughts on Same-Sex Marriage." *Law and Sexuality* 1 (summer 1991): 31–61.

Emerson, Thomas. "In Support of the Equal Rights Amendment." In "Equal Rights for Women: A Symposium on the Proposed Constitutional Amendment." *Harvard Civil Rights–Civil Liberties Law Review* 6 (Mar. 1971): 225–33.

Ervin, Sam J., Jr. *Preserving the Constitution: The Autobiography of Senator Sam J. Ervin, Jr.* Charlottesville: Michie, 1984.

Eskridge, William N., Jr. *The Case for Same-Sex Marriage: From Sexual Liberty to Civilized Commitment.* New York: Free Press, 1996.

———. "A History of Same-Sex Marriage." *Virginia Law Review* 79 (Oct. 1993): 1419–1511.

Ettelbrick, Paula L. "Since When Is Marriage a Path to Liberation?" *Outlook* 2, no. 9 (fall 1989): 9–17.

———. "Wedlock Alert: A Comment on Lesbian and Gay Family Recognition." *Journal of Law and Policy* 5, no. 1 (1996): 107–66.

Faderman, Lillian. *Odd Girls and Twilight Lovers: A History of Lesbian Life in Twentieth-Century America.* New York: Columbia University Press, 1991.

Ferrar, Derek. "Sleeping with the Legislature." *Honolulu Weekly,* 23 Feb. 1994.

Firestone, Shulamith. *The Dialectic of Sex: The Case for Feminist Revolution.* New York: Morrow, 1970.

Fowler, David H. *Northern Attitudes towards Interracial Marriage: Legislation and Public Opinion in the Middle Atlantic and the States of the Old Northwest, 1780–1930.* 1963; New York: Garland, 1987.

Fox, Richard, and James Kloppenberg, eds. *A Companion to American Thought.* Oxford: Blackwell, 1995.

Franke, Katherine M. "The Central Mistake of Sex Discrimination Law: The Disaggregation of Sex from Gender." *University of Pennsylvania Law Review* 144 (Nov. 1995): 1–99.

Freeman, Jo. "How 'Sex' Got into Title VII: Persistent Opportunism as a Maker of Public Policy." *Law and Inequality* 9 (Mar. 1991): 163–84.

Friedman, Alissa. "The Necessity for State Recognition of Same-Sex Marriage: Constitutional Requirements and Evolving Notions of Family." *Berkeley Women's Law Journal* 3 (1987–88): 134–70.

Gallagher, John. "Marriage Compromised." *Advocate,* 27 May 1997.

———. "Marriage: Hawaiian Style." *Advocate,* 4 Feb. 1997.

"Gay Marriage 'Boom': Suddenly, It's News." *Advocate,* 5–18 Aug. 1970.

"Gay-Wed Bill: Can It Be Upheld?" *Honolulu Advertiser,* Feb. 1994.

Glendon, Mary Ann. *The Transformation of Family Law: State, Law, and Family in the United States and Western Europe.* Chicago: University of Chicago Press, 1989.

Gornick, Vivian, and Barbara K. Moran, eds. *Woman in Sexist Society: Studies in Power and Powerlessness.* New York: Basic Books, 1971.

Greer, Germaine. *The Female Eunuch.* New York: McGraw-Hill, 1971.

Halley, Janet E. "The Politics of the Closet: Towards Equal Protection for Gay, Lesbian, and Bisexual Identity." *UCLA Law Review* 36 (June 1989): 915–76.

Haraway, Donna J. "'Gender' for a Marxist Dictionary: The Sexual Politics of a Word." In *Simians, Cyborgs, and Women: The Reinvention of Nature,* 127–48. New York: Routledge, 1991.

Harrison, Cynthia. *On Account of Sex: The Politics of Women's Issues, 1945–1968.* Berkeley: University of California Press, 1988.

Harvard Law Review. *Sexual Orientation and the Law.* Cambridge: Harvard University Press, 1990.

"Hawaii Could Be First State to OK Same-Sex Marriage." *San Francisco Examiner,* 20 Feb. 1994.

"Hawaii Court Revives Suit on Gay Marriages." *Los Angeles Times,* 7 May 1993.

Heeb, Jennifer. "Homosexual Marriage, the Changing American Family, and the Heterosexual Right to Privacy." *Seton Hall Law Review* 24 (1993): 347–93.

Homer, Steven K. "Against Marriage." *Harvard Civil Rights–Civil Liberties Law Review* 29 (summer 1994): 505–30.

"Homosexual Marriages Defended by U.N. Aide." *New York Times,* 11 Aug. 1970.

"Homosexual Weddings Stir Controversy in Colorado." *New York Times,* 27 Apr. 1975.

Hunter, Nan D. "Marriage, Law, and Gender: A Feminist Inquiry." *Law and Sexuality* 1 (summer 1991): 9–30.

Hutchinson, Darren Lenard. "Out yet Unseen: A Racial Critique of Gay and Lesbian Legal Theory and Political Discourse." *Connecticut Law Review* 29 (winter 1997): 561–645.

"Jack, Mike Lose on Job, Marriage." *Advocate,* 10 Nov. 1971.

Johnston, Jill. *Lesbian Nation: The Feminist Solution.* New York: Touchstone, 1973.

"Judge Blocks 2 Marriages." *Advocate,* 6–19 Jan. 1971.

"Judge Upholds Denial of Marriage." *Seattle Post-Intelligencer,* 28 Apr. 1972.

Kelley, Jon-Peter. "Note: Act of Infidelity: Why the Defense of Marriage Act Is Unfaithful to the Constitution." *Cornell Journal of Law and Public Policy* 7 (fall 1997): 203–53.

Koedt, Anne, Ellen Levine, and Anita Rapone, eds. *Radical Feminism.* New York: Quadrangle Books, 1973.

Koppelman, Andrew. "The Miscegenation Analogy: Sodomy Law as Sex Discrimination." *Yale Law Journal* 98 (Nov. 1988): 145–64.

———. "Why Discrimination against Lesbians and Gays Is Sex Discrimination." *New York University Law Review* 69 (May 1994): 197–287.

Law, Sylvia A. "Homosexuality and the Social Meaning of Gender." *Wisconsin Law Review* (1988): 187–235.

"The Legality of Homosexual Marriage." *Yale Law Journal* 82 (Jan 1973): 573–89.

"License Fight Reaches Minnesota High Court." *Advocate,* 13 Oct. 1971.

"Louisville GLF Pickets Bar, Backs Suit." *Advocate,* 19 Aug.–1 Sept. 1970.

Mansbridge, Jane. *Why We Lost the ERA.* Chicago: University of Chicago Press, 1986.

Marcus, Eric. *Making History: The Struggle for Gay and Lesbian Equal Rights, 1945–1990: An Oral History.* New York: HarperCollins, 1992.

"Marriage Bid Rejected; Pair Appeal." *Advocate,* 14–27 Apr. 1971

"Marriage Suit Shunned by Tribunal." *Advocate,* 8 Nov. 1972.

Mathews, Donald G., and Jane Sherron De Hart. *Sex, Gender, and the Politics of ERA.* New York: Oxford University Press, 1990.

May, Elaine Tyler. *Homeward Bound: American Families in the Cold War Era.* New York: Basic Books, 1988.

Meyerowitz, Joanne, ed. *Not June Cleaver: Women and Gender in Postwar America, 1945–1960.* Philadelphia: Temple University Press, 1994.

Millett, Kate. *Sexual Politics.* New York: Ballantine Books, 1969.

"Move to Kill Bill on Same-Sex Unions Greeted with Cheers." *Honolulu Advertiser,* circa 30 Mar. 1994.

"Nixon Nixes Same-Sex Marriages." *Advocate,* 2–15 Sept. 1970.

"No More Social Experiments." *Honolulu Advertiser,* 7 Feb. 1994.

"'Non-Believers' Seek License to Wed." *Advocate,* 10 Nov. 1971.

Pascoe, Peggy. "Miscegenation Law, Court Cases, and Ideologies of 'Race' in Twentieth-Century America." *Journal of American History* 83 (June 1996): 44–69.

———. "Race, Gender, and the Privileges of Property: On the Significance of Miscegenation Law in the U.S. West." In *Over the Edge: Remapping the American West,* ed. Valerie Matsumoto and Blake Allmendinger, 215–30. Berkeley: University of California Press, 1998.

Polikoff, Nancy D. "We Will Get What We Ask For: Why Legalizing Gay and Lesbian Marriage Will Not 'Dismantle the Legal Structure of Gender in Every Marriage.'" *Virginia Law Review* 79 (Oct. 1993): 1535–52.

"Request on Marriages." *Honolulu Advertiser,* 8 Jan. 1994.

"Rights Group Backs Homosexual Marriages." *New York Times,* 28 Oct. 1986.

Rubin, Gayle. "Thinking Sex: Notes for a Radical Theory of the Politics of Sexuality." In *Pleasure and Danger: Exploring Female Sexuality,* ed. Carol S. Vance, 267–319. Boston: Routledge and Kegan Paul, 1984.

Rubin, Gayle. "The Traffic in Women: Notes on the 'Political Economy' of Sex." In *Toward an Anthropology of Women*. ed. Rayna R. Reiter, 157–210. New York: Monthly Review Press, 1975.

Saks, Eva. "Representing Miscegenation Law." *Raritan* 8 (fall 1988): 39–69.

"Same-Sex Ban Is Approved." *Honolulu Advertiser,* 13 Apr. 1994.

"Same-sex Marriage Ban on Track." *Honolulu Advertiser,* 4 Feb. 1994.

"Same-Sex Marriage: Don't Get Bogged Down on It." *Honolulu Advertiser,* 2 Feb. 1994.

Schwarzchild, Hannah. "Same-Sex Marriage and Constitutional Privacy: Moral Threat and Legal Anomaly." *Berkeley Women's Law Journal* 4 (1988–89): 94–122.

Scott, Joan Wallach. "Gender: A Useful Category of Historical Analysis." *American Historical Review* 91 (Dec. 1986): 1053–75.

Sedgwick, Eve Kosofsky. *Epistemology of the Closet.* Berkeley: University of California Press, 1990.

"Senate Approves Measure Banning Gay Marriages." *Los Angeles Times,* 12 Aug. 1977.

Sherman, Suzanne, ed. *Lesbian and Gay Marriage: Private Commitments, Public Ceremonies.* Philadelphia: Temple University Press, 1992.

"Socialite Son Sues." *Advocate,* 2 Feb. 1972.

Stouffer, Robert. "Another View of Same-Gender Marriage." *Island Lifestyle,* Jan. 1994.

Strasser, Mark. "Family, Definitions, and the Constitution: On the Antimiscegenation Analogy." *Suffolk University Law Review* 25 (1991): 981–1034.

———. *Legally Wed: Same-Sex Marriage and the Constitution.* Ithaca: Cornell University Press, 1997.

Sullivan, Andrew, ed. *Same-Sex Marriage: Pro and Con.* New York: Vintage Books, 1997.

"Terrance Tom Answers Questions from the Honolulu Gay Support Group." *Gay Community News,* Jan. 1994.

"Till Death Do Us Part: A Hawaii Court Upholds a Challenge to the Denial of Same-Sex Marriages." *Advocate,* 15 June 1993.

Trosino, James. "American Wedding: Same-Sex Marriage and the Miscegenation Analogy." *Boston University Law Review* 73 (Jan. 1993): 93–120.

"Twentieth Annual Survey of Developments in Virginia Law, 1974–75." *Virginia Law Review* 61 (Dec. 1975): 1732–51.

"Two Men Refused License to Marry." *Seattle Post-Intelligencer,* 21 Sept. 1971.

United Nations Commission on the Status of Women. *Legal Status of Married Women.* New York: United Nations, 1958.

"Upsurge in Men Who Want to Marry Men." *San Francisco Chronicle,* 29 May 1970.

U.S. House of Representatives, Committee on the Judiciary, Subcommittee

No. 4, Hearings on H.J. Res. 35, 208, and Related Bills and H.R. 916 and Related Bills. *Equal Rights for Men and Women 1971,* 92d Cong. 1st sess., March 24, 25, 31 and April 1, 2, 5, 1971.

U.S. President's Commission on the Status of Women. *American Women: The Report of the President's Commission on the Status of Women and Other Publications of the Commission.* New York: Scribner's, 1965.

————. *Report of the Committee on Civil and Political Rights.* Washington: Government Printing Office, 1963.

U.S. President's Task Force on Women's Rights and Responsibilities. *A Matter of Simple Justice* (Apr. 1970). Reprinted in *Women and the "Equal Rights" Amendment: Senate Subcommittee Hearings on the Constitutional Amendment, 91st Congress,* ed. Catharine Stimpson. New York: R. R. Bowker, 1972.

U.S. Senate, Committee on the Judiciary. Hearings before the Subcommittee on Constitutional Amendments. *The "Equal Rights" Amendment,* 91st Cong., 2d sess., S.J. Res. 61, 5–7 May 1970.

————. Hearings on S.J. Res. 61 and S.J. Res. 231, *Equal Rights 1970,* 91st Cong., 2d sess., 9–15 Sept. 1970.

"A Vote to Ban Gay Marriages." *San Francisco Chronicle,* 22 Apr. 1977.

"Wants Gay-Marriage Ban." *Honolulu Advertiser,* 14 Feb. 1994.

"The Wedding Is Off." *Advocate,* 17 May 1994.

"Welfare Thinks They're Couple, but License Bureau Won't Agree." *Advocate,* 29 Sept.–12 Oct. 1971.

Weston, Kath. *Families We Choose: Lesbians, Gays, Kinship.* New York: Columbia University Press, 1991.

Wisensale, Steven K., and Kathlyn E. Heckart. "Domestic Partnerships: A Concept Paper and Policy Discussion." *Family Relations* 42 (Apr. 1993): 199–204.

Wolfson, Evan. "Crossing the Threshold: Equal Marriage Rights for Lesbians and Gay Men and the Intra-Community Critique." *New York University Review of Law and Social Change* 21 (1994–95): 567–615.

"Women Ask License." *Advocate,* 17 Oct. 1971.

"Women to Fight for Kentucky License." *Advocate,* 5–18 Aug. 1970.

Part II

Storytelling

Sites of Empowerment, Sites of Exploitation

Storytelling is a site for the construction of personal and collective identity—and for the critical interrogation of those identities. Stories can also be tools—of empowerment or domination—as well as valuable commodities. The essays in this part explore questions about who tells stories to whom, whose labor is expressed in and through the stories, how stories are appropriated or reclaimed, who has a right to tell certain stories, and how stories function to construct, challenge, or deconstruct our personal and collective identities.

Within feminism, storytelling has been one of our talismans of self-creation. The stories in these essays, although rooted in traditions and specific communities, also hark back to a particular moment in feminism, when the most popular stories—both within academia and in the broader media as well—reflected dominant American myths about the self-made man. Slogans like "I am a woman giving birth to myself" were popular because they seemed empowering. Such a vision of total self-creation was less radical than we had hoped because while denying ourselves the resources of traditional stories and traditional communities, we were helping ourselves to the conceptual resources of liberal individualism. In these essays, however, although strains of individualism are implicit, their embeddedness in traditional communities and traditional storytelling is at the very heart of their political radicalism.

We might also consider Muriel Ruykeyser's famous lines, "What would happen if one woman told the truth about her life? / The world would split open" (103), which reflect the excitement women felt at that time about the radical potential of speaking truths. Without diminishing the very real potency of speaking openly about one's experience, we must note that such stories were often assumed to reflect reality in uncomplicated ways—and thus, race and class got separated out from many of the mainstream (and academic) stories, which inevitably failed to recognize that some women were being ignored and others were being consigned to background status. Similarly, goddess stories, because they were purported to be available to any woman, regardless of her cultural background, suggested that there was a generic pool from which any woman might reshape her own story. Carol Christ, for instance, saw stories as the key for women's self-discovery:

> Women's stories have not been told. And without stories there is no articulation of experience. Without stories a woman is lost when she comes to make the important decisions of her life. She does not learn to value her struggles, to celebrate her strengths, to comprehend her pain. Without stories she cannot understand herself. Without stories she is alienated from those deeper experiences of self and world that have been called spiritual or religious. She is closed in silence. The expression of women's spiritual quest is integrally related to the telling of women's stories. If women's stories are not told, the depth of women's souls will not be known. (*Diving Deep and Surfacing* 1)

Storytelling as a mode of theorizing draws our attention both to particulars and to connections among them. It thus serves to counter the tendency on the part of privileged theorizers to overgeneralize from their own experiences—as well as the tendency to evade responsibility by telling only one's own story, as though it were pretheoretically pure and detached from the stories of others. Feminism on a global scale is achieved—we want to argue, and the essays in this part persuasively demonstrate—not by universal theory but by concrete reciprocal engagement and by accountability to the diverse communities in which we are variously invested and which we variously affect. Such engagement and accountability emerge when our attention shifts from stories or theories as finished products to the modes of their production—the agency behind them, including the interweaving of resistance and privilege—and to the modes of their consumption—to the multiple uses to which they are put, to their benefits and harms.

Because the academy would "other" her and her research, which refuses the patriarchal, Eurocentric notion of the "other," Kath Weston argues that it turns her into a "virtual" anthropologist. Produced by her discipline as a Native Ethnographer, one engaged in queer studies, the virtual anthropologist finds herself in a "hybrid" category and her work judged as suspect, not on the basis of its argument or analysis, but because it is not considered authentic or "the real thing." As a lesbian doing research in the homosexual community, Weston finds her position within the academy and within her own texts scrutinized. If she writes about her own "community," she is seen as doing inside, "easy" research; but Weston shies away from identifying herself as a voice for a particular community, or from using the voices of the "communities" she studies as speaking for the whole. Weston's autobiographical account reflects the essays in part 1 in its effort to transcend categories and stereotypes and to transform a discipline.

Mrinalini Sinha's essay asks us to look at how non-Western women's histories are told, and how feminism is commonly narrated: why and how might differently situated women bring their conflicting stories into critical engagement? She argues in favor of historicizing contemporary debates around feminism, stating that the study of history cautions against any response to the current crisis of feminism that simply validates a multiplicity or plurality of feminisms. The question of the meaning of feminism has become especially contested as many feminists in non-Western cultures reject the label of "feminism" as westernized, and as many white Anglo-American feminists, stung by criticisms of the racism and Eurocentrism of feminism, abandon cross-cultural critiques by invoking cultural difference. This essay suggests that such a move—which would lead us logically to a supermarket of feminisms to cater to every taste—evades rather than confronts the challenges of feminism today. Through a historical study of feminism in Britain and in India, Sinha demonstrates how historicizing feminism and its challenges allows us to understand the production of cultural differences historically and to respond to the current crisis of feminism in more mutually engaged and productive ways.

Cheri Register's essay is a memoir about the women who work "on the sliced bacon" and an analysis of her fear of ending up like them, her relationship with the feminist community, and her decision to leave academia. This is an essay about the importance of class and one's connections to one's people. She argues for a "collective voice," while interrogating her own place in relation to the women whose stories she works to tell. It is in large measure through the interwoven stories of their lives and hers that she enacts the accountability toward them that is at the heart of her feminism.

Kathryn Shanley begins her essay with a story about working at a restaurant with other American Indian women as a means of understanding the gulf that exists between feminism as we theorize and practice it in the academy and the way women live their lives. In order to discuss what American Indian women's history might look like, what kind of history they have written themselves, we need to come to something approximating common terms: what, for instance, is meant by "subjectivity" and "agency" in the context of American Indian women's lives? Shanley describes the dangers inherent in subsuming "race" into "ethnicity" in maneuvers that hasten to link us together without a proper understanding of our differences. She emphasizes the importance of understanding the role of kinship bonding and warns against the tendency to look at American Indian culture as "sightseers," "touring the exotic country," trying to "capture" their essence. The importance of lovingly telling the stories of the women she lived and worked with is shadowed by her knowledge of the appropriative commodity value these stories have for white America.

Edén E. Torres shows how her grandmother's stories and the traditional proverbs that she radically transformed into teaching tools for her granddaughters come to bear on the practice of art in the Chicana/o community. Although academic work plays an important role in her life, Torres finds that the university also obscures some of the lessons of her grandmother, separating her from the community where her bonds are deepest, yet paradoxically, always in danger. Torres explores the relationship of Chicana "professional intellectuals" to the Chicana/o community—in particular to other Chicanas doing work that does not carry the privileges of intellectual labor. She considers several Chicana writers whose work, which remains closely tied to working-class roots, nevertheless challenges dominant values and reconfigures familiar stories of such mythic figures as La Llorona and La Malinche, thus liberating women's status from patriarchal narratives. Because the call for multiculturalism has not led to fair or even representation, Torres demonstrates the revolutionary intent and content of Chicana writing against the obscuring of those themes when the work is taught by mainstream academics, who mine it for comfortable "universal" themes. One way Torres works to counter this appropriation is by bringing the published writings of Chicanas to women in the community, in whose lives the stories are rooted but who are likely to feel estranged from the published word. Grounded in those readings, Torres's own discussions close the circle, deflecting the centripetal pull of the academy. For Torres, maintaining connections, through literature and personal contact, allows intellectual Chicanas to keep a vigilant eye on the mainstream "bosses" and to aid in the ongoing struggle for social justice.

All these essays reveal the centrality of storytelling to social justice work, particularly as people struggle to shape identities that are responsive to and responsible for different communities. In *Woman, Native, Other,* Trinh T. Minh-ha writes that "The story depends upon every one of us to come into being. It needs us all, needs our remembering, understanding, and creating what we have heard together to keep on coming into being" (119). Although she is referring in part to stories told by the elders, particularly the women, of a community, she reminds us that we all need to tell our stories. Furthermore, those of us whose stories are now familiar refrains need now to hear other stories, and all of us need to find ways for our stories to speak to each other. In passing on others' stories we become guardians for both the stories and the communities from which the stories come; thus, some stories may not be repeated or must be repeated only in certain ways, coded or privately:

> The story . . . does not really belong to me, and while I feel greatly responsible for it, I also enjoy the irresponsibility of the pleasure obtained through the process of transferring. Pleasure in the copy, pleasure in the reproduction. No repetition can ever be identical, but my story carries with it their stories, their history, and our story repeats itself endlessly.(122)

The stories that were told in the 1970s helped to bring feminism into existence, but the stories told and reflected on in these essays emerge from a reflexivity in which we become figures in each other's stories about feminism. If we imagine that reflexivity to be a spiral that allows us to look back through our individual and collective histories, then we are better able to see what was true all along—that no story is transparent or unmediatedly effective. Rather than "one woman" telling one "truth," we must pursue the relational aspects of our stories to other women's. Every time a woman writes her story, questions about why she is writing—as political act, as resistance, as self-indulgence—are forming the next level of the spiral. No story is detachable from its telling, and all stories are implicated in the teller's life and in her community.

WORKS CITED

Christ, Carol P. *Diving Deep and Surfacing: Women Writers on Spiritual Quest.* Boston: Beacon Press, 1980.
Minh-ha, Trinh T. *Woman, Native, Other: Writing Postcoloniality and Feminism.* Bloomington: Indiana University Press, 1989.
Rukeyser, Muriel. *The Speed of Darkness.* New York: Random House, 1968.

Chapter 5

The Virtual Anthropologist

Kath Weston

What walks like an ethnographer, talks like an ethnographer, packs a tape recorder, jots incessant notes, publishes, travels to conferences, and applies for jobs just like an ethnographer, even begs and blunders and cajoles like an ethnographer, but is not and never can be a "real" ethnographer? Welcome to the netherworld of virtual anthropology, the state to which the field methodically consigns its "unfit," a mode of inhabiting the discipline that substitutes ceaseless interrogation for all the comforts of home. How can you expect to teach based on this sort of fieldwork? Why didn't you study genuine families? Real women and real men? Authentic (pure, isolated, acceptable) natives? How can you have any perspective as an "insider"? Do you really call this anthropology?

The virtual anthropologist is the colleague produced as the Native Ethnographer.[1] Fixed as the one who sets out to study "her own," she attracts, disturbs, disorders. She may have acquitted herself with highest honors during her professional training. She may have spent long hours in the field, carefully researching a topic central to the intellectual history of the discipline. If she is lucky, she will carry with her a pedigree from an outstanding graduate program. (Being advantageously positioned in terms of class hierarchies helps.) If she is very smart and very, very lucky, she may eventually secure a position at a top-ranked university (although precisely because she has been rendered virtual she is less likely to garner such accolades). In short, she may have gone through all the motions expected to bring about professional legitimacy, and, with it, access to what resources the profession has to offer (salary, students, coastal residence, travel, grants).

Yet her work will remain suspect, subject to inspection on the grounds of authenticity rather than intellectual argument or acumen.

Too often described as a marginal figure, unfairly exiled to the periphery of the discipline, the virtual anthropologist actually moves through the professional landscape as a creature of another order. She is irredeemably Other, but not as the result of anything so blatant as an operation of exclusion based on race, sex, class, ethnicity, nationality, or sexuality ("We don't hire/serve/need [epithet of choice] here"). Instead, oppression operates obliquely to incarcerate her within a hybrid category. It is as the Native Ethnographer that the virtual anthropologist finds her work judged less than legitimate, always one step removed from "the real stuff."

Curiouser and Curiouser: The Case of Queer Ethnography

Back in graduate school, when I first decided to study lesbians and gay men in the United States, the faculty members who mentored me pronounced the project "academic suicide." I found it hard to disagree. Before I could proceed, I had to reconcile myself to the possibility (probability?) that I would never get a job in "my field." (At least, I thought, I would get a book out of it: a way to present my research to a wider public.) One glance at the gloomy employment picture for ethnographers who had studied "homosexuality" reinforced this assessment. Almost none of them held appointments in anthropology, if they had jobs at all.

Is it simply that people were more likely to bow down before that spectral figure, homophobia, back in the early 1980s? I don't think so. Graduate students still write to me, torn between the desire to run off with their first love, queer studies, and the advice of elders to accept the more sensible arranged marriage with "another culture" that would move them securely into "mainstream" anthropology. While job prospects may have improved ever so slightly, the structural circumstances that undercut the legitimacy of queer researchers who study queer topics remain. Anthropology's colonial heritage has formed a field that disciplines its natives in a society that nativizes its queers.

The points at which I have been and continue to be produced as a Native Ethnographer tend to be points of evaluation. These are the sites at which the discipline fields its ethnographers: not just job interviews, but conference presentations, book reviews, skewed readings of published research, and the many small interactions that mint that coin of the academic realm, national reputation (reputation as what?). Comments on such occasions range from the generic dismissal ("Fieldwork with gay people is not fieldwork") to the more refined art of the backhanded compliment ("When I saw the title for your talk, I thought it would be a really flaky topic, but you've just transformed my whole notion of kinship"). More often, those reactions remain unspoken, coiled back into the reception of essays like this. Which is your first inclination as a reader: to reduce the essay to a protest against the discrimination aimed at certain "kinds" of people or to read it for its theoretical contribution to debates on identity, subjectivity, and ethnographic writing?

Reactions to the threat posed by the hybridity of the Native Ethnographer may be couched as expressions of concern: "Some people (not me, of course, I'm your friend) think that if we were to offer you a job here, you would become an advocate." (Don't we all advocate for something?) Then there is the repetitive deployment of that thoroughly neutral category, "fit," as in, "We love your work, but you just wouldn't fit into this department." (Ever wondered why?)

For a change of pace, inventive sorts resort to the thinly veiled objection on methodological grounds: "Lesbians and gay men are too small a segment of society for your results to be meaningful." (As opposed to research on that multitude, the Yanomami?) "Well, there aren't many x left, but when you study the x you are studying an entire social system." (Even Marx, who aspired to a systems analysis, sought a point of entry—alienation, commodity fetishism—that offered a unique line of sight into the whole.) "But why bother with queer theory? It's just a passing fad." (Like the Sapir-Whorf hypothesis? Or game theory? How about that onetime razor's edge of anthropological analysis, structuralism?) Every bit as disconcerting as the historical and political ignorance embedded in such a litany is the utter lack of irony with which otherwise astute colleagues pose these questions.

My dance with professional death would have been humorous if it weren't so costly. Anyone who brings the wrong color or area of competence to her work is familiar with the pressures of having to do more and better than peers to get ahead. But it's difficult to describe the unsettling experience of watching your job history recast as a cautionary tale for the benefit of graduate students still in training. Or the sense of moving through the world more ghost than legend in one's own time. Or the slow and painful realization that the portable inquisition is likely to follow you even if you someday manage to secure a "good" position. Not that the vagaries of the job market make it easy for most applicants to land the job of their dreams (Nelson; Roseberry). Still, in my case, there was the telltale specificity of the grounds for incredulity and dismissal: Explain why you call this anthropology.

Mistakenly concluding that my subjection to reality checks in an interrogative key was the consequence of conducting research on a stigmatized topic, mentors devised tactics to mitigate the effects of a risky focus of study. Arranged in chronological order, their advice went something like this: As long as you do theory, everything will be okay. Write your way out. Just finish your dissertation. Just get your degree. Once you sign a book contract, things will start to change. Just wait until the book is in press. Wait until the book comes out in print. Wait until people have time to read the book. Maybe that second book manuscript will turn the tide. Perhaps if you broadened your geographic area a bit (say, from lesbians and gay men in the United States to Western Civilization)?

What these routinized strategies for establishing professional credentials failed to take into account are the processes that can render an anthropologist virtual. For that peculiar anthropological subject/object, the Native Ethnographer, career strategies that rely solely on meritocracy or a move to the disciplinary center necessarily prove inadequate.[2] To the degree that queerness is read not only through your research but through your body, hybridity becomes impossible to ignore.

Going Ethnographer

If one is not born an anthropologist, neither is one born a native. Natives are produced as the object of study that ethnographers make for themselves (Appadurai; Fabian). Coming of age "there" rather than "here" is generally enough to qualify you for this anthropological makeover. Expatriates, of course, need not apply: suitable candidates must be able to lay claim to the ethnicities and nationalities assigned to their place of origin. In Europe and the United States (anthropology's "here"), attribution of native status becomes a bit more complicated. Assignees tend to occupy a sociohistorical location that makes them suitable for exoticization. Darker skin and deviance are always a plus.

With their self-absorption, sexual obsession, love of pageantry, celebration of the body, and party-going nature (please!), queers could have been sent over from central casting to play the savages within. Stereotypes all, but stereotypes that are remarkably continuous with the construction of the primitive in the annals of anthropology.[3] Much as accusations of idleness placed European beggars in a structurally analogous position to those certifiable savages, the "Hottentots" (Coetzee), so the facile reduction of fieldwork among lesbians and gay men to "an extended vacation" evokes the frivolous childlike behavior in which barbarians everywhere wallow.

Of course, lesbians and gay men do not offer the "best" natives for study. In representation, if not in action, they appear too modern, too urban, too here and now, too wealthy, too white.[4] Below the perceptual horizon are queers with rural origins, immigrant status, empty pocketbooks, racial identities at variance with the Anglo. Ironically, the gay movement's problematic tendency to draw analogies between sexual and racial identity—as though all gays were white and people of color could not be gay—has encouraged even white queers who study queers to be taken as "insider" ethnographers in a way that heterosexual white anthropologists studying their "own" communities are not.[5]

Unlike "primitive" or "savage," the term *native* has made something of a comeback in recent years. This particular return of the repressed has occurred after a pluralist fashion that takes little notice of the power relations that produce different types of nativity. (I'm a native, you're a native, we're a native, too.) But each nativizing move can be understood only in its specificity. As the century turns the corner, queers are constructed not just as natives tethered to the symbolics of residence or birth, but as natives-cum-savages. Like primitives, who got such a bad rep after ethnologists decided they had not evolved to the point of practicing monogamous marriage, queers have been saddled with a sexuality that is popularly believed to evade the strictures of social control. For lesbians and gay men of color, these representations become overdetermined, given the racist legacy that primitivizes and hypersexualizes everyone but the Anglo.

As postmodern-day savages, queers have only a few, mostly unsavory, choices: they can be lazy or restless, noble, self-indulgent, or cruel. The articulate presence of these domestic but not domesticated natives is doubly disturbing because it disrupts the homogeneity of "home," that imagined space of sameness and security that shadows "the field."[6] To the degree that the queer who studies queers has been nativized, she joins a long line of African American, American Indian, South Asian Indian, Mexican, and Brazilian anthropologists trained in "American" universities.[7] Like it or not, she is bound to incite professional insecurities about a changing world in which natives not only read the ethnographies that purport to explain them, but also threaten to show up in a graduate program near you.

So it is not surprising that the aspiring anthropologist who is known to be "that way" finds herself reduced to her sexuality with the presumption that queer nativity is a prior attribute she brought with her into higher education. Forget for a moment the complexities of history and circumstance that undercut the utopian vision of a perfect native. Ignore the possibility that our anthropologist may not interpret her sexuality in terms of identity categories and identity politics. Table every theory you know that tells you identities do not produce transparent, shared experiences waiting to be expressed. Set aside the differences of race and religion and class and nationality that guarantee she will never be the consummate "insider" familiar with every nuance of a bounded community. Never mind that her own discipline is implicated in constructing the (queer) native as an internally homogeneous category. When she embarks on a career in anthropology, she is likely to be seen as native first, ethnographer second.

Now bring the set-asides in the preceding paragraph back into focus. The complications they introduce into one-dimensional portraits of "the ethnographer" or "the native" describe precisely what is at stake when I characterize the Native Ethnographer as a hybrid.

"Hybridity" is a term that has lost in precision what it has gained in popularity as it has found its way into discussions of multiculturalism.[8] Although many writers have begun to use "hybrid" and "mixed" interchangeably, hybridity technically describes a process that compounds rather than mixes attributions of identity. If you want to understand the conflicts, suspicion, and general volatility of social relations that surround the lucky incumbent of the Native Ethnographer position, this distinction becomes indispensable.

Think back to that mystical moment in chemistry class when the instructor explained the difference between mixtures and compounds.[9] A mixture is something like a teaspoon of salt stirred together with a spoonful of pepper. Given lots of time, good eyes, and a slightly maniacal bent, a person can sort a mixture back into its original components, placing the pepper, grain by grain, in one pile, and the salt in another. A compound is another matter altogether. Compounds also combine disparate elements, but they join those elements through a chemical reaction that transforms the whole into something different from either of its constituent parts. Water is a compound of oxygen and hydrogen. Put the two together in certain proportions under particular conditions and you will find a liquid where you might expect a gas. Trying to divide water into its elements mechanically, molecule by molecule, drop by drop, would be a fool's errand. Assuming that you understand the properties of water because you once inhaled "pure" oxygen could lead to early death by drowning.

So hybridity is not the sum of an additive relationship that "mixes" two intact terms (Native + Ethnographer). A person cannot understand what it means to be positioned as a Native Ethnographer by reading an essay or two on representations of savagery and then brushing up on the latest in interview techniques. Attempting to grasp each term in isolation is as fruitless as trying to spot the elements of hydrogen and oxygen in your morning cup of coffee. If you come up with anything at all, it is likely to be your own reflection.[10]

But if hybridity is not an additive relationship, neither is it the joining of two terms by a Lacanian slash (Native/Ethnographer). The slash is really nothing more than a variant of the mixture model that problematizes the relationship between the terms. A Native/Ethnographer would be someone who moves, more or less uneasily, between two fixed positions or "worlds" (professional by morning, queer by night). But no two identities attributed to the same body are that separable, that discrete. Nobody checks identities at the door. Whether or not the Native Ethnographer embraces the categories that define her, she is not a split subject, but a hybrid who collapses the subject/object distinction (more on this in a moment).

To continue the science analogy, if there is a chemical reaction that creates the Native Ethnographer as a particular sort of hybrid, it is the act of studying a "people" defined as one's own.[11] Or more accurately, it is the performance of this research activity in the context of the same set of social relations that produces inanities like the characterization of "insider" fieldwork as one long party. (I don't know what kind of parties you go to, but spin the bottle looks pretty good next to 350 days of fieldnotes.) All of this is a social product. Studying "one's own" is no more a matter of natural affinity than nativity is the consequence of birth.

Whether someone becomes nativized—much less primitivized—depends on matters of history and power that extend well beyond the academy. (To repeat: darker skin and deviance are always a plus.) The mere act of surveying someone with an anthropological (or sociological, or historiographic) gaze is not enough to transform her into a native or credit her with membership in "a people." Veterans who study warfare are not nativized in the same way as queers who study sexuality, and the work of these veterans is much less likely to be read off their bodies.[12]

Because our youthful hero has been produced as a virtual anthropologist only in relationship to her object of study, her ethnography will be perpetually interpreted through her (now increasingly essentialized) nativity. "Evidence" of her sexuality pops up in her work in unexpected places, like Elvis at a road rally or Our Lady of Sorrows in Vegas. And this double-edged process does not require ignorance or ill will to wreak the havoc it does.

Through it all, the Native Ethnographer grapples with the instability of the terms that represent her. Colleagues who misrecognize hybridity as an additive relationship find themselves disturbed by the native's apparent ability to morph into the anthropologist.[13] Imagining that the two parts coexist side by side within her, they ask questions that are the equivalent of trying to separate a compound by mechanical means. Their insistence on establishing a standard for "real" fieldwork and "real" anthropology attempts to ferret out the native in the anthropologist like the pepper in the salt. Surely somewhere there must be an advocate hiding behind the professional mask, the savage in ethnographer's clothing. Meanwhile, the anthropologist who finds herself mired in nativity in the eyes of colleagues can attempt to extricate herself by "going ethnographer": emphasizing observation over participation, or insisting on the authenticity of her research ("I did fieldwork, too, you know").

Although these offensive and defensive moves may seem opposed in the high-stakes game of authentication, they share an insistence on the importance—indeed, the possibility—of separating the ethnographer from the native. But the two terms cannot be neatly distinguished once the discipline has brought them into a relationship of hybridity. As a compound state, hybridity represents something more complex than an "intersection" of separate axes of identity. The operations that transform the whole into something qualitatively different from the sum of its parts make it impossible to tease out the various ways in which research area and nativization combine to provide a basis for discrimination.

Was it studying the United States or the way you stood with your hands in your pockets (too butch) that led the interviewer to pose that hostile question about "real fieldwork"? Funny, another guy asked the same thing when the job specified a geographic focus on the United States, so maybe it's not geographic area after all. But if it wasn't area and it wasn't the hands in the pockets (still not sure about that one), maybe it was because you couldn't put to rest those lingering fears that, if appointed, you would become a crusader for "your people."

There are plenty of grounds these days for charging someone with a failure to perform "real anthropology." Studies of Europe or the United States, studies that traverse national borders, studies "up" instead of "down," studies of "one's own," studies that refuse to exoticize the stigmatized: all have been dismissed, at one time or another, as less than legit. But there is a pattern and a specificity to the occasions on which anthropologists have rallied to the real. In periods of disciplinary complacency as well as the current era of budget cuts and postcolonial reflection, the anthropologist known as the Native Ethnographer has repeatedly been taken to task for passing herself off as the genuine article and falling short of authentic practice.

When Native Ethnographers attempt to prove themselves real in the face of the inevitable interrogation, they face the old duck dilemma: however convincingly they may walk and talk, quack and squawk, as they perform the time-honored rituals of professional legitimation, they will look *like* an ethnographer before they will be taken as (a real) one. As hybrids, they are continuously produced in the cyberspace of the virtual. As hybrids, they compound subject with object. As hybrids, they become at once hypervisible and invisible, painfully obtrusive and just as readily overlooked.

In the course of professionalization, Native Ethnographers emerge from graduate programs that promise to transform the benighted Them (natives) into the all-knowing Us (anthropologists). On the job market, Native Ethnographers labor under the suspicion that greets shape shifters, those unpredictable creatures who threaten to show up as Us today, Them tomorrow. The very presence in the discipline of queers who study queers could complicate this dichotomy between Us and Them in useful ways. But in the absence of the thoroughgoing reevaluation of the anthropological project that an understanding of hybridity entails, the irresolvable question that faces the virtual anthropologist remains: How are *these* ethnographers to make their Other?

I, Native

To be taken seriously as a scholar, it is not enough to author ethnographies: our aspiring anthropologist must establish herself as an authority. But as a hybrid, she will find that she cannot authorize herself through recourse to the same time-tested rhetorical strategies that other anthropologists have employed to create professional credibility. The instability of hybridity and the discomfort it inspires make it well-nigh impossible to speak or write from the subject position of "I, Native Ethnographer." Social relations inside and outside the profession pull her toward the poles of her assigned identity, denying her the option of representing herself as a complex, integrated, compound figure. Instead of writing as "I, Native Ethnographer"—or some equally compound subject position—she ends up positioned as *either* "I, Native," *or* "I, Ethnographer." The nuance of the two as they are bound up together is lost.

"Why not try objectivity?" you ask. This distancing device served well enough to secure the reputations of anthropologists in days gone by. Surveying her subjects with an omniscient gaze, the virtual anthropologist sometimes attempts to prove herself real by setting out to occupy the "I, Ethnographer" position with a vengeance. It's bad enough to study a fringe topic; why risk calling attention to an ethnicity shared with "informants" or committing a stigmatized sexual identity to print? Far better to play God. To remind the reader that society casts the Native Ethnographer as "one of them" would be to acknowledge that the author has helped create the universe she observes. Come to think of it, even gods have been known to spin a creation myth or two. Strictly empiricist anthropologists (good girls) don't.

Now this objectivist stance is not bad as a form of resistance to the ways nativization reduces people to one-dimensional representatives of "their" putatively homogeneous society or community. But the author who writes as "I, Ethnographer" ignores at her peril the impact of her specific social positioning on her research. And she pays a price when she bows to pressures to disembody herself in order to disavow nativity.

All right, then. Let's turn to the strategy of explicitly inserting oneself into the text, a gambit popularized by what has been dubbed the reflexive turn in anthropology. Writing under the ethnographic "I" means that the author must write *as* someone or something: a situated "self." What's in a pronoun? In reflexive writing, the narrator—as distinct from the author—generally situates herself in terms of identities that carry weight in Euro-American societies. Gender, ethnicity, class, nationality, and (once in a while) sexuality come to the fore.

Of course, reflexivity does not automatically confer credibility. (Witness a friend's reaction when she first leafed through my book on gay kinship ideologies, *Families We Choose*: "There certainly are a lot of 'I's' in your book! Is this supposed to be social science?") But reflexivity has the advantage of calling attention to differences that make a difference. If you set out to study a former colony from the former metropole, it just might affect how you are received. If your parents once numbered themselves among the colonized, your reception may shift accordingly. If people "in the field" code you as a woman with money to spend, that assessment can affect your research in ways that bear examination. If you have never done drag but the person you're interviewing has, a "shared" gay identity may or may not affect the results you get on tape. But it is probably worth noting.

Reflexivity reminds the reader to view the circumstances of the anthropologist in relation to the circumstances of the people studied. It also highlights the ways the ethnographer's hand, however light, shapes the presentation of data from the field. Still, so much attention to identities can foster a dangerously reassuring belief in equality ("We're all 'I's' here") in situations where serious disparities prevail. All the pious calls for dialogue and mutual respect between the ethnographer and her subjects cannot change the fact that socially structured inequalities do not dissolve under the influence of ac-knowledgment and understanding. Reflexivity is not, in itself, an equalizing act.

Here lies the danger that reflexivity poses for the Native Ethnogra-pher. To the extent that she uses identity categories to describe herself in her scholarship, she will most likely be read as speaking from the "I, Native" rather than the "I, Native Ethnographer" position. *Her* use of "I" splits the hybridity of the Native Ethnographer by giving nativ-ity pride of place over professional standing. This nativization is the effect not of authorial intent but of power relations in the wider soci-ety. Even as I sit at my desk calling attention to the ways nativization writes people out of the discipline, I am aware that the use of the first person in this chapter may end up reinforcing a tendency to view my work through the narrowing lens of an ascribed lesbian identity.[14] Why else would I be sent manuscripts for review on anything to do with queers (lesbians and ecology, anyone?), but so little material on the theoretical questions about ideology and identity that inform my research?

For the anthropologist who gets nativized as lesbian, gay, or bisex-ual, "coming out" when she writes up her data can create more prob-lems than it resolves. By and large, the critique associated with reflex-ivity has addressed power relations between anthropologists and their "informants."[15] But what about the power differentials embed-ded in relationships with professional "peers"? Which do you think would be harder to reveal: your positioning as a middle-class hetero-sexual white male, or as some deeper shade of queer? The price of methodological responsibility is higher for people positioned lower. Or, as Lady Macbeth might have said about much of the reflexive soul searching to date, "What need we fear who knows it, when none can call our power to account?"

When the Native Ethnographer writes about how constructions of her gender or ethnicity or sexuality affected her research, she may provide insights that are crucial for interpreting her results, but she also subjects herself to an insidious sort of surveillance. Although sexualities need not be inscribed *on* bodies (no, Ethel, you can't always know one when you see one), the publications the virtual anthropologist produces will begin to be read *through* her body. Now thoroughly ensconced in nativity, she is likely to be credited with the "instant rapport" that is but one of the illusory attributes of the insider: zap and cook, stir and eat, point and shoot, speak and be in accord, listen and understand. Culturally marked aspects of her identity flag "like" identities among her research subjects, while attributes that place her within the magic circle of domination encourage other aspects of her work to be overlooked.

Since the publication of *Families We Choose,* I have been intrigued by the patterned ways it is read and not read. As part of my research for the volume, I conducted a year of fieldwork in San Francisco, getting to know a wide range of gay men, lesbians, bisexuals, "don't-categorize-me's," and even the occasional heterosexual. The parameters of my field research are clearly laid out in the book, both in my words and in the voices of people I interviewed. Yet readers often transform *Families We Choose* into a lesbian text, turning me into a researcher who studies lesbians (what else?) and effectively erasing 50 percent of an interview sample composed of equal numbers of lesbians and gay men. Meanwhile, the racial diversity of the sample goes unremarked, despite its rarity amid the largely white social science studies of homosexuality. Each of these characterizations of the book filters my research through my placement in fields of identity and fields of power. *Families We Choose* is the product of a hybrid "I" who has been nativized in particular ways within and without the text: as a white (unmarked), lesbian (most certainly marked) scholar.

When the politics of reflexivity engage with the complex representation that is the Native Ethnographer, they end up looking more retro than radical. As though stigmatization and skewed readings were not enough, the forced retreat to an "I, Native" subject position embroils the writer in an inhospitable economy of disclosure and revelation. Leaving aside for the moment the associations of moral culpability attached to the confessional form, the concept of coming out of the closet implies the existence of a coherent, prefabricated identity waiting to be expressed for the pleasure of the viewing audience. Yet historical and cross-cultural research emphasizes the cultural specificity of the identity categories ("the" homosexual) that organize sexuality into a domain in Anglo-European societies (Weston, "Lesbian/Gay Studies").

What is it, then, that can render even well-read scholars stupid in the face of identity politics? With a rudimentary knowledge of the literature on identity, how can they persist in asking such questions as "What was it like to work as an insider ethnographer?" (Inside what? An unbounded, heterogeneous population that can be neither counted nor defined?) Rhetorical questions, to be sure. The point is this: Coming out in print, however artfully executed, can too easily be misinterpreted as a public statement of the "truth" about a sexuality that is supposed to create automatic solidarity with at least some of the people encountered in the field.

Interestingly, the "coming out" passage in *Families We Choose* is barely that. I read it now as a failed attempt to resist nativization without obscuring my implication in identity categories that affected my field research:

> "Are you a lesbian? Are you gay?" Every other day one of these questions greets my efforts to set up interviews over the telephone. Halfway through my fieldwork, I remark on this concern with the researcher's identity while addressing a course in anthropological field methods. "Do you think you could have done this study if you weren't a lesbian?" asks a student from the back of the classroom. "No doubt," I reply, "but then again, it wouldn't have been the same study." (Weston, *Families* 13)

While this passage recounts a "real-life" incident, I strategically selected that incident and crafted the passage with care. Students and potential research subjects supply the categories (lesbian, gay) that cast my sexuality in the mold of identity. No variant of "homosexual" passes my lips, although it could be argued that I tacitly assent to those categories with a response ("No doubt") that leaves their terms intact. To round things off, the setting—a methods class!—introduces an element of irony that beckons the reader to reflection.

What else might a close reading of this passage suggest? My departure from an identity politics that credentials certain people as "insiders" and insists that only "authentic" members of a group may speak.[16] My belief that power and positioning matter. My impatience with identity-based constructions of sexuality that cannot accommodate a range of intimacies and attractions.

Too subtle, perhaps? But what rhetorical devices besides the ethnographic "I" are available to the hybrid who cannot reconcile herself to the fate of having her professional persona endlessly recycled through nativity? After she has exhausted the possibilities of authorizing herself through strategies of objectivity and reflexivity, what's a virtual anthropologist to do when it comes to the thankless task of getting people to read her work through something besides persona and physique?

In a pinch, there's always reportage with an eyewitness twist. Nothing like building the implicit claim "I was there" (Sorry, pal, you weren't) into an ethnographic narrative to lay claim to special insights inaccessible to the general reader (see Clifford; Geertz). Of course, that claim depends on maintaining a clear separation between there and here, a separation usually worked out by mapping categories of people onto place. Natives are the ones who are always there, always embodied, always open to scholarly inspection. Ethnographers are the ones who go there ("the field") to study natives with every intention of returning here ("home"), whether "here" lies across the seas or in a co-op apartment on the other side of town (see Clifford; see also chapter 1 of Gupta and Ferguson). The odd anthropologist out has been known to jump disciplinary ship by "going native," but that hardly counts as an option for the ethnographer already located as a native. Because the virtual anthropologist's hybridity blurs the distinction between researcher and researched, she cannot create ethnographic authority by distancing herself in time or space from the people she studies. There is now, here is there, and we are them.[17]

Like an eagle caught far from its range, the Native Ethnographer's wings become tangled in the power lines that join two senses of "my people": the colonialist's "*my* people" and the activist's "my *people*." It's hard to say which formulation is more problematic: the first with its hierarchy of racial and labor relations left intact, or the second with all the limitations of the nationalist vision of an imagined community that undergirds identity politics.[18] The virtual anthropologist once again finds herself in an untenable position, unwilling or unable to produce "*my* people" (the Other of anthropological inquiry), and incapable of extricating herself from the grip of the professionally dangerous perception that she should "naturally" call some nativized group "my *people*." Understandably loath to exoticize that which she cannot leave behind, she is less likely than most of her colleagues to build professional credibility on the backs of "informants" through an orientalizing move.

If all else fails, then, our ever-resourceful anthropologist can attempt to make the best of nativization by taking a stand on native authority.[19] Barely articulated notions of informant expertise have been embedded all along in the process of making ethnographic writing credible. Natives are the ones with a corner on the academic market for (genuine) experience, the kind worth documenting and transcribing and playing the voyeur to. Natives are well known to have bodies and practical knowledge, the better to filter their nativity through. For the real anthropologist, in contrast, experiential authority and embodiment end with the "return from the field."

No visible work discipline attaches to the visceral, concrete labor of "writing up." When books and essays make the ethnographer's body visible, they depict its toils and deprivations in the field, seldom at the keyboard. Where in experimental ethnography are the endless cups of tea or coffee, sore muscles, aching head, and stiff hands from hours bent over a text? When did the work of producing a monograph count as real experience, or for that matter, manual as well as mental labor? With the demise of armchair anthropology, who ever heard of an anthropologist, reflexive or otherwise, establishing credibility by proclaiming, "I was there . . . for years . . . in my study"?[20]

If the labor of writing disappears for the ethnographer, the arduousness of research tends to fade from view for the native who "goes to the field." Working in a country or community portrayed as one's own becomes "not work," much as teaching a language is assumed to require no training for people labeled "native speakers." This ethnographic variant of natural rhythm (note the racialized and sexualized subtext) casts the virtual anthropologist once again as instant insider, accepted with open arms into the ethnographic utopia of a homogeneous community. Her experience as a native—the only experience about which she can speak authoritatively from the "I, Native" position—is taken to be familiar and complete, yielding knowledge acquired with little or no effort.[21]

Savaged again, and to what avail? Disappointingly, native authority doesn't get the virtual anthropologist very far. In a scholarly world that places a premium on explanation, the meaning of experience must remain opaque to the native in order to be revealed by that privileged interpreter, the social scientist. Being university trained, the virtual anthropologist can always pull the old hat trick (today native, tomorrow ethnographer; now you see the native, now you don't). But she will be hard put to write from the Native Ethnographer position, much less to work through its contradictions.

So the virtual anthropologist goes through her long- or short-lived—career constantly being pulled toward one or the other of the poles of her hybridity. Try as she might, she will not be able to produce a fully legitimized account of her field research. Why can't she authorize herself in the same way as the real anthropologist? Because most of the rhetorical strategies that establish ethnographic authority are predicated on a separation of object from subject. And the prescribed cure for this mind/body split—reflexivity—does not free the author from the trap. Even the most celebrated of experimental ethnographies end up reinstating a division between you and I, native and ethnographer, Other and Self, often at the very moment they "allow" people from the field to speak.[22]

There is, of course, one final (though limited) strategy familiar to informants everywhere who have exercised their perfect native authority with witty abandon. Whether ad-libbing "traditional" songs and stories or making jokes at the anthropologist's expense that are received in all seriousness and duly recorded for publication, natives have always participated in an improvisatory construction of what is "empirically" available for study, including their own nativity (see Limón; Paredes; Rosaldo; and Sarris, "What I'm Talking About"). Instead of letting parody pass as realism, the Native Ethnographer can be "true" to the hybridity forced upon her by creating parodies—rather like this essay—that are marked as such. Anthropologists may be nativized or virtualized, hybridized or realized. But camp is camp is camp.[23]

The problem with the Native Ethnographer, though, is that she won't stay put: the slippery rascal keeps sliding over from the object (Native) into the subject (Ethnographer) position. Hybridity is disconcerting precisely to the degree that it collapses the subject/object distinctions that work to insulate "us" from "them." Because the categories that nativize her combine with professional identity to yield a hybrid compound, she encounters a double bind when it comes time to write. To produce anthropology at all, she must treat the components of her hybridity as merely additive (Native + Ethnographer) or split (Native/Ethnographer) by writing from only one subject position at a time, unless hybridity itself becomes the focus of the piece. And each time her work submits to this double bind, as it must, it surrenders the intricate operations of hybridity to the oversimplifications of nativity or objectivity.

Just in case legions of readers inspired by the density of the last paragraph find themselves moved to set out on a quest for a better formula for ethnographic writing, let me add that this is a case where rhetoric is not enough. In the end, ethnographic authority is more than "affected" by race or gender or sexuality or a host of other identities (cf. Gordon). Those identities filter through both hybridity and a subject/object divide produced in social arenas apart from the text. Through it all, the legitimacy of the generic, unmarked anthropologist is read into reality by the very power relations that read the virtual anthropologist out.

Peripheral Re-Vision

Although being read out of "real" anthropology increases the chances that the Native Ethnographer will be marginalized within her discipline, the two processes are actually distinct. Not that there has been any noticeable expansion of appointments for queers who study queers in anthropology departments at top-ten universities. But virtuality does not assign the Native Ethnographer a particular position—be it center or margin—in the metaphorical space of the field. Instead, virtuality consigns her to the unnerving experience of moving through the professional landscape as something just short of genuine, regardless of where she plants her professional feet. It's about becoming not-real, though not quite imitation either, in ways that make her unmappable.[24]

Marginality models import the geopolitics of empire into the cyberspace of academic politics. Bemidji State becomes to the University of Michigan what the imperial outpost is to the metropolis (see Ashcroft, Griffiths, and Tiffin; hooks, *Feminist Theory*; and Spivak). Prestigious departments occupy the symbolic center of the academic universe, and their centrality, far from insulating them behind ivory-tower walls, grants them a high degree of control over the resources necessary to do the kind of anthropology that confers professional credibility. Hierarchies of practice and place ensure that aspiring anthropologists who "don't make the grade" are shipped off to the colonies ("the margins"), where long hours, temporary status, lack of leave time, too many committees, too many classes, high student-teacher ratios, and research conducted on the fly make a ticket to the center more improbable with each passing megawork day.

Yet the virtual is not the marginal. Why else would the Native Ethnographer remain virtual, regardless of whether she occupies the center or periphery of the academic world? She cannot make herself "real" by changing the theoretical topic she studies or the institution she serves. A time-tested focus like politics, the latest in transnationalism, Stanford or Podunk U.—it's all the same when it comes to hybridity. The compound position from which the Native Ethnographer speaks leaves her somewhere between subject and object, Us and Them, pedestrian reality and "here comes trouble."

In this sense, the process of hybridization that renders someone virtual is not equivalent to growing up on the wrong side of the tracks or enrolling in a school on the wrong side of the Mississippi. The upwardly mobile scholar who migrates from the periphery to an elite institution may work hard to maintain her marginality by writing on behalf of "her people" or remembering what it was like to come of age on the wrong side of town (hooks, "Choosing the Margin").[25] But the virtual anthropologist who comes into the intellectual's equivalent of an inheritance needs no reminder. She remains virtual at the very moment she wins the all-expenses-paid trip to an institution at the heart of the discipline. Purveyors of digs and doubts will track her down, even in her endowed chair. The girl could be responding to questions at the press conference called to celebrate her receipt of a MacArthur award (dream on!), and she would be kidding herself if she believed it impossible for some joker to rise up out of the audience to say, "Your work's very interesting, very interesting indeed, but why do you call it anthropology?"

With a little luck, the virtual anthropologist *may* live to pursue her career as an "outsider within," in Patricia Hill Collins's sense of a person assigned to a subordinate position in the belly of the beast.[26] Surely you've run across her: the lone member of the faculty allotted a windowless office, the one "inadvertently" dropped from the invitation list to departmental functions, or the one relentlessly included on the invitation list to departmental functions (where she can expect to have the pleasure of being shown off as the embodiment of her colleagues' liberality and goodwill). But the virtual anthropologist is just as likely to pass her days as the outsider without: jobless, piecing together academic appointments, crisscrossing the globe in her search for admission to the tenured elect, consigned to the academy's back of beyond, eventually giving up or giving out.

Excised or tokenized, the virtual anthropologist inherits much of the loneliness associated with the outsider-within position, but little of its fixity. Her problems do not stem from being a dyke out of (her) place in academe, but from those seemingly unpredictable shifts from Native to Ethnographer and back again. What makes her virtual is neither a fixed identity (the house queer) nor a fixed location (at center or margins), but a compounding of identity with research that sets her in motion as a Native Ethnographer. At issue is not who she "is" or where she stands, but whether onlookers see her as a Native rising up out of the community she studies. If they do, the game's up: she'll be rendered virtual, going under to that telltale hybridity, another casualty of the kind of Othering that sends its targets ricocheting between subject positions.

No surprise, then, that virtuality does not yield to protests against exclusion from the center or efforts to jockey for a better position. Strategies of inclusion attempt to better the lot of the marginalized professional by confronting the forces of discrimination that have pushed her to the periphery. Strategies of critique rely on the keen insight and creativity that some scholars believe accompany the view from the edge (see hooks, "Choosing the Margin"). Both tactics keep in place a territorial model for conceptualizing power relations. Both keep the long-suffering aspirant oriented to the field's metaphorical center, whether she adopts the stance that says, "Let me in!" or the voice that admonishes, "Let me tell you what's problematic about being in!"

A virtual anthropologist cannot pin her hopes on the search for a level playing field or a place in the sun, because these spatial metaphors keep intact the process of nativization that is her bane.[27] Natives in, natives out: the same pieces are shuffled around the board with nothing to challenge their construction. But the polymorphic character of the virtual anthropologist makes her a shape shifter at center or margin. Our hero's heightened visibility *as* a Native Ethnographer is the very condition of her invisibility. Now you see her, now you don't, because when you do see her, you can view her only through the lens of hybridity.

Though the topic may be academic suicide, the implications of being rendered virtual do not stop at books left unwritten and derailed careers. Being read out of reality transports the nativized scholar who studies "her own" into a different dimension of meaning altogether. The Native Ethnographer, in the full glory of her hybridity, confronts the conventional definition of anthropology as the study of (the hu)man, or even the study of cultural differences, with the possibility that the field might be more appropriately conceptualized as a site for the *production* of difference. Unlike headhunters and firewalkers from days gone by, safely contained "over there" in "the field," the virtual anthropologist's location "within" the discipline threatens to expose her inquisitors' participation in the power relations that fuel the process of nativization.

In the libraries and in the halls, queers who study queers find themselves grouped with other Native Ethnographers whose bid for professional status entails being reduced to the categories (sexuality, ethnicity, what have you) that are supposed to organize their identities. It's easy to forget that these one-dimensional representations feed back into the communities ethnographers study. At a time when "natives" worldwide resort to quoting ethnographies to explain their "traditions" to the state and to themselves, the virtual anthropologist is the ghost in a disciplinary machine whose finest documentary efforts have doubled as exotica, intervention, and spectacle. If anybody can help anthropology retool, she's the one.

NOTES

An earlier version of this chapter was presented in 1995 at the colloquium series in the department of anthropology, Princeton University. The essay has benefited greatly from a series of conversations with Deb Amory, Jared Braiterman, Susan Cahn, Rebecca Etz, Kristin Koptiuch, Yasumi Kuriya, Thaïs Morgan, Geeta Patel, Suzanne Vaughan, participants in the 1994 Anthropology and "the Field" conference organized by Jim Ferguson and Akhil Gupta at Stanford University and the University of California, Santa Cruz, and participants in the 1994 Thinking, Writing, Teaching, and Creating Justice conference hosted by the Center for Advanced Feminist Studies at the University of Minnesota. Smadar Lavie read the manuscript and offered many thoughtful suggestions, not all of which could be incorporated here. Special thanks to VéVé Clark for the irreverent comments and heartfelt exchange that helped make this essay what it is today. Finally, my thanks to colleagues like Celia Alvarez, Jean Comaroff, John Comaroff, Tim Diamond, Smadar Lavie, Sylvia Yanagisako, and above all the late David Schneider, who have all challenged in productive ways the processes that can render someone virtual.

1. "Native" is a problematic term that keeps people in their place by essentializing their characters, bounding their communities, and otherwise subjecting them to the disciplinary legacies of racism that emerged from colonial rule (Bhabha, "Of Mimicry"; Narayan). In this chapter, I capitalize Native Ethnographer to underscore the category's status as representation rather than birthmark.

2. Whether the production of the scholar who studies "her own" as a particular sort of hybrid obtains for fields like literature or sociology, I leave to colleagues from those disciplines to determine. In some respects, the Native Ethnographer is a subject position peculiar to anthropology, with its long history of participation in the colonial ventures that produced "the native" as an object of Euro-American subjugation. Yet the processes of nativization unleashed by colonialism proceed apace within the academy as well as the world at large. Scholars of color who work in "ethnic studies" have found themselves produced in analogous fashion for the viewing (dis)pleasure of colleagues. As a candidate for the top position on a university campus, Arturo Madrid confronted the question, "Why does a one-dimensional person like you think he can be the president of a multidimensional institution like ours?" (10). Lisa Duggan ("The Discipline Problem") fielded similar insults from colleagues who wondered aloud how she, a "gay historian" (note the collapse of subject researcher into object research), could possibly be qualified to teach "generic" topics in American history. With regard to anthropology, Ruth Behar eloquently conveys the effects of an identity politics that filters scholarship back through bodies whenever the bodies in question are marked as Other:

> You mainly read women anthropologists for their critiques of androcentrism, and you mainly read anthropology or cultural criticism by people of color for their particular accounts of local places, or at best, as grist for your already grinding theoretical mill. You don't read either for "high theory," the sort of understandings that are supposed to be of such translocal importance that they can serve as grids for work anywhere. The more neutralizing the translation of local accents, the better. Ironic, isn't it? Can this be the discipline whose legitimacy is so wrapped up in foreign languages and worlds? (299)

3. This nativization of gay men and lesbians across race is quite evident in *The Gay Agenda,* a video produced by a right-wing group in California and widely distributed to libraries across the United States. The video intersperses footage from the annual San Francisco gay and lesbian pride parade with talking heads who are trotted on screen to present unfounded statistics about "cure" rates and sexual habits of homosexuals. Against a visual montage of gyrating bodies, naked body parts, and sexual innuendo, a narrator intones dire warnings about the out-of-control sexuality and insatiable hunger for political power lurking behind the mild-mannered facade of gay rights groups. These hypersexualized and hyperbiologized representations of queers draw on a long and racist history of depicting imagined threats to civilization as "we" know it, from portrayals of African Americans during Reconstruction to characterizations of aliens in horror films (Bukatman 262).

4. Anthropologists have tended to construct morally graded variants of the (ideal but vanishing) native along continua from good to bad, genuine to faux, traditional to modern, rural to urban, inner-city to suburban, living in pristine isolation to having been corrupted by the lures of Western civilization (see Gupta and Ferguson, chapter 1). Because the ideal native is also the native considered most suitable for study, it is not so surprising that, despite the recent nativization of lesbians and gay men, there has been no rush of anthropologists to the gold fields of queer studies.

5. This is not to say that queers of color and white queers in the United States occupy the same position, even vis-à-vis queerness, as a result of nativization. Witness the anger and discomfort voiced by several members (most of them people of color) of the Society of Lesbian and Gay Anthropologists when the group sold T-shirts that read, "These natives can speak for themselves." In this instance the term *native* became a contested site, with distributors of the T-shirt arguing that they had *reappropriated* the term *native* and critics decrying what they regarded as an *appropriation* of ethnicity carried out by a predominantly white group (Bustos-Aguilar 164–65). Bustos-Aguilar presents a thoughtful, impassioned critique of the ways white gay ethnographers have colluded in (not-yet-post-) colonial relations. His remarks are particularly scathing on the subject of the colonialist presumptions that continue to infuse research projects on same-sex eroticism and on the tendency for fieldwork "abroad" to edge over into sex tourism or surveillance.

6. Patel ("Home, Homo, Hybrid: Gender and Sexuality in South Asia") and Raiskin ("Inverts and Hybrids") discuss how processes of nativization undercut the complexity of ambiguously sexed/raced/nationalized bodies by tethering people to fixed social locations. On the discomfort and ambivalence associated with the racialized and sexualized colonial stereotype that helps produce the native, see Bhabha ("Of Mimicry and Man" and "The

Other Question: Difference, Discrimination, and the Discourse of Colonialism"). For a feminist critique of home as a locus of safety and familiarity, see
Martin and Mohanty, and M. B. Pratt ("Identity"). Visweswaran (101–4) takes
the feminist critique one step further with her concept of "homework."
Homework is not a matter of conducting "fieldwork at home," but a rejection
of fieldwork in favor of a method and a politics of location in which "home"
marks the site(s) from which a person writes, studies, and speaks (see also the
discussion of Visweswaran's work in Lavie and Swedenburg).

7. "Joins," that is, if colleagues have not already located her in this lineage
by virtue of ethnicity, religion, and/or nationality. For authors who write explicitly, though not always contentedly, from the position of "native anthropologist" or "insider ethnographer," see Abu-Lughod; D. Jones; Limón;
Narayan; Sarris, "What I'm Talking About" and *Mabel McKay*; and Zavella.

8. Gloria Anzaldúa ("borderlands" and "*mestizaje*"), Homi Bhabha ("Of
Mimicry"; hybridity as a product of colonial encounters), and Gerald Vizenor
("cross-bloods") have laid much of the theoretical groundwork for discussions of identities that will neither stay pure nor stay put. For examples incorporating the concepts of hybridity and *mestizaje* into scholarly discussions of
multiculturalism, see Lavie and Swedenburg; Lowe; Lugones; and West. Hale
explores the complex relationship between *mestizaje*, nationalist ideologies,
and the state, as well as the contention that *mestizaje* represents a "new form
of colonialism" for people who identify as *indígenas* (18). In the intellectual
borderlands where academic and popular audiences meet and meld, Lisa
Jones (*Bulletproof Diva*) and Greg Tate (*Flyboy in the Buttermilk*) have also challenged readers to grapple with the historical contingencies of raced categories. M. B. Pratt (*S/he*) deftly conveys the slipperiness of terms like woman,
man, and lesbian sexuality. Asad; Crenshaw; and Weston ("Get Thee to a Big
City") explore some of the material consequences of an identity politics that
depends on bounded, mutually exclusive categories like "sex" and "race" for
its (in)effectiveness.

9. Nancy Hewitt has also used the distinction between mixtures and compounds to clarify matters of difference and identity in the United States. I am
grateful to Rebecca Etz for calling this to my attention.

10. Narayan uses the term "hybridity" in her thought-provoking essay on
the so-called native anthropologist, but in the sense of an additive rather than
a compound relationship. In Narayan's account, hybridity brings two static,
given social locations into a relationship, producing what I describe here as a
mixture. Her discussion of "enactments of hybridity," which turn everybody
into a hybrid with respect to something, includes a valuable exploration of
the ways identities are selected and highlighted contextually. Yet this emphasis carries with it the danger of glossing over the power relations that historically have marked particular people as particular sorts of hybrids. I see hy-

bridity as a process that, once contextually invoked, not only locates but also subordinates people by encouraging most things they do or say to be interpreted through the compound category taken to define their hybridity.

11. The operations of hybridity may also help explain the anecdotal evidence that people who simultaneously claim a queer identity and study queer communities have greater difficulty finding employment than individuals who do one or the other. See also Newton, "Lesbian and Gay Issues in Anthropology."

12. "Natives" may be construed as objects for study, but not all objects of study are construed as natives. Anderson's now classic work on nationalism and imagined communities explores the processes that affiliate certain identities (but not others) with membership in "a people." For more on the impact of the fantasy of primitivism on anthropological practice and popular imagination, see Kuper.

13. In this sense, hybridity has the potential to disrupt processes of nativization that attempt to fix subjects and hold them steady. On morphing and shape shifting, see Bukatman; and Smith. On hybridity as a "space" of productivity, see Muñoz. But see also Young, who cautions that the concept of hybridity can subtly reinforce (neo)colonialist fears of miscegenation and lend credence to efforts to police the boundaries of ostensibly pure (often racialized) categories. Awkward (*Negotiating Difference*) insightfully explores tensions between the instability of categories of gender or race (or class or sexuality) and the tendency to treat these categories of difference as though they were set in stone. For some of the ways in which naturalizing identity works to naturalize power, see Yanagisako and Delaney.

14. I am grateful to Susan Cahn, always up for a good paradox, for helping me articulate this point.

15. But see Newton, "My Best Informant's Dress," who has taken reflexive anthropology to task for its failure to acknowledge that sexuality can be another arena in which ethnographers wield power over people "in the field."

16. Coombe offers an excellent critique of simplistic mappings of "voice" onto identity, standpoint, authenticity, or authority to speak on behalf of a group.

17. For further discussion of these authorizing devices, see Fabian on temporal distancing; Clifford, Geertz, and M. L. Pratt on geographic distancing; and Appadurai on the rhetorical mapping of people onto place entailed in nativization. Lavie and Swedenburg discuss the breakdown of distinctions between "home" and "field," researcher and researched, in the wake of diasporas and resistance movements.

18. On the relationship between imagined communities and identity politics, see Anderson; Bhabha, "DissemiNation"; and Berlant and Freeman.

19. Here again, however, the virtual anthropologist's extremely high level

of education limits the legitimacy achievable with this tactic by rendering her a less than ideal native.

20. On the topic of the "manual" work discipline attached to "mental" labor, I am indebted to a series of discussions with Thaïs Morgan.

21. The point is not that social positioning and experience make no difference, but rather that they are not transparent and do not lead to effortless understanding or instant rapport (Behar; Sarris; Scott). Narayan offers an excellent critique of the misleading implications of the term insider "anthropologist."

22. In Behar's *Translated Woman,* for example, the author's "I" frames Esperanza's first-person account, effectively transforming Esperanza's "I" into a "you" (similarly for Shostak with Nisa, Crapanzano with Tuhami, and a host of others). The framing devices of authorship, introductions, and moments of reflexivity that have the power to interrupt the flow of a narrative undermine the apparent egalitarianism of first-person pronouns by smuggling in old dichotomies. The resulting accounts, however innovative, end up consolidating "I, Native" and "I, Ethnographer" as mutually exclusive positions from which to speak and write. It's Self and Other, Us and Them, anthropologist and informant all over again. For the virtual anthropologist, in contrast, recourse to the ethnographic "I" makes nativization, exoticization, and stigmatization that much more likely to ensue. I am grateful to Geeta Patel for clarifying and queering my thinking about the work of pronouns in a text.

23. See Newton (*Mother Camp; Cherry Grove*) and Román for analyses of camp as a form of intervention and resistance. Ross is more cautious, noting the link between camp and capitalist forms of commodity fetishism.

24. On the distinction between the virtual, the simulated, and the imitative, see Rheingold; and Woolley.

25. But see Bhabha's guarded response to revisionist interpretations that treat marginality as a potential site for resistance as well as victimization. Perhaps, he comments, scholars have been too quick to celebrate the virtues of exile ("DissemiNation" 292).

26. Collins grounds her concept of "the outsider within" in African American women's work as slaves and domestic servants. She argues that the conditions of oppression responsible for locating black women's labor squarely in the domestic space of white families afford African American women a distinctive (and potentially subversive) perspective on white elites. More infiltrator than member, the outsider within occupies a vantage point that allows her to see things veiled from the privileged themselves.

27. Hybridization as a Native Ethnographer is a more complex operation than the exile that results from "discrimination," because hybridization is not an unmediated consequence of bearing the stigmata of nativity (cf. D'Emilio). Neither do center/periphery models, with their concomitant strategies of in-

clusion and critique, disrupt the process of nativization. This is a case in which Lefebvre is right to reject the geometric bent in the scholarly imagination that turns everything into a "space."

WORKS CITED

Abu-Lughod, Lila. "Writing against Culture." In *Recapturing Anthropology: Working in the Present*, ed. Richard G. Fox. Sante Fe: School of American Research Press, 1991.

Anderson, Benedict. *Imagined Communities: Reflections on the Origin and Spread of Nationalism*. London: Verso, 1983.

Anzaldúa, Gloria. *Borderlands/La Frontera: The Mestiza*. San Francisco: Spinsters/Aunt Lute, 1987.

Appadurai, Arjun. "Putting Hierarchy in Its Place." *Cultural Anthropology* 3.1 (1988): 36–49.

Asad, Talal. *Genealogies of Religion: Discipline and Reasons of Power in Christianity and Islam*. Baltimore: Johns Hopkins University Press, 1993.

Ashcroft, Bill, Gareth Griffiths, and Helen Tiffin. *The Empire Writes Back: Theory and Practice in Post-Colonial Literatures*. New York: Routledge, 1989.

Awkward, Michael. *Negotiating Difference: Race, Gender, and the Politics of Positionality*. Chicago: University of Chicago Press, 1995.

Behar, Ruth. *Translated Woman: Crossing the Border with Esperanza's Story*. Boston: Beacon Press, 1993.

Berlant, Lauren, and Elizabeth Freeman. "Queer Nationality." In *Fear of a Queer Planet: Queer Politics and Social Theory*, ed. Michael Warner, 193–229. Minneapolis: University of Minnesota Press, 1993.

Bhabha, Homi K. "DissemiNation: Time, Narrative, and the Margins of the Modern Nation." In *Nation and Narration*, ed. Homi K. Bhabha, 66–84. New York: Routledge, 1990.

———. "Of Mimicry and Man." In *The Location of Culture*, 85–92. New York: Routledge, 1994.

———. "The Other Question: Difference, Discrimination, and the Discourse of Colonialism." In *The Location of Culture*, 66–84. New York: Routledge, 1994.

Bukatman, Scott. *Terminal Identity: The Virtual Subject in Postmodern Science Fiction*. Durham: Duke University Press, 1993.

Bustos-Aguilar, Pedro. "Mister Don't Touch the Banana: Notes on the Popularity of the Ethnosexed Body South of the Border." *Critique of Anthropology* 15.2 (1995): 149–70.

Clifford, James. *The Predicament of Culture: Twentieth-Century Ethnography, Literature, and Art*. Cambridge: Harvard University Press, 1988.

Coetzee, John M. "Anthropology and the Hottentots." *Semiotica* 54.1-2 (1985): 87–95.

Collins, Patricia Hill. *Black Feminist Thought: Knowledge, Consciousness, and the Politics of Empowerment.* New York: Routledge, 1990.

Coombe, Rosemary. "The Properties of Culture and the Politics of Possessing Identity: Native Claims in the Cultural Appropriation Controversy." *Canadian Journal of Law and Jurisprudence* 6.2: 249–85.

Crapanzano, Vincent. *Tuhami: Portrait of a Moroccan.* Chicago: University of Chicago Press, 1980.

Crenshaw, Kimberlé. "Mapping the Margins: Intersectionality, Identity Politics, and Violence against Women of Color." In *After Identity: A Reader in Law and Culture,* ed. Dan Danielsen and Karen Engle. New York: Routledge, 1995.

D'Emilio, John. "Not a Simple Matter: Gay History and Gay Historians." In *Making Trouble: Essays on Gay History, Politics, and the University.* New York: Routledge, 1992.

Duggan, Lisa. "The Discipline Problem: Queer Theory Meets Lesbian and Gay History." *GLQ: A Journal of Lesbian and Gay Studies* 2.3 (1995): 179–91.

Fabian, Johannes. *Time and the Other: How Anthropology Makes Its Object.* New York: Columbia University Press, 1983.

Geertz, Clifford. *Works and Lives: The Anthropologist as Author.* Stanford: Stanford University Press, 1988.

Gordon, Deborah A. "The Politics of Ethnographic Authority: Race and Writing in the Ethnography of Margaret Mead and Zora Neale Hurston." In *Modernist Anthropology,* ed. Marc Manganaro, 145–62. Princeton: Princeton University Press, 1990.

Gupta, Akhil, and James Ferguson, eds. *Anthropological Locations: Boundaries and Grounds of a Field Science.* Berkeley: University of California Press, 1997.

Hale, Charles R. "Between Che Guevara and the Pachamama: Mestizos, Indians, and Identity Politics in the Anti-Quincentenary Campaign." *Critique of Anthropology* 14.1 (1994): 9–39.

hooks, bell. "Choosing the Margin as a Space of Radical Openness." In *Yearning: Race, Gender, and Cultural Politics,* 145–53. Boston: South End Press, 1990.

———. *Feminist Theory: From Margin to Center.* Boston: South End Press, 1984.

Jones, Delmos J. "Toward a Native Anthropology." *Human Organization* 29 (1970): 251–59.

Jones, Lisa. *Bulletproof Diva: Tales of Race, Sex, and Hair.* New York: Doubleday, 1994.

Kuper, Adam. *The Invention of Primitive Society: Transformations of an Illusion.* New York: Routledge, 1988.

Lavie, Smadar, and Ted Swedenburg. "Between and among the Boundaries of

Culture: Bridging Text and Lived Experience in the Third Timespace." *Cultural Studies* 10.1 (1996): 154–79.

Lefebvre, Henri. *The Production of Space.* Oxford: Basil Blackwell, 1991.

Limón, José. "Representation, Ethnicity, and the Precursory Ethnography: Notes of a Native Anthropologist." In *Recapturing Anthropology: Working in the Present,* ed. Richard G. Fox. Sante Fe: School of American Research Press, 1991.

Lowe, Lisa. "Heterogeneity, Hybridity, Multiplicity: Marking Asian American Differences." *Diaspora* 1.1 (1991): 24–44.

Lugones, Maria. "Purity, Impurity, and Separation." *Signs: Journal of Women in Culture and Society* 19.2 (1994): 458–79.

Madrid, Arturo. "Missing People and Others Joining Together to Expand the Circle." In *Race, Class, and Gender,* ed. Margaret L. Anderson and Patricia Hill Collins, 6–11. Belmont, CA: Wadsworth, 1992.

Martin, Biddy, and Chandra Talpady Mohanty. "Feminist Politics: What's Home Got to Do with It?" In *Feminist Studies/Critical Studies,* ed. Teresa de Lauretis, 191–212. Bloomington: Indiana University Press, 1986.

Muñoz, José. "The Autoethnographic Performance: Reading Richard Fung's Queer Hybridity." *Screen* 36.2 (1995): 83–99.

Narayan, Kirin. "How Native Is the 'Native' Anthropologist?" *American Anthropologist* 95.3 (1993): 19–34.

Nelson, Cary. "Lessons from the Job Wars: Late Capitalism Arrives on Campus." *Social Text* 13.3 (1995): 119–34.

Newton, Esther. *Cherry Grove, Fire Island: Sixty Years in America's First Gay and Lesbian Town.* Boston: Beacon Press, 1993.

———. "Lesbian and Gay Issues in Anthropology: Some Remarks to the Chairs of Anthropology Departments." Paper presented at the annual meeting of the American Anthropological Association, Washington, D.C., November 1993.

———. *Mother Camp: Female Impersonators in America.* Chicago: University of Chicago Press, 1979.

———. "My Best Informant's Dress: The Erotic Equation in Fieldwork." *Cultural Anthropology* 8.1 (1993): 2–23.

Paredes, Americo. "On Ethnographic Work among Minority Groups: A Folklorist's Perspective." In *New Directions in Chicano Scholarship,* ed. Ricardo Romo and Raymund Paredes. La Jolla, CA: Chicano Studies Monograph Series, 1978.

Patel, Geeta. "Home, Homo, Hybrid: Gender and Sexuality in South Asia." *College Literature* 24 (1997): 133–50.

Pratt, Mary Louise. "Fieldwork in Common Places." In *Writing and Culture: The Poetics and Politics of Ethnography,* ed. James Clifford and George Marcus, 27–50. Berkeley: University of California Press, 1986.

Pratt, Minnie Bruce. "Identity: Skin, Blood, Heart." In *Rebellion: Essays, 1980–1991.* Ithaca, NY: Firebrand Books, 1991.

———. *S/he.* Ithaca, NY: Firebrand Books, 1995.

Raiskin, Judith. "Inverts and Hybrids: Lesbian Rewritings of Sexual and Racial Identities." In *The Lesbian Postmodern,* ed. Laura Doan, 156–72. New York: Columbia University Press, 1994.

Rheingold, Howard. *Virtual Reality.* New York: Summit Books, 1991.

Román, David. "It's My Party and I'll Die if I Want To: Gay Men, AIDS, and the Circulation of Camp in U.S. Theater." In *Camp Grounds: Style and Homosexuality,* ed. David Román, 206–33. Amherst: University of Massachusetts Press, 1993.

Rosaldo, Renato. *Culture and Truth: The Remaking of Social Analysis.* Boston: Beacon Press, 1989.

Roseberry, William. "The Unbearable Lightness of Anthropology." Radical History Review 65 (1996): 5–25.

Ross, Andrew. "New Age Technoculture." In *Cultural Studies,* ed. Lawrence Grossberg, Cary Nelson, and Paula A. Treichler, 531–48. New York: Routledge, 1992.

Sarris, Greg. *Mabel McKay: Weaving the Dream.* Berkeley: University of California Press, 1994.

———. "What I'm Talking about When I'm Talking about My Baskets': Conversations with Mabel McKay." In *De/Colonizing the Subject,* ed. Sidonie Smith and Julia Watson, 20–33. Minneapolis: University of Minnesota Press, 1991.

Scott, Joan W. "Experience." In *Feminists Theorize the Political,* ed. Judith Butler and Joan W. Scott, 22–40. New York: Routledge, 1992.

Shostak, Marjorie. *Nisa: The Life and Words of a !Kung Woman.* Cambridge: Harvard University Press, 1981.

Smith, Stephanie A. "Morphing, Materialism, and the Marketing of Xenogenesis." *Genders* 18 (1993): 67–86.

Spivak, Gayatri Chakravorty. *The Post-Colonial Critic.* New York: Routledge, 1990.

Tate, Greg. *Flyboy in the Buttermilk: Essays on Contemporary America: An Eye-Opening Look at Race, Politics, Literature, and Music.* New York: Simon and Schuster, 1992.

Visweswaran, Kamala. *Fictions of Feminist Ethnography.* Minneapolis: University of Minnesota Press, 1994.

Vizenor, Gerald. *Crossbloods: Bone Courts, Bingo, and Other Reports.* Minneapolis: University of Minnesota Press, 1990.

West, Cornell. *Race Matters.* Boston: Beacon Press, 1993.

Weston, Kath. *Families We Choose: Lesbians, Gays, Kinship.* 2nd ed. New York: Columbia University Press, 1997.

———. "Get Thee to a Big City: Sexual Imaginary and the Great Gay Migration." *GLQ: A Journal of Lesbian and Gay Studies* 2.3 (1995): 253–77.

———. "Lesbian/Gay Studies in the House of Anthropology." *Annual Review of Anthropology* 22 (1993): 339–69.

Woolley, Benjamin. *Virtual Worlds: A Journey in Hype and Hyperreality.* Oxford: Basil Blackwell, 1992.

Yanagisako, Sylvia, and Carol Delaney, eds. *Naturalizing Power: Essays in Feminist Cultural Analysis.* New York: Routledge, 1995.

Young, Robert J. C. *Colonial Desire: Hybridity in Theory, Culture and Race.* New York: Routledge, 1995.

Zavella, Patricia. "Feminist Insider Dilemmas: Constructing Ethnic Identity with 'Chicana' Informants." *Frontiers* 13.3 (1993): 53–76.

Chapter 6

How History Matters

Complicating the Categories of "Western" and "Non-Western" Feminisms

Mrinalini Sinha

Feminism has been productively challenged in recent years by a politics that thematizes "difference" and diversity. The erstwhile representation of Western (or Anglo-American) feminism as "normative" has been displaced by the recognition of a multiplicity of feminisms. In the current pluralistic context, therefore, "non-Western" feminisms have acquired a certain cachet for their capacity to challenge the Eurocentrism that has long dominated "Western" feminism. In large part the centrality of notions of "difference" and diversity within feminism today is a measure of the success of centuries-long struggles of women of color, "Third World" women, women of the laboring classes, and gays and lesbians. Yet the frameworks within which the notions of "difference" have entered academic and popular consciousness are not strictly tied to their original articulations. From curricular changes and the demand for more "multicultural" education in the academy to the "cultural sensitivity" workshops run by transnational corporations to maximize profits worldwide, the question of "difference" occupies center stage in strikingly different arenas and for widely differing agendas.[1]

It has thus never been more urgent than at the present for critical political scholarship and for social movements interested in transformatory social change to reexamine the contemporary deployment and circulation of notions of "difference." For those of us committed to such a politics, the meanings we attach to notions of difference, as much as our understanding of difference itself, have great political urgency today. For feminists in the United States, for example, questions about "difference" have emerged on a variety of issues. Should women in the U.S. army stationed in Saudi Arabia during the Gulf War have been expected to be sensitive to, and comply with, the host country's strictures on appropriate female behavior? Should the U.S. Congress disregard claims on behalf of certain so-called traditional cultural rituals and pass legislation to prohibit the performance of such rituals as female genital surgery by certain immigrant communities in the United States? The forms in which these questions often emerge—as a choice between a respect for different cultural traditions and a feminist critique of the treatment of women in different cultures—are themselves an indication of the limitations of contemporary understandings of "difference." And how does one distinguish between such widely differing agendas as those served in the following invocations of the magical buzzword "difference": (1) the agenda of many feminists themselves who use it to question the hegemonic assumptions of a "normative" white, middle-class, and heterosexual feminism; (2) the agenda of right-wing groups in "Third World" countries who deploy it to discredit the feminist-activists in their countries as out-of-touch Westernized feminists; and (3) the agenda of some leading women activists in "Third World" countries, like Madhu Kishwar of India, who disclaim the label "feminist" to represent their own political struggles as distinct from those waged by feminists in the West (see Kishwar)?

These questions are an indication of the current impasse in responses to the politics of difference; in addition, such questions reflect the centrality of notions of difference in the academic and popular discourses in the present times. If feminism's response to the call for more non-Western feminisms is inadequate under these conditions, the inadequacy arises precisely because feminist thought often does not historicize sufficiently the material conditions under which notions of "difference" are raised. The current concern with "difference" is also determined in contradictory ways by the contemporary historical moment: the imperatives of a U.S.-dominated "new world order" and its international allies; the deflection of internal social tensions in developing and developed nations in the rise of religious fundamentalisms and in the anti-immigrant and antiminority backlash; the patrolling of the boundaries of culture and community through control over women's bodies and women's sexualities; the increasing polarization between the North and the South or the "First" and "Third" Worlds after the collapse of the socialist "Second" World; the displacement of older forms of social movements with a new politics more sensitive to "local" contexts and to the intersections of racial, class, gender, sexual, and ethnic identities; and, above all, the precariousness of a viable and forward-looking politics of difference in the era of late capitalism marked by globalizing and homogenizing impulses, on the one hand, and the underpinning of a variety of "ethnic absolutisms"[2] on the other. The task for a critical and effective politics of difference today lies in relating the production and circulation of difference—as academic and popular commodity, as political slogan, as lived experience—to contemporary material conditions.[3]

The discipline of history, and imperial historiography in particular, provides us with models for responding to this challenge. The recent historiography of nineteenth- and twentieth-century Britain and India contains some crucial implications for contemporary responses to the politics of difference. The intersections of the histories of Britain and India in the history of imperialism illustrate the limits of challenging the Eurocentrism of "Western" feminism by simply calling for more "non-Western" feminism. Indeed, the histories of feminism in Britain and India demonstrate not only the inadequacy of a model that merely contrasts Western and non-Western feminisms, but also the necessity of revising feminism as a whole from a "global" perspective.[4]

First of all, the history of feminism in Britain exposes the full implications of the politics of difference for an understanding of Western feminism. Feminism in Britain bears the inescapable traces of its "imperial location." It exposes as inadequate efforts to give token acknowledgment to, and thereafter separate, the imperial and racial legacy of Victorian and Edwardian feminism as if they were merely discrete elements of the feminist past. Victorian and Edwardian feminism in Britain was at every level the product of an imperial social formation (see especially Burton). The lessons of history, then, require consideration of how the current understanding of feminism has been shaped by feminism's imperial location. Indeed, coming to terms with feminism's imperial legacy necessarily entails a revising of feminism itself.

The imperial dimension of British feminism has only recently begun to attract full attention. So long as the historiography of British imperialism has been dominated by a "centrifugal" model of imperial influence radiating from Britain to its colonies overseas, the impact of imperialism on the *domestic* history of Britain itself has remained somewhat obscured.[5] Hence it is only recently that the full implications of imperialism for the history of women in Britain—extending to the very character of British feminism itself—have begun to receive any serious attention. New trends in both imperial and feminist history—and their productive coming together in the most provocative recent histories of British feminism—have made it impossible to ignore the inseparability of middle-class women's activism (and early feminism generally in Britain) from the imperial context from which it emerged.

Even the significance of white women to the empire, moreover, has been a relatively new field of interest. Traditional imperial historiography has long subscribed to the view that if the British Empire was not quite acquired in a "fit of absence of mind," it was nevertheless acquired in a "fit of absence of wives."[6] The stuff of imperial mythology in India, therefore, has been built typically on the "masculine" world of the British in the late eighteenth and early nineteenth centuries, before the arrival of white women in large numbers, and on the romance of the "frontier" provinces, where white women were conspicuous by their absence almost up to the end of the empire itself. When white women were mentioned at all, it was usually to bemoan the impact of their arrival on the "easy" social and sexual mores of the expatriate British community in India. Since the arrival of white women in India also came on the heels of a number of reforms that regulated the expatriate British society and brought it into greater conformity with the changing norms of a "Victorian" British society, white women were made into convenient scapegoats in both imperial mythology and traditional imperial historiography for the (male) ambivalence toward these changes (see Strobel; and Midgley). The widening of the "racial gulf" between indigenous and Victorian British society, for example, was often attributed to women's greater inherent capacity for racism[7] and, in more recent variations of the same theme, to the "strident puritanical" bent of feminists in particular who lobbied to limit the field of "sexual opportunity" once available to white men as compensation for risks incurred in the Great Game of empire.[8]

Even with the burgeoning of "women's history" scholarship on white women and the empire, there was at first little interest in bringing the impact of empire back "home" to Britain. Until very recently, therefore, the historiography on white women and imperialism was limited to the history of white women who actually went out to the colonies or who had some direct connection to the colonies. Much of this early scholarship, in fact, was primarily concerned with compensating for the representation of white women in traditional imperial historiography; it was preoccupied with the task of rescuing white women in the empire from the disdain of posterity.[9] In recent years, however, there has been a shift away from this earlier more celebratory approach to the history of white women in the colonies. The current scholarship on white women and empire has been largely structured around the twin poles of "complicity and resistance"—and often both simultaneously—to illustrate the contradictions arising from the peculiar intersection of racist and sexist dynamics in the colonial context.[10] White women's roles in the colonies, as *memsahibs* or housewives, as social reformers, as missionaries, and as activists for one cause or another, have been reassessed through this paradigm. The current scholarship, moreover, points out the importance of white women to the "patriarchal racism"[11] that sustained the construction and projection of whiteness in the colonies. Indeed, as Ann Stoler has argued, the control of white women was the central basis for the drawing and policing of racial boundaries, for the race- and class-specific self-identification of "whites" in the colonies.

It has been impossible, moreover, for the historiography on women and feminism in Britain to remain immune to the vastly expanded domain for the study of white women and the empire. At its best, the history of white women in the colonies has always had implications for stay-at-home women in Britain. So, as the historian Janaki Nair has shown, white women's writings on the *zenana* or the female quarters in elite and upper-caste homes in northern India reveal more about the climate of women's reform in Britain than about the *zenanas* themselves: in the first half of the nineteenth century, white women tended to compare the *zenana*, seen as the symbol of outdated tradition and superstition, most unfavorably with the more enlightened domestic arrangements in Britain. By the end of the century, however, the antifeminist backlash in Britain produced a more sympathetic picture of the *zenana* as a testimony to the high spiritual ideals of service and sacrifice of the Hindu wife (see Nair). The history of women and women's reforms in nineteenth-century Britain and India demonstrate, as Kumkum Sangari writes, "that colonial states and cultural formations established under the aegis of imperialism have spread across 'national' boundaries."

That British women's *own* emancipation may have been shaped by Britain's imperial connection with India, however, is perhaps the most important insight to emerge from the historiography on women and imperialism. Antoinette Burton, more than most other scholars, has attempted to establish the nature of this connection. Burton argues that stay-at-home British feminists, perhaps even more than the usual suspects (white female missionaries, philanthropists, social reformers, and *memsahibs* who actually went out to the colonies), were active collaborators in the ideological work of empire. British feminists—as much as other British women social reformers and missionaries—adopted a position that Barbara Ramusack has aptly called "maternal imperialism" in their relations with Indian feminists and Indian women. The very self-representation of liberal middle-class feminism in nineteenth- and twentieth-century Britain was tied to the imperial connection. The leading feminist journals of the time were constant reminders to their growing numbers of readers of Britain's imperial mission: there were advertisements for jobs and opportunities for white women in the far corners of the empire; periodical progress reports on the good work being done by white women overseas; and constant appeals to the "white woman's burden" in bringing civilization to an assorted group of benighted native sisters. That feminist literature from this period was suffused with discussions of the "long suffering Indian woman" is not in itself surprising. More interesting, perhaps, is Burton's argument that the representation of the "Indian woman" had less to do with the uplifting of Indian women per se and more with the emancipation of British women themselves. The image of the helpless Indian woman in British feminist literature served the purpose, above all, of legitimizing the claims of British women suffragists to political agency and to the moral responsibility they had for representing their colonial sisters in India.

What is important to note, however, is not just that feminist journals and organizations in Britain were saturated with imperial rhetoric nor that British feminists justified their own demands on the basis of their imperial responsibilities, but that the imperial alliance had serious consequences for the realization of the radical potential of feminism for white, middle-class British women themselves. The failure to connect patriarchal privileges at home with "patriarchal racism" abroad allowed feminist challenges to be easily recuperated for the reordering of a hierarchical social order. In 1883 feminist circles in Britain publicly endorsed white women's unprecedented mobilization in India in defense of their racial privileges—a movement that was based on the argument that white men alone could be the "natural" protectors of white women. The negative impact of this legacy on the development of feminism in Britain thus went well beyond the failure to commit feminism to racial equality (see Sinha, "Lineage"). Here British feminists, in aligning themselves with the racial ideology of imperialism, were also limiting the demand for autonomy even for white, middle-class British women. That imperial ideology was hardly conducive to the emancipation of even white middle-class women would become clear not long after, when imperialists like Lord Curzon and Lord Milner invoked the empire in defense of their diehard antisuffrage stand in Britain (see Harrison). It was the imperial connection, moreover, that enabled the "New Woman" to be recruited for eugenics-based movements and for reactionary glorifications of "motherhood" in the early twentieth century in Britain (see Davin). Recent feminist historiography has thus made inescapable the implications for British feminism of its location in an imperial social formation. The feminist engagement with imperial history, then, takes the challenge of "difference" to the very heart of Western feminism itself. It illustrates that only a feminism fully reconceived from a global perspective can respond to the imperial and racial legacy of the nineteenth- and twentieth-century feminist past.

Second, and no less crucially, the history of feminism in colonial India illustrates the importance of engaging more fully with "non-Western" feminisms in their particular contexts. When non-Western feminisms are invoked simply to counter the dominance of Western feminism, the specificity of non-Western feminisms themselves in terms of their own social location is seldom engaged. Defined purely through their binary opposition to "Western" feminism, so-called non-Western feminisms are inevitably reified into tokens of "diversity." In such a capacity, then, Indian feminism gets invoked merely to resolve an "identity crisis" of a feminism wanting to prove its non-racist credentials. A serious engagement with the histories of non-Western feminisms, however, would quickly reveal that non-Western feminisms in themselves cannot offer any panacea for revising feminism as a whole.

While the recent historiography of feminism in colonial India has offered sophisticated analyses of Indian feminism's relationship with British imperialism, Indian nationalism, and British and Western feminism, its major contribution lies in the recognition that "nowhere can or have reforms been directed at patriarchies alone, but they have also been involved in re-aligning patriarchy with social stratification (both existing and emerging) and with changing political formations" (Sangari and Vaid). Much of the early feminist historiography on feminism in colonial India, however, examined Indian feminism against the background of a normative Western model of feminism and found the former wanting. Scholars like Kumari Jayawardena thus concluded that the symbiotic relationship between Indian feminism and Indian nationalism prevented the development of a "revolutionary feminist consciousness" in colonial India. Yet the point of historicizing feminism, whether in Britain or in India, should be to go beyond ahistorical models of some normative feminism and to locate each feminism in the context of the historical conditions of its emergence.

The nature of the relationship between Indian feminism and Indian nationalism was shaped by a variety of historical factors, including the contradictions of the colonial state. During much of the nineteenth century in India, the colonial state supported a variety of social reform legislation for women in India in keeping with its civilizing mission. While in nineteenth-century Indian society the question of women's reform was initially debated almost exclusively in male social reformer circles, both orthodox and educated middle-class women slowly began to produce their own contributions to the reform debate (see Forbes). Some individual women and women's journals and reform organizations in India went on to support reform legislation, often against male cultural nationalists, who, by the end of the century, had become much more defensive about colonial interference in indigenous cultural and religious practices.[12] The example of Pandita Ramabai, Ramabai Modak, Kadambini Ganguly, and the numerous women's meetings held in support of the controversial Age of Consent Act of 1891, despite the widespread nationalist agitation against the measure led by the nationalist leader Bal Gangadhar Tilak, is a case in point (see Anandhi; Rani; Pickering). While Indian women and their organizations also cooperated with the nationalist movement against the colonial state on a number of occasions, throughout the century women activists were just as likely to turn to the colonial state for protective legislation for women. The withdrawal of the colonial state from the field of social reform and its effort to consolidate support for the colonial state from orthodox and reactionary elements in indigenous society disillusioned women activists about the "modernizing" role of the colonial state. In the early twentieth century the organized women's movement in India, even when it maintained its independence from one or the other of the political parties in India, was forced to recognize the obstructionist role of the state and turn to modernizing groups within the Indian National Congress and other independent Indian legislators for securing the passage of reform legislations for women (see Sinha, "Lineage").

The symbiotic relationship that developed between the organized women's movement and the official nationalist movement, especially after the emergence of M. K. Gandhi as the leader of the nationalist movement in India in the 1920s, had important consequences for the shape of middle-class Indian feminism. The energies of the Indian women's movement in colonial India were directed much more successfully toward dismantling the orthodox indigenous patriarchy than toward challenging the "new nationalist patriarchy" that was being set in place by a middle-class and upper-caste–dominated nationalist movement (see Sinha, "Lineage"). Despite official histories of the close alliance between the nationalist movement and the organized women's movement, the struggles of individual women as well as the discussions in Indian feminist journals of the time reveal a much greater divergence of views than has been presumed. Feminist critiques of nationalist patriarchy in India have received far less attention partly because they always had to negotiate simultaneously with the more dramatic confrontations between nationalism and imperialism. Feminist historiography still needs to pay much more attention to the less visible and less public side of the feminist movement in colonial India.

The point of reassessing Indian feminism in colonial India, however, is not to set up a heroic alternative either to nationalist patriarchy or to an imperialist Western feminism. Instead, the point is precisely to historicize Indian feminism in the context of the material conditions of its emergence. From such a perspective the alliance between Indian feminism and Indian nationalism was as much about the empowerment of women of particular class and caste backgrounds as about the co-optation of feminism by nationalism. Indian nationalism thus empowered the vision of Indian women against both British women and Indian men for the emancipation of women in India. While Indian feminists frequently turned to British feminist and international feminist networks to support their struggles in India, they also waged a constant struggle for equality and respect within these feminist communities. Indian feminists frequently protested the "maternal imperialism" of Western feminists. In the 1920s the representatives of the organized women's conference in India protested their second-class status at an international women's movement in Geneva by unfurling the national flag of India and insisting on taking their place as equal members of the conference (cited in Sinha, "Women's Suffrage"). When the leading British feminist Eleanore Rathbone organized a conference in London on the nature of the responsibility of British women's organizations for the advancement of women in India, Indian feminists in London publicly denounced the exclusion of Indian feminists from the conference platform as a feminist variation on the theme of the "White Man's Burden." Dhanvanthi Rama Rao, a member of three major all-India women's organizations in India, insisted that the work for women in India had to be done by Indian women's organizations themselves, to which British women could only offer assistance (cited in Sinha, "Reading Mother India"). It was due to the success of the nationalist challenges posed by Indian feminists that most British feminist organizations were forced by the 1930s to work with representative Indian women and with the organized women's movement in all matters concerning women in India. The national framework allowed the elite women's organizations in India to emerge as the legitimate representative of all Indian women. In turn, the elite Indian women's organizations also helped consolidate official Indian nationalism against the challenges posed by nonelite or subaltern movements in colonial India. The ideology of nationalism had allowed the predominantly elite/middle-class and upper-caste women in the organized women's movement in India to claim a position for themselves in a male-dominated public sphere; it also served to consolidate the dominance of their class and caste in the nationalist construction of India.

What has received less attention until recently, however, is precisely how this alliance between nationalism and feminism also marginalized alternative constructions of the nation and visions of women's emancipation in various subaltern or nonelite movements (see Geetha and Rajadurai). Several of the subaltern movements, like the anti-caste Self-Respect Movement of Madras, offered stringent critiques of their own of the gender as well as the caste and class privileges in the dominant nationalist construction of India (see Anandhi; Rani; Pickering). The anti-caste Self-Respect Movement tended to see caste and gender hierarchies as inseparable in their critiques of the dominant nationalist construct of India. The organized women's movement, however, still tended to frame its critique of gender hierarchies within a dominant nationalist framework, which ultimately aligned the women's movement with official Indian nationalism behind a more inegalitarian social order. The history of Indian feminism thus cautions us against simply celebrating the challenge that non-Western feminisms pose to Western feminism. When the history of non-Western feminisms is engaged seriously, as is the history of Western feminism, it becomes necessary to qualify the radical potential in simply substituting a multiplicity of non-Western feminisms for a singular normative feminism. The engagement with history demands that we reconceive feminism—Western and non-Western—to engage adequately with the challenge of the politics of difference.

Finally, and perhaps most importantly, the history of the reconstitution of "Hindu" culture in colonial India raises some important questions about the now sacrosanct notion of cultural difference preserved in such dichotomies as Western and non-Western feminisms. The image of the Indian *sati*, the upper-caste Hindu widow who immolates herself on her husband's funeral pyre, became for generations of imperialists and nationalists alike the symbol of Hindu and/or Indian cultural difference. More than a century after the practice of *sati* has been made illegal, certain Hindu fundamentalist and other right-wing organizations in India not only defend a woman's right to commit *sati*, but label its opponents deracinated and Westernized Indians (see Rajan; Oldenburg). The recent feminist historiography on *sati,* however, exposes how "Hindu" culture was in fact reconstituted under colonial rule to make *sati* into a contested symbol of cultural authenticity for Hindus.

The unprecedented epidemic of *satis* in eighteenth- and early-nineteenth-century Bengal was not some manifestation of a timeless "Hindu" culture, but a response to the social, economic, and political uncertainties of the period. Although self-immolation existed as one among many options prescribed for upper-caste widows in some ancient Brahmanical texts in India, it had never assumed anything like a general prescription for even elite and upper-caste women in India. Historians like Ashis Nandy have tried to offer materialist explanations for the emergence of the *sati* epidemic in Bengal (see Nandy). The period of uncertainty after the decline of the authority of the Bengal Nawabs and before the consolidation of the power of the British East India Company was one of great social stress. Under the changing economic times, widows in Bengal—the one province where widows could inherit the property of their deceased husbands—were often encouraged by family members to immolate themselves so that it was the family who retained control over the widow's property. The rise of parvenu native groups who profited in connection with their relation to the East India Company, moreover, led more traditional elite groups to retain their status through the rediscovery of certain upper-caste rituals as *sati.*[13] The timing of the *sati* epidemic and its location—mainly in the province of Bengal, where the British had begun the task of consolidating their colonial regime—supports the political and material explanations for the practice.

Yet, until recently, the historiography on *sati* as much as the popular debate over *sati* has focused only on ahistorical cultural explanations. This is due at least in part to the ways culture itself got reconstituted in India under the aegis of colonialism. Eighteenth-century Europeans were captivated with both horror and admiration for the Hindu wife's gruesome proof of her devotion to her husband even after his death (see Mani, "Production" and "Contentious Traditions"). Humanitarian condemnation of the practice by British and Indian reformers, however, urged some form of intervention on the part of the colonial state. While the colonial state rightly deserves credit for eventually abolishing the practice in 1829, it also carries the dubious distinction of having been the first and only all-India power to provide a positive legal sanction for *sati* in an earlier legislation of 1813. The 1813 colonial legislation, while disallowing "bad" *satis* that entailed force and coercion, allowed "good" *satis* that did not entail the use of force and were allegedly in accordance with the prescriptions of ancient Brahmanical scriptures. The state officials, as they had to monitor the use or absence of force in individual *satis,* now became directly involved in the performance of *sati.* The subsequent rise in the number of *satis,* as well as the persistent protests from Indian and British reformers, led the government to abolish *sati* finally in 1829.

The real legacy of the colonial intervention on *sati,* as demonstrated in Lata Mani's highly influential work, was the particular reconstitution of Hindu culture: it promoted a "textual" interpretation of Hindu culture based on ancient scriptural texts as opposed to the actual customs and practices of the people.[14] Out of both political and administrative imperatives during the early years of Company rule, British scholars-cum-administrators were engaged in codifying "Hindu" and "Islamic" scriptural texts to provide the basis for civil legislation under colonial rule. In the very process of codifying ancient scriptures and converting them into rulebooks for understanding contemporary culture, the colonial state drastically altered both the scriptures themselves and the natural evolution of culture from the interaction of tradition with actual historical practices. Confronted with the necessity of an official response to *sati,* therefore, the colonial state first turned to Brahmanical scriptures for precedents. Moreover, as Lata Mani has shown, colonial officials sought clarity and certainty from the scriptures and were thus impatient with the more ambivalent responses of their native informants on the status of *sati* in the scriptures. The 1813 legislation reflected not only the authoritative colonial interpretation of *sati* as a practice sanctioned by the scriptures, but also an important step in putting into practice the colonial "textual" interpretation of Hindu culture. The result of the nature of the colonial intervention was that the subsequent debate on *sati* in India got framed purely in terms of a scriptural authority that ignored the political and material conditions for *sati.* Both Indian reformers who supported the abolishing of *sati* and orthodox Indians who defended the practice now sought to defend their respective positions primarily on the basis of centuries-old textual authorities. This textual interpretation of Hindu culture became the new "common sense" among Britons and Indians alike. It was from this understanding of Hindu culture—based on the timeless authority of ancient scriptural texts—that *sati* could be converted into a crucial terrain for competing definitions of an unquestioned and essentialist Hindu (and often Indian) cultural identity. The recent feminist historiography on *sati* in colonial India—especially the contributions of Lata Mani—forces us to reexamine the reification of cultural difference either in defensive arguments about cultural purity and authenticity or in paternalist arguments in favor of a hands-off cultural relativism.

From a global perspective, furthermore, it becomes instructive to compare the trajectory of the historiography on *sati* in eighteenth-century India with that of the witch-hunts in Europe and North America in the sixteenth and seventeenth centuries. Although both the *sati* and the witch-hunt epidemics were manifestations of larger political and social upheavals of their times, they have occupied very different places in understandings of Indian and Euro-American cultures respectively. The nature of the colonial intervention and the subsequent politicization of culture in colonial India—shaped alike by colonialist denunciations and nationalist defenses of indigenous culture—ensured that the dominant debate on *sati* remained within the limited framework of a timeless cultural misogyny. The point of much recent feminist historiography on *sati,* therefore, has been to examine the debate on *sati* in colonial India in terms of discontinuity rather than continuity with indigenous tradition. The major aspect of the discontinuity, as Mani's work demonstrates, was that the debate on *sati* in colonial India was not really about women as such, but about competing understandings of Hindu tradition and culture.

The thrust of the recent feminist historiography on the European witch-hunts, however, has been in an opposite direction. Since, as the feminist historian Elspeth Whitney points out, the standard historiography has tended to see the European witch-hunts mainly in terms of such factors as early modern "state-building, economic and social stresses, and the relationship of folk and elite culture," gender has "fallen out" as a category of analysis in explanations of the hunt. The point for Whitney and others, therefore, is to re-emphasize the place of women and the significance of misogyny in explanations of the hunts. From this perspective, moreover, the witch-hunts appear less as a new phenomenon and more as part of a continuing tradition by which various outsider groups had been persecuted in early modern Europe. Viewed thus, the truly new or distinctive aspect of the witch-hunts compared to the earlier persecutions was precisely that so many of the witches were women. The recent feminist historiographies on the witch-hunts and *sati* have been important in their own—very different—ways in challenging received assumptions about the witch-hunts and *sati*. Yet there is a further point to be made in bringing these two different historiographical traditions together: they point to the historical contingency for predominantly "culturalist" or "materialist" explanations for such phenomena as *sati* and witch-hunts. Indeed, together they foreground how different locations within the imperial social formation have widely different implications for the production and circulation of notions of cultural difference.

The study of history from a global perspective, indeed, shows the limits of such halfway measures as the contemporary "affirmation" or "celebration" of difference. The real challenge of the politics of difference consists not in merely celebrating "difference," but in situating difference in a truly global history. The construction of cultural difference itself is always the product of particular material histories. This means that contemporary efforts to revise feminism in response to the politics of difference must go beyond the binary opposition between Western and non-Western feminisms. To take the categories of Western and non-Western as given is to efface their mutually imbricated history. It is important that we pay attention to that history precisely because it contextualizes difference and demonstrates the mutual constitution of what gets understood as Western as well as non-Western within what must now be analyzed as a single imperial social formation.

NOTES

I would like to thank Clement Hawes and Lynn Lyerly for their critical reading of this essay.

1. For a discussion of the problematic implications of the commodification of "multiculturalism," see Shohat and Stam.
2. The phrase is from Gilroy.
3. For a critique of these trends, see Dirlik.
4. For an argument for a "global social analytic," see Hennessy.

5. For an early articulation for a "centripetal," rather than a "centrifugal," model for the study of imperialism, see Mackenzie.

6. The original phrase, of course, is by J. R. Seeley, the doyen of British imperial history. Ronald Hyam plays on Seeley's phrase in *Britain's Imperial Century*.

7. For the prevalence of this myth in the historiography of British India, see Spear 140.

8. See Hyam, "Empire and Sexual Opportunity" and *Empire and Sexuality: The British Experience*. For an insightful critique of an earlier formulation of Hyam's thesis, see Berger.

9. For a critique of this literature, see Haggis.

10. For a discussion of this scholarship, see Formes.

11. The phrase is from Loomba.

12. For a history of nationalist retreat from social reform, see Heimsath; and Chatterjee.

13. The above argument is from Nandy.

14. The above argument is drawn from Mani, "Production of an Official Discourse" and "Contentious Traditions."

WORKS CITED AND CONSULTED

Anagol-McGinn, Padma. "The Age of Consent Act (1891) Reconsidered: Women's Perspectives and Participation in the Child-Marriage Controversy in India." *South Asia Research* 12.2 (1992): 100–18.

Anandhi, S. "Women's Question in the Dravidian Movement c. 1925–1948." *Social Scientist* 19.5-6 (1991): 24–41.

Berger, Mark T. "Imperialism and Sexual Exploitation: A Response to Ronald Hyam's 'Empire and Sexual Opportunity,'" *Journal of Imperial and Commonwealth History* 17.1 (1988): 83–99.

Burton, Antoinette. *Burdens of History: British Feminists, Indian Women, and Imperial Culture, 1865–1915*. Chapel Hill: University of North Carolina Press, 1994.

Chakravarti, Uma. *Rewriting History: The Life and Times of Pandita Ramabai*. New Delhi: Kali, 1998.

Chatterjee, Partha. "The Nationalist Resolution of the Women's Question." In *Recasting Women: Essays in Indian Colonial History*, ed. K. Sangari and S. Vaid, 233–53. New Brunswick: Rutgers University Press, 1990.

Davin, Anna. "Imperialism and Motherhood." In *Tensions of Empire*, ed. F. Cooper and A. Stoler, 87–153. Berkeley: University of California Press, 1997.

Dirlik, Arif. *The Postcolonial Aura*. Boulder: Westview, 1997.

Forbes, Geraldine. *The New Cambridge History of India: Women in Modern India.* Cambridge: Cambridge University Press, 1996.

Formes, Malia B. "Complicity versus Resistance: Recent Work on Gender and European Imperialism." *Journal of Social History* 28.3 (1995): 629–41.

Geetha, V., and S. V. Rajadurai. "One Hundred Years of Brahminitude: Arrival of Annie Besant." *Economic and Political Weekly* 30.28 (1995): 1768–73.

Gilroy, Paul. "'The Whisper Wakes, the Shudder Plays': 'Race,' Nation and Ethnic Absolutism." In *Contemporary Postcolonial Theory: A Reader,* ed. Padmini Mongia, 248–74. London: Arnold, 1996.

Haggis, Jane. "Gendering Colonialism or Colonising Gender? Recent Women's Studies Approaches to White Women and the History of British Colonialism." *Women's Studies International Forum* 13 (1990): 105–15.

Harrison, B. *Separate Spheres: The Opposition to Women's Suffrage in Britain.* New York: Holmes and Meier, 1978.

Heimsath, Charles. *Indian Nationalism and Hindu Social Reform.* Princeton: Princeton University Press, 1964.

Hennessy, Rosemary. *Materialist Feminism and the Politics of Discourse.* London: Routledge, 1993.

Hyam, Ronald. *Britain's Imperial Century.* Basingstoke: Macmillan, 1993.

———. *Empire and Sexuality: The British Experience.* Manchester: Manchester University Press, 1990.

———. "Empire and Sexual Opportunity." *Journal of Imperial and Commonwealth History* 14.2 (1986): 34–89.

Jayawardena, Kumari. *Feminisms and Nationalism in the Third World.* London: Zed Books, 1986.

Kishwar, Madhu. "Why I Do Not Call Myself a Feminist." *Manushi* 61 (1990): 2–8.

Loomba, Ania. *Gender, Race and Renaissance Drama.* Manchester: Manchester University Press, 1989.

Mackenzie, John. *Propaganda and Empire.* Manchester: Manchester University Press, 1984.

Mani, Lata. "Contentious Traditions: The Debate on Sati in Colonial India." *Cultural Critique* 7 (1987): 119–56.

———. "The Production of an Official Discourse on Sati in Early 19th Century Bengal." *Economic and Political Weekly* 21.17 (1986): WS32–WS40.

Midgley, Claire. *Gender and Imperialism.* Manchester: Manchester University Press, 1997.

Nair, Janaki. "Uncovering the Zenana: Visions of Indian Womanhood in Englishwomen's Writings, 1813–1941." *Journal of Women's History* 2.1 (1991): 8–34.

Nandy, Ashis. "Sati: A Nineteenth Century Tale of Women, Violence and

Protest." In *At The Edge of Psychology: Essays in Politics and Culture,* 1–31. New Delhi: Oxford University Press, 1980.

Oldenburg, Veena Talwar. "The Roop Kanwar Case: Feminist Responses." In *Sati, The Blessing and the Curse,* ed. John Stratton Hawley, 101–30. New York: Oxford University Press, 1994.

Pickering, Natalie. "Recasting the Indian Nation: Dravidian Nationalism Replies to the Women's Question." *Thatched Patio* 6 (1993): 1–20.

Rajan, Rajeswari Sunder. "The Subject of Sati: Pain and Death in the Contemporary Discourse on Sati." *Yale Journal of Criticism* 3.2 (1990): 1–23.

Ramusack, Barbara. "Cultural Missionaries, Maternal Imperialists, Feminist Allies: British Women Activists in India, 1865–1945." In *Western Women and Imperialism: Complicity and Resistance.* ed. M. Strobel and N. Chaudhuri, 119–36. Bloomington: Indiana University Press, 1992.

Rani, Prabha. "Women's Indian Association and the Self Respect Movement in Madras, 1925–1936: Perceptions on Women." Paper presented at the Third National Conference on Women's Studies, Chandigarh, October 1986.

Sangari, Kumkum. "Relating Histories: Definitions of Literacy, Literature, Gender in Early Nineteenth Century Calcutta and England." In *Rethinking English,* ed. Svati Johsi, 32–123. New Delhi: Trianka, 1991.

Sangari K., and S. Vaid. "Recasting Women: An Introduction." In *Recasting Women: Essays in Indian Colonial History,* ed. K. Sangari and S. Vaid, 1–26. New Brunswick: Rutgers University Press, 1990.

Shohat, Ella, and Robert Stam, eds. *Unthinking Eurocentrism: Multiculturalism and the Media.* New York: Routledge, 1994.

Sinha, Mrinalini. *Colonial Masculinity: The "Manly Englishman" and the "Effeminate Bengali" in the Late Nineteenth Century.* Manchester: Manchester University Press, 1995.

———. "The Lineage of the Indian Modern: Rhetoric, Agency and the Sarda Act in Late Colonial India." In *Gender, Sexuality and Colonial Modernities,* ed. A. Burton. London: Routledge, 1999.

———. "Reading Mother India: Empire, Nation and the Female Voice." *Journal of Women's History* 6.2 (1994): 6–44.

———. "Women's Suffrage and the Modernization of the Imperial State: Enfranchised Women in Britain and India." *Elusive Sisterhood: Citizenship, Nation and Race in the British Empire,* ed. I. Fletcher, P. Levine, and L. Mayhall. London: Routledge, forthcoming.

Spear, Percival. *The Nabobs.* London: Oxford University Press, 1963.

Stoler, Ann. "Making Empire Respectable: The Politics of Race and Sexuality in 20th Century Colonial Cultures." *American Ethnologist* 16.4 (1989): 634–60.

Strobel, Margaret. *Gender, Sex and Empire*. American Historical Association pamphlet, 1993.

Whitney, Elspeth. "International Trends: The Witch 'She'/The Historian 'He': Gender and the Historiography of the European Witch-Hunts." *Journal of Women's History* 7.3 (1995): 77–101.

Chapter 7

Bringing It All Home to the Bacon
A Ph.D. (Packinghouse Daughter)
Examines Her Legacy

Cheri Register

For several years, I balked at writing a memoir that nevertheless struggled onto my computer screen in the form of loosely connected vignettes and essays. I cringed with embarrassment when people asked what I was working on. A memoir in middle age is the literary cliché of the moment. Imagine a whole Baby Boom's worth of personal confessions! In Minneapolis, where I live, the midwestern coming-of-age story is especially scorned, like Wonder Bread shelved among tastier, grainier loaves. I harbor plenty of internal critics, as well. One scolded that if I were a better writer, I would do this as fiction. Another, my academic self, insisted that with more scholarly patience, I could turn it into historical research. Then I could take comfort in accuracy and give up my compulsive pursuit of an elusive literary truth.

The truth I had set out to recover is itself inhibiting. The culture of my upbringing, which I mean to describe truthfully, does not listen eagerly to voices that set themselves apart. "She's always been real differ'nt," I can hear my classmates and neighbors intone. The self-presentation at the heart of the memoir genre is heard as self-aggrandizement where I come from: Albert Lea, an industrial town of eighteen thousand in the southern Minnesota corn-and-soybean belt. I left Albert Lea at eighteen, equipped with several scholarships, to lead the Life of the Mind, extolled in the University of Chicago's recruitment literature as the noblest of human endeavors. As a writer, I retrieve words and images from my mental catalog, take frequent strolls through my memory, and draw on my subconscious for inspiration. The mind is where I live now. I only visit Albert Lea. That puts my entitlement to the story I am telling in question.

I came of age in Albert Lea's working class in the 1960s. My Mom worked part-time as a dollar-an-hour salesclerk, and my Dad is a retired packinghouse worker, employed for thirty years at Wilson and Company, at that time Albert Lea's major industry. The blue-collar culture of my childhood is easily stereotyped and steadily disappearing, two facts that compel me to write about it. The packinghouse itself is a casualty of industrial "downsizing" and corporate flight. The slaughter operation has been closed down, leaving less than a quarter of the peak workforce to process meat trucked in from low-wage suppliers. The way of life from which my habits and values spring is becoming a figment of middle-aged memory, and memoir may be the most suitable form to contain it.

As I ventured to show pieces of my memoir to friends and writers of other backgrounds, I learned that the story I tell is somewhat exotic. The public image of working-class life has been distorted by a mythology I first encountered at the University of Chicago in the politicized sixties. The packinghouse families of my childhood neither endured Dust Bowl poverty nor engaged in radical politics, nor were they urban or "white ethnic," unless you stretch the term to include second- and third-generation Scandinavian Americans. Towns like Albert Lea have never been a likely subject for literature, though readers may think that Sinclair Lewis's *Main Street* or Garrison Keillor's Lake Wobegon says it all. My preliminary readers, friendly critics to whom this story is fresh and unfamiliar, urged me to drop my hesitation and proceed.

I am not the best person to tell this story, only the most likely. I have never worked in the packinghouse, nor in any other blue-collar job. I am thirty years removed from working-class life—an escapee, in fact, who once sought refuge from the divisiveness of social class in the neutrality and objectivity of academe. My education marks me as an outsider now and limits my access to this place where I once belonged. I barely know the story I long to tell, yet it has shaped the life story I have been telling myself all these years. I *can* write with authority and authenticity about leaving home—in a larger, more turbulent sense than geographic relocation—and about rediscovering the aspects of home I unwittingly carried with me. The packinghouse, "the plant" in local lingo, does occupy the center of that story. Though I was allowed inside only once, on an eye-bulging, nose-pinching, ambition-boosting sixth-grade field trip, it dominates my memories of Albert Lea. Its smoky stench, its noon whistle, its mooing and squealing truckloads of freight, its radio livestock market broadcasts find their way into my writing, as image and as atmosphere. Sometimes they carry meaning. Sometimes they are simply there, as given features of daily life.

All along, I have wanted to narrate this story in a collective voice, to make it a much less selfish "documentary-memoir." I began by interviewing high school classmates about the Sixties, intending to challenge the current nostalgia for that era, which generally omits the experience of working-class youth, except perhaps as fatalities of the Vietnam War. That topic proved to be of little interest to my interviewees. I found myself listening most intently as they talked about their parents' work and its impact on their life's decisions. Bob, who designs bridges and freeway interchanges, talked of seeing his father on that field trip, trimming fat off a hunk of beef in a room that felt intolerably cold and damp. Bill, chair of the fine arts department at a large institution, told me the only clue he had to what his dad did all day was the odor of the closet where he kept his work clothes. I could tell the story of upward mobility, I realized, and of survivors' guilt, an emotion tainted with condescension. But I didn't want to disregard Steve, who was longing, in his forties, to get out of the packinghouse before they carried him out, nor his coworkers who have held on, despite the high rate of injury, because processing food is necessary, honest work that, until the 1980s, also paid decently—for a blue-collar wage.

A friend and fellow writer helped me see that I was already using a collective voice. My narrative blends "I" and "we," which usually stands for "we Albert Lea kids" as I remember "us." Besides, memoir is an internally collective process. The retrospective adult voice must collaborate with several younger, and often contentious, selves, who resist facile truths. My liveliest collaborator is a fourteen-year-old narrative persona whose consciousness has been aroused and assumptions provoked by a violent strike that has put her family in jeopardy and divided her town into hostile camps. "Tell *that*, tell *that*!" she begs.

More and more, that strike became a focal point of my writing. The

most formative event of my adolescence, it was the moment at which
I realized that I was living in history, as a member of a social group
that needed to be better represented in our country's vision of history.
My fourteen-year-old self demands that I use my skill with words to
set the record straight. She offers justice as the central motive for the
memoir and would even like to title it *Unfair*, a word she read on a
picket sign.

The strike by the United Packinghouse Workers of America against
Wilson and Company meatpacking—also known as the lockout, Wilson's attempt at union-busting—brought national media attention to
Albert Lea in the cold, overcast days of mid-December 1959, one
month after it began. To quell the violence that erupted when the
company severed negotiations with the striking workers and hired
permanent replacements, Governor Orville Freeman, by executive
order, closed the packinghouse and placed the city under martial law.
This act was decried in newspaper editorials across the country as an
illegal seizure of property, morally equivalent to Governor Orville
Faubus's stand in the schoolhouse door. Within weeks, a federal court
concurred in that judgment and ordered the plant reopened.

This is not what I first recall about the strike. I know its legal and
political dimensions mostly from the archival research I have done.
What I actually remember is the blue jewelry box I got as a Christmas
present from a family at Hormel's in Austin that drew my name, the
loaded shotgun my Dad stored in the front closet in case we were
"visited" by nightriding scabs (he says this isn't true), the marshmal-
lows we shoved onto the antennae of National Guard jeeps in a
thrilling, flirtatious act of girl vandalism, and the debates vehemently
whispered across public library tables about who should control the
packinghouse: the people who put in long overtime hours of physical
labor or the people who invested money they had probably only inherited. We were not allowed to discuss this issue at school. Any
mention of the strike was cause for discipline.

My curiosity about the strike led me to a document I could barely
have hoped to discover, one that requires me to examine my place as
a female inhabitant of this outwardly masculine culture. It is a metic-
ulously maintained scrapbook about five inches thick, containing
daily newspaper articles, letters from the company urging employees
to return to work and threatening them with replacement, leaflets
and posters, a button proclaiming, "The Wilson label disgraces your

table" (a variation on the company's advertising slogan), and earnest, eloquent position papers composed by members of the local union. The scrapbook was left in the care of United Food and Commercial Workers Local P-6, the successor to the UPWA, after the death of Hazel Gudvangen, a sausage worker at the time of the strike. It is not yet in great demand. Whenever I come to the Union Center to look at it, the secretary has to climb on a chair to lift it down from the top cupboard. As I carry it down the hall and into the conference room where I will sit and page through it, it feels as precious as an Egyptian papyrus.

Hazel Gudvangen has become, in effect, a collaborator in this project. Had she not believed that a daily record of the strike was of lasting value, I would find it much more difficult to compose my memoir. I have come to rely on her scrapbook both to spark and to check my memories. I don't know that she would be a willing coauthor, however. I don't know that she would trust me, a Ph.D. with my head in the air, to share in the storytelling; Hazel didn't take any guff from anybody, my Dad says. He remembers her as a short, heavyset woman with a quick temper. She was an eager picket, I know, because of the many holes punched into her duty card, which is pasted inside the front cover of the scrapbook. When the strike ended in February, her name appeared, along with my Dad's, on the "craplist," the roll of those who were not immediately hired back because of alleged strike violations. Hazel had slapped a woman in a brawl with some scabs at a gas station. She claimed she was only pushing the woman out of harm's way, before someone else hit her with a board. Although a court referee accepted that story, she was kept out of work until December, one of the last two strikers hired back, and the only woman punished in this way.

I don't mean to depict Hazel as a radical heroine. Political ideology is not the issue here. It's a matter of right and wrong. I know, because I grew up with those clear distinctions. A faithful working person is entitled to decent treatment. A scab, who lays selfish claim to someone else's job, is immoral. "Scab" was the only word I knew for such a person until I read "replacement worker" in the newspaper. I never thought of it as loaded or partisan, just descriptive, like "liar" or "thief." This was Hazel's understanding as well, and she just happened to be hotheaded in enforcing morality. Neither do I want to portray her as a long-suffering victim. She did the job she was paid to do, making sausage casings that would be stuffed on down the line, and she found community with her coworkers in the union. There is no special virtue in her tolerance of that work, one of the most secure and best-paying women's jobs in town. She earned benefits unavailable to my nonunionized mother, who stood on her feet for hours in a busy fabric store, breathing in fumes from the dyes. Operating the casing machine was a more skilled position than "eggbreaker" at DeSoto Creamery and Produce, a job title that appears behind many women's names in the Albert Lea city directory of 1959.

It is ironic that Hazel Gudvangen should be my guide on this journey home through memory. She was one of the women who scared me away at eighteen—not Hazel herself but the image she and her female coworkers at the packinghouse embodied—and I still feel a bit quaky in her presence. By fifteen or sixteen, I knew I could not live in Albert Lea as an adult. The strike had taught me that the "educated" people I might like to be numbered among were largely unsympathetic to industrial workers who made demands on their employers. Becoming upwardly mobile at home was both unlikely and unappealing. As far as I could tell, a young working-class woman had roughly two choices. Either I would find a husband who was a good provider and didn't drink, or I would probably end up "on the sliced bacon," the primary women's job in the packinghouse. To avoid this fate, I would have to work hard in school, watch my behavior (i.e., not get pregnant), and leave town. The women on the sliced bacon served as the specter of the future that drove me from home, and they have kept their grip on my life as the ghosts of possibilities past, the standard against which I measure all proposed truths about the category "women." While I seek to demythologize the perception of working-class life I encountered in academe, I realize that I have enshrouded the female packinghouse workers in a mythology of my own making. I will have to get to know Hazel Gudvangen on her terms. If only her husband hadn't burned the diaries she kept for years.

Maybe Hazel Gudvangen wouldn't begrudge me the right to portray midwestern working-class life at midcentury. She might rather welcome me home as a success story. Among the documents on file at the Minnesota Historical Society is a letter written by Mrs. Tuberty, the daughter and wife of Albert Lea packinghouse workers, thanking Governor Freeman for stopping the violence. In the letter, she names her children: a captain in the army, a doctor of optometry, a nun who heads a department at a nursing school. "It was a long hard struggle for us to give to our children the educations they each received," she closes, "but we were always entertaining high principles and did not wish to see our children have to work as hard as their father had to make a living."[1] Sending children away to improve their lot is a mixed source of pride and sorrow for working-class families. When my Dad introduces me around town, he brags about my Ph.D., but he has also said of my brother-in-law, "He's such a nice guy you wouldn't even know he was educated." That embarrassing Ph.D. of mine can, I realize, also stand for Packinghouse Daughter. I am doubly credentialed—academically and experientially—for re-creating the history Hazel Gudvangen and Mrs. Tuberty and I all lived, each in her own way. I don't know their stories well enough to speak on their behalf, but I am getting to know my own, and I offer a condensed version of it here:

When I left Albert Lea for the University of Chicago, I expected a smooth transition. I was already leading the Life of the Mind, I figured, reading e.e. cummings, composing poems in my head as I walked gravel roads at the edge of town, and writing earnest editorials on the major issues of the day in the school newspaper. I had fashioned an identity for myself, Girl Intellectual, that transcended social class by locating its measures of virtue in the metaphysical realm. The University of Chicago would be a much more congenial environment for this refined persona of mine than a town surrounded by cornfields, with a packinghouse smoking at its periphery and class animosity seething under its placid surface.

My awakening from this fantasy was, indeed, rude. I came back from class one day to find my roommate and another friend rummaging through my dormitory closet looking at the labels in my clothes. There were not many to find, because my mother sewed nearly everything I wore. Spotting "J. C. Penney" in my underwear, my roommate told me, with the glee of reverse snobbery, that the city council in her phony, pretentious Long Island suburb had refused a building permit to Penney's because it was lower-class. Her tone confused me. She spoke scornfully of her own origins, while also letting me know where I stood on her social scale. Mind was presumably not all that mattered to my new friends. The two of them passed off the closet escapade as preparation for a joke they intended to play. In the sophomoric teasing typical of close-quarters dorm life, my working-class upbringing served both as the butt of jokes and as the object of a condescending solicitousness. When my Dad mailed me boycott lists from *The Packinghouse Worker*, my friends memorized the product names as though they were curious phrases in a foreign language.

By winter break, I had learned that the way to fit in physically and be left alone to lead the Life of the Mind was to grow my hair out, pierce my ears, roll my jeans up my calves, and wear, amazingly, a blue workshirt. I planned to buy one in Albert Lea, from my Aunt Vivian at Montgomery Ward, another lower-class store. I have written about this event elsewhere (see "The Blue Workshirt"), lending it all the drama it is due, but here I will only tell what happened. When my Dad heard that I wanted a workshirt, he offered to get me one himself. He brought me his own, which was stained with hog blood. Girl Intellectual came thudding down to earth, and I returned to campus with a painful self-awareness that colored everything I experienced.

The University of Chicago prided itself on its commitment to pure scholarship and its avoidance of "applied" fields that we could just as well study at our state universities. Here we were offered literature, not journalism; physics, not engineering. Our education was based on an assumption of shared values that had little to do with the life I had lived thus far. "We," I came to understand, enjoyed a level of aesthetic appreciation never attained in "popular" culture. One instructor, fortunately not mine, used as his code for the isolated and unenlightened not "the Boondocks" or "Hicksville," but "Albert Lea, Minnesota." He presumably remembered it from coverage of the strike four years before. What irony that Albert Lea High School's humanities program, which had introduced me to classical music and Renaissance art, was later acclaimed as a national model for secondary education in the humanities.

My greatest love, literature, was, I learned, to be read as formal artistry, without regard to historical context or author intention (The Fallacy!) or reader response. Of course, there were instructors who departed from this formalist norm or who applied it with subtlety and sensitivity. Nevertheless, the prevailing critical mode proudly titled "the Chicago school" settled on student discussion, as high theory often does, in its most vulgar, reductionist form: To draw comfort or knowledge or inspiration from literature was stupidly utilitarian. I couldn't say why this judgment felt skewed to me, as well as humiliating. I was embarrassed to let people know that I grew up in a house with very few books, and I was too disheartened to draw the obvious connections between reading and leisure time. My mother treated my reading habit the way I regard my children's TV-watching: "Can't you find something to do?" Except for Lillian Roth's *I'll Cry Tomorrow* and the infamous *Peyton Place*, her reading was limited to magazines, which she could get through in a hurry, she said. In the time it took to read a novel, she could whip up a beautifully tailored corduroy suit. My Dad, in his spare time, built us a house that still has square corners and level planes forty-five years later. He worked crossword puzzles for relaxation, but the only novel I could ever persuade him to read was Upton Sinclair's *The Jungle*. "If it wasn't for the union," he told me, "Wilson's would still be just like this." "Muckraking" was the dismissive label the formalists applied to this book that had helped save my family from literally crushing poverty.

Outside class, I was contending with a blue-workshirted New Left that invoked the oppression of the working class while betraying its ignorance of how the working class actually lived. I took the same stand they did on the issues—Civil Rights, the War in Vietnam—but limited my activism to showing up anonymously to fill out the crowd at meetings and demonstrations. I had grown uncharacteristically shy in this strange environment, and I was afraid that identifying myself would require me to challenge the working-class mythology. I was greatly disappointed with myself, since politics had always been at the center of my life. My earliest memories of leafletting and door-knocking for the DFL (the Democratic-Farmer-Labor party, Minnesota's Democrats) date from the 1952 elections, when I was seven. My Dad was even urging me to major in political science, to prepare myself to run for office, his ideal of achievement. I began to feel resentful, as though a vital part of my identity had been appropriated by "rich kids" pretending not to be.

I found refuge in another aspect of my identity that I first discovered away from home: my Scandinavian ethnicity, which was commonplace in Albert Lea. Curiosity about my heritage and an interest in language propelled me into an impractical but intriguing major, Scandinavian languages and literatures, which I followed through to a Ph.D. Here was the neutral environment I had counted on: a tiny enclave within the university where literature was read as aesthetic form, as historical document, as personal testimony, and as a vehicle for social change. The Golden Age of Scandinavian literature is, after all, the Modern Breakthrough of the 1880s, which produced socially engaged drama and prose, much of it written by women and/or about "the woman question." In Sweden, where I frequently did research and lecturing, I felt safe talking about social class, partly because the Social Democratic movement beginning in the late nineteenth century had established class as a legitimate subject for debate, and partly because I had no personal stake in the outcome. Curiously, however, nearly all the Swedish academics I got to know were of *borgerlig*—bourgeois—origin.

My association with women's studies began in a Scandinavian setting. For my final presentation at a summer language institute at the University of Uppsala in 1968, I chose from a list of suggestions the topic "the status of women in your country." I heard myself reciting, in impassioned, spontaneous, and surprisingly fluent Swedish, the injustices suffered by me, my mother, Betty Friedan, AFDC mothers, and the women on the sliced bacon. Back at the University of Chicago in the fall, I began attending a consciousness-raising group made up primarily of Bruno Bettelheim's beleaguered graduate students, an activity cut short by my near death in the Hong Kong flu epidemic in December. That winter, I teamed up with three other students to ask for a seminar that was "relevant" to our interests, unlike the one listed in the schedule. We ended up with "Feminism in Scandinavian Literature," taught by a visiting professor from Sweden—one of the very first women's studies courses on record.

"Relevance" was, of course, sweeping academe at that time, reforming or undermining, depending on your point of view. The concept fit very nicely with the standard I had set for myself as a way of reconciling my academic pursuits with my childhood loyalties. I could live in the mind as long as the product of my mental work had some practical use in the world. My Ph.D. dissertation was a model of usefulness and relevance. Entitled "Feminist Ideology and Literary Criticism in the United States and Sweden," it investigated the uses to which female readers of feminist persuasion were putting literature written by women, both rediscovered texts and newly written ones. In addition, it included intensive readings of three rather neglected Swedish works that I thought worthy of feminist attention. I am proud to have helped generate a revival of interest in the author Tora Dahl, whose series of autobiographical novels about a working-class girl's encounter with academic life was reprinted in paperback prior to her death at age ninety-five in 1982.

Pressed by a concerned faculty member to specify what critical method I would be applying to the texts I examined, I had to scramble to find one. The term "feminist literary criticism" had barely been coined and was being tossed around without definition. I figured I would have to make up my method as I went along, deriving it mainly from book reviews in feminist periodicals and the rare articles on women's literature published in academic journals. I ended up describing feminist criticism as a three-part endeavor: (1) analyzing the image of women in literature, (2) examining the existing body of criticism of female authors, and (3) setting standards to determine which literary works are "good" from a feminist point of view. "Prescriptive feminist criticism" was the tentative label I put on this third mode, actually my synthesis of the mostly implicit standards by which feminist book reviewers and literary scholars seemed to be evaluating the feminist content of a literary work. Unaware of the dangers of reification, I called these standards "functions": the role-model function, the sisterhood function, and so on. That's a decision I've lived to regret.

I finished in 1973—the grand year of first feminist dissertations—and was awarded honors with my degree. The department chairman, a Swedish philologist and place-name researcher nearing retirement, was happy to oversee scholarship that was new and bold and adventurous. Only the Marxist critic on my committee was skeptical of feminism. The dissertation made its public appearance as a somewhat revised and "popularized" book in Sweden and as a single chapter standing alone—a "bibliographical essay"—in an anthology in the United States (see Register, "American Feminist Literary Criticism," and *Kvinnokamp och litteratur*). That essay has since been memorialized in Jane Gallop's *Around 1981* as "an idea presented before its time" (see Gallop 101–18). I have come to think of it as The Essay That Will Not Die. A ghostly version of myself apparently haunts the history of feminist criticism, prescribing what female authors may and may not write. Naive and trusting as I was—and eager to publish—I did not think about the dangers of submitting a chapter apart from its comparative Scandinavian/American context and separate from the dissertation's introduction, which states clearly, "My intention was to be *descriptive* rather than *critical*, to describe what the critics in question are saying and what their concerns are, rather than to justify their

statements or determine their truth." I was surprised by the controversy engendered by my claim that feminist criticism might be prescriptive and perplexed by the few critics who dismissed my linkage
of ideology and literature as utilitarian or even programmatic. What
else could an avowedly feminist literary criticism, born of women's
discontent with the social order, possibly be?

As a women's liberation activist and a non–tenure-track, "soft
money" assistant professor in the experimental women's studies program at the University of Minnesota, I took for granted that women's
studies teaching and research bore a direct relationship to the life of
women in the world, mediated by the liberatory goals of the women's
movement. My test of usefulness grew ever more precise: What does
this have to do with the women on the sliced bacon? After a conversation with my dad about his sister's dismal work situation, it became
further refined: How will this benefit my Aunt Mary Jean, who
debones chickens for Banquet pot pies? Of course, my own teaching
and research often flunked this test, though I was adept at drawing
road maps between Swedish feminist-pacifists of the 1910s and working-class women in Albert Lea. Sometimes I took compensatory measures, such as teaching a course on working-class women in America
for which I had no proper academic credentials. The students I remember best are a cocktail waitress who has since moved on through
union leadership to elective office; a young man of hippie appearance
who was really just a working-class kid like me, saddened by his
growing distance from home; and an aristocratic young German
woman who faulted me for not knowing Feuerbach and Habermas.
Had she known Hazel Gudvangen, she might not have given me so
much guff.

In my seven years of teaching, matters of social class emerged frequently in classroom discussion. When students newly awakened to
feminist consciousness asserted the primacy of work over domesticity, I felt compelled to point out how, without defining "work" more
precisely, that hierarchy might cast liberation up against obligation.
The sliced bacon was not necessarily a freeing or freely chosen career,
I argued. The women who worked there might prefer to keep it temporary and part-time, as necessity dictated. Hearing the familiar defense of domesticity, "being a housewife is just a matter of choice," I
would inhale deeply and wish it truly were. My mother had made
that choice retroactively. "I'm so glad I stayed home to raise you

kids," she told me once, though I remember being rushed through breakfast by my older sister, who often saw me off to school in the primary grades. Mom was already sewing at Munsingwear by that time of the morning. But that was only for a little while, she protested when I reminded her, because Munsingwear closed down and moved South where wages were lower. Every job my mom ever held was only for a little while, no matter how long she had to keep working.

In scholarly exchanges about the theoretical underpinnings of women's studies, I could not set aside my experience of social class. My view of the patriarchy and the mechanisms of gender inequality was filtered through that bloodstain on my dad's workshirt. I have vivid recall of a session at the Modern Language Association where Adrienne Rich spoke to us about the power of her father's culture and the dominance of the fathers' language. She envisioned the books lining her father's study and read the canonical authors' names from their spines. Meanwhile, I saw the image of my dad stretched out supine on the living room floor, easing the pain in his back after a day's work. When he fell asleep, my sisters and I would merely step over him to get where we had to go. I had rid myself well before then of the fathers' language. I knew enough to say "almost" instead of "pret' near."

Jane Gallop's essay ends dramatically, "Register spoke out of turn and was dismissed," as though I suffered retribution for audaciously proclaiming that feminist criticism is prescriptive. It might be fun to play martyr-to-the-truth, but that is not the truth. My departure from the university in 1980 is a complex matter that can be reduced to a simple fact: The Women's Studies Program was granted permanent status as the Women's Studies Department, but the budget allotted contained no "line" for my position. I could have waited for the allocation of additional, temporary funds and stayed on year by year for as long as the department chose to make such use of its money, but I had no enthusiasm for continuing as a hardworking stringer while my colleagues got promotions and tenure and insurance coverage and all the rest. Because of other personnel problems that had created a serious crisis of morale, no one stepped forth to protest my leaving as a loss to the program/department, and there was no union to make my case. Only lately, as I watch academic friends take bold measures to advance their careers, have I realized that I could have fought for a permanent position. Advocating for myself is a lesson I have never learned, though I can struggle as tirelessly as anyone on behalf of a group or a cause. Maybe it's a stretch to attribute this to my working-class upbringing, but I see no model in my life for career ambition.

I had decided to treat this unfortunate circumstance as an opportunity to be more faithful to my own vision. For years, I had longed to "write in my own voice," which was exactly how I put it. I was troubled by the appearance of a new jargon within women's studies and literary criticism, in particular, and joked about the difficulty of turning Derrida into an adjective. (The *Signs* editors removed that joke, and all the others, from my review essay on literary criticism, published in 1980, which I regarded as my swan song to feminist criticism.) To justify its institutionalization as an academic (inter)discipline, women's studies seemed to be undergoing a shift in values, veering away from advocacy and accountability to the women's movement or a larger community of women. Papers presented at conferences were sometimes so esoteric and abstract that I found myself muttering the sliced bacon test under my breath. I knew my hour was up when a woman in the back of the audience at a panel I was on described my *Signs* essay as "millennial." I seemed to believe, she said, that feminist criticism was supposed to change the world.

Of course, I have some regrets about leaving academe. I miss the easy access to colleagues, the instant identity, the income, the travel perqs, the free-food schmoozing opportunities, the library privileges, the discounts on computers and cultural events, the linkage to Internet, and, especially, the access to funds to support research and writing. With regard to money and prestige, the direction of my mobility is drastically downward. But I have never stopped working at my profession, and the work I have done generally measures up to my standard of usefulness. I have written a book on the experience of chronic illness that brings in letters and phone calls from people who say, "You've told my story" (see *Living with Chronic Illness*). After adopting my two daughters from Korea, I wrote a book addressing the ethical questions that arose for me during the adoption process and that continue to come up as we live our lives as an interracial family (see *"Are Those Kids Yours?"*). I credit the women on the sliced bacon for helping me keep in mind the young, unmarried women in the garment and electronics factories in South Korea.

These books have provided me with a new vocation: the pursuit of "the un/common story," a term I coined for a literary rendition of a fairly unusual experience that is not, however, unique to the author. It uses autobiography not for self-exposure, but as a source of truth about shared experience, which can be most movingly told in a specific, personal voice. I teach a course on the un/common story at the Loft, a writers' center in Minneapolis, where I offer what guidance I can to people writing about illness, job loss, ethnicity, infertility, the birthmother's experience of adoption, exile. . . . Students come to improve their writing, without the motivation or limitation of grades and degrees. Some, of course, nourish the standard writer's hope of immortality. Whether the students' work leads to publication or is done for its therapeutic value, I walk out of the classroom feeling very useful. I only wish that the Loft, a "soft money" organization, could provide the job stability and salary of an academic institution.

If asked to account for my standard of usefulness, I would trace it back beyond the "relevance" of the sixties to my working-class childhood. It would be a simplification, however—and romanticism—to locate its origin in the mere circumstance of class. I learned it, in fact, by instruction and example. I wish, for this audience, that I could call it a maternal inheritance, but my Dad deserves most of the credit. He was the one who showed me how to find purpose in work that others might dismiss as unfortunate or meaningless. If you spend your work life in a packinghouse, you do the most skilled work you can and you work through the union to secure the best conditions you can get for everybody. If you are bothered by the indignities faced by "ordinary working people" (his term for working class), then you'd better speak up. At fifty-two, my Dad ran for political office and became the first laborer elected to the Albert Lea city council. If you're going to get old, well. . . . At eighty-three, he was distributing surplus commodities to "old people" and lobbying through the union for national health insurance. Now eighty-seven and relocated to a retirement complex, he is determined to expose the profiteering in services for the elderly.

The most pressing un/common story I have left to tell is the one about midwestern blue-collar life, about the packinghouse, about the strike that placed my town, my family—me—at the center of the world. Once my memoir is in print, I have a chance of educating the pitifully small audience that reads literary memoir and history about the inadequacy of working-class stereotypes. But how useful is that? And how will it benefit the women on the sliced bacon, not to mention my Aunt Mary Jean, who is, mercifully, retired? I want to give something back to the people who have lived this story, something as valuable as Hazel Gudvangen's scrapbook. Maybe it is a chance to tell the story themselves, to join with many highly specific, personal voices, my own included, in pursuit of a shared truth. With public grant money, I am also collecting the pieces of the story as oral history. Unfortunately, many of the key players are already gone.

I began by interviewing the president of the union local during the strike, who had worked as a "gutsnatcher" at the plant. My intention in that interview was simply to check out the interpretation of events that I had derived from reading archival material at the Minnesota Historical Society. But every interview contains its unexpected bonus. As the union president sought to explain how Wilson's lockout of its employees had come about, he gestured to his wife and said, "Tootie worked out there at that time." "I was in bacon," Tootie joined in, "and I'd come in in the afternoon, and this one day when I came in, somebody had been fired in bacon. The day girls would not get off their seats for us night girls to take over, because they were protesting this firing . . ."

The collective voice I seek has grown more audible as I write my way closer to home and begin to tune in other voices. And I can smell the smoky, pungent, yet comforting packinghouse aroma in the air.

NOTE

1. Letter from Mrs. James H. Tuberty, December 15, 1959, in *Governor Orville Freeman: Records Relating to the Wilson Company Strike.*

WORKS CITED

Gallop, Jane. *Around 1981: Academic Feminist Literary Theory.* New York: Routledge, 1992.

Governor Orville Freeman: Records Relating to the Wilson Company Strike. Minnesota State Archives, Minnesota History Center, St. Paul, Minnesota.

Register, Cheri. "American Feminist Literary Criticism: A Bibliographical

Essay." In *Feminist Literary Criticism: Explorations in Theory,* ed. Josephine Donovan, 1–28. Lexington: University of Kentucky Press, 1975.

———. *"Are Those Kids Yours?" American Families with Children Adopted from Other Countries.* New York: Free Press, 1991.

———. "The Blue Workshirt." *Hungry Mind Review,* spring 1995.

———. *Kvinnokamp och litteratur i USA och Sverige.* Stockholm: Rabén och Sjogren, 1977.

———. *Living with Chronic Illness: Days of Patience and Passion.* New York: Free Press, 1987. Rpt. New York: Bantam, 1989, 1992. Updated and republished as *The Chronic Illness Experience: Embracing the Imperfect Life.* Center City, Minnesota: Hazelden Books, 1999.

———. "Review Essay: Literary Criticism." *Signs: Journal of Women in Culture and Society* 6.2 (winter 1980): 268–82.

Chapter 8

Blood Ties and Blasphemy
American Indian Women and the Problem of History

Kathryn Shanley

> The discourse of history dramatizes the struggle between the impossibility of totalization and the possibility of a meaningful representation of totalization produced through narrative closure.
> —Julia V. Emberley, "'A Gift for Languages':
> Native Women and the Textual Economy
> of the Colonial Archive"

> Writing is an act of courage for most. For us, it is an act that requires opening up our wounded communities, our families, to eyes and ears that do not love us. Is this madness? In a way it is—the madness of a Louis Riel, a Maria Campbell, a Pauline Johnson, a Crazy Horse— a revolutionary madness. A love that is greater than fear. A love that is as tender as it is fierce.
> —Beth Brant, *Writing as Witness*

Writing and speaking about American Indian literatures, histories, and cultures, as I so frequently do, does not trouble me nearly as much as writing about American Indian *women* does. Yet it seems I have been writing this essay all my life. I am Indian because of blood ties, my ancestral links to a people who have lived—indeed thrived— on the Plains long before they were gathered up on the Ft. Peck Reservation to live a different kind of life.[1] (My grandmother was the first person in my family to be born on the reservation, a little over a century ago.) But my "Indianness" is more than blood heritage—it is a particular culture, Nakota, and a history of the place where I grew up and much more. I am also a mixed-blood, though I prefer Gerald Vizenor's term, "crossblood" (Vizenor 13). What owning the term "crossblood" implies, in part, is that I am also Indian (or tribal) because of blasphemy, my position on one side of a binary opposition, which connotes resistance—a "not that" on the other side of a dubious Christian "blessing." Oppositional pairs such as native/white, pagan/Christian, primitive/civilized, or savage/citizen bespeak the historical relations that have shaped me—all of that Indianness is, largely, easy to talk about, since it is fueled by the madness of which Beth Brant speaks. Woman, however, is the first skin around me, and I do not know entirely what it is or even how to talk about it. I do know it is not my story alone; my story belongs also to my mother, grandmothers, sisters, friends, relatives, and so many others, including non-Indians, and all their perspectives must be respected in whatever I say. So my approach to the subject of American Indian women and history requires a shifting discourse, one that circles its subject and even circles my own subjectivity.

In their introduction to *Feminisms: An Anthology of Literary Theory and Criticism,* Robyn R. Warhol and Diane Price Herndl remark that "[B]eginning with a personal anecdote is practically obligatory" (ix); they say, "There are good reasons for this: feminism holds that 'the personal is political,' and that feminists believe that the traditional academic boundaries between professional and personal experience ought to be undermined" (ix). While I agree with Warhol and Price Herndl about the imperative to undermine boundaries between personal and professional experiences, an imperative the theoretical term "subject position" is meant to capture, I also believe that both epistemological and ontological realms differ considerably for American Indian women, in comparison to non-Indian women, so much so that audience becomes a problematic in the positioning of oneself to speak. Moreover, an Indian woman speaking out risks being seen as a representative of Indian women; I must disavow that role, yet I hope to share thoughts from an Indian woman's perspective that will be helpful in feminist discussions.

Simply put, Americans need to embark on a general reeducation in order to know how to situate new perspectives and voices wisely, because misinformation and mythologies about native women's lives and experiences prevail in such abundance (particularly in popular culture media). We need a common knowledge base, something more than television perspectives or single-issue alliances (i.e., antihomophobic or sexual abuse activism), that at the very least illuminates governmental policies toward American Natives and proceeds with a recognition of basic differences between tribal and Christian worldviews. Clara Sue Kidwell, a Choctaw/Anishinaabe historian, offers a useful set of questions to begin:

> The mythology of Indian women has overwhelmed the complexity of roles in the history of Indian and white contact. Indian women stand in history as stereotypes such as the hot-blooded Indian princess, a la Pocahontas, or the stolid drudge, the Indian squaw plodding behind her man. They are not real people. The myths of colonialism and manifest destiny raise questions about their associations with European men. Their roles must be interpreted in two cultures. If American history portrays them as saviors and guides of white men and agents of European colonial expansion, were they explicitly or implicitly betraying their own people? Were they driven by passion, or were they victims of fate, forced to submit to men of a dominant society? (Kidwell 98)

One thing is certain, their voices "are not heard in the written documents or in the history books," a fact that leads Kidwell to conclude, "we must attempt to recreate the cultural context of their actions and to move beyond the myths that have been woven around their lives" (Kidwell 98).

Inquiries into the cultural contexts of the lives of historical figures such as Pocahontas, Doña Marina (La Malinche), or Sacajawea, begun or continued by scholars such as Kidwell, still leave a gap between those Indian women's lives and the lives of women living today. A similar gap exists between the notable Indian woman non-Indians tout and those women who serve Indian communities first and foremost.[2] With the aim of reopening the destructive and stereotypical narrative closures surrounding contemporary Indian women, I will begin with a story, a sort of truncated Indian version of *Fried Green Tomatoes at the Whistle Stop Café*. It is a story about women working to survive, to find ways to raise their families, to make meaning of their places in the world.

When I was nineteen, a year out of high school, I worked as a waitress at Skelly's truck stop in a town thirty-some miles off the reservation—it was truly one of the only jobs open to me. There I met a woman I will call Dorothy.[3] She was one of several cooks who rotated onto the day shift. Dorothy was on the chubby side, nervous, even driven, and she was, for the most part, toothless. Although she could not have been much more than fifteen years older than I was at the time, the egocentrism of my youth prevented me from seeing any relationship between who she was and who I was, other than our both being Indian—let alone who she was becoming in relation to my goals and directions.

She was married to an abusive man, an alcoholic, a fact I only knew by-the-way—or perhaps I intuited it, since my mother was also married to an alcoholic. Dorothy and I did share, however, in our commiseration over our working conditions. Later, I would remember my time at Skelly's when I read Richard Wright's story in *American Hunger* of how he moved north and took a job at a restaurant, read of his flight toward freedom and his subsequent disillusionment. The rules seemed to work against the employees, and the employees, in turn, worked against the rules and the boss—an old story of class struggle. Dorothy and I were the exceptions, both too sincere (also read: naive) and too driven to become something else to recognize that things were set up to prevent us from doing that. For example, the boss—the brother of the man who had before managed the restaurant part of the business, but who ran away to Alaska, leaving a stack of bills behind—was understandably worried about his profit margin. He had limited Dorothy in her preparation of the "daily special": she could use either fruit or whipped cream in the dessert, but not both, so Dorothy made Jell-O on cookie sheets, then cut the Jell-O into little cubes. A neat trick, I thought, and she looked so proud when she gazed on those thick parfait glasses filled with ruby red cubes, topped (of course) with whipped cream—with the powdered substitute the boss passed off as whipped cream.

Dorothy was honest, unlike one cook, Sandy, who sometimes had her husband drive up in back at the end of the afternoon shift to load up packages of frozen chicken and steak; or another cook, Ralph, who drank on the job and, I imagine, spit in the stew, like the immigrant woman character in Richard Wright's book. Another cook, Linda, was married to a one-armed man, a handsome, burly, mixed-blood Canadian Indian who worked for the state as a crew boss in road construction. Linda was a stunningly beautiful blond, despite her being marked as lower-class by the nicotine stains on her teeth and fingers. Her complexion was creamy white and her figure a perfect hourglass. And she was only two years older than I was, I discovered when she told me she had been in the eighth grade with my older brother (the year she dropped out of school). She loved to tell me of her battles with her husband, usually resulting from his fierce jealousy—how one time after he beat her severely for taking a dollar tip from a truck driver who felt she had cooked his T-bone just right, she got her revenge by packing him a thermos of coffee with a cup of sugar in it and a sandwich consisting of two slices of Wonder Bread filled with dead flies she had harvested from the windowsill. Out sixty miles from town and hung over, he would have to think about a few things, she said. Another time, she tied him up after he had passed out from drinking, and showed him what it feels like to be beaten. The destructiveness of their bond was most daringly played out when he would meet her after work so that they could race the five miles home in their separate vehicles.

Few employees could be trusted to handle the till. Sherry, one of the senior waitresses, wasn't safe within a mile of the cash drawer, any vacated table with a tip lying on it, or our purses, which we kept unlocked in the back room. I knew she stole, but couldn't, didn't dare try to, prove it. She was "one tough lady," as they say, and I didn't mess with her. She also made extra money at night in the bunk area where truckers slept while their rigs were being serviced, or so I was told. She too was Indian, and a single parent with four children.

Ten years later, I moved back home to take care of my mother, who had to have surgery; she was living alone then. By that time, I had grown up, had made my own mistakes, had worked at many different jobs—I had sold Avon, been a legal secretary, an outreach worker in a high school for what we now call "at-risk" kids, a secretary for the Dominican Sisters of the Sick Poor, and, finally, had gone back to school to become a registered nurse. A marriage, a divorce, and two nursing jobs later, I returned home with child in tow, the memories still vivid of the folks I had worked with at Skelly's. Now as I recount those memories, the phrase, popular nowadays in the academy, "intersections of 'race,' class, and gender," echoes in my head. Inasmuch as any single phrase can describe a psychosocial reality, I suppose that one does; but for me it will always be a matter of the heart, of "survivance," as Vizenor terms it: the mornings Sandy (the cook I told you about who stole food from the boss) would show up for work with her eyes blackened and her temper sharpened; she was non-Indian and married to an unemployed Indian man with whom she shared five kids. I remember the days Ralph (the best cook among them) didn't show up to open the place and was nowhere to be found—not in the sleazy boardinghouse where he lived nor among the men in the early-morning bar crowd—how I worried what he would do if he lost his job, how he loved to kid me and would cook anything for me that my heart desired. (I stayed away from the soup.) I remember the days when Sherry stole the tip I earned from waiting on the entire staff of the local telephone company.

I found out that Dorothy had moved away, and that Sandy had become a licensed practical nurse. I never found out what happened to the others—Linda, Ralph, or Sherry. But I ran into my buddy, Violet, the waitress I most liked to work with, at the local Woolworth lunch counter. She had gotten her two girls through high school, and like the plodding, devoted Mole in the Coyote tales of the Okanogan, she had to struggle against her trickster husband to do so. She too is Indian, a Chippewa displaced to Trenton, North Dakota, one of many Chippewas who were shut out of allotment on Turtle Mountain Reservation largely because it was situated on a tract of land desirable for Euroamerican settlement.

I tell this story, just one of many I could tell, and not one of the worst, as a way of describing the gulf we all know that exists between feminism as we theorize and practice it in the academy, American Indian women's history as we conceive of it—if we do in fact conceive of it at all—and the way women live their lives in (post)colonial times and places. In communities where these women work, jobs for Indians in the banks or white-owned stores and businesses are few or none. Indian women living on reservations have many different stories to tell; some of them like the stories of these women, and some focused on links to past generations and continuing religious and cultural practices (though religion and cultural worldview are one and the same in my estimation). The "old ways" stories, tales of exotic Indian life ways, always seem to interest wider audiences the most. Urban Indian women no doubt offer another set of stories entirely, however, not without common ties to their sisters' stories from rural America, for working-class experience and continuing traditions may provide common denominators.

In regard to urban Indian experience and all the stories associated with that experience, more literature is available.[4] Whether living off-reservation in rural America, on-reservation in America's internal colonies that would be sovereign, or in America's cities, Indian women and their histories cannot be adequately represented or understood if we do not also understand their centuries-old oppressions. Answers to questions of why some families stay on the reservation, why some leave never to return, and why some go back and forth lie in understanding the allotment decades before the 1920s, tribal government under the Indian Reorganization Act of the 1930s and 1940s, and the Termination Policy years of the 1950s, and all against the backdrop of specific cultural histories. Canadian Native history also must be explored; many Canadian Native families like Brant's migrated to U.S. cities to find work in factories.

American Indian and Canadian Native women's stories remind us that social oppression based on class, gender, and "race" is by no means a thing of the past, despite the laudable gains the women's movement has made. But I do not need to tell you that changes have occurred or that oppressions continue: we now have new words, phrases, and metaphors in our vocabularies to connote those changes and the continuing need for change: "sexual harassment," "glass ceilings," "battered women and children's shelters," "sexual predators," "homophobia," and so on. What I do hope to make clear is how the means for and terms of realizing gains against gender/"race"/class oppression differ for American Indian women—a point I hope to make implicitly if not explicitly. Nevertheless, I fully recognize that "From the outside 'feminism' may appear monolithic, unified, or singularly definable," and I agree with Warhol and Price Herndl that "the more one sees the multiplicity of approaches and assumptions inside the movement," the clearer it becomes that feminist projects can provide "a model for cultural heterogeneity" (x). Dialogues and coalitions must be encouraged to grow.

In order to discuss what American Indian women's history might look like, what kind of history they have written themselves or carried within their hearts, we need to come to something approximating common terms: what cultural differences between Indians and non-Indians persist in (post)colonial situations; who are American Indians and American Indian women to themselves; what would social justice be in regard to American Indian women's history; what are "subjectivity" and "agency" in the context of American Indian women's lives; and what constitutes activism? Through an exploration of what I mean by "race"/class/gender, I hope that the issues outlined above will take on a more particularized meaning, although more suggestively than prescriptively so.

Who is the/an American Indian? By now we know "race" to be more of an ideological construct than a fact of essential biological difference. While the terms "class" and "gender" are in some senses as ideologically constructed as is the term "race," I would argue that "race" as a term stands apart, not as the greatest in a hierarchy of oppressions, but as an overarching global designation tied to a particular colonial history of economic power and privilege. In other words, the legacy of racism among postcolonial people along with continued oppression have created a reality for "race," far beyond any genuine biological differences. Gender and class oppressions, in my opinion, can be equally destructive to groups and individuals, but how those oppressions are "racially" configured shapes them in primary, paradigmatic ways.

Books such as Michael Banton's *Racial Theories,* Stephen Jay Gould's *Mismeasure of Man,* and other, more recent works, such as Henry Louis Gates's edited anthology, *"Race," Writing, and Difference,* and Dominick LaCapra's edited anthology, *The Bounds of Race,* amply establish how scientific studies of "racial" difference are most often used to create a superior/inferior distinction between groups. Such theoretical clarity remains theoretical, however. There remains a gap between such academic discussions and the people most affected by constructs of "race," between theory and the practice of justice. This gap should be apparent by recent controversial legal decisions, such as the Rodney King and O. J. Simpson verdicts, and subsequent discussions of whether justice is possible from a jury of one's peers. To add another layer to the complexity, that gap between theory and practice is itself shaped by "race," gender, and class. What Russel Barsh notes about American Indian studies in his article "Are Anthropologists Hazardous to Indians' Health?" could be said of many scientific and scholarly enterprises as well: "Like missionaries, anthropologists were frequently conspicuous in the front lines of colonialism" (1). Barsh attributes anthropologists' cultural blindness to what he sees as their frequent failure to "appreciate the difference between their field as a 'science,' which has so often helped justify manipulation of indigenous cultures, and their field as a philosophy, which has been more positive" (1). One might add theorists' blindness to their failure to recognize their subject positions as philosophers of culture.

Barsh's remarks, admittedly vitriolic, nevertheless serve to bracket the information gathered mostly by Anglo-Saxon males on American Indian women, information contaminated by both missionary zeal and a dishonest claim to scientific objectivity. The problem with those perspectives, Barsh argues, is that

> Anthropological evidence is particularly elusive because it is based on an individual subjective interpretation of a wide variety of qualitative impressions, rather than counting discrete, concrete events. It is a study of a people's style, and difference of professional opinion cannot be resolved by any objective standard, such as statistical analysis. (14)

Lack of "objectivity," however, is only one side of the problem—objectizing human "subjects" is the other.

For a fuller picture of American Indian life, feminist scholarship that incorporates "race" as a term connoting an aspect of oppression must take kinship into account as well, in its most tribally specific, qualitative dimensions. Discussion of blood ties must be set against the idea of blasphemy or sin that has been associated with tribal social practices in missionary and anthropological renderings of tribal life and women's roles in those societies. The sexualities of individuals informed by identities that are other-than-heterosexual have likewise suffered distortion under the missionary's and scholar's gaze.

What do we mean by "race" then? Werner Sollors, the author of *Beyond Ethnicity* and editor of *The Invention of Ethnicity,* provides a conflicted jumping-off place. He argues that "it is most helpful not to be confused by the heavily charged term 'race' and to keep looking at race as one aspect of ethnicity" (*Beyond Ethnicity* 39). Eventually, he argues, we must also abandon the term "ethnicity," for "we may be better served by the vocabulary of kinship and culture codes than by the cultural baggage that the word 'ethnicity' contains" (*Beyond Ethnicity* 39). While I agree both with the general principle of moving beyond "race" as a construct (an effort that may ultimately render "racism" less ideologically powerful) and with his impetus for also replacing "ethnicity" with terms that capture a greater complexity of being, I would argue that racism maintains material/real boundaries between "racially" designated groups and other Americans and that those boundaries figure essentially in the groups' culture codes (Shanley). While strong in his undoing of "race" as a biological denotation, Sollors is weak in accounting for the ideological power that "race" categories have carried and continue to carry with them; he perhaps believes (certainly more than I do) in a trickle-down of academic theorizing and philosophizing to the level of institutional and cultural spheres of influence.

I see another problem in Sollors's leap to a different terminology—the leveling effect of ethnicity or its less loaded equivalents designating all matters of cultural difference. Euroamericans have, in many respects, invented an ethnic identity around the Indian presence in their history, often based on, as Sollors notes, "a presumptuous reconstruction of American kinship" (*Beyond Ethnicity* 125). In order for such appropriations of American Indian cultural identities to be effective, however, a simultaneous silencing needs to occur. Vizenor remarks on the phenomenon of Euroamerican silencing, appropriation, and absorption of tribal realities, using the adjective "scriptural" in a deconstructionist mode to describe the stature such constructions have had and continue to have in American national consciousness:

> The various translations, interpretations, and representations of the absence of tribal realities have been posed as the verities of certain cultural traditions. Moreover, the closure of heard stories in favor of scriptural simulations as authentic representations denied a common brush with the shimmer of humor, the sources of tribal visions, and tragic wisdom; tribal imagination and creation stories were obscured without remorse in national histories and the literature of dominance. (Vizenor 16)

For Vizenor, visions and wisdom arise from humor; humor, in turn, keeps representations shimmering with life and unpredictability, while science is based on predictability.[5] Appropriations of Indian culture, whether under the guise of anthropological objectivity or New Age religiosity, invariably take themselves very seriously. Vine Deloria, Jr., in his book *Custer Died for Your Sins*, humorously comments on how many proud and serious-minded non-Indians announce that they, too, have Indian heritage, and always through a Cherokee grandmother (10-11). (There are, by the way, living Cherokee people who suffer from such generalizations.) A female ancestor must be infinitely more palatable in the blood ties equation than would be the "brutish and savage" (albeit noble) Indian male. Deloria employs a scathingly ironic humor in speaking of such appropriations. Sollors comments on the hegemonic nature of such gestures, noting that "the popular image of the Indian exists in a web of subdued love relationships" (Sollors, *Beyond Ethnicity* 127).

Historical figures such as Pocahontas ("the first mythical Indian," as Betty Louise Bell refers to her) have become Euroamericans, common ancestor with Natives, a usurpation tied with love in the American representational economy—"the white ventriloquism of her motives and desires . . . have made her a metaphor for the colonizing of native identity by settler imagination" (Bell 67). Sollors rightly identifies the European originary structure of such narratives:

> From Pocahontas to the hundreds of stories—supposedly of Indian origin, but invariably products of the Euro-American imagination—which are associated with America's many lovers' leaps, Indians remain connected with love in the American imagination and, more specifically, with the imagery of chivalric courtly love of the European Middle Ages. (*Beyond Ethnicity* 127)

While such appropriations and romantic constructions continue in Walt Disney's recent feature-length cartoon *Pocahontas*, actual Indians have difficulty obtaining the health care they need or the education promised them by their treaties, because the government has constructed a mound of red tape requiring proof of Indian identity, and legal jargon as to whether their identity is to be determined by ancestry and to what degree, or by tribal affiliation.[6] Tribes themselves struggle for clarity in approaching the government. Sharon O'Brien writes of the complex and convoluted nature of Indian law, "Scholars have written several major works and over 1300 articles on American Indian law in their attempts to explain and define" the relationship between the United States and tribal governments (O'Brien 1462).

On the one hand, the Supreme Court has emphasized that the government's relationship with tribes "is not defined by race, but is of a political nature" (O'Brien 1462). On the other hand, as of 1978 "federal legislation contained thirty three definitions of Indians" (O'Brien 1485), based on various racial and cultural formulas. The government's fiduciary responsibility toward Indians (its trust relationship based on treaties and other agreements, as well as on legal precedents) falls subject to the conflicts between the branches of government, when Congress by its fiscal principles and politics (determining who actually gets served with monetary appropriations) decides to support the interests and concerns of non-Indian constituents over and above those of Indians. Such conflicting positions on Indians illustrate why it is important not to subsume "race" into the larger category of ethnicity. Regardless of whether or not the Supreme Court decides over and over again that Indians are political entities, the legislative and executive branches of the government deal with Indians according to Indians' degree of Indian blood and Indians' ability to document that blood, rather than as individuals and nations with whom the government has a special relationship and toward whom it has a special charge. (The Bureau of Indian Affairs, for example, continues to manage millions of dollars worth of American Indian resources, and it has a poor record of doing so honestly and ethically.)[7] "Race" determines the particulars of many Indian lives, through government regulations, as O'Brien notes:

> The most outstanding (although largely historical) use of race is in regard to competency. Whether or not the Bureau was willing to declare an Indian competent, thereby capable of alienating his or her land, depended upon the person's possession of one-half or more blood quantum. Individuals possessing less than one-half Indian blood were considered "more competent" than those with one-half or more. (O'Brien 1483–84)

Competence has always meant different things to the Washington-appointed bureaucrats than it has to tribal people themselves. Being Indian, culturally setting oneself apart as such in Indian communities within quasi-sovereign nations, depends to a large extent on tribes' being able to make gains in economic development; their ability to educate Indian citizens to acquire the skills necessary to live productive, satisfying lives and, in turn, to enable those citizens to serve their communities; and a nation's hope to provide for the health and social needs so pathetically underserved.[8]

Urban Indians present similar needs, and have largely ended up in cities because their home communities are lacking in economic opportunities. Unrelenting efforts on the part of the U.S. government over the past century to assimilate Indians into the mainstream, or simply to make them disappear from America's bureaucratic landscape and ledgers, involve perceptions of who Indians were and who they are today—contemporary "poor relatives" who represent a continuing burden, one President Bush declared he could "terminate" at will. Back in 1969, Deloria described a situation that continues to this day.

> With so much happening on reservations and the possibility of a brighter future in store, Indians have started to become livid when they realize the contagion trap the mythology of white America has caught them in. The descendant of Pocahontas is a remote and incomprehensible mystery to us. We are no longer a wild species of animal loping freely across the prairie. We have little in common with the Mohicans. (Deloria 33)

Meanwhile, as of the latest census, more and more Euroamericans choose to identify as Indian, while "livid" Indians struggle to set the terms of membership in their own spheres of life and influence. Tribes often employ self-destructive blood quantum measures to determine who is Indian in an effort to prevent shrinking tribal resources from going to wannabes. It is often a lose-lose situation.[9]

American Indian women figure centrally in vague, blood-tie identities, as I have noted above, but Indian women constructed in popular culture media have difficulty surviving to the end of the movie. In *Legends of the Fall,* for example, a film based on a novella by Jim Harrison, we are supposed to identify Colonel William Ludlow as a hero, because as a former military officer who had been involved in the wars against Indian people of the Dakotas, he speaks out against the government's injustices toward Indians; after resigning from the military, he even writes a book about unethical and immoral government policies and about the slaughter of Indian women and children. Yet no mention is ever made of how he acquired his homestead, where he lives with his three sons and his hired hands, One Stab, Decker, Beth (Decker's Indian wife), and Isabel (the Deckers' daughter). Although in many ways the portrayal of the Ludlow family, of which Decker, Decker's family, and One Stab are vital and beloved members, accords dignity and a certain degree of credibility to Cree traditions (the Cree language is spoken, for example) and humanity to the Indian characters, the women's roles follow along old stereotypical veins.

The plot fulfills itself and completes the Pocahontas paradigm when the son, Tristan Ludlow, with the soul of an Indian and the troubled heart of a bear, marries Isabel Decker, a girl of a mere thir-

teen when the movie begins. She is killed accidentally in a confrontation between her husband and the police who are protecting their
bootlegging liquor interests, but not before she leaves him two children who have absorbed her bloodline. Throughout the film,
Decker's wife can be found in almost every scene with a broom in her
hand or silently—obediently, one imagines—beating a rug or cooking
a meal. None of the women fares well in *Legends of the Fall* (a name, by
the way, that evokes a nostalgic association with the impossibility of a
return to "prelapsarian" Indian life), since Susannah, the genteel
paramour of all three brothers, dies by her own hand. Her fate also
fits well in the homoerotic American hero paradigm elucidated by
Leslie Fiedler, while the Indian women follow the Pocahontas paradigm in painfully explicit terms. Indian women fulfill their mytho-
logical purpose only in liaisons with white men. As Rayna Green
notes of Pocahontas legends,

> Whether or not she saved John Smith, her actions as recounted by
> Smith set up one kind of model for Indian–White relations that per-
> sists—long after most Indians and Anglos ceased to have face-to-face
> relationships. Moreover, as a model for the national understanding of
> Indian women, her significance is undeniable. With her darker, nega-
> tively viewed sister, the Squaw—or, the anti-Pocahontas, as Fiedler
> called her—the Princess intrudes on the national consciousness, and a
> potential cult awaits to be resurrected when our anxieties about who
> we are make us recall her from her woodland retreat. (Green 700–701)[10]

The virgin/whore dichotomy is nothing new and is so essentially a
part of the American Christian worldview that it dies hard, but its implications for Indian women and Indian people in general are chilling
in their genocidal potential. The American Indian woman, Green concludes, "[a]s some abstract, noble Princess tied to 'America' and to
sacrificial zeal . . . has power as a symbol" (emphasis added), but her
binary sister, the Squaw, represents a repugnance for Indian sexuality.
Green writes,

> As the Squaw, a depersonalized object of scornful convenience, she is
> powerless. Like her male relatives she may be easily destroyed without
> reference to her humanity. (When asked why he killed women and chil-
> dren at Sand Creek, the commanding general of the U.S. Cavalry was
> said to have replied, "nits make lice.") As the Squaw, her physical re-
> moval or destruction can be understood as necessary to the progress of

civilization even though her abstracted sister the Princess, stands for that very civilization. (713–14)

Yes, she stands for that very civilization, but only in myth, as doomed progenitor of Americans. In that respect, the Indian Princess is not a virgin, or rather she embodies a virgin's worthiness prior to her being conquered, but eventually conquered she must be for the myth to work. She substitutes for the more "permanently" pristine woman of European heritage, with the amendment that, being a creature of nature, Indian women (both princesses and squaws) also embody sexual knowledge. Providing us with a problematically mixed metaphor, the Princess is the biological means to the creation of the new American. In her fallen state, the state she is supposedly born into as an Indian woman, particularly on the frontier, she represents a whore.

Norman Maclean similarly exoticizes Paul's "girl" in *A River Runs through It,* such that he moves her quickly through Princess to Whore; he tells how she "felt that she had had a disappointing evening and had not been appreciated if the guy who took her out didn't get into a big fight over her" (28). In the protocol of the Last Chance Gulch Saloon, the "girl's" honor seems a trifling thing; however parodically portrayed, she is a princess nonetheless. He goes on to describe Paul's relationship to her, without offering her given name:

> I called her Mo-nah-se-tah, the name of the beautiful daughter of the Cheyenne chief, Little Rock. At first she didn't particularly care for the name, which means, "the young grass that shoots in the spring," but after I explained to her that Mo-nah-se-tah was supposed to have had an illegitimate son by General Armstrong Custer she took to the name like a duck to water. (29)

How peculiar that "Paul's girl" had not heard of Mo-nah-se-tah, since the legend has, in fact, been kept alive over the years by Cheyenne people themselves! But it is no less peculiar than the fantasy that she would want to be named for the woman who allegedly bore Custer's "illegitimate" son, a child and wife he abandoned for his "civilized" partner. Could it be that she expects disrespectful treatment by others or that she read Paul's dubbing as his attempt at flattery, however misguided? Maclean's closure of the narrative on "whore" prevents us from readily seeing any other possibility.

Making use of the Indian Princess image is not limited to masculinist movies or Anglo male writers, however. In "Who Is Your

Mother? Red Roots of White Feminism," Paula Gunn Allen recounts how Eva Emery Dye co-opted the image of Sacajawea to be used as a feminist heroine in the late-nineteenth-century women's movement (Allen). Sacajawea functioned as a cultural mediator, no doubt, but much controversy surrounds the particulars of her life and her role on the expedition. The questions raised by the historian Kidwell, quoted earlier, resurface when one reads accounts of Sacajawea's abuse by her husband, Charboneau, guide to the Lewis and Clark expedition. Sally Roesch Wagner reconstructs another of the early American feminist movement's connections to Native women's lives in her article "The Iroquois Influence on Women's Rights." According to Wagner, the antebellum suffragettes around Seneca Falls, New York, were influenced and inspired by their neighbor clanmothers among the Haudenosaunee. Such alliances were not always exploitative or appropriative, but rather were based on mutual benefit and respect. Wagner's research provides a model for feminist scholarship on Indian women.

More recently, however, Mary Dearborne, who draws on Werner Sollors's work for her book *Pocahontas' Daughters,* gropes toward a definition of "female ethnicity," beginning with American Indian women, and along the way poses the question, "Did Pocahontas know that she was an ethnic woman?" Because Pocahontas did not leave a written record of her thoughts and experience, Dearborne concludes, we cannot know. Aside from the privileging of textual records implied in Dearborne's conclusion, how could Pocahontas *not* know that she was viewed by colonists differently than European women were viewed?[11] For one thing, as the favorite daughter of Powhatan, she was kidnapped by the English and held for over a year as ransom for demands that Powhatan met; the English continued to wage war nonetheless, and Pocahontas was not returned to her father (Vaughan 114). Moreover, if there are parallels to Phillis Wheatley, an eighteenth-century black woman slave who did leave a written record in her poetry, one would have to say, yes, Pocahontas knew she was "other," "heathen," in the eyes of many. In her earlier historical moment, Pocahontas was set apart by her "race," no doubt, despite her marriage to a European man, just as Wheatley was considered black, and therefore subject to slavery on the earthly plane, despite her Christian salvation—racism dictates no less. In other words, even in well-intentioned works by capable scholars, such as Dearborne, a sort of theoretical blindness to America's racist history occurs.[12]

One of the more chilling recent representations of Indian women appears in a recent publication aimed at youth. The author of a new comic book, *Ghostdancing*, presents an Indian princess/whore, dancing nearly naked in a prison cell in a "furious fit of dementia. A death rattle."[13]

> She wants to scream . . . but that is not her way. . . . Instead she grinds her teeth hard through her lip. There is no pain and, after a while, everything is still and dead again. (Delano and Case 13)

The erotic images accompanying the prose revive the tragic view of Indian women's existence, at the same time as they make her "yours for the taking," depicting her as scantily rag-clad and voluptuous. The author takes refuge in what he sees as his right as a writer to appropriate Indian sacred traditions toward his own ends. After explaining that he has "read *Bury My Heart at Wounded Knee,* and all the other 'Indian books' I could lay my hands on," he states,

> Doubtless with countless other pseudo-hippie romantics, I fantasized a Utopian, dignified nomadic coexistence with the land, and heaped opprobrium on the callously indifferent heads of our colonial ancestors— almost ignoring, in my arcadian reverie, the contemporary extermination of Native Brazilians. History repeats itself endlessly. The Christian cultures rob and pillage instinctively. It's depressing.
>
> So what do *I* do? I write a mad, symbolic, apocalyptic drama—a millennial western epic, in which I animate representations of beings sacred to various Native American mythologies. I put words in their mouths, and feelings in their hearts. I distort their context and use them to express my own prejudices, preconceptions, and guilts.
>
> But that's what writers do. We rob and pillage instinctively. We're cultural and emotional pirates. . . .
>
> But hey, we don't mean any harm. We're just passing through. (Delano and Case 25)

I am not sure whether Delano's recognition of his own egregious appropriation makes him better than a Lynn Andrews or a Jamake Highwater (the former claiming her "right" to appropriate Indian spirituality through a vision, and the latter claiming his "right" to represent Indians through a vague blood heritage, seriously in dispute), but I tend to think not.[14] More to the point, what most would-be-Indian frauds and writing "pirates" often have in common is their desire to reach into

Indian cultures and histories for gender and spiritual constructions more appealing than those they apparently see before them in their own cultures or histories. They are akin to grave robbers, under whose "pirating" acts Indians have also suffered long and hard. But if we follow Delano's rationalized ethos, what the hey, they're dead anyway. Delano's woman is "dead inside," so maybe it is not such a stretch to connect such sentiments with grave robbing as well as with salvage anthropology and other academic "traditions" that claim the right to capture Things Indian before those things are lost.

By these examples, we can see the dangers inherent in subsuming "race" into "ethnicity," maneuvers that hasten to link us all together in multicultural America without a proper understanding of our historical differences. While the definition of Indians as peoples historically set apart in a "racial" category by themselves is a generalization that by no means fully incorporates the urban Indian communities that have grown considerably over the past several decades, nor the individuals deracinated through adoption, Indian sovereignty movements of necessity define "Indianness" as a personal and tribal identity—in other words, an identity that cannot be claimed without corroboration by the tribe, band, or nation. Within those definitive boundaries, terms such as "fiduciary" and "fiscal" take on special meanings or simply retain the meanings Indians invested in them when they made those treaties with the Great White Father in Washington—treaty making as quasi-kinship bonding, which also apparently meant different things to the parties involved.

A well-documented aspect of the fiduciary or trust institution *within tribal societies* encompasses an intricate network of kinship relations. Among the Lakota, such ties are referred to as the *tiyospaye* (literally, a circle of tipis), which is a reference to extended families who camped together. Kinship ties are established through blood ties, marriage, and ceremonies of adoption, such as those of the *kola* and *hunka*. While generalizing from one tribal tradition to something one might designate as a pan-Indian perspective can be dangerous, I believe it is not a stretch to generalize that all indigenous tribes organize themselves around kinship. On the other side of the continent, Mary Jemison, a white woman captured at the age of fifteen, went through Haudenosaune (Iroquois, specifically Seneca) adoption rituals, so that she could be made into a relative to replace a brother who had died. Of that experience she writes,

I afterwards learned that the ceremony I at that time passed through, was that of adoption. The two . . . [sisters] who had lost a brother in Washington's war, sometime in the year before, and in consequence of his death went up to Fort Pitt, on the day on which I arrived there, in order to receive a prisoner or an enemy's scalp, to supply their loss. . . . It was my happy lot to be accepted for adoption. . . . I was ever considered and treated as a real sister, the same as though I had been born of their mother. (Seaver 77)

Neither "race" nor biological sex factor into the Haudenosaune need to create this bond. Moreover, Jemison's descriptive phrase "happy lot" suggests much about the belonging that kinship ties can bring. She died at age ninety-nine, a Seneca grandmother. I do not mean to diminish the trauma she experienced seeing relatives killed and then being captured and taken from her own family and home; nevertheless, I would add that Jemison was one of many "white Indians" who preferred Indian life to their repressive and oppressive positions in non-Indian colonial societies—a topic beyond the scope of this essay.[15] Nonetheless, the trust implied in such ties exceeds not only "race," but class loyalties of a capitalist, profit economy. In *The Gift: Imagination and the Erotic Life of Property*, Lewis Hyde argues that such "erotic bonding" involving people as "commodities" of exchange functions as the center of gift-giving cultures. "Erotic," in the context of Hyde's argument, stands for bonding that is consummately dynamic and vital, the stuff that holds communities together.

In her novel *Waterlily*, Ella Cara Deloria, a Lakota anthropologist, offers a unique perspective on the practice of kinship bonding among the Lakota, the "buying" of wives—a practice considered the most honorable way to be married. As the aunt of the protagonist, Waterlily, attempts to put an end to speculations about whether Waterlily will accept the offer of marriage, made through the presentation of horses and other gifts placed at Waterlily's tipi by the young man's female relatives, the cultural values become clear:

Dream Woman spoke up, "We do not yet know how our niece will decide, of course. But if she says no, we must accept it. That is as it should be. Some families, who set greater store by things than by kinship, might force their girls to marry. In our family, Father says, no girl need marry unless she wishes. And he is right." (151)

Although the people in the novel and their way of life are idealized, Deloria succeeds in her intention to make some of her people's ways sensible to the non-Indian readership of the 1940s. Not only does Waterlily "sacrifice" for the kinship bond, she also enables her uncle to replace the horses he lost that were intended as give-away items at her grandmother's ghost-releasing ceremony; it was nonetheless a difficult decision for her to make. Generosity is one of the four essential Lakota virtues (the others being fortitude, bravery, and gratitude), and as a beloved child, a *hunka,* it was Waterlily's role to be generous in all ways. Men had equally demanding social roles.

While these examples of gift-giving may seem dated, out of some distant idyllic past, it is not so. Valuing generosity and personal sacrifice was a vital aspect of the training I received as a child, as was respect for elders. In the late nineteenth century, laws were passed to prohibit Indians from communal practices such as give-aways and their attendant rituals. Even before the passage of the American Indian Freedom of Religion Act in 1978, tribes across the country began reviving their ancient traditions. A couple of summers ago, I attended an annual celebration in my home community, and was pleased to see that the *heyoka* (sacred clowns) had come back to taunt the people and to beg money for the poor.

These sacred clowns, however, are in some ways a cleaned-up version of their foremothers and -fathers. In times past, they were a sexually outrageous lot, often imitating lewd sexual acts to the entertainment of all, but because such spectacles offended the missionaries and government officials, they were made to cease. As "contraries" who did things backwards and even mocked the sacred during ceremonies, *heyokas* fulfilled a unique role in tribal communities; humor functions centrally in many indigenous religious practices as a force to check pomposity and to highlight both human frailty and absurdities in the human condition. Sacred themselves, they were not to be contradicted or in any way harmed, no matter how outrageous their antics. They also represented a unique gender category, since they seldom married—indeed, they were greatly feared because of their Thunder Being dream power—and they "played" at traditional male and female roles. *Winktas* (men who chose to take on women's roles in society) and manlyhearted women (women who chose to take on men's roles in society) also died away with religious and government censorship, or at least were shamed from public view.[16] I suspect that, given the homophobia in American society in general, it will take a while for *heyokas* (or whatever the equivalent would be among other indigenous peoples) to return to the full power they once had and for alternative gender roles to be fully accepted. Many Indians today are Christian themselves and slow to see the oppressive legacy of the Christian worldviews forcibly imposed on them and their ancestors.

I hope that my discussion of "race," class, and gender gives a sense of the complexity of how those terms have come to bear on American Indian women. Appropriations of American Indian women's experience and stereotypes of our identities, historical and contemporary, pose serious obstacles to realistic and humane renderings of our lives. In order for class differences and struggles, such as in my story of Skelly's truck stop, to be understood adequately, we must make sure that "racial" history and cultural kinship values enter our thinking. Regional histories must also be given their due.

However clarifying, my own writing risks seeming both like a "tour of the exotic country" and like the voice of "the imperial tongue." I do recognize my own privilege as one who lives and works among the writing elite; nevertheless, my deepest loyalties lie elsewhere. True knowing grows slowly, and sometimes we cannot see the thing we are looking for *because* we are looking for it—looking as sightseers do. Walker Percy has an amusing way of describing the sightseer's dilemma, as he imagines a tourist couple's paradoxical delight and disappointment in discovering an Indian village off the beaten path:

> "This is it" and "Now we are really living" do not necessarily refer to the sovereign encounter of the person with the sight that enlivens the mind and gladdens the heart. It means that now at last we are having the acceptable experience. The present experience is always measured by a prototype, the "it" of their dreams. "Now I am really living" means that now I am filling the role of sightseer and the sight is living up to the prototype of sights. This quaint and picturesque village is measured by a Platonic ideal of the Quaint and Picturesque. (53)

They will return, Percy surmises, with their ethnologist friend to "certify their experience as genuine" (53).

Indian cultures are growing and changing today as they always have been; hence, we would do well to avoid the sightseer's mistake in trying to "capture" (as with a photograph) their essence. Rather, our inquiries need to involve us as dynamically as possible in listening, without succumbing to the temptation of hasty closures of mind or lapses into national mythologies. Reflecting on Emberley's words in the epigraph, recognizing the "impossibility of totalization" in the writing of American Indian women's history does not preclude the possibility of "meaningful *representation* of totalization through narrative closures," as long as the drama of such intellectual balancing acts is staged and Indian "subjects" have their ample share of the speaking parts in such textual dramas.

What I call "subjectivity" and "agency" approximates what Percy calls "personal sovereignty," a willing abandonment of preconceived packaging of ideas, coupled with a delightful and liberating empowerment in discovering truth. My sense of "personal sovereignty" also includes tribal sovereignty, a strong link to the concerns of a people much greater and more important than myself. I must confess, to tell a public story of my own personal suffering would make me ashamed of myself, both because my sufferings seem like nothing in relation to the sufferings of others I have known and because to focus on myself that way would seem inappropriate. A full story of my mother's and my grandmother's lives deserves to be told, and mine folded into theirs, but I would rather postpone that telling until I can sufficiently cloak it in fiction and humor so as to celebrate their strengths as well as to probe their failures. Yet I honor those Indian women who do and can tell stories about the oppressions they have suffered *as women and as Indians,* their stories and the ones they carry for others; all those stories need to be told. Certain stories can eat a hole in the center of our being, trying to get out. As Beth Brant tells us, "The secrets I am told grow in my stomach. They make me want to vomit. They stay in me and my stomach twists—like [Betty Osborne's] lovely face—and my hands reach for a pen, a typewriter to calm the rage and violence that make a home in me" (*Writing as Witness* 13).[17]

Such a writing response goes beyond compassion or empathy to commitment. In the Lakota language, the term *cante ista* means "the heart's eye," a way of seeing that comes from both the deepest of emotional and spiritual experiences and the awe, humility, and compassion engendered by suffering. "Heartfelt" would, I suppose, be the English equivalent, but "cordial" also means "heartfelt." *Cante ista* connotes something more than the individualistic way in English we customarily use "heartfelt" to designate a knowledge based on experiences that have moved us. *Cante ista* implies responsibility toward others, a trajectory of feeling into action for the greater good, the good of others. Humiliation and shame (in the Lakota sense of *unsiga*, frequently translated as "pitifulness"), which are at the core of ceremonies of deprivation and flesh offerings, liberate the religious seeker into generosity and sacrifice as a means of both giving back and belonging once again to a world of relatives—"relatives" includes all other living beings.

Of all the people I knew at Skelly's truck stop, knowing Dorothy has moved me to the depths of my being. When I returned ten years later, Dorothy had moved away to go to school, but her daughter Bobbie had become a good friend and helper to my mother. She was also taking care of her grandparents. Bobbie became my best friend— we were bound to one another through gift-giving and sacrifice. She was bright, had been valedictorian of her high school class. Her three-hundred-pound body was exceeded in abundance only by her sense of humor and generosity. That spring, as the tadpoles grew into baby frogs, she went to the river and gathered up a handful, then headed for her grandparents' trailer home. She knocked on the door and when Grampa opened it Bobbie smiled, liberating a mouthful of baby frogs in one green streak. I tell of that afternoon to honor her, her memory and her life. But despite her being wise beyond her years, she despaired, feeling there was no place for her in the world. That summer, drunk, she drove her car into a cement wall—it was probably on a dare, since she took three other young people with her.

Several years ago Doreen, my sister Indian-way, drank herself to death, leaving five children for her no-good husband to raise. We were the same age. Throughout our childhoods growing up on the reservation, we vowed that we would make something of ourselves. I would like to be able to tell you more of her story, to honor her in that way, but the time is not right to do that. As Brant says, to do so takes courage, a courage to open up "our wounded communities, our families, to eyes and ears that do not love us" (*Writing as Witness* 53). To tell Doreen's story would require "the shimmer of humor . . . tribal visions . . . and tragic wisdom" Vizenor calls for to thwart "scriptural simulations" in the "literature of dominance." Doreen was known for her sense of humor, and deserves that sort of story. I name her here to

mark a place in the world, in writing, for her story—not as a sensa-
tional, sentimental, or tragic example of pain, but as my heart's punc-
tuation mark for the importance of remembering to remember. I
know I live too much with a survivor's grief and guilt. But survivors
carry more than grief and guilt—they must live their dreams doubled, perhaps multiplied many times over. I would rather close with a
happier story, a story of empowerment: Dorothy now has a Ph.D. She
is happily remarried and working actively in Indian education.
Skelly's burned down sometime in the 1970s, but I am sure Dorothy
remembers as I do what it meant to work there.

Activism for me means first hearing and telling stories "seen" with
the *cante ista*. When stories of a people's heroism and suffering are
presented as a transparent history—an old, safe story, another legend
of "the Indian's" fall from dignity in history—no new insights into
our common humanity are possible. The most important conclusions
to be made about the lives of the women whom I worked alongside at
Skelly's are first their own, and unlike Pocahontas or Sacajawea or
Bobbie or Doreen, they may still be able to make their stories known,
in their own words.

NOTES

1. I use the terms "American Indian," "Native American," "Native," "indigenous," and "tribal" fairly interchangeably in speech, as a sign to my listeners that they need not struggle for the politically correct term. But I do make a
distinction in my thinking and in my writing. "American Indian" or simply "Indian" is my preferred term for indigenous peoples in the lower forty-eight
states; Alaskan and Canadian Natives often prefer those name designations.
Differences in the historical and legal backgrounds of Alaska Natives and Native Hawaiians require that they be seen in their own distinct political and cultural contexts and referred to by their terms for themselves. This essay is primarily about indigenous peoples in the lower forty-eight states. "First Nations"
is also used by groups and individuals in Canada and the United States. "Native American" came into usage with the political movements of the 1960s and
1970s and began more or less in the academy among Indian educators and activists. Most of the American Indian peoples I know refer to themselves by their
tribally (band-, community-, or clan-) specific names first, then to themselves as
"Indian." See Matthew Snipp, *American Indians: The First of This Land* for a fuller
discussion of the issue of naming and Indian identity, as well as for demo-
graphics on American Indians and tribes.

I am an enrolled member of the Assiniboine (Nakota) tribe of the Ft. Peck Reservation, a reservation that is also home to Dakota people.

2. M. Annette Jaimes and Theresa Halsey, in their article "American Indian Women: At the Center of Indigenous Resistance in North America," present a compelling story of the Indian women who are heroines among Indian people today.

3. All the names of the women in this story are fictitious, but the events are true from my point of view. Special thanks to David L. Moore for his comments on this manuscript and his unwavering support, and to Beth Brant for our many discussions about the issues contained here and for inspiring me to believe that it is not oxymoronic to see writing as a "brilliant and loving weapon of change."

4. In particular, Beth Brant's stories in *Mohawk Trail* and *Food and Spirits* offer portrayals of urban life.

5. "Pure" science in Western traditions strives for results that can be predicted and duplicated. Indigenous people similarly conduct such experimentation and study in their realms, though they may be guided by decidedly different interpretations of outcomes and predictions of possible outcomes.

6. The difficulty in interpreting the Native American count through the U.S. census illustrates the trouble one can get into in accounting for the various ways of identifying as Indian. While in the 1980 and 1990 census figures many researchers associated inflated numbers of Native Americans with positive media portrayals of Indians, those planning for the year 2000 census fear the opposite, that 10 to 20 percent of the actual Native American population will be missed.

7. Secretary of Interior Babbitt, in his testimony during the recent suit against the BIA, admits that the fiduciary responsibility of the federal government toward tribes and Native American individuals who own trust lands has been woefully neglected if not criminally violated.

8. Casinos and other forms of gambling are relatively new to Indian tribes and have barely begun to provide the capital necessary for building a sustaining infrastructure for a few Indian nations. Largely through the efforts of Donald Trump, Congress is attempting to tax casino profits—a move that flies in the face of the sovereign nation status tribes assert for themselves. Moreover, tribal gaming comprises 8 percent of the total gaming in the United States, and 85 percent of tribal casino employees are non-Indian, according to Richard Hill, head of the Indian Gaming Commission in a speech before Congress.

9. For a fuller account of the blood-quantum dilemma, see M. Annette Jaimes, "Federal Indian Identification Policy: A Usurpation of Indigenous Sovereignty in Contemporary North America."

10. It is interesting to note that the stereotypical Indian male is of Plains

origins—never from a Pueblo tribe, for example—while stereotypical Indian females most often belong to woodlands tribes. Plains Indian women apparently do not conform to non-Indian ideals of beauty and femininity; while, in the economy of American image-making, Plains Indian men represent the rugged individualism non-Indians hope to achieve.

11. Two recent pieces on Pocahontas provide enlightening readings on her life: Jennifer Gray Reddish, "Pocahontas"; and Beth Brant, "Grandmothers of a New World," in *Writing as Witness*.

12. According to Alden T. Vaughan, in *Roots of American Racism*, Pocahontas's people were not easily subdued by the English. Vaughan argues that in an effort to end Indian resistance to English colonization in the time immediately preceding Pocahontas's kidnapping, the English military commanders "rapidly abandoned all regard for customary rules of war and gained much of their success by guile and merciless treatment of captives" (114).

> [Thomas] Gates lured some Indians into the open with a music-and-dance act by his drummer, then slaughtered them. Percy routed the Paspahegh tribe, destroyed its village and fields, and allowed his men to throw the Indian queen's children into the river and shoot their brains out for sport. Lord De La Warr wanted to burn the queen; Percy convinced him to let her die by the sword instead. (114)

13. Special thanks to Juan Mah y Busch, a doctoral student at Cornell University, for bringing the comic book to my attention. Other recent studies of indigenous American gender relations and constructions include Sue-Ellen Jacobs, Wesley Thomas, and Sabine Lang, eds., *Two-Spirited People*; Sabine Lang, *Men as Women, Women as Men*; Laura Klein and Lillian A. Ackerman, eds., *Women and Power in Native North America*.

14. Ward Churchill discusses the works of Lynn Andrews and Jamake Highwater in his book *Fantasies of a Master Race*, and mentions the two in his more recent work, *Indians Are Us?*: "Think about the significance of charlatans like Carlos Castaneda and Jamake Highwater and Mary Summer Rain and Lynn Andrews churning out 'Indian' bestsellers, one after the other, while Indians typically can't get into print" (82). Of Lynn Andrews, Churchill writes in *Fantasies*,

> And, as if all this were not enough, we are currently treated to the spectacle of Lynn Andrews, an air-head "feminist" yuppie who once wrangled herself a weekend in the company of a pair of elderly Indian women of indistinct tribal origin. In her version of events, they had apparently been waiting their entire lives for just such an opportunity to unburden themselves of every innermost secret of their people's spiritual knowledge. They immediately acquainted her with such previously unknown

"facts" as the presence of kachinas in the Arctic Circle and the power of "Jaguar Women," charged her with serving as their "messenger," and sent her forth to write a series of books so outlandish in their pretensions as to make Castaneda seem a model of propriety by comparison. Predictably, the Andrews books have begun to penetrate the "popular literature" curriculum of academe. (189)

Also see Kathryn W. Shanley, "The Indians America Loves to Love and Read." A version of my discussion of the term "race" as it appears in the present essay first appeared in the above-cited article.

15. For a fuller accounting of "White Indians," people captured by various tribal groups who did not want to return to non-Indian life, see James Axtell, "The White Indians of Colonial America."

16. Walter L. Williams, in *The Spirit and the Flesh,* explores the topic of gay sexual orientation in traditional North American Indian, Alaskan Native, and Mexican Indian cultures, and also touches on Indian lesbian sexuality and gender construction. Also see Evelyn Blackwood, "Sexuality and Gender in Certain Native American Tribes: The Case of Cross-Gender Females"; and Claude E. Schaeffer, "The Kutenai Female Berdache: Courier, Guide, Prophetess, and Warrior."

17. Beth Brant began her career as a writer after editing an anthology of North American Indian women's writing, *A Gathering of Spirit.* In commencing that project, she decided she had to draw together the voices of all Native women, not just those recognized for their literary achievements, so she contacted tribal communities, prisons, and every other place where Indian women are likely to be. Her efforts resulted in an extraordinary collection of writings, but also in her becoming the repository for many Indian women's stories and secrets, as a friend and sometimes a lone confidant.

WORKS CITED

Allen, Paula Gunn. "Who Is Your Mother? Red Roots of White Feminism." In *The Sacred Hoop: Recovering the Feminine in American Indian Traditions,* 209–21. Boston: Beacon Press, 1986.

Axtell, James. "The White Indians of Colonial America." In *The European and the Indian: Essays in the Ethnohistory of Colonial North America,* 168–206. New York: Oxford University Press, 1981.

Banton, Michael J. *Racial Theories.* New York: Cambridge University Press, 1998.

Barsh, Russel. "Are Anthropologists Hazardous to Indians' Health?" *Journal of Ethnic Studies* 15.4 (1988): 1–38.

Bell, Betty Louise. "Pocahontas: 'Little Mischief' and 'the Dirty Men.'" *SAIL* 6.1 (spring 1994): 63–70.

Blackwood, Evelyn. "Sexuality and Gender in Certain Native American Tribes: The Case of Cross-Gender Females." *Signs* 10.11 (1984): 27–42.

Brant, Beth. "Preface: Telling." In *Food and Spirits,* 11–17. Ithaca, NY: Firebrand Books, 1991.

———. *Mohawk Trail*. Ithaca, NY: Firebrand Books, 1985.

———. *Writing as Witness: Essay and Talk*. Toronto: Women's Press, 1994.

———, ed. *A Gathering of Spirit*. Toronto: Women's Press, 1984; 1989.

Churchill, Ward. *Fantasies of a Master Race: Literature, Cinema, and the Colonization of American Indians,* ed. M. Annette Jaimes. Monroe, ME: Common Courage Press, 1992.

———. *Indians Are Us? Culture and Genocide in Native North America*. Monroe, ME: Common Courage Press, 1994.

Dearborne, Mary. *Pocahontas' Daughters: Gender and Ethnicity in American Culture*. New York: Oxford University Press, 1986.

Delano, Jamie, and Richard Case. *Ghostdancing* 1 (March 1995) (DC Comics).

Deloria, Ella C. *Waterlily*. Lincoln: University of Nebraska Press, 1988.

Deloria, Vine, Jr. *Custer Died for Your Sins: An Indian Manifesto*. 1969; Norman: University of Oklahoma Press, 1988.

Flagg, Fannie. *Fried Green Tomatoes at the Whistle Stop Café*. New York: Random House, 1987.

Gates, Henry Louis, Jr. *"Race," Writing, and Difference*. Chicago: University of Chicago Press, 1985, 1986.

Gould, Stephen Jay. *Mismeasure of Man*. New York: Norton, 1981.

Green, Rayna. "The Pocahontas Perplex: The Image of Indian Women in American Culture." *Massachusetts Review* (autumn 1975): 698–714.

Hyde, Lewis. *The Gift: Imagination and the Erotic Life of Property*. New York: Vintage Books, 1983.

Jacobs, Sue-Ellen, Wesley Thomas, and Sabine Lang, eds. *Two-Spirited People: Native American Gender Identity, Sexuality, and Spirituality*. Urbana: University of Illinois Press, 1997.

Jaimes, M. Annette. "Federal Indian Identification Policy: A Usurpation of Indigenous Sovereignty in Contemporary North America." In *The State of Native America: Genocide, Colonization, and Resistance,* ed. M. Annette Jaimes, 123–38. Boston: South End Press, 1992.

Jaimes, M. Annette, and Theresa Halsey. "American Indian Women: At the Center of Indigenous Resistance in North America." In *The State of Native America: Genocide, Colonization, and Resistance,* ed. M. Annette Jaimes, 311–44. Boston: South End Press, 1992.

Kidwell, Clara Sue. "Indian Women as Cultural Mediators." *Ethnohistory* 39.2 (spring 1992): 97–107.

Klein, Laura, and Lillian A. Ackerman, eds. *Women and Power in Native North America.* Norman: University of Oklahoma Press, 1995.

LaCapra, Dominick, ed. *The Bounds of Race: Perspectives on Hegemony and Resistance.* Ithaca: Cornell University Press, 1991.

Lang, Sabine. *Men as Women, Women as Men: Changing Gender in Native American Cultures.* Austin: University of Texas Press, 1998.

Maclean, Norman. *A River Runs through It.* 1976; New York: Pocket Books, 1992.

O'Brien, Sharon. "Tribes and Indians: With Whom Does the United States Maintain a Relationship?" *Notre Dame Law Review* 66:5 (1991): 1461–1502.

Percy, Walker. "The Loss of the Creature." *Message in the Bottle: How Queer Man Is, How Queer Language Is, and What One Has to Do with the Other,* 46–63. New York: Farrar, Straus, and Giroux, 1975.

Reddish, Jennifer Gray. "Pocahontas." *Tribal College* 6.4 (spring 1995): 22–33.

Schaeffer, Claude E. "The Kutenai Female Berdache: Courier, Guide, Prophetess, and Warrior." *Ethnohistory* 12.3 (summer 1965): 193–236.

Seaver, James E. *A Narrative of the Life of Mrs. Mary Jemison.* Edited by June Namias. Norman: University of Oklahoma Press, 1992.

Shanley, Kathryn W. "The Indians America Loves to Love and Read." *American Indian Quarterly.* 21.4 (1997): 675–702.

Snipp, Matthew. *American Indians: The First of This Land.* New York: Russell Sage Foundation, 1989.

Sollors, Werner. *Beyond Ethnicity: Consent and Descent in American Culture.* New York: Oxford University Press, 1986.

———, ed. *The Invention of Ethnicity.* New York: Oxford University Press, 1989.

Vaughan, Alden T. *Roots of American Racism: Essays on the Colonial Experience.* New York: Oxford University Press, 1995.

Vizenor, Gerald. *Manifest Manners: Postindian Warriors of Survivance.* Hanover: Wesleyan University Press, 1994.

Wagner, Sally Roesch. "The Iroquois Influence on Women's Rights." *Akwe:kon Journal* (spring 1992): 4–15.

Warhol, Robyn R., and Diane Price Herndl, eds. *Feminisms: An Anthology of Literary Theory and Criticism.* 1977; New Brunswick: Rutgers University Press, 1991.

Williams, Walter L. *The Spirit and the Flesh.* Boston: Beacon Press, 1986.

Wright, Richard. *American Hunger.* 1977; New York: Perennial Library, 1983.

Chapter 9

Ella Que Tiene Jefes y No Los Ve, Se Queda en Cueros
Chicana Intellectuals (Re)Creating Revolution

Edén E. Torres

My grandmother rearranges common sayings to fit her experience and her perspective on the world. The title of this essay is one of her reconfigured proverbs. As I grew up, I often found myself in arguments with people who would utter these sayings in their customary forms. Not only had I heard them differently, but my grandmother's versions made more logical—as well as emotional and intuitive—sense to me. The above adage in its conventional form warns male employers to distrust their workers, and to guard against employee theft. (El que tiene peones y no los ve, se queda en cueros.) But my grandmother changes the masculine pronoun to a feminine one, and replaces the word *peones* (peons), with *jefes* (bosses). Her rendition says, "She who has bosses and does not see them is left naked."

The first substitution reflects her delightful inclination toward switching genders, turning traditional dichos into teaching tools for her granddaughters. Ironically, these messages were spoken in the kitchen as we prepared meals for an active—as in volcanic—extended family.[1] Yet it is clear that she hoped and/or expected sus nietas (her granddaughters) to go into the world with whatever knowledge she could pass on. The second change counsels us to see power where it exists—to keep our eye on the boss. Though my grandmother remains a traditional Mexican woman in many ways, I can easily trace the source of my rebelliousness to her.

My grandmother's wisdom lies at the center of this essay. It informs my vision of Chicana intellectualism and its relationship to social justice. The words, and the circumstances under which I heard them, frame the major themes that wind through and intertwine in this meandering river of a composition. (Thus, I hate to list them sequentially.) Readers may find other themes more useful, but I intend to speak about the importance of the knowledge we acquire through our ties to the Mexican American community. Significant also is the function of ethnic loyalty across class divisions in our personal/professional life. I also want to talk about the social responsibilities of Chicana intellectuals and the way our unique perspective challenges dominant paradigms. Related to this is a discussion of how Chicana writers represent lived experience *and* express political ideology. Who interprets and/or teaches this material is an unavoidable part of such commentary.

As a newly appointed assistant professor, I frequently struggle to maintain my sanity—the core of who I am. Learning is my seducer. Though it is often warm and joyous, it can also be a cruel and abusive lover separating me from my family and friends. It is most dangerous when I become too intimate with institutional forms of education. Remembering my grandmother's wise counsel prompts me to remain aloof, even as I continue to use formal scholarship. Knowledge has many alternative sources. Applying them keeps my connection to my grandmother (and thus my culture) strong. This will not allow me to stray too far from home—from the figurative and literal neighborhood where social transformation is an obvious and glaring need. From this perspective, my individual socioeconomic situation is unimportant.

Loosely described, my primary work is a study of the way Chicana writers use, define, represent, and (re)create Chicana and Mexican American ethnicity and culture. In writing about Chicanas, I use "(re)" as a prefix to words like create, claim, construct, interpret, and so on. In parentheses it signifies something done over again or changed slightly in the process of creating something original. Though the writers act as a focal point, my concerns include culture studies, ethnic environments, and social transformation.

Because I care about the relationship between intellectual production and the women in our community, my work has included interviews with working-class women who are not writers, have not read the literature I discuss, and in most cases are not aware that it even exists. While some scholars choose to emphasize the split between Chicana writers and "real" women in the community, I focus on the unbreakable bond between us.[2] These conversations provide evidence of a shared context, of authentically created characters and fictional responses to similar social environments. I do not disregard possible differences based on class, education, and levels of acculturation, but illuminate a viable space between writers and nonwriters. Comparing the women allows for an exploration of the depth and function of implicit knowledge, the information gained in daily life and expressed in a variety of social locations. But I do not study culture apolitically.

For me, the word "Chicana" signifies not only Mexican American ethnicity but the resistant, political awareness of "El Movimiento"— the Chicano Brown Power movement of the late 1960s and early 1970s. While it is true that the legacy of El Movimiento carries with it tiresome traces of nationalist imperialism and hypermasculinity, it is not difficult to find competing strains of feminist criticism and resistance, as well as nationalism, that have more to do with cultural loyalty than political hegemony. Our contemporary role, as it has been throughout our history, is to cast a critical eye on the bosses—to resist the impulses of the empire—to be wary, cynical, suspicious, and constantly on guard, or we will all be left naked. How Chicanas and Chicanos choose to do that may vary.

One of our strengths in this endeavor is our culture—the memories of things to come—the timeless relationships between grandmothers and granddaughters. Throughout most of my academic endeavors, that bond sustains me.[3] I have rarely spoken to family and friends about my life in the academy in anything other than joking and disparaging ways. Their gentle teasing eases our fear of separation. But in the dark and lonely days of researching and dealing with university bureaucracy, I have purposefully sought out more serious conversations with Mexican American women outside the academy. Because they remind me of my family members, I do not relate to them as a scholar, but as a Chicana—una nieta—who happens to be a teacher.

My original motivation for interviewing working-class women as part of my research did not arise out of a desire to collect social science data nor the impulse to become an ethnographer. I simply regard them as experts on the context that I attempt to describe. But even this notion

comes as a secondary result of feeling alienated from formal scholarship, philosophical inquiry, and traditional research methods. Though
this anxiety is eternal, one pivotal event made clear the emotional force
of my attachment to the community.

In the early 1990s I attended a Chicano scholars conference in San
Antonio. During a plenary session luncheon, we heard passionate
speeches about the dominant culture, the oppression of people of
color, and the exploitation of Mexican American workers. When an
unscheduled speaker from the community—a Chicana union orga-
nizer—addressed the session, she received little attention from the
audience. Abstract lectures on classism garnered more interest than
this firsthand experience. We were a room full of academics, making
good salaries or acquiring the skills to do so. Many of us were there
because universities were paying some or all of our expenses. Few
were listening to the speaker describe the plight of factory workers.

Similarly (and disgustingly), no one acknowledged or seemed to
notice that we were being served by Mexican/Mexican American and
African American waiters. These men were not listening either. They
were working. It was a stressful situation in which the Anglo boss
took them aside and chastised them for not making sure the coffee
was hot, not refilling bread trays, and not getting the desserts out
faster. All of this was in response to complaints from some of the conference participants. I felt sick, dizzy with shame and appalled that
few of my colleagues seemed to sense the frightening irony of it.
Thinking of the women in my family who had worked in hotels made
me desperate to escape. I walked out of the conference and into the
street to regain my balance. In playful, familiar conversation with a
local woman, my sense of dislocation disappeared.

While intellectualism is part of my everyday life, I know that the
institution can be dangerous to my perspective. Constant immersion
in academic language weakens my code-switching skills. Once this
occurs, the bosses of the world become less visible. This, above all
else, frightens me, and the struggle to stay connected to my community is eternal. Thus, I continue to long for the wisdom of my grandmother—for conversations in the kitchen. Similar battles of the soul
abound in the work of the writers I am studying. Clearly, we must remind ourselves that the bond between us and the working-class reality of much of our community is deep and insoluble—yet paradoxically, always in danger.

Too often, those of us who are successful as writers, educators, and critical theorists feel guilty about our accomplishments. Or we experience a sense of alienation in relationship to (not necessarily from) our communities. However ludicrous, we internalize messages about what constitutes a "real" or "authentic" Chicana and feel awkward because our reality so rarely matches the narrow definitions we hear. These images come from both inside and outside the community— images that we, ironically, help to construct. They also descend from racist or ethnocentric critics whose stereotypes of Mexican Americans do not include academic excellence, intellectualism, or mainstream audience recognition. Though it is often a rejection of elitism on our part, we sometimes unwittingly absorb and recapitulate the same sentiments.

So thoroughly have we as a community consumed our lessons in hierarchical structures and social stratification, that we believe intellectuals to be somehow "above" those who have not been published, attained academic degrees, or participated in society at the institutional level. Once status of this nature has been acquired we imagine that the person no longer has an interest in or fidelity to the community. Furthermore, we believe that Chicana identity will become little more than an occasional colloquialism. When we become writers or scholars, tension is created between what we believe status brings and what we know ourselves to be.

While it may be true that some individuals abandon their ethnic loyalties and the fight for social justice with the acquisition of increased social status, it is not the inevitable outcome of intellectual activity, commercial success, or institutional recognition. To assume that one cannot be both Chicana and intellectual is to support the stereotype that Mexican Americans lack the capacity to be cerebral. It denies a long history of Mexican and Amerindian creativity and thought. To presuppose that we will leave our historic, political concerns behind is to waste the talents and skills we have developed. Accepting the premise that relative social privilege or economic prosperity automatically signals sympathy with the status quo is to reject the possible usefulness of having an agent inside a strategic location. But these emissaries must take care not to forget the origins of their social conscience.

While I believe Audre Lorde's (by now proverbial) statement that "the master's tools will never dismantle the master's house" (112), I think we do a disservice to Lorde's message if we define intellectualism as the master's exclusive property. Certainly alternatives exist to the assumption that intellectuals must be apolitical or impotent as activists. The philosopher Nancy Fraser tells us to "think of . . . intellectuals first and foremost as members of social groups and as participants in social movements . . . rather than free-floating individuals who are beyond ideology" (108). No one could read the work of Gloria Anzaldúa without recognizing political conviction *and* intellectualism. Nor can we question the authenticity of her experience as a member of a specific ethnic group.

Openly critical of sexism and homophobia within the Chicana/o community, like Anzaldúa, other writers celebrate the mutual dependence communal life creates rather than the isolation of dominant/subordinate relationships.[4] We see nurturing alliances between women in countless characterizations. Individual achievement is rarely separate from the positive benefits to the community. In her poem "Para Teresa," Inés Tovar writes of individual paths stemming from the common desire to resist and survive racism. Her protagonist fights from within the system, but keeps resolute her connection to a classmate outside it. She recognizes that each Chicana acts on behalf of the larger group.

Similarly, Mary Helen Ponce's short story "The Permanent" details the social and political awakening of Altagracia Diaz. Ponce shows the slipperiness of class distinctions and the illusionary nature of privilege for middle-class Mexican Americans. Her protagonist comes to understand the dangers of feeling comfortable in mainstream culture and the bitter realities of disconnecting from one's ethnic group. Altagracia speaks with pride only when she (re)connects with her Mexicanness in an intense confrontation with racism and classism. Readers thus contemplate the importance of ethnic loyalty across class divisions, as well as the role passionate response plays in the realization of social justice for the larger community.

Like these characters, Chicana intellectuals must remain cynical in our dealings with institutional power and its agents. Simultaneously, we must place our trust in blood ties and find hope in our kinship. We cannot let the combative styles we learn in fighting for justice infect our personal and communal relationships. We must act among friends and family out of love and good will instead of fear and suspicion.

Throughout my academic career family and friends have kept me sane. Like Tlazolteotl, communal spirits continue to cleanse the filth of public debate from my heart.[5] Without them, I could never suffer through the "delusional grandeur" of becoming a professor. My conversations with women who clean hotel rooms for a living, wait on tables, or strip feathers from turkeys in processing plants help me maintain stability through the shifts in consciousness I must make every day. They confirm and expand my conceptualizations about the nature of the relationship between professional and working-class intellectuals.

In order to discuss the points at which women in different social locations converge and separate, I have always felt forced to set up a clear dichotomy—or at the very least to see us at opposite ends of a continuum. Yet I am uncomfortable positing one group as "intellectuals" and the other as "working-class women." The Chicana in me—not so far removed from the latter category—rebels against the idea that working women do not exercise their intellects. Similarly, the scholar I have become resists the notion that my "labor" is immune to exploitation. It seems clear that though we may suffer them in different social locations and to varying degrees, we share many of the common elements of oppression. Chicana writers describe these commonalities in fictional narratives, poems, historical research, and expository or theoretical essays.

Scholars are subject to established criteria, which many women of color challenge, refusing to write conventional texts. As professional intellectuals we should not allow ourselves to be seduced into studying working-class women from a top-down model. Nor should we be expected to produce studies that add to our understanding of Chicana/o culture but do little to expose the source of social injustice. However we incorporate community experience into our work, we must keep our focus on subverting imperial, masculinist power. Our skills should be used to critique and dismantle the existing oppressive structures, not to satisfy the voyeuristic curiosity of an elite audience. How we choose to do that—to see the boss as my grandmother counseled—is an individual choice. As Henry Louis Gates, Jr., said in a lecture at the University of Minnesota, "there are a thousand different ways to help." And, I might add, a thousand potential methods—which may not always duplicate currently accepted approaches, but will not make pimps of Chicana intellectuals.

To choose to work against established power in an intellectual arena—through scholarly work, public discourse, or creative writing—is not a lesser moral choice than social organization. It is a different one. Both are important, require special skills, and serve vital functions. If a Chicana's natural inclination, talent, and acquired knowledge make her ideally suited to a specific location, then that is where her potential as a transformative agent is most likely to be realized.[6] But such a struggle requires subjective dedication. Ethnic loyalty is vital, as is the ability to remain viscerally moved by injustice. Maintaining our ties to the community sustains such passion.

I see in revolutionary Chicana literature and theory a place where intellectual women express a continued allegiance to, and a strong connection with, a specific ethnic community. It is Chicana writers who (re)invent "Chicanisma." The word itself has its roots in the political ideology and scholarship of the Chicano movement. Here it acts as a political declaration that is purposefully female (much like my grandmother's deliberate switching of genders when reciting proverbs). In some ways it reflects the tension between professional intellectualism and an ethnic identity. "Chicanisma" sounds strange to both English and formal Spanish speakers, as well as apolitical Mexican Americans. It is slang with a specific ethnic consciousness used by Chicana feminists. Thus it describes our unique position as simultaneous insiders and outsiders of both the academy and our communities.

The term "Chicanisma" is not widely used in everyday life by Mexican Americans, many of whom regard the label Chicano and all its derivatives—Chicanisma included—in much the same way that mainstream culture thinks of "special interest" groups. Many women, for instance, eschew the terms "feminist" and "feminism" because they fear being linked to what has been characterized as uniformly radical politics.[7] Yet the spirit of feminism permeates the larger culture in many ways. Women who would never use the term nevertheless demonstrate feminist behaviors and political beliefs. Chicanisma simply means Chicananess—the essence or spirit of being a Chicana—Mexicanness with an added political conviction.[8]

While Mexican American women may not commonly use the term, they perform acts of Chicanisma in their daily lives. My grandmother's ritual of sneaking cigarettes despite my grandfather's specific instructions not to smoke is an example of Chicanisma—resistance to and subversion of despotic power. This is a woman who, when I was eight years old, whispered through her tears that women cry at weddings not because they are happy for the bride, but because "they are regretting her future."[9] This counternarrative may seem like a small and insignificant act of rebellion. But for the granddaughter watching and listening, who understood the tyranny of her grandfather, the symbolism was huge.

We generally think of revolution and revolutionaries in national or global terms—like radical shifts in economic systems or transformations of formally organized power structures. But "revolutionary" can also apply to changes in a variety of social relationships and informal systems of oppression—many of them interpersonal. The lessons we learn in our families and communities—about bosses and our relationship to them—have a great deal to do with how we will respond to them as adults. Such informality, while not directly governed by specific laws, is nevertheless supported by the institutional forms of power to which the family is subject.

In my work I have linked the voice of Chicana writers to the legendary figure of La Llorona, for several reasons. Most basic is that the narratives remind me of the Llorona stories I heard long ago, the life I lived as a child in a family of influential women, and the kitchen table lessons I absorbed. Also, La Llorona is a folkloric figure—familiar to all Mexican Americans, professional intellectuals as well as working-class women. Because she has not been used by paternal organizations as a symbol, I believe—as does the anthropologist and Mexican American folklorist José Limón—that the image of La Llorona has the most potential to represent the revolutionary spirit of Chicanas (399).

Unlike Malintzin Tenepal and La Virgen de Guadalupe, La Llorona has not yet been appropriated by institutions—neither the state nor the Catholic Church.[10] She has not been used to form a cohesive national identity, and does not serve as an example of virtuous womanhood in the socialization of young women. Because La Llorona remains at the level of folklore, unencumbered by any systematic retelling, she is not an instrument of institutional control. Her potential has not been reduced to an easily duplicated and disseminated code. Consequently, many of the lessons in Llorona stories are subjective and implicit rather than objective and explicit. Like my grandmother reshaping proverbs, women at every level have the power to (re)shape the legend of La Llorona.

This is not something new. Many variations of the story exist, and Chicana writers have produced their own interpretations with an obvious revolutionary intent.[11] Whatever version of La Llorona's tale you hear, her cries have the power to arouse fear in an otherwise comfortable existence—and thus challenge the established order. Whether you respond with terror and apprehension or empathy and understanding is largely a reflection of how you imagine your role in her pain (or your relationship to power). This is likely to be different for women than for men.

While the myth resembles—and indeed some versions stem from—Western mythology, it is also rooted in Aztec legend and Amerindian traditional knowledge. A similar omen appeared to Moctezuma, who saw and heard the wailing woman wandering the streets of Tenochtitlan crying for her lost children. This has generally been interpreted as one of the signs predicting the arrival of the Spanish and the conquest of the Mexica empire. The "lost and murdered children" in this case would have been the Aztecs following the conquest.

In most folkloric renditions, Llorona is imagined to be wandering the banks of a river or stream at the edge of town. Never a part of the community, she nevertheless haunts and disturbs its residents. In her nightly ritual she wails for her lost children—who have been murdered, drowned, or stolen away. Her ghostly voice warns listeners not to wander too far from home, nor too near the river. Though the children are often victims of infanticide, Llorona usually kills them out of desperation and in response to her oppressive mistreatment by a man. Regardless of the method or motivation, it is always she who is left eternally suffering their deaths.

Chicana writers emulate the cries of La Llorona—testifying to a state of perpetual marginality, suffering the loss of something precious, and crying for justice or demanding redress for past wrongdoing. La Llorona's lament echoes the eternal grief we feel when we see our literal and figurative children lost to a host of adversaries, as well as our desire for atonement. Such storytelling acts as a transmitter of cultural and historical knowledge. Literary narratives, in addition to political rhetoric and individual expression, can be seen as communal ceremony or ritual performance. Yet the writers also exemplify the socially conscious creator and the politically transformative agent—the person who does battle with the enemies of our community.

(Re)claiming, (re)inventing, or (re)interpreting history and culture, the author is grandmother, storyteller, priestess, and revolutionary. The process resembles the gender and class shifting I talked about at the beginning of this essay. Of course textual representation is no longer oral tradition because it carries with it the burden of semipermanency. Yet Chicana writers draw on the cultural shifts occurring in the community as well as the personal impulse to subvert established paradigms in the same way that my grandmother did. In fact, some writers make noticeable changes in their previous work when it is republished, reflecting at least some of the character of oral storytelling.[12] Those of us who read and then (re)tell the stories to other members of the community, or to the children in our families, have the power to (re)turn them to oral tradition.

Writers reflect and create cultural shifts as they (re)claim historical figures. Sylvia Alicia Gonzales, in these lines from a long poem entitled "Chicana Evolution," writes: "I am Chicana / Waiting for the return / of la Malinche, / to negate her guilt . . . I am Chicana / Waiting for the coming of Malinche / to sacrifice herself / on an Aztec altar / and a Catholic cross / in redemption of all her forsaken daughters" (418–26).

The references Gonzales makes to sacrifice, the Aztec altar, Catholic cross, and redemption all connote ritual (as well as the syncretism of Aztec and Catholic religious performance). Her reference to La Malinche and wanting to negate her guilt expresses the Chicana's desire to (re)construct Malinche's identity—thus subverting Mexico's masculine elite portrayal of Malinche as the betrayer of Mexico and the lascivious mother of the "bastard race." Though she uses the pronoun "I," Gonzales is speaking collectively as she brings into question the nature of patriarchal definitions of women. She takes her challenge outside the interpersonal sphere and into the institutionally constructed realm of Spanish and Criollo (or European colonial) versions of recorded history. In (re)configuring Malinche, Gonzales acts as a storyteller—and as a priestess with the power to redeem all Chicanas. She is, she says, waiting to sacrifice herself for all Malinche's daughters—removing any fabricated social categories that might separate women.

The Chicana feminist Norma Alarcón has little patience with this image of unfulfilled redemption, and sees this revision of Malinche's image as "gloomy." We are, she says, left waiting for the dream (199). While this assessment is an astute one, and I understand the impatience, I do not think that unrealized hope renders the poem useless as symbolic resistance. Gonzales is not constructing a dream with a happy ending any more than my grandmother ever directly confronted authority. But she is advocating change, praying for redemption, and suggesting an end to oppressive constructs. In that sense, Gonzales successfully executes her professed intention to "mirror" society and "to voice the needs" of Chicanas. Like Llorona, that voice is a restless one.

While our grandmothers, as well as our contemporaries, may practice relatively small rebellions, the example is filled with potential. When observed over a lifetime, or witnessed daily in the community, these gestures compose a significant body of resistance. One of the prerequisites to a life of advocacy and fighting for social justice is the absorption of such information. The responsibility of the Chicana intellectual—writer or scholar—is not necessarily to interpret, translate, or disseminate that knowledge to a larger audience, but to use it to subvert unjust systems. It is not enough to record the voices and insights of women in the community. We learn from and with them how the spirit survives. But we must also understand what continues to make that survival difficult, and where we belong in the struggle. This does not mean apologizing for who we are.

In the United States, artists are seen as eccentrics—people at the margins of the "real world" of labor, commerce, consumerism, and bureaucracy. Increasingly, intellectuals have come to be seen in a similar way. Mainstream culture has little respect for critical thinking. Creativity is of value only as popular entertainment, or as a way of producing new material goods for the marketplace. But in Latin America, artists and writers command not only respect, but veneration as the political vanguard.

Part of this respect has its origins in Europe, where formal art and literature have a long history of social importance. But it is also tied to folkloric creation—art that comes out of oral cultures, where ballads and stories act as historical memory, instruments of socialization, and news services (political as well as social). This is related to a history of colonization and brutal dictatorships. Art may (though not always) be disseminated where directly confrontational rhetoric will get you killed. Politically charged prose and poetry can be distributed and read by many people before it commands the attention of the state. Of course the reverse is also true. Artists and writers can be under immediate scrutiny by the government precisely because the state understands the power of imagery to inspire revolution and communicate its goals.

In her book *The Last Generation,* Cherríe Moraga speaks of a time when science was secondary to music and art—when poets were highly respected for their knowledge. "Metaphor," she says, "expressed what the intellect suffered" (186). Though she is talking about ancient Mexico, the same can be said about relatively recent history throughout Latin America. Long before the ideas of Michel Foucault washed up on the shores of the American academy, Latin Americans understood the power of public discourse.[13] What they also understand is that art arouses emotions, provokes insight, spurs discussion, and challenges ideas—political as well as personal.

This is what we share with, and inherit through, La Raza (our people)—respect for the artist and acceptance of the link between literary expression and political ideology. From the beginning of the Brown Power movement, writers and painters were involved, not as the entire voice of the revolution, but as a significant part of it. Like their predecessors, contemporary Chicana writers like Gonzales, Anzaldúa, Moraga, Castillo, Lorna Dee Cervantes, and others creatively express the needs of the people. They can do this only because they come out of and/or remain close to communities in need of social justice.

Spiritually, these writers rip open their chests and expose their still beating hearts to *and for* us. Their autobiographical prose and poetry, as well as theoretical writing, often defy conventional category. Narratives explode with revolutionary spirit. But they are also intensely personal. This too has always been the nature of Latin American literature and politics. Like Neruda, Chicana writers understand the connection between the hunger of the body for bread and the yearning of the soul for freedom and beauty. They know we must have food, justice, *and* art to live. We must be able to express our rage and cynicism as well as our love and hope to survive. Whether we are writing books or dancing to Tejano music, art is often the jalapeño touch that spices an otherwise intolerably distasteful life.

As romantic as this might seem, it is not naïveté. We are fully aware of the necessary demands of our physical bodies. But we do not separate mind, spirit, and body. We know from our experience with imperialism that the endurance of a people involves the part of us that lives to reproduce as well as the part of us that survives to transmit our culture. For Chicana/os, both parts of the equation require the creativity, labor, and ethnic identity or cultural loyalty of all members of the family—professional intellectuals and working-class women alike. All participants have stories to tell, as well as lessons to learn and pass on.

Because our connection to the community is necessary to our ethnic identity, Chicana writers seldom resemble an intellectual aristocracy separate from the people. The complexity of this identity is astonishing. Constantly in flux, it is made up of multiple, blended cultures—Indian, Spanish, Mexican, and U.S., as well as local, regional, national, and socioeconomic variety. While scholars interpret, analyze, and theorize such intricacy—looking for elaborate explanations of its meaning—women in the community simply live it. One valuable aspect of fiction and poetry is that they can creatively represent this complexity. In work of this kind, an author like Sandra Cisneros hides her interpretive and analytical skills in a deceptively simple narrative of lived experience.

Occasionally, readers expect writers to be more directly confrontational of stereotypes than they are. In every class where I have used Mary Helen Ponce's novel *The Wedding*, white students have expressed concern that it seems to reinforce negative stereotypes of Chicano youth. Yet Chicana/o students generally enjoy the book, and some think it's hilarious. They say that it reminds them of various family members, or that they have been part of similar relationships.

The difference is that white students only see this as a literal or explicit representation. But Mexican Americans "know" the story at the implicit level. They understand that the characters and situations certainly exist among them, but that such descriptions do not represent all Chicanos any more than Philip Roth's characters represent the totality of Jewish life. Because they come out of similar communities, Mexican American students understand the core elements that are the basis for certain exaggerations, that is, they get the joke. At the (usually) subconscious level, they also understand the poignancy with which the portraits are created. Like old photographs de la vida loca (of the crazy life) present somewhere in our histories, they provoke a certain nostalgia we cannot explain to outsiders.

The other thing white students seem to miss is the criticism present in such portrayals—the author's careful use of satire, which in this case critiques male posturing, U.S. consumer culture, as well as economic realities and socialization processes that limit choices for women. Obviously, the writer must have close contact with this existence in order to accurately portray it, and to use satire effectively.

For self-consciously "Chicana" writers, the creative part of such representation goes beyond the ability to produce aesthetically pleasing prose. Conveying messages to the reader is part of the process. The ability to "show, not tell" is what makes the writer an artist. Yet few Chicana writers, completely cognizant of socioeconomic stratification and constructed hierarchical systems, separate art from politics. Most authors show *and* tell. Realistic images of lived injustice and the language of a disenfranchised people impart political messages. They show us a community (not just an individual) in conflict with mainstream society. As readers, we know the promise of democratic pluralism, yet here is an entire group of people for whom the promise is unfulfilled. This is not so much the literature of victimization as it is the proof of a pledge not kept.

Most literary studies focus on aesthetics—lyricism, metaphor, style, and so forth. Chicana literature is also viewed in contrast and comparison to other "ethnic" women writers, or against "universal" (read: white) themes, or as a cultural artifact. While these approaches can be useful, they only scratch the surface of complex social locations and multidimensional experience. Because our literature is sometimes in the classroom even when we are not, the political messages often go undetected and/or undisclosed. Though some thought may be given to examples of social agency in a subculture, little or no exploration of revolutionary ideology takes place. This often occurs because conventional scholarship is terrified of radical ideas and the subversive/subjective knowledge of colonized peoples.

The promise of multiculturalism—more diversity in the core curriculum as well as the faculty—has bogged down after limited success. This means that the narratives of people of color now routinely show up on lists of required texts, while money for hiring diverse faculty has evaporated, and affirmative action has been dismantled on many fronts. As a result, far too many courses are taught by professionals with no tie to the community being discussed.

In such conversations—where largely mainstream individuals

discuss marginalized ethnic groups—talk often turns to the way the individual writer's experiences and feelings mirror those of Euro-Americans.[14] Unfortunately, it is seldom accompanied by a self-deprecating critique of mainstream culture's culpability for the group's marginalized position. More likely is a critique that emphasizes or blames "pathology" within the group for its social location. The implicit knowledge of a culture and the depth of resistance reflected in the narrative usually go unnoticed. Visceral responses to oppression—which can best be conveyed by those who have experienced it—will not be present if a participant in the community, willing to teach, is not in the classroom.[15]

This is not a criticism of an individual instructor. It is directed at an institutional culture that thinks food coloring changes the taste of the frosting. It does not recognize the need for a whole new cake. Bringing in texts, but not the people they represent, is not an effective change of the surface decoration, much less the core. Explicit information about any group, as well as conventional theory and methodology, can be taught by anyone with an interest in doing so. Chicana literature can be read, analyzed, interpreted, and discussed by anyone, anywhere, at anytime. (Algo es algo.) But this alone does not necessarily qualify as a social transformation, diversity, or multicultural understanding.

Though a Chicana narrative is a "visceral response" of sorts, much of what we learn about lived experience is not available in written texts or detached lectures. It is conveyed through body language, the tone of the voice, facial expressions, and so on. The skill or art of storytelling is essential. While no individual can speak for an entire community, s/he can give a human voice to the emotional toll oppression takes. S/he can also see and challenge privilege and authority from the bottom up. This is teaching that cannot generally be duplicated by an uninvolved observer, no matter how educated or sympathetic to the experience they may be. Sometimes the only participant voice in the classroom is the text itself.

In the work of writers like Roberta Fernández, Helena Viramontes, and Mary Helen Ponce, we can see knowledge subjectively acquired through day-to-day living within Mexican American communities. Like the writers, their protagonists grow up in cultures where gender, racial, and class identities develop in tandem. This experience is inextricable from living in a larger society sick with "isms" or doctrines of hatred. They are subject to an economic system that requires a reserve and easily exploitable labor force—as well as constant expansion and the continued accumulation of wealth—to be considered healthy.

In contrast, the narratives of Cherríe Moraga, Sandra Cisneros, and Edna Escamill show us voices that (re)claim cultural histories weakened and obscured through acculturation and forced assimilation. (For many Chicanas, this reality is not consciously chosen, but exists as part of our history in an occupied land—a history of imperialism and colonization.) These authors reassert their ethnicity, resisting further erosion of their cultural identities.[16] As Cherríe Moraga says, "I am the white girl gone brown to the blood color of my mother" (Loving 60). Yet they too experience dominant culture from a subordinate position.

Threatened also are class identities to which the authors feel loyal. Class is not just a matter of economics or changes in one's social location. It is also about culture—where you think you belong or feel most comfortable. Narratives reflect particular allegiances, whatever the contemporary situation of the author. This means that writers and academics are likely to identify with the socioeconomic situation of their childhood—especially in confrontations with authority figures or institutions that have significantly different social environments. When threatened we will always revert to the safety of our affective cultures. This is also true when we are trying to express deeply felt alienation from the mainstream.

Sandra Cisneros demonstrates a similar involution to Moraga's (re)clamation of a home culture, though it is not as directly stated.[17] Her early poetry barely contains any references to her ethnicity. Yet her later book, *Woman Hollering Creek,* is filled with ethnically specific language, Mexican mythology, and traditional themes. Though these references are not universally recognized or accepted by many Mexican American readers—especially community members unfamiliar with codified history and scholarly research—they nevertheless reflect a conscious assertion by Cisneros of her Mexican/Mexican American identity.

We could be cynical about this transformation, and assume that Cisneros is merely following the cash-producing trend toward "ethnic" literature. But anyone who knows Sandra and/or her work will tell you that less explicit signs of this identity were obvious in her earlier novel, *The House on Mango Street.* Her move to San Antonio and her immersion in its Tejano culture, as well as its vital Mexican American artistic community, have deeply affected her sense of self. They have had a profound impact on the way she sees the world, her relationship to Mexico, her personal life, and thus on her work.

We now see less of Sandra Cisneros, the individual woman alone in a world of love and loss, and more of the community—the fictive kin who have become her characters. This too was evident in *Mango Street,* but her later work contains more images of ethnicity as a consciously described feature. For her characters, it remains relatively invisible because it is so ordinary. But for the reader—even the Mexican American women I have interviewed during my research—it is clearly a conscious declaration by the author. Rather than simply reflecting semi-autobiographical experience, Cisneros has become the storyteller—the symbolic grandmother reconfiguring proverbial knowledge. This gives the writing an implicitly political quality. Though *Woman Hollering Creek* is published by a mainstream press, it represents a challenge to the homogeneous, dominant culture. Yet the narratives remain highly personal portraits of intimate miseries and quiet revolutions.

More directly political than Cisneros, Cherríe Moraga weaves together the strands of evolving self-awareness and continuing political consciousness in her book *Loving in the War Years,* published in 1983. Like Gloria Anzaldúa and other Chicana feminists, Moraga criticizes the hierarchies and oppressive practices within Chicana/o culture. Refusing to make excuses for sexist and homophobic behaviors within the community, she nevertheless remains loyal to her ethnic identity. Though she is equally impatient with discrimination ten years later, the publication of *The Last Generation* shows that Moraga has expanded beyond gender, beyond Chicanisma, and beyond the U.S. border. While much of her knowledge still springs from her relationship to her Mexican mother, she has stepped into an international arena to demand social justice for all oppressed people.

Moraga calls the book "a prayer written at a time when I no longer remember how to pray . . . 500 years after the arrival of Cristóbal Colón" (1). She ends it with a piece she calls "Codex Xerí: El Momento Histórico." This title refers to the hieroglyphic pictorials used by the Aztecs to record their history, and "Xerí" is the Nahua (Aztec language) spelling of Moraga's first name. It was written, she says, "amid the fires of the Los Angeles Rebellion, on the eve of a fading

Quinto Sol and a rising new época" (184). Here Moraga links the af-
termath of the Rodney King decision to the ancient prophecies of
Mayan and Aztec people. Like other indigenous groups, they predicted not only the arrival of the Spanish, but a future in which European rule would end on this continent. "El Quinto Sol," the Fifth Sun
or current age, is supposed to end with a series of earthquakes. The
transition between the Fifth and Sixth Epochs, Moraga says, is now
taking place.

She uses images and symbols specific to the Mexican American
community of East Los Angeles and other California locations, which
demonstrates the importance of community and ethnicity in the formation of political ideology—the Chicana/Azteca perspective that
allows her to write a codex. The codex, she says, is "a portrait of our
daily lives." Her resistance does not grow out of a sense of personal
entitlement—as conservatives argue—but out of a heightened awareness that the Mexican American community continues to exist and
(re)create itself in contrast to U.S. mainstream culture. This is a response to colonization, not fragmentation.

Moraga also shows the unconscious deconstruction of "gringo history" as she describes the way knowledge is passed on within the
barrio. She calls graffiti "modern day hieroglyphs," and Chicano
slang an "urban guerrillero tongue." This is a tribute to communication that takes place outside the understanding of mainstream culture. Such modern/urban folklore resembles La Llorona's usefulness
as a symbol of the restless spirit—dangerous and demanding justice—grieving for what we have lost, expressing sorrow for the re-
grettable acts we have committed out of our frustration.

Like other Chicana writers, Moraga takes issue with the Catholic/
European culture of rape and conquest. Her codex demands retribution—the return of Aztlán, the mythical Chicano homeland or the occupied territory of northern Mexico—now the southwestern United
States. Much of this chapter is reminiscent of the nationalism expressed during the Brown Power movement, yet Moraga's feminist
sensibilities are present throughout. Clearly she has written a political manifesto that is also personal and deeply felt.

Moraga offers the piece as a prayer "for the last generation to suffer white rule" (184). As Norma Alarcón has pointed out, this kind of
subjectivity is not the solitary, self-determined subject found in mainstream literary theory. Nor is it the fragmented self of feminist theory.

This voice does not resemble the diva's aria, but the chorus. Like Gonzales waiting to redeem all Chicanas, Moraga prays for all colonized people.

Subjects found in Chicana narratives inhabit communal border regions—the spaces so brilliantly described by Gloria Anzaldúa in *Borderlands/La Frontera*. This is a complex and multidimensional identity that defies boundaries. Anzaldúa's notion of living in the space in-between and embracing a life of ambiguity might be mistaken for postmodernism, or the dissolution of the center. But this is a meaningless construct for women in the Mexican American community and for most Chicana intellectuals. As I've heard several times in casual conversations between Chicana/o scholars, "postmodernism" was invented in ancient Mexico. For the community, multicultural existence is nothing new. Our centers have been dissolving for thousands of years, yet we always seem to know where we are. Our geographical location as a people in the landscape of our origin "grounds" us physically and psychologically.

Anzaldúa and other Chicana writers are not ambiguous about who has suffered oppression. In this regard, we know who dominates and who is pushed to the edges of society. We know that social justice is not a reality in our communities. It is the responsibility of Chicana intellectuals to keep this knowledge a part of public discourse in whatever way our particular talents dictate. Writers let us know—in voices loud and clear, sweet and angry—that race, ethnicity, gender, class, and sexual identity are not just relative categories, that a dominant/subordinate paradigm is not just a tension between diverse cultures, or a naturally occurring phenomenon between groups who do not understand each other. It is not the inevitable result of majority and minority populations. It is a model of injustice—the crimes of the powerful against the outnumbered, outgunned, and/or outfinanced. An arrogant war against the exploitable but ever resistant "other."

While this sense of positioning is based on our history, as well as our contemporary experience with various forms of supremacy and influence, Gloria Anzaldúa's notion of borderland space rejects the singularity of the "other" category. It is too vulnerable a condition to accept. To be so easily categorized is to be promptly controlled. Thus, it is in our best interest to reject such labels, even as we simultaneously understand their meaning and relevance to our social reality. Insisting on a complex identity eliminates the handhold of simple identifiers. Thus, the poet Bernice Zamora declares, "my divisions are infinite" (78).

This is one of the reasons creative, thoughtful individuals—who contribute to public discourse—are so necessary, and why our knowledge and/or inspiration must originate in the community. If we do not resist easy categories by constantly slipping out from under them or continually inventing new language, we are susceptible to dismissal. Creative energy is absolutely essential to any struggle for social justice, because the language and categories we create will always be co-opted at some point and used against us. Or they will simply diffuse—lose their significance and power with common usage.[18] If everyone is "other," then no one is. As with most popular cultural shifts, inventiveness is not located in the mainstream, but outside it. Once the creation gets to the mainstream, it's dead. The freshness, the wonder, and the passion are sucked out of it.

As Chicana intellectuals, we must keep our memories of our grandmothers alive in our work, yet remain selective about what we reveal. The covert nature of our struggle demands the protection of our sources. Culture that is appropriated and devoured provides little comfort or inspiration. Regalar la verdad es perder el corazón. We must keep our eye on the bosses we encounter (even if they claim to be our brothers and sisters), our hearts open to the artistry and passion of the street, and our minds (re)creating proverbial knowledge.

We share with everyone in the community the experience of contact with mainstream culture, its institutions, and its socioeconomic machinery. Thus we are all exposed to the common elements of oppression. Yes, significant differences exist between the women working in clothing factories and women who sit at computers. Showing up for work to discover that your plant's operations have moved to Costa Rica is different from receiving a rejection notice from a publisher. But before we draw definite boundaries between women we must remember that the divisions within our community are as infinite as Zamora and Anzaldúa describe them. Whether we are what Sandra Cisneros has called "migrant professors" or migrant workers, we are all "authentic" Chicanas.

There are class differences we cannot ignore, and professional Chicanas should not coldly abstract and exploit the experiences of working-class women simply to further their careers. But as fiction writers, poets, and/or theorists we have an obligation to know the effect of public policy on our communities if we expect to critique lawmakers, institutions, and mainstream culture. Our particular burden is that we have to know it from both sides. We must sit in kitchens listening to the latest chisme (gossip) *and* find time to study and understand the full implications of welfare reform, English-only at the federal level, NAFTA, and GATT.

We also have to invest in social transformation on many fronts. Not content to simply inherit and maintain Mexican or Chicano culture unexamined, we cast a cynical eye on the "bosses" within our culture. Whether it is done by our grandmothers, remembered and recorded by writers, or incorporated in theoretical essays, it should be part of a community-wide distilling process. In the case of women challenging masculine privilege or tyranny, traditional culture is blended with revolutionary consciousness. Change is an essential component of cultural survival. Lo que no cambia se pudre. (That which does not change, rots.)[19] Yet as we foster change we must remember the importance of the survival strategies and the subversive techniques we acquire through day-to-day existence in Mexican American communities.

Broadening our definitions of authenticity so that the Chicana/o community includes intellectuals from many social locations—the hotel, the academy, the writer's desk, and the factory—makes us less susceptible to being singularly defined. For this to be successful we must demystify scholarship—be able to translate our work into a variety of languages. We can become Malinche without being a slave to the conqueror. In some cases this means diffusing the ego that initially propelled us toward a cerebral life, but makes us vulnerable to being recruited into a position of authority *over* others. If that happens we are likely to find ourselves speaking about the community without participating in it. This is not what my grandmother advised.

Keeping our ties to the community strong and remaining loyal to our ethnicity are centering mechanisms. But so too is the cultivation of "infinite divisions," or as George Lipsitz says, "sophisticated capacities for ambiguity." While this seems on the surface a dissolution of the center, I agree with Anzaldúa's characterization of such capacity, which, I know from experience, means that once you learn to live with paradox and ambiguity it becomes resolute. Any artist knows the importance of negative space—what the eye does not see is just as significant as what it does see.

In the same way that my ancestors produced solid adobe out of formless clay, I make a firm center out of the multifocal perspective I have inherited. If it is true that postmodernism was invented in ancient Mexico, we know that cultural survival and change exist simultaneously. Chicanas understand that tradition continues even as the disruption of existing social relationships occurs. Science tells us that adobe will eventually disintegrate, yet much of it still stands in the desert long after its creation. But even when that takes place, the mud simply returns to the earth.

De la tierra, a la tierra. Y gracias a la vida Chicana, hacemos el mismo.

NOTES

1. As a child I rarely saw my grandmother outside the kitchen— except when she sneaked to the outdoor toilet to smoke cigarettes, which my strict grandfather had forbidden her to do.

2. Obviously, most Chicana writers and scholars are not far removed from working-class lives. Many have done manual labor, come from families where most members still do this work, and continue to participate in the struggle against poverty and injustice. But the question of how scholarly and literary writing is relevant to working-class women arises constantly. Whenever cerebral conversation and professional jargon start to flow someone is sure to ask, "So how does this relate to 'real' women?" as if Chicanas who write are not "real" women (nor Chicana ethnically speaking). To paraphrase Sojourner Truth y bell hooks, "¿soy Chicana, no?"

3. In fact, all the titles in my dissertation come from my grandmother's sayings. This was not something I imposed on the text. As the thesis evolved, the wisdom imparted long ago returned to my consciousness and demanded inclusion.

4. I use "Chicana/o" rather than simply "Chicano." While the rules of Spanish dictate using the masculine form when speaking of both men and women—as in the English use of the word "man" to mean all humans— many writers are now using both masculine and feminine endings. This specifically or purposefully includes women rather than subsuming them under a masculine construction.

5. Tlazolteotl–Aztec (possibly Huaxtec in origin) was a goddess who ate the sins of the people.

6. This does not mean we cannot also be activists, community facilitators, or group advocates. What I am talking about is maintaining an effective focus.

7. Feminists, of course, know that "The Movement" actually runs the political gamut—from supporting the status quo with only minor changes to calls for a profound shift in our culture, institutions, and economic system. Most people fall somewhere in between. Diversity exists among feminists in the same way it appears in all groups.

8. The word "Chicanisma," like its male counterpart "Chicanismo," is part of a living language—Caló, or Español Chicano.

9. "Es su futuro las mujeres sienten." In a similar act of resistance, after a lecture from a nun about keeping ourselves pure for our future husbands, my great-grandmother told my girl cousins and me that we would only learn to howl if we hung around with coyotes.

10. Malintzin Tenepal, also known as La Malinche and Doña Marina among other things, is the historical woman given to Cortes as a slave when she was fourteen. In elite, masculine history, she is seen as being responsible for the downfall of the Aztec empire. Conversely the Virgin of Guadalupe was associated with the goddess Tonantzin in an effort to make Catholicism more palatable to Indians. She also became a symbol of independence as Mexico fought to free itself from Spain. Where Malinche came to symbolize betrayal and the inherent evilness of women, La Virgen came to represent nurturing and motherhood.

11. La Llorona's sovereignty as an uncodified, folkloric figure may be in jeopardy. In 1987 Cinco Puntos Press of El Paso published a children's book called *La Llorona: The Weeping Woman,* written by a man named Joe Hayes. The cover proclaims it "An Hispanic Legend." The book is printed in both English and Spanish. While it contains beautiful illustrations, I would hate to see it replace the spontaneous oral presentations of the story by our mothers, abuelitas, tías, madrinas, y hermanas. Hopefully it is out of print by now.

12. See, for example, the ending of Helena Viramontes's short story "Growing" in her collection *The Moths and Other Stories,* and the ending of the same story in *Cuentos: Stories by Latinas,* ed. Alma Gómez, Cherríe Moraga, and Mariana Romo-Carmona. See also the revised edition of Ana Castillo's novel *Sapagonia* in comparison to the original published by Bilingual Press. Some changes simply reflect further editing; others are more significant. Once a piece is published in book form, it is unusual for authors to make such changes in a fictional or poetic text.

13. Unlike Foucault, Latin Americans generally, and poor and indigenous people specifically, fully understand the despotic reality and supreme power of the state. While I concede that power is also located in community and interpersonal relationships, which play a role in what the state eventually becomes, a regime is an overwhelming enforcer against which, my grandmother and Thomas Jefferson would agree, we must remain ever vigilant.

14. My friend Tamara Buffalo has a joke: "How do you make a white

woman feel multicultural?" Answer: "Stand an African American woman next to her while she (the white woman) talks about herself." In the case I've described, the Chicana narrative is standing next to the mainstream participants in the classroom.

15. This means someone who has *chosen* to teach the class—not one of its students. Certainly students can learn from their classmates, but the *responsibility* for teaching should not fall on any student's shoulders just because they happen to be a member of a specific community. Neither should the student's experience be ignored or dismissed should she choose to reveal it. This situation is not easy; it's a "ring of fire" for everyone involved.

16. Escamill changed her name between the publication of her novels *Daughter of the Mountain* and *The Storyteller with Nike Airs and Other Barrio Stories* from Edna Escamill to Kleya Forté-Escamilla. Though I have little clues to the change of her first name, the addition of the *a* to her last name rejects a more English compatible sound in favor of its Mexican/Spanish origin. When I used her earlier book in a class, Mexican and Mexican American students were initially (and remained) skeptical of the novel because they saw her Anglicized name as a betrayal of her Mexican heritage. Thus they questioned her ability to write about Mexican/Indian experience. It will be interesting to see how the name change affects students' reactions to the material.

17. I use "involution" as opposed to "evolution," which generally connotes only linear or progressive movement. Involution connotes a folding in on one's true self, or turning back to an original source, that is, a nonlinear movement.

18. "Diversity" is an example of a word that has lost its significance as it has become part of corporate and institutional culture. New language, new names, and (re)claimed concepts add energy to a movement grown stale, refocus attention on an old struggle, or take off in a more productive direction. Feminism—though it rarely changes its base name—is constantly redefining itself. The terms "second-wave" and now "third-wave" feminism have been attempts to make room for new voices, as well as invigorate beleaguered ones. Alice Walker's definition and use of "womanist" as opposed to "feminist" can be seen as an example of inventiveness—slipping out from under what, for her and many African American women, was or had become a meaningless category. While some saw this as a divisive development, it actually expanded the fight for gender equity—made the whole movement less susceptible to dismissal and control. Such change often stimulates new passion for social transformation.

19. Republican victories in 1994 and the 1999 victory of the Reform Party candidate Jesse Ventura were attributed to the desire for change. In reality, they were not calling for change at all, but a reaffirmation of white/male/ power at the top of the pyramid, standing on the backs of everyone else. Hopefully the rotting will take place soon.

SOURCES

Alarcón, Norma. "Excerpts from Traddutora, Traditora: A Paradigmatic Figure of Chicano Feminism." In *Changing Our Power: An Introduction to Women Studies,* ed. Jo Whitehorse Cochran, Donna Langston, and Carolyn Woodward. Dubuque: Kendall/Hunt, 1988.

Anzaldúa, Gloria. *Borderlands/La Frontera: The New Mestiza.* San Francisco: Spinsters/Aunt Lute, 1987.

Calderón, Héctor, and José David Saldívar, eds. *Criticism in the Borderlands: Studies in Chicano Literature, Culture, and Ideology.* Durham: Duke University Press, 1991.

Castillo, Ana. *Sapagonia.* Tempe: Bilingual Press/Editorial Bilingüe, 1990.

———. *Sapagonia.* Rev. ed. New York: Anchor Doubleday, 1994.

Cisneros, Sandra. *The House on Mango Street.* Houston: Arte Público, 1989.

———. *Woman Hollering Creek and Other Stories.* New York: Random House, 1991.

Escamill, Edna. *Daughter of the Mountain.* San Francisco: Aunt Lute, 1991.

Escandon, Carmen Ramos. "Alternative Sources to Women's History: Literature." In *Between Borders: Essays on Mexicana/Chicana History,* ed. Adelaida R. Del Castillo. Ventura: Floricanto Press, 1990.

Fernández, Roberta. *Intaglio: A Novel in Six Stories.* Houston: Arte Público, 1990.

Forté-Escamilla, Kleya. *The Storyteller with Nike Airs and Other Barrio Stories.* San Francisco: Aunt Lute, 1994.

Foucault, Michel. *Power/Knowledge,* ed. Colin Gordon. New York: Pantheon, 1980.

Fraser, Nancy. *Unruly Practices: Power, Discourse and Gender in Contemporary Social Theory.* Minneapolis: University of Minnesota Press, 1989.

Gómez, Alma, Cherríe Moraga, and Mariana Romo-Carmona, eds. *Cuentos: Stories by Latinas.* Latham, NY: Kitchen Table Press, 1983.

Gonzales, Sylvia Alicia. "Chicana Evolution." In *The Third Woman: Minority Women Writers of the United States,* ed. Dexter Fisher. Boston: Houghton Mifflin, 1980.

Hayes, Joe. *La Llorona: The Weeping Woman.* El Paso: Cinco Puntos Press, 1987.

Limón, José E. "La Llorona, the Third Legend of Greater Mexico: Cultural Symbols, Women and the Political Unconscious." In *Between Borders: Essays on Mexicana/Chicana History,* ed. Adelaida R. Del Castillo. Ventura: Floricanto Press, 1990.

Lipsitz, George. *Time Passages: Collective Memory and American Popular Culture.* Minneapolis: University of Minnesota Press, 1990.

Lorde, Audre. *Sister Outsider: Essays and Speeches by Audre Lorde.* Trumansburg, NY: Crossing Press, 1984.

Moraga, Cherríe. *The Last Generation: Prose and Poetry.* Boston: South End Press, 1993.

———. *Loving in the War Years: Lo Que Nunca Pasó por Sus Labios.* Boston: South End Press, 1983.

Padilla, Genaro M. *My History, Not Yours: The Formation of Mexican American Autobiography.* Madison: University of Wisconsin Press, 1993.

Pharr, Suzanne. *Homophobia: A Weapon of Sexism.* Little Rock: Chardon Press, 1988.

Ponce, Mary Helen. *Hoyt Street: An Autobiography.* Albuquerque: University of New Mexico Press, 1993.

———. *Taking Control.* Houston: Arte Público, 1987.

———. *The Wedding.* Houston: Arte Público, 1989.

Rebolledo, Tey Diana, and Eliana S. Rivero, eds. *Infinite Divisions: An Anthology of Chicana Literature.* Tucson: University of Arizona Press, 1993.

Saldívar, Ramón. *Chicano Narrative: The Dialectics of Difference.* Madison: University of Wisconsin Press, 1990.

Tovar, Inés. "Para Teresa." In *The Third Woman: Minority Women Writers of the United States,* ed. Dexter Fisher. Boston: Houghton Mifflin, 1980.

Viramontes, Helena. *The Moths and Other Stories.* Houston: Arte Público, 1985.

Zamora, Bernice. "So Not to Be Mottled." In *Infinite Divisions: An Anthology of Chicana Literature,* ed. Tey Diana Rebolledo and Eliana S. Rivero. Tucson: University of Arizona Press, 1993.

Part III

Starting Here, Starting Now
Challenges to Academic Practices

One of the central contradictions we face as feminist scholars concerns our social location in the academy. Patricia Hill Collins reminds us that "Scholars, publishers, and other experts represent specific interests and credentialing processes, and their knowledge claims must satisfy the epistemological and political criteria of the contexts in which they reside" (751). We teach, write, and administer in ways that we hope will promote social justice and foster understanding of diversity, even though we find ourselves in an institution that, despite its stated democratic commitments, works to maintain and reproduce gender, racial, and class inequality. Is it possible to contribute to social justice in such a problematic environment, and if so, how? To the extent that the academy is reproducing itself and failing to foster critical thinking or awareness, it is rendering itself irrelevant. Many of the essays also speak to the issue of alienation within the academy. Writing from very different social locations with regard to the academy—from former student to tenured professor—as well as from diverse racial, ethnic, class, and sexual identities, the authors come to strikingly similar conclusions about how the university fails them. In failing them, it also fails to live up to the democratic ideals that are supposed to undergird liberal education in the United States.

The "university gaze" (Diana Vélez's term) often obliterates realities that do not fit easily into its own research and developmental agendas. The essays in this part consider ways of disrupting and diverting that gaze, while for the most part recognizing our inability to escape it. In fact, our ability to help students in their project of getting through the university—and even more, to aid them in their own struggles with social justice—is enhanced only when we remain conscious of and resistant to the university's hegemonic and homogenizing tendencies. None of these essays could have been written without the authors' deep commitment to students, whether this means personally helping them surmount and remove racist, classist, and homophobic hurdles, or challenging the infrastructure that holds those barriers in place.

Sharon Doherty argues that the best way to work toward social justice in academia is to challenge the individualism that dominates scholarly practice and teaching. The costs of individualism to a social justice agenda are threefold: a competitive mentality encourages people to get ahead by knocking others down; specialization with no concern for tying research to social needs leads to an emphasis on form over substance; and the use of exclusionary language encourages the perspective that knowledge exists for its own sake, rather than to serve real human and global needs. Resisting individualistic notions of human life and maintaining substantive connections with and accountability to our communities are necessary to transform the university, where current efforts to achieve social justice are at loggerheads with the university's efforts to maintain the status quo.

Mary Romero analyzes the responses of disappointed graduate students in sociology who entered programs because of a commitment to social justice, but who find their way impeded at every step—from a paucity of courses offered on race, to blatant disapprobation by professors and administrators. How can a field that helps us understand families and other institutions, social groups, and movements fail to promote racial understanding, when all of those families and institutions and movements are shaped by attitudes about race?

The university gaze when it does attend to race often misses the mark. In the case of the Moynihan report and others like it, the Black family is pathologized. This study, notorious as it is among some scholars, appears in a new light in Rhonda Williams's essay. Williams uses her own coming out to students in class and in university student publications as the site for a critique of conflicting ideologies of "Blackness" and queerness. Resistance to the ways signs of Black "dysfunction" are regularly recycled in political culture, marking men as criminal and women as hypersexual, combines with a strong nationalist desire to claim a male-dominated, Afro-defined heterosexual family. Comparing Black nationalist ideology and white racist narratives of Black familial pathology (such as the Moynihan report), Williams demonstrates the ways heterosexuality is normalized, Black women blamed for cultural chaos, and queerness cast as a "white thing." Black queerness thus interrupts "a longing for a stigma-free Black sexuality" and opens the way for new discussions of the Black family that don't rely on rigid heterosexist "Afro" or white racist formulations.

While Williams's commitment to students involves challenging their received notions about sexuality and Blackness, Diana L. Vélez speaks about serving students from another angle. She wonders whether it is possible to serve students or contribute to social justice in any other way in an environment as noxious as she finds the university. Vélez argues that the "grasping anger" and resentment that permeate academic departments defy attempts to bring about social justice, and that the only way we can bring about change is by beginning with individual efforts to resist anger. Using her own training in Buddhism, Vélez shows how mindfulness would transform academics' stressful lives by allowing them to live in the present rather than perpetually juggling ambition, commitment, and personal feelings. In contrast to Audre Lorde's position in "The Uses of Anger," which Vélez addresses, she sees anger as a barrier to social change because anger clouds judgment and keeps us focused on ourselves rather than on the issues we claim to care about and the people we claim to serve.

In contrast to Vélez's plea for mindfulness and control of anger, Joanna Kadi demonstrates that anger can very effectively challenge the limited knowledge production accomplished in most schools and with most professors. Kadi points directly to the systematic ways the university maintains its class privilege, perpetuating myths about the "stupidity" of working-class people and strengthening its own location as a center for "intelligence." How can academics theorize about social justice without challenging the class oppression embedded in their home institution? While Romero addresses the difficulties of achieving social justice from within departments of sociology that fail to offer resources for training and mentoring for students interested in social justice, Kadi reveals the university's means of perpetuating class oppression. By addressing her own experience as a working-class student, Kadi draws our attention to the overlooked resources in the skills and knowledge of construction workers and janitors.

Each of these writers demonstrates the merging of theory and practice through risk taking and personal narrative. Vélez and Williams, for example, have taken risks—not only in using personal narrative but in allowing themselves to be vulnerable to the very subordinating practices that their essays are designed to expose. Vélez's framework stands in direct contrast to how and what academics are supposed to think and, more importantly, what they are supposed to write. She publicly names as noxious the very place that provides her financial security. Williams's writing, on the other hand, calls attention to heterosexism in Black communities, risking being misunderstood by well-meaning and not so well-meaning academics to perpetuate racialized thinking about African Americans. By coming out in such public ways and promoting greater understanding of social justice as it concerns gays and lesbians of all groups, Williams takes considerable personal risks. Kadi and Romero also run the risk of being either misunderstood or branded as troublemakers, or both. But by taking these risks, these writers merge practice and theory to work for social justice for our students and colleagues.

Another recurring theme is the ways the production of knowledge in universities is undermined. The experiences that these writers divulge and criticize demand our attention, since they reveal gaps, silences, and invisibility in what passes for knowledge. Within the academy and within movements for social change, what are the roles of silence? Who is silenced and who is doing the silencing? In these days of loud and disingenuous complaints from the privileged that they are being "silenced" (meaning that their words are met with vocal and focused criticism rather than unquestioningly absorbed), it is salutary to hear, in telling detail, what true silencing feels like, how it works, and whom it harms and benefits. For Kadi and Romero, the concerns of white working-class students and students of color are ignored—either intentionally or because the kind of knowledge required is precisely the kind that has been denied. For Williams, the most compelling pressure comes from conflicting ideologies that nonetheless silence both gay and lesbian students and professors. In Doherty's work, the production of knowledge is so individualized that there is an enormous gap in what students can learn about collaboration and alliance building. Kadi and Romero also address the issue of "theory for theory's sake." For Kadi, it is the postmodern theorist who produces her greatest frustration: in the name of theory and distancing rhetoric, the postmodernist turns the lives of real people and their knowledge into an object to be studied for the sake of study. In Romero's study of graduate students of color in sociology, it's clear that the enormous absence, silence, and invisibility of training in race issues promote a racially and ethnically homogeneous university, not social justice.

WORK CITED

Collins, Patricia Hill. "The Social Construction of Black Feminist Thought." *Signs* 14.4 (1989): 745–73.

Chapter 10

Being Queer, Being Black
Living Out in Afro-American Studies

Rhonda M. Williams

Graduation day, Afro-American studies program, 1991: I remind my-self that there are ruptures in my being an out lesbian on campus. My colleagues and superiors know I'm a dyke, as do some, but clearly not all, of our students. Two of my former students—both campus ac-tivists, both proponents of a distinctly masculine cultural nationalism circa 1990s—launch into a tirade against queers. One young man worries about what to do about the fags, and suggests putting them (me?) on a spaceship bound for outer space. He also ruminates on the possibility of a few good gay-bashings. I am disarmed and afraid, and do not name my queerness. As I question their hostility toward lesbians and gays, our conversation lurches from pillar to post: they inform me that queers are a detriment to our race, that "they" are selfish, unnatural, anathema to the building of a strong Black nation.[1]

My question begins to crystallize: why is heterosexuality so central to these young men's notions of Blackness?

This essay uses my coming out/living out to Black students at Col-lege Park as an occasion to reflect on the racialization of heterosex-ism. I begin with a documentation of student responses to my "com-ing out," first in the student newspapers, and then in a large lecture course in Afro-American studies. This discussion foregrounds the is-sues that structured the coming out conversations. I am interested in dialogues that articulate either heterosexuality's centrality to some notion of "Blackness," or the racialization of sexual discourse, includ-ing the notion that homosexuality is a "white thing."[2] The essay then engages the nexus of sexuality and race, suggesting that Black queers interrupt a longing for a stigma-free Black sexuality, a longing forged in the fires of racist ideology. It begins to formulate an explanation of what is at stake when one particular oppressed nationality confronts visible queerness. I preliminarily posit that racialized discourses lend a specificity to some African American heterosexisms. For some African Americans, the issue is not simply sexual orientation, but Blackness itself.

Being Seen

The University of Maryland is a historically white public university that now has a larger African American population than most traditionally white universities. The Black student population includes more than two thousand African Americans, who have created a host of academic, cultural, social, and political organizations. They are a varied lot, and are joined on campus by more than sixty tenured and tenure-track Black faculty and more than one thousand staff and administrators.

There were few out gay and lesbian faculty in the spring of 1992; those who were out are white. As I thought about the absence of visible Black lesbians and gays on campus, I speculated that this void bolstered and empowered those in the African American community who harbor sexuality-based fears and hostilities. Such was the thinking behind my consent to being named as a lesbian in the *Diamond Back,* the student newspaper with the largest readership. This initial article (March 1992) described an upsurge in antigay activity on campus. Two members of the faculty and three students condemned the harassment and called for an administrative response.

Phase two of my coming out: Shannon Murray, an editor for the *Eclipse* (one of our two Black student papers), requested an interview for Women's History Month. She wanted to feature three professors in a spread on Black women. Shannon is a former student; I agreed to the interview. She interviewed straight and gay folk who spoke candidly about homophobia in Black communities. Two Black lesbians named the pain of rejection by their Black peers; a young gay man lamented Black heterosexism, but was quoted under an assumed name. Steve Palmer, then president of the campus chapter of the NAACP, cautioned that "Homosexuals have a spiritual and moral problem that they have to deal with. I do not believe anyone should be physically bashed, but the Black community needs to take a stand on homosexuality and stop being shaped by white standards" (*Eclipse,* March 23, 1992, 4).

Palmer articulated a familiar cultural nationalist perspective. His critique of homosexuality was moral, racialized, and informed by notions of sharp boundaries between Black and white community standards. According to Palmer, the Black community should affirm (does affirm?) a morality that precludes homosexuality. In his broad defense of heterosexism, Palmer assumed the voice of authoritative Blackness—his words became central to subsequent journalistic exchanges.

Phase three: the classroom. My syllabus for "Introduction to Afro-American Studies" included a unit entitled "Black Families, Black Kin: Beyond the Discourse of Pathology" and a subsection on homophobia in Black communities. These lectures compared racist narratives of Black familial pathology to cultural nationalist discourse on Black homosexuality. Each set of conversations normalizes heterosexual, two-parent family life: whereas racist narratives naturalize the two-parent heterosexual family and stigmatize Black female-headed households, the cultural nationalists normalize and privilege heterosexuality at the expense of queerness. Each conversation universalizes the perspectives and analyses of those defining and naming pathology—white (and some Black) social scientists, Black heterosexuals. In what follows, I will suggest connections between the two conversations.

Several departmental staff and a professor attended the lecture in a show of solidarity. I presented, then challenged, the writings of Nathan and Julia Hare, Haki Madhubuti, Amiri Baraka, and Frances Cress Welsing.[3]

These writers share a common nationalist perspective on Black gays and lesbians: our behavior is both a consequence of one or more strains of white supremacy and a threat to kinship and family:

> Unlike the white male, the Black male does not arrive at the effeminate bisexual or homosexual stance from any deeply repressed sense of genetic weakness, inadequacy, or disgust, which I refer to as *primary effeminacy* (effeminacy that is self-derived and not imposed forcibly by others). Instead, the Black male arrives at this position *secondarily,* as the result of the imposed power and cruelty of the white male and the

totality of the white supremacy social and political apparatus that has forced 20 generations of Black males into submission. This pattern of imposed submission is reinforced through every institution within the white supremacy system, but especially in the fundamental social institution of the family or, in this case, the Black survival unit. (Welsing 86)

Those students who asked questions were somewhat surprised by the tone and content of the nationalist authors; many had neither heard of the authors nor read their works. For those willing to speak publicly of these matters, the nationalist discourse was no more than an interesting curiosity. In that setting, no one affirmed Palmer's view. Those who spoke agreed that the reduction of Black sexuality to white racism was an unwarranted denial of Black subjectivity and agency.

Subsequent private conversations with students confirmed my suspicion that more students than not affirmed cultural nationalist sentiments. They were uncomfortable voicing such views in the classroom (in my presence?), but would speak their minds to one another. I learned through the grapevine and in my office of the parameters of the debates. Some students again claimed that homosexuality is a "white thing," worthy of condemnation by those true to authentic Blackness. Some reaffirmed biblical sanctions against homosexuality; others voiced resentment toward those white gay activists who draw comparisons between heterosexist and racist oppression. In subsequent issues of both the *Eclipse* and the *Black Explosion,* the campus community debated the issue. Each paper published letters and editorials from those who condemned queers and from those who critiqued heterosexism.

My concerns for the remainder of this essay are the more explicitly racialized components of Black heterosexism. In other words, I will explore the social constructions of race that mediate some African American heterosexisms and homophobias.

Being Black

I take as a given the pervasiveness of racial representations in U.S. culture and, indeed, throughout the Western world. I understand these representations to be nonstatic, shifting, contested, gendered, and class-specific.[4] Western racist discourse frequently constructs

"Blackness" as a negative problematic. In so doing, the architects of cultural and (social) scientific racism historically have represented Black communities, Black families, and Black bodies as the bearers of stigma, disease, danger, violence, social pathology, and hypersexuality. I am particularly interested in the racialized stories that address Black families and sexuality. Black families have long functioned as markers in the white racist public imagination: they generally signify and manifest a morally problematic sexual agency, a cultural degeneracy. The conventional social scientific wisdom is clear: "the problem" is that so much Black sexuality and kinship formation transgresses the boundaries of married (healthy) heterosexuality.[5]

However, social managers and engineers do not have a monopoly on the generation and propagation of deeply gendered familial tropes. In their musings on the well-being of "the Black nation," African American nationalists have long invoked family metaphors. Martin Delany—often identified as the father of Black nationalism— was among the earliest nationalists to embrace an explicitly patriarchal domestic ideal. Writing in the nineteenth century, Delany believed that masculine authority in both the home and the political institutions that organized citizenship was essential for the well-being of the exiled Black nation (Gilroy, "Family Affair" 23–24). In what follows, I will suggest that family tropes are vital today, and function in part to circulate specific notions of racial authenticity.

Today's African American college students have come of age in a political culture that regularly recycles the signs of Black dysfunction: antisocial Black (male) criminality and (female) sexuality are the behavioral manifestations of contemporary Black cultural chaos. Scholarly and journalistic treatises on the underclass anchored race talk in the 1980s and 1990s; they often spoke the language that distinguishes the aberrant underclass from the striving middle class.[6] As long as they aver affirmative action and other race-based policies, the middle classes are potentially (though suspect) members of the community of citizens. In sharp contrast, the behaviorally deviant underclass compels vigilant monitoring, discipline, and control.[7]

A magazine article from the early 1990s retells the story of Black families in trouble. The August 30, 1993, issue of *Newsweek* featured a lengthy lamentation on the decline of marriage among African Americans. The author of "Endangered Family" made much of noting the ubiquity of Black family crisis: declining marriage rates and out-of-wedlock births are not restricted to the Black poor. Across the board, African American men and women are at odds with one another:

> Black men say black women are "Sapphires," trying to dominate, explains Harvard psychologist Alvin Poussaint, referring to the wife of Kingfish in "Amos 'n' Andy," who epitomized the bitchy, bossy black woman. But Boston anchorwoman Liz Walker believes that many black men mistake self reliance for highhandedness. (Ingrassia 20)

The spectacle of a conflicted Black heterosexuality saturated the pages, and the theme is familiar: there were/are too many female-headed households. Social scientists are left to weigh the relative importance of structural and cultural explanations. The author, Michel Ingrassia, summoned the authority of empirical social science to trash the notion that female-headed families, whatever their "cause," are potentially viable and life-enhancing, as good as "the nuclear unit": "The evidence comes down solidly on the side of marriage. By every measure—economic, social educational—the statistics conclude that two parents living together are better than one" (21). The author recycles some of the evidence: children of Black single mothers are 3.5 times more likely to grow up in poverty than children of married Black couples, children in "intact" families learn commitment, children in one-parent homes are educationally at risk, boys in particular need role models unavailable in female-headed homes. Two-parent homes are, by definition, heterosexual.

Readers familiar with this narrative are not surprised to (re)learn that African American women are the primary carriers of Black familial pathology—ours are the homes that nurture violent Black sons and daughters seemingly in rebellion against male power. In Valerie Martin's home in Washington, D.C., the signs of trouble are already apparent:

> Latoyia, who's going into fifth grade, gets A's and B's, but this articulate girl who seems so calm at home was suspended three times last year for getting into fights. George . . . had to repeat first grade. He seems only mildly rambunctious, but Valerie says he's getting hard to discipline. (18)

Martin's three children have three different (and nameless) fathers. Her relationships with the fathers faltered when Latoyia's got bossy, and George's started to "act stupid." Valerie's story is familiar and comforting to readers already attuned and receptive to cultural explanations of Black distress: the welfare-dependent single mother embodies and reproduces heterosexual confusion in poor, urban African American communities.

Martin has her counterparts among working Black women not receiving AFDC. Here too we find single mothers, raising their children, struggling to make ends meet. Sylvia Berry works for wages outside the home, but the consequences for her son are nonetheless dire. Marcus is "stuck in solitary" while his mother works: his home is a prison, because his neighborhood (the Shaw district, again in the nation's capital) is unsafe. Restless and bored, he plays in school and earns low grades.

Black students read these stories—they bring them to me, offerings that, for them, personalize William J. Wilson's thesis of a crisis-ridden, aberrant underclass. Many African American undergraduates at Maryland do not know that this narrative predates their birth. They experience it as a new and powerful truth. Some read it as a call for a new movement, one that strives for Black economic independence. For others, these narratives are a comforting palliative, stories that help them differentiate themselves from the "others"—the hated and feared African American underclass. When compared to the Martins and Berrys, many of their families emerge as shining examples of domestic bliss. For yet another group, these texts concretize a class-specific missionary zeal: here are the lumpen folk to whom they can offer the gift of racial uplift. Whatever the particular read, many students weave these stories into their customized brands of social conservatism.

Wahneema Lubiano discusses the power of these stories, the saliency of the meanings deployed and circulated in the juxtapositon of welfare and working mothers. Her analysis of the gendered pathology discourse begins with the Clarence Thomas/Anita Hill hearings:

> the flip side of the pathological welfare queen . . . is the black lady, the one whose disproportionate overachievement stands for black cultural strangeness and who ensures the underachievement of "the black male" in the lower classes because "ours [the United States] is a society which presumes male leadership in private and public affairs." (335; quotation from Moynihan Report, 1965)

Lubiano catalogues the narratives mobilized by Hill's opponents: they sought to discredit her professional status by invoking affirmative action and/or by casting her as the living embodiment of a spurned/lesbian womanhood. She is most compelling in her interpretation of the development of Black hostility to Hill:

> Blackness, as an abstraction, did battle for Thomas because few people actually belonging to the group "black" or "African-American" [here referred to by Lubiano as a taken for granted social fact] would have gone to war on behalf of Thomas the corrupt judge, Thomas the bigot, Thomas the incompetent head of the EEOC. But for Thomas the black male victim of "Sapphire"—black female emasculation and betrayer of black men and carrier of black family pathology—well, the African American legions would and did rise to battle against her. Out of the ooze of his past record climbed Thomas, the *real black* thing. (345)

I quote Lubiano at length because her ideological critique illuminates some of the issues at stake in Black heterosexism. Her thesis presumes that many African Americans affirmed the racialized and gendered narratives of Black pathology. To the extent that she is right, Lubiano provides us a means to conceptualize the stakes in Black reluctance to embrace gays and lesbians in our own communities.

In the ideologies of contemporary cultural nationalism, families are *the* sanctioned site for the reproduction of authentic racial ethnic culture. Healthy families are monogamous, are dedicated to masculine authority, and affirm traditional gender roles; unwell families include sexually promiscuous adults and foster female dominance. Recalling "Endangered Family," women are the primary reproductive agents in this narrative, and their dysfunctional families spawn a crisis-ridden racial community populated by carriers of a disabled masculinity and an aggressive femininity. However, redemption is possible: "the crisis of black masculinity can be fixed. It is to be repaired by instituting appropriate forms of masculine and male authority, intervening in the family to rebuild the race" (Gilroy, "Family Affair" 312).

Like Sapphire, Black queers betray the quest for healthy Black families, a regulated and normalized Black sexuality. Whether viewed as the products of broken families or betrayers of family life altogether, Black gays and lesbians are a potential anathema to straight African Americans whose resistance to racist narratives inspires them to "clean up" images of Black sexuality. When these African Americans publicly reject homosexuality, they do so in a social context that persistently regenerates public images and discourses of sexual perversion and familial

damage. For those seeking to sanitize and normalize popular perceptions of Black sexuality, the public affirmations of queerness—a category marked with the stains of hypersexuality, promiscuity, and danger—can only serve to further the stigmatization of Blackness.[8]

Racist narratives that pathologize our families and sexualities also
diminish heterosexual privilege within Black communities—communities already constructed in racist discourse as the reproducers of an
unnatural heterosexuality, already beyond God's law and nature's
logic. Accordingly, the redemption of African American families requires the harnessing and disciplining of Black sexual behavior. Hypersexual heterosexuals can, in principle, change or be changed. As
noted above, the solution is a communal recommitment to the male-
dominated and sexually restrained domestic unit. However, queerness is not so easily reined in—indeed, according to the nationalists,
it is a pathology that totally destabilizes the parameters of social life
and thwarts the building of a strong Black nation.

Many African Americans have expended copious amounts of energy resisting/transforming the discourses that pathologize heterosexual Black families and kinship systems.[9] This essay questions the
contours of that resistance: do they reify Black families and sexualities, or historicize them as complex, diverse, and flexible? My contention is that many cultural nationalist projects reject this complexity. Thus efforts to affirm "Blackness" generate a contradictory narrative: although nationalists seek to remove stigma, they offer in its
place a terrifyingly rigid and tyrannical notion of "family." Shane
Phelan's critique of lesbian essentialism is apropos: "When one is presented with a stigmatized identity, it makes sense to challenge the
stigma surrounding that identity. This serves, ironically to reinforce
the solidity of that identity even as the stigma is rejected" (773). Can
one resist the stigmatization of Black families and sexuality without
consenting to normative and demonizing notions of race, community,
and culture?

Insofar as they reinscribe rigid boundaries of Blackness, nationalist
efforts to destigmatize display at least three noteworthy tendencies.
The first is an identification with Africa that is, as Paul Gilroy notes,
both partial and selective ("Family Affair" 307). For example, Nathan
and Julia Hare's advocacy of polygamous families idealizes co-wife
cooperation and male support, but "ignores cross-generational conflict and intrafamily rivalry" (White 75). In a similar spirit of oblitera-

tion, nationalists who embrace the autonomous, monogamous, conjugal heterosexual family as the domestic ideal suppress their indebtedness to European and Euro-American nationalist notions of proper family life. Their vision of kinship is radically different from the consanguinity and polygamy practiced by many of African America's ethnic ancestors (Sudarkasa).

The second tendency is the aforementioned essentialism—the notion that there is one true African American and/or African diaspora consciousness, one Black ontology that crosses state boundaries and ethnic groups. bell hooks's essay "Postmodern Blackness" speaks to the genealogy of essentialist longings in African America:

> The unwillingness to critique essentialism on the part of many African Americans is rooted in the fear that it will cause folks to lose sight of the specific history and experience of African-Americans and the unique sensibilities and culture that arise from that experience. . . . There is a radical difference between a repudiation of the idea that there is a black "essence" and recognition of the way black identity has been specifically constituted in the experience of exile and struggle. (Yearning 29)

This same tendency also emphasizes similarities between Africans and African Americans, but silences the many and important historical differences.

A third current runs steadily through many nationalist polemics: the notion that Black queerness is fundamentally an epiphenomenal consequence of white supremacy (Madhubuhti 73–74; Welsing 86). The invocation of white racism constructs a mythical and asocial queerness. The gays and lesbians who stalk their pages are not members of Black churches, clubs, schools, and neighborhoods (they are, of course, products of dysfunctional homes). Thus Lubiano's analysis lends itself to a deeper analogy: just as an abstraction of "Blackness" as victim rallied community sympathy for Clarence Thomas, so an abstraction of queerness enables the cultural nationalist line.

Consider the extent to which some straight African Americans partake of "don't ask, don't tell," offering acceptance of queers in return for the silence, shame, and terror of the closet. Lesbians and gays who consent to this form of heterosexism are not so easily viewed as beyond the boundaries of "Blackness." However, when recast as marked carriers of white oppression, these same folk can elicit Black condemnation.

In locating the genesis of Black homosexuality outside Black communities, both cultural nationalists and those not so specifically identified restore the possibility of a normal, healthy Black sexuality. Restoration of health requires recovery from the allegedly corrosive influences of white supremacy that have weakened patriarchal heterosexual bonds in African American communities. The supposed consequences of weakened heterosexual bonds are numerous and pernicious, but the allegations of Black male emasculation and familial breakdown resonate most powerfully within this context.

The stigmatization of Black families and sexualities has been/remains a crucial component in the constitution of Black consciousness. Unlike their white counterparts, African Americans live in a national culture that historically withholds the benefit of an assumed familial and sexual wellness. Individual white families can and do manifest numerous and myriad behaviors, but dominant narratives rarely read such events as revelation of an intrinsic, racial-ethnic cultural chaos. The racist presumption of Black sexual deviance nurtures African American predispositions to keep at arm's length those individuals and behaviors that may reconfirm aberration. It sustains selective and convenient appropriations of Africa, essentialism, and the white causality model. Thus racialized discourses of families and sexuality profoundly mediate the meanings of queerness for many African Americans. The stakes are not merely homosexuality, but Blackness itself.

My conversations with students suggest that many are unfamiliar with nationalist texts.[10] Nonetheless, they often experience queerness as something emanating from, associated with, white peoples. In other words, they affirm the third nationalist tendency. But if not the nationalists, whither the cultural processes that support their racialized constructions of sexuality? I suggest that we have no shortage of recent popular representations that code gay "white."

First and perhaps foremost, many images of gay rights activists visible in the nonqueer media are white images, a phenomenon partly caused by white gay racism but enabled by closeted Black gays and lesbians. For example, in the Clinton-led 1993 debate/debacle on gays in the military, I cannot recall either a single news report that featured a gay Black soldier or a set of talking heads that included African American queers. The visible faces were uniformly white and mostly male. Former army sergeant Perry Watkins is Black and the only openly gay serviceman to have successfully challenged the military's antigay policy. Yet according to Watkins, the "anointed" (white) leadership in the gay movement ignored him during the fight to allow gays to be out in the service.

Margaret Cerullo suggests that campus affirmative action battles also code gay white. Cerullo reports being queried as to whether "gay/lesbian" should be recognized as an affirmative action category.

> It took me a while to think that idea through, but what I eventually realized was that in such suggestions, "gay/lesbian" is being opposed to race, and implicitly therefore being constructed as white. Within an affirmative action search, then, say for a sociologist, the effect (goal?) would be to increase the possibility of hiring a white man or woman. (Harper et al. 32–33)

She goes on to reflect on the constructions of "gay male" in the AIDS epidemic. Despite the fact that in 1987, 50 percent of Black men and Latinos with AIDS had gay or bisexual conduct as their primary risk factor, images of gay men remained white. Cerullo argues that this construction continues, and is aided and abetted by AIDS activists who separate (and thereby repress the intersections of) the "gay epidemic" from the "epidemic among people of color." The national media reported in the autumn of 1994 that AIDS is now the leading cause of death among young African American men. And still, discussions of sexuality remain largely suppressed or marginalized in many Black communities.

Widely circulated representations that code queer white also emanate from the ranks of organized heterosexism. Media messages from those opposed to gay civil rights suggest that all the queers are white and all the Blacks are straight. Here I have in mind the media campaigns waged during the fall 1993 electoral season. In Colorado, for example, the antigay movement challenged the thesis of heterosexist oppression by circulating income tables that purportedly "show" that gays have higher family incomes than African Americans. This strategy, directed in particular at Black audiences, intends to weaken African American support for gay civil rights.[11] Taken individually, each of these practices functions to make Black queers invisible to straight folk of all races. Viewed collectively, they constitute a powerful and highly visible cultural message consumed by our students and the public at large.

Being Political

Several African American students at the University of Maryland—all male—addressed the Black student population on the dangers of a narrowly confined Blackness. David Terry opined that "homosexuality is not a burdening problem in the Black community. . . . If there is a problem within the Black community, it is on the part of 'we' the heterosexual members" (Terry 2). Timothy Dixon lamented the "small-mindedness" and "stupidity" of his peers (Dixon 2). Two young men came to my office to share with me their personal support and to let me know that they were taking up the queer cause in the dormitories. I noted the absence of young women visitors, the dearth of young women who challenged heterosexism in the Black papers. I am reminded of Makeda Silvera's essay on the invisibility of Afro-Caribbean lesbians:

> Negative responses from our heterosexual Black sisters, although more painful [than similar responses from the men], are, to a certain extent, understandable because we have no race privilege and very, very few of us have class privilege. The one privilege in our group is heterosexual. We have all suffered at the hands of this racist system at one time or another and to many heterosexual Black women it is inconceivable, almost frightening, that one could turn her back on credibility in our community, and the society at large by being lesbian. These women are also afraid that they will be labeled "lesbian" by association. It is this fear, that homophobia, which keeps Black women isolated. (531)

I wonder to what extent masculine privilege empowered the young men who publicly affirmed my sexual orientation. Would they have felt equally at liberty to speak out if the queer in question was a gay brother?

As one semester passes into the next, I regularly encounter students responding to the news of my queerness. First-year students no longer hear it in the large lecture course, but may receive a briefing from their older peers. Those who frequent the Afro-American studies office witness a small community of folks struggling to embrace (sometimes with more ease than others) the diversity of our collective. The departmental space provides many students an example of how they might live and work in principled solidarity with their queer brothers and sisters. Conversations about sexuality are more frequent and less tense. On campus, the 1998–99 president of the undergraduate student queer organization was a Black woman; and the 1998 NAACP was in the forefront of student organizations rallying in solidarity with the lesbian and gay community after two violent heterosexists murdered Matthew Shepard in Wyoming in the fall of 1998. I take these as hopeful signs of change.

NOTES

I thank Katie King, M. V. Lee Badgett, and the editors at the Center for Advanced Feminist Studies at the University of Minnesota for insightful comments. An extended version of this essay appears in W. Lubiano *The House That Race Built: Black Americans, U.S. Terrain* (Pantheon, 1997).

1. This paragraph employs a diversity of self-referential terms: "lesbian," "dyke," "queerness." My use of these terms has shifted over the years, and not in some ideologically recognizable pattern. My current penchant for "queer" reflects my delight in the term's definitional fuzziness, its overdetermination. I draw inspiration from Phillip Brian Harper's assertion that "queer includes within it a necessarily expansive impulse" (Harper et al. 30), and Oscar Montero's proposition that "Queer theory skirts identity, sometimes literally, and brings other identities, ethnic, racial, and national into play" (Montero 17). I would also add that many homophobes and heterosexists use the term as well. Their use connotes a generally transgressive sexuality, and gender particularities are not always relevant.

2. In their 1981 dialogue, Barbara Smith and Beverly Smith previewed some of the issues raised here. Barbara Smith suggests that racist sexual stereotypes shape homophobia in Black communities; Beverly Smith conjectures that racism's dichotomies give Black folks the option of coding lesbianism white. This essay revisits these issues and seeks to extend and amplify their earlier observations (Smith and Smith 124).

3. Simmons concisely and critically reviews cultural nationalist positions on Black homosexuality.

4. The literature on racial representations, racial meanings, and the racializations of Western political economies and cultures continues to grow. For important examples, see Omi and Winant, Gooding-Williams, Butler, Goldberg, Christian, hooks, and Jewell.

5. 1994–95 marks the thirtieth anniversary of the publication of Daniel P. Moynihan's book *The Negro Family: The Case for National Action.* Now known as "the Moynihan report," this monograph popularized the notion that slavery had created a Negro American subculture that is matriarchal and therefore pathological. According to Moynihan and his disciples, it is this familial

dysfunction that impedes Black social development, and not contemporary forms of economic and cultural racism. The sociologist William J. Wilson's 1987 treatise, *The Truly Disadvantaged*, affirmed the prevalence of pathology among the Black urban poor, but argued that deindustrialization, not slavery, is the source of female-headed households (i.e., the loss of manufacturing jobs for high school educated men devastated the employment possibilities for those same men, resulting in a decline in marriage rates). Challenges to Moynihan and Wilson abound. Reed provides a solid contemporary example.

6. Wilson focused much underclass debate in the late 1980s and early 1990s. For a compelling discussion of "the underclass" as a racialized and gendered ideological discourse, see Reed.

7. Dumm discusses the intensification of state monitoring and control of urban Black America.

8. I thank Elizabeth Seydi for articulating this contradiction so clearly in our conversations about sexuality and race and thereby sending me in the directions developed in this essay.

9. In this context, "kin" refers to a group of people who consider themselves family or relatives. The rules for defining kin vary widely across cultures, time, and place, but often imply notions of responsibility and obligation.

10. They are equally unfamiliar with Black lesbian feminist critiques of nationalist-inspired homophobia in Black communities. In past semesters, I have included either Audre Lorde ("I Am Your Sister") or Cheryl Clarke ("The Failure to Transform") in their readings.

11. I thank M. V. Lee Badgett for reminding me of these campaigns. She notes that the gay samples from which these data emerge are biased and non-random, thereby overrepresenting high-income gays.

WORKS CITED

Butler, Judith. "Endangered/Endangering: Schematic Racism and White Paranoia." In *Reading Rodney King, Reading Urban Uprising*, ed. Robert Gooding-Williams. New York: Routledge, 1993.

Christian, Barbara. "What Celie Knows That You Should Know." In *The Anatomy of Racism*, ed. David Goldberg. Minneapolis: University of Minnesota Press, 1990.

Clarke, Cheryl. "The Failure to Transform: Homophobia in the Black Community." In *Home Girls: A Black Feminist Anthology*, ed. Barbara Smith. Latham, NY: Kitchen Table, Women of Color Press, 1983.

Dixon, Timothy. "Choosing Sides." *Eclipse* (University of Maryland at College Park), April 6, 1992.

Dumm, Thomas. "The New Enclosures: Racism in the Normalized Community." In *Reading Rodney King, Reading Urban Uprising,* ed. Robert Gooding-Williams. New York: Routledge, 1993.

Freeman, Brian. "Pomo Afro Homos Presents Fierce Love." *Outlook* 4.2 (1991).

Gilroy, Paul. *The Black Atlantic: Modernity and Double Consciousness.* Cambridge: Harvard University Press, 1993.

———. "It's a Family Affair." In *Black Popular Culture,* ed. Gina Dent. Seattle: Bay Press, 1992.

Goldberg, David. "The Social Formation of Racist Discourse." In *The Anatomy of Racism,* ed. David Goldberg. Minneapolis: University of Minnesota Press, 1990.

Gooding-Williams, Robert. "Look! A Negro." In *Reading Rodney King, Reading Urban Uprising,* ed. Robert Gooding-Williams. New York: Routledge, 1993.

Gresham, Jewell Handy. "The Politics of Family in America." *Nation,* July 24–31, 1989.

Harper, Phillip Brian, Margaret Cerullo, and E. Frances White. "Multi/Queer/Culture." *Radical America* 24.4 (1990).

hooks, bell. *Black Looks: Race and Representation.* Boston: South End Press, 1992.

———. *Yearning: Race, Gender, and Cultural Politics.* Boston: South End Press, 1990.

Ingrassia, Michele. "Endangered Family." *Newsweek,* August 30, 1993.

Jewell, K. Sue. *From Mammy to Miss America and Beyond.* New York: Routledge, 1993.

Lorde, Audre. "I Am Your Sister: Black Women Organizing across Sexualities." In *A Burst of Light.* Ithaca, NY: Firebrand Books, 1988.

Lubiano, Wahneema. "Black Ladies, Welfare Queens, and State Minstrels: Ideological War by Narrative Means." In *Race-ing Justice, En-gendering Power,* ed. Toni Morrison. New York: Pantheon, 1992.

Madhubuti, Haki R. *Black Men: Obsolete, Single, Dangerous? The Afrikan American in Transition: Essays in Discovery, Solution, and Hope.* Chicago: Third World Press, 1990.

Montero, Oscar. "Before the Parade Passes By: Latino Queers and National Identity." *Radical America* 24.4 (1990).

Omi, Michael, and Howard Winant. *Racial Formation in the United States from the 1960s to the 1980s.* London: Routledge, 1986.

Phelan, Shane. "(Be)Coming Out: Lesbian Identity and Politics." *Signs* 18.4 (1993).

Reed, Adolph. "The Underclass as Myth and Symbol." *Radical America* 24.1 (1990).

Silvera, Makeda. "Man Royals and Sodomites: Some Thoughts on the Invisibility of Afro-Caribbean Lesbians." *Feminist Studies* 18.2 (1992).

Simmons, Ron. "Some Thoughts on the Challenges Facing Black Gay Intellectuals." In *Brother to Brother*, ed. Essex Hemphill. Boston: Alyson, 1991.

Smith, Barbara, and Beverly Smith. "Across the Table: A Sister-to-Sister Dialogue." In *This Bridge Called My Back: Writings by Radical Women of Color*, ed. Cherríe Moraga and Gloria Anzaldúa. Latham, NY: Kitchen Table, Women of Color Press, 1981.

Sudarkasa, Niara. "African and Afro-American Family Structure: A Comparison." *Black Scholar*, November–December 1980.

Terry, David. "My Brother, Black Is Black." *Eclipse* (University of Maryland at College Park), April 6, 1992.

Welsing, Frances Cress. "The Politics behind Black Male Passivity, Effeminisation, Bisexuality, and Homosexuality." In *The Isis Papers*. Chicago: Third World Press, 1991.

White, E. Frances. "Africa on My Mind: Gender, Counter Discourse and African American Nationalism." *Journal of Women's History* 2.1 (1990).

Williams, Rhonda M. "Living at the Crossroads: Explorations in Race, Nationality, Sexuality and Gender." In *The House That Race Built: Black Americans, U.S. Terrain*, ed. Wahneema Lubiano. New York: Pantheon, 1997.

Wilson, William J. *The Truly Disadvantaged*. Chicago: University of Chicago Press, 1987.

Chapter 11

Learning to Think and Teach about Race and Gender despite Graduate School

Obstacles Women of Color Graduate Students Face in Sociology

Mary Romero

As I walked out of a graduate course on social movements and collective behavior in the mid-1970s, the instructor approached me in the hall to comment on my research proposal. "There is too much passion in the proposal. You don't have enough distance and objectivity to study the Chicano movement from a sociological perspective. You need to learn sociology first and then you will be able to do Chicano-related research." He then changed his demeanor to a more paternalistic stance and said, "You are a good student. You are different from the other Chicano graduate students. They are not going to finish. You can—if you don't get involved in politics."[1] I was stunned. I responded with silence.

After our encounter, I played the scene over and over again in my mind. What was wrong with having passion and commitment? Why do research if it does not matter? Why should I continue in a field just for the sake of learning a sociological perspective? As a college student during the height of the Chicano movement in Denver, I entered graduate school in sociology with the goal of doing research on Chicano-related social issues. I had selected sociology as a means to understanding the Chicano experience and as a way to make a contribution toward social justice.

I felt sickened by the attempt to separate Chicano graduate students from each other. Being the only student or the only one of two students of color was difficult, particularly in an environment that attributed my achievements to affirmative action and where faculty interest was a response to my ethnicity and a need to affirm their liberalism.

I had not thought about these experiences for nearly a decade. Having taught primarily undergraduate courses in predominantly white institutions in the Midwest and the Pacific Northwest, I was removed from the shared accounts of graduate students of color in sociology. Listening to the papers presented by women of color graduate students at sociology conferences and discussing their research with them, I had assumed that my isolated graduate experience was a reflection of the early years of affirmative action—after all, there were now many more Chicana/o and African American sociologists. In pursuing research on women of color graduate students, however, I discovered otherwise.

When I served on the social issues committee of the Sociologists for Women in Society (SWS), the absence of domestic women of color (Latina, African American, Asian American, and Native American) was identified as a concern of the association. Several national regional sociological associations had already conducted studies on the status of women in the profession.[2] Our committee agreed to study the situation. I volunteered to study graduate students and began collecting data. Compiling a list of women of color graduate students from the American Sociological Association's (ASA) list of minority fellows and names provided by graduate programs responding to inquiries, I mailed 165 questionnaires in 1989. Sixty-six women responded. One of the items on the questionnaire asked the respondents whether they would be willing to participate further in the study by being interviewed. In 1991 twenty-six follow-up telephone interviews were conducted with women of color graduate students in various stages in their Ph.D. programs in sociology.[3] Thirty-nine percent were enrolled in graduate schools in the West and another 39 percent were in the East, 15 percent enrolled in the South, and 8 percent in the Midwest.[4]

All the interviews were transcribed and then coded in general categories of mentoring, financial assistance, networking, decision for selection of graduate programs, relationships with faculty and students, teaching and publishing opportunities, and the issues they identified as barriers. I recoded the data in each category based on the themes that emerged. In response to the two most common complaints the women made about graduate school, my analysis turned to detailed descriptions of how graduate programs socialize students to the profession. The two complaints were (1) the lack of training available in the area of sociology of race and gender, and (2) the degree to which the curriculum had not been transformed to include race and gender.[5] Both complaints are consistent with other critiques of graduate programs that appear in the literature. For instance, in his introduction to the special issue on "Racial Diversity in Becoming a Sociologists" published by the *American Sociologist,* John Stanfield described the "organizational life of professional sociology" as "quite conservative politically and socially." Nevertheless, the descriptions of graduate programs without courses in race and gender are alarming, considering the extensive efforts made by scholars, teachers, and students to develop multicultural requirements, revise the curriculum, and transform the discipline.[6] The lack of race courses in the sociology graduate curriculum is even more shocking, given today's screaming headlines about ethnic cleansing, race riots, anti-Semitism, and the rise of neo-Nazi groups.

I further investigated their claims about the curriculum by conducting a survey of Ph.D. programs in sociology (Romero and Margolis). The quantitative data bore out the women's stories: less than a quarter of all departments included the study of race in the required theory courses and more than a quarter of all departments did not offer a single graduate course on race. Of the departments that offered graduate courses on race, about half (54 percent) of all graduate race relations courses had not been offered in the last year. Furthermore, many of these classes identified as "race relations" were actually courses on Latin America and other non-European societies.[7] It appears that many graduate programs consider courses dealing with international issues part of their race specialty; however, courses on international topics do not necessarily address race relations or race theory. Yearly offerings of courses that covered race relations in the United States or race theory were clearly not the norm. The survey data support the claims that race remains a secondary category and is far from the center of the discipline.[8]

I was shocked to discover how little graduate school had changed

since I was a graduate student in the 1970s. Given the numerous curriculum revision programs throughout the country and the move to
add diversity requirements to undergraduate education, I had simply
assumed that any responsible graduate program included, if not required, a course on race. The data clearly suggest that the profession
is not preparing the next generation of sociologists to meet the challenges posed by the increasing numbers of students of color and
racial issues affecting society. The ASA survey of graduate departments reported similar findings and concluded that "academic programs are created and maintained without any concern about the
characteristics of their students" (Mayrl and Mauksch 16–17).

I returned to examining the socialization process operating in
graduate programs and looked at the type of training future sociologists are in fact receiving (Margolis and Romero). I wondered
whether women of color were still mentored away from their own
political commitment to racial justice. Had they given up any hope of
studying race relations in the United States? Was the sociology of race
relations presented as an area to avoid—an area that would limit their
opportunities in the profession? Or were they developing strategies
to obtain the training and support to do research and teaching shaped
by their commitment to struggles for racial justice?

The women's narratives are quite appropriate for exploring issues
related to social justice because each of them mentioned in their interview that they entered sociology graduate programs with these issues
in mind. Patricia Gurin and Edgar G. Epps would classify these
women as committed-achievers; that is, they are motivated by both
individual and collective aspirations. The following excerpt from a
student of color is a typical response given for selecting sociology and
the struggles encountered as a result:

> The reason I chose sociology was that after I had gotten out of high
> school, I worked for some social welfare organizations. One of them I
> worked for in particular was a federally funded program that was
> called "Model Cities." I became very excited about the idea about mak-
> ing social and structural changes that made a difference in people's
> lives. . . . Very often women of color are interested in doing the kinds of
> research that has some real policy implications and that's really ori-
> ented toward problem solving issues. And at the program in ———
> University it's the kind of research that's almost disdained and it's al-

most looked down upon. People have been very kind about my little research project here but I know that it's not the kind of thing—I mean they place a much higher value and premium on things that are purely theoretical types of studies. . . . So for me right from the beginning there was that focus on how to translate everything that we know, all the sociological wisdom that we say we have into something that's practical and into something that makes a difference. . . . In this particular program that kind of orientation does not get a lot of respect.[9]

The ASA survey also noted tension in establishing applied sociology and concluded that "The bulk of graduate education involves talking about sociology rather than doing sociology" (Mayrl and Mauksch 17).

Focusing on the experiences of women of color graduate students in sociology builds on the growing literature on women[10] and minorities[11] in higher education and the sociology of sociology. I am particularly interested in research that attempts to use a sociological perspective to understand our own circumstances in academia.[12] While many of these studies restrict their goals to the evaluation of graduate education and training, others have moved toward a "sociology of the discipline."[13] One area of focus in the literature has been to identify patterns of bias and how they operate at various levels that reproduce knowledge and its practitioners.[14] An early study of this type was conducted by Julius A. Roth, who interviewed faculty advisors at the University of Chicago about their conceptions of "good" and "poor" graduate students. He found consistent descriptions that "create a restricted culture in which students with certain characteristics will thrive, while others with negatively valued characteristics will run into repeated stumbling blocks" (350).[15] Originality was used as a measure of intellect; however, "when a student's originality carried him outside the limits" of the mainstream, s/he was defined as "bizarre" rather than as a potential scholar. If this situation holds true today, we would expect that women, working-class students, and students of color who attempt to use "standpoint" theory or interdisciplinary approaches are not likely to be defined as "good" students.[16] Furthermore, the characteristics identified in the study (assertiveness, confidence, independence, adjustment) place women, working-class students, and students of color at a disadvantage.[17] Janet Malenchek Egan's work on self-concept and graduate school identifies the relationship between these characteristics and social structure:

> In my definition, high self-esteem is contingent on a view of oneself as
> a competent, worthwhile person, deserving of acceptance and expect-
> ing to succeed. Individuals assess whether they possess these qualities
> according to the standards and the frame of reference provided by their
> culture. If this self-view is challenged by structural features of the so-
> cializing organization, the possibility exists for a lowering of individual
> self-esteem. (201)

The situation is further worsened by the high degree of competition
(Kleinman; Egan) and isolation (Sherlock and Morris; Egan) characteristic of graduate school.

Investigating the structure of the department is essential in identifying how valuable resources (primarily mentoring and financial assistance) are distributed and controlled.[18] Faculty members are responsible for admitting new students, awarding teaching and research fellowships, and writing letters of recommendation. They are
also central to graduate students' success in acquiring research experience and publishing opportunities. Consequently, mentoring is a
key feature of success in graduate school. Given the cloning aspects
of the mentorship, faculty rarely engage in such relationships with
students who are different—placing women and minority students at
a disadvantage.[19]

A second area of concern that these "self-reflective" studies have addressed is the internal structure of sociology departments. The studies
most relevant to the research at hand, however, are those that analyze
the complex position of graduate students within the department and
their socialization process toward professionalization.[20] For instance,
Charles Crothers's study of sociology departments included an analysis of graduate students' position in the formal and informal structure
and their relationships with faculty. He notes that graduate students as
a group experience "status degradation" as they are stripped of their
past identities and treated as "baby sociologists."[21] Egan goes even further and argues that graduate students undergo a resocialization
process: "currently lacking professional self-image and scholarly world
view, it [professional socialization] alters the past rather than merely
building on it" (201). Little systematic help is built into the formal structure to move graduate students from the transition from being a directed student to being a self-directed researcher or toward developing
a professional or disciplinary identity.[22] The status of graduate students
changes as they move from course work to qualifying exams to Ph.D.

candidacy. Their needs, as well as their involvement, also differ at various stages. Graduate programs lack the formal or informal structure for "covering professional skills and the acquisition of professional skills" (Crothers 340). Ronald M. Pavalko and John Holley's study of professional self-concept among graduate students supports previous research on the relationship between opportunities and the socialization toward professional identity. Carin Weiss's research on the socialization process in graduate and professional schools underlines the importance of informal interaction with faculty in developing a high professional role commitment. Yet graduate programs seldom recognize this interaction as a component of the students' education or as faculty responsibility.

Research on the sociology of sociology identifies the ways sociologists reproduce themselves and mainstream sociology, but rarely discuss the implications for women of color as students, faculty, or scholars. Research has begun to address how socialization impacts white women but not students of color, particularly women of color. Discussion about professional identity assumes a race norm, that is, a white (and frequently male) professional identity. For instance, D. Stanley Eitzen's proposed syllabus for a course on the "Introduction to Graduate School" includes a discussion of the status of women and minorities in the profession but does not address how to handle racism and sexism as a graduate student or later as a faculty member; nor is there a discussion of how to socialize white students to work and learn in a diverse workplace.

The women shared stories of frustration, struggle, and achievement. They described hurdles not typically addressed by affirmative action or retention programs, barriers in the curriculum and in the distribution of critical resources. These hidden barriers and policies function as obstacles to diversity and multicultural education. I will employ their narratives to identify the patterns of socialization affecting the training available to teach and do research aimed at furthering social justice. Their struggles include the fight for a more equitable distribution of resources in graduate school and for an end to racist practices in sociological knowledge and social relationships between faculty and other graduate students. The women's descriptions of their graduate education also include the wide range of strategies employed to obtain an education fulfilling their needs by going outside the formal organization of their program. Before turning to a discussion of the socialization process, I will summarize the environment in which graduate students learn to become sociologists.

Monocultural Learning Environment

The most common single factor in the women's descriptions of Ph.D. programs in sociology is the lack of diversity in faculty, students, and curriculum. First of all, students are confronted with the glaring absence of people of color.[23] One graduate student recalls her first day in the department:

> The first time I walked into the campus, one of the secretaries—who turned out to be a really nice person in the long run—she just kind of had this startled look, "Can I help you?" In the kind of way when somebody thinks you're going to rob them and they figure they better help you before you help yourself. She kind of looked and saw this Black woman standing there and usually the only other Black person to come to the building is the woman who sweeps the floors. I thought, "Oh boy, this is a really good start." The second thing that shocked me was, they have these wonderful pictures lining the stairwell of every graduate since 1901. The first Black woman I saw in that lineup graduated the year I got there. So I was Black woman number two or Black woman number three. I thought, "Good god, I didn't realize it was this bad."

This student's experience is not unique. Many women spoke about being the "lone" woman graduate student of color. Several students noted the presence of international students from Third World countries, but the source of "loneliness" and isolation was the absence of other domestic students of color.

> I'm like the first Black African American student I guess that they've had in the past eleven years now. They do get a lot of foreign students but not Americans. In fact as far as American minority students go, as far as I can tell there are none other than me. I never see them [other women graduate students of color] and I never talk to them. They're just not around at all. I think they had such a horrible experience that they just stay off campus and come in only when necessary.

The kind of "loneliness" and isolation that women of color identified is quite different from the experience of the "lone scholar" (Becker;

Hood) or individualism (Kleinman) addressed in previous studies. They experienced not only an absence of other graduate students of color but also an absence among the faculty in the department. The following is a typical inventory:

> The department has between forty to forty-five graduate students and about ten to fifteen faculty persons. It's a very conservative department. All White men are professors except for about two women. Only one tenured female faculty. One junior faculty that's Black. One minority woman who is on leave and she's a junior faculty. So the power structure of the department is very male and very white and very old and very conservative.

Second, the absence of diversity among students and faculty is also reflected in the curriculum. This included course offerings, subject matter in required and elective courses, and required readings for courses and exams. One graduate student described the exclusion of race as making people of color invisible:

> For example one class I took on gender focused on theoretical issues. The readings that we did—there were five or six required books—and none of these books, not any sections of these books, really focused on the Black female experience although it was a class in gender. . . . Another example, an aging class that I took—very little focus on race. . . . If you are looking at comparative historical or theoretical stuff and the focus is on the major social thinkers, there's not even an opportunity to bring up issues that necessarily relate to racial minorities. So there's a lot of invisibleness in the overall program.

Gloria Jones-Johnson echoed a similar assessment in her article on Black women sociologists in academe:

> Unfortunately, sexist, racist, cultural-bound and middle-class assumptions held by faculty result in the omission of the perspective of women of color, biased teaching, limited learning and myopia in sociological pedagogy. Sociological knowledge has assumed both a masculine and white perspective, however. (315)[24]

In response to the question, "Would you recommend the program to another woman of color?" a student appraised the learning environment women of color face in graduate school:

> If you're talking about a Black student who is interested in some level of discussion or something [interaction] with other students, I couldn't

recommend this program for her. If she were interested in the possibility that she might form some kind of mentoring relationship with the faculty then I couldn't really recommend this program. . . . if she were looking for some satisfying level of social interaction with either faculty or students, I couldn't say that she would find it here. . . . If they just wanted to get a good education in sociology and learn a lot about theory, a generally good program, I'd say yeah, come to ——— University. But if they're looking for something else, a rounded out good experience, not just the academic, but something that recognized racial ethnic issues and offered some level of social interaction for minority students then I couldn't say this would be the program.

This appraisal points to an important process of socialization involving students of color internalizing the mainstream definition of what constitutes a "good" program or a quality education. Training in race and ethnicity in a multiracial environment becomes defined as something special rather than a criterion for any program to train competent sociologists. In sum then, these women entered Ph.D. programs with the intention of making social change and contributing to the struggle for social justice. They felt isolated from persons of their cultural background or who shared similar racial experiences, and encountered a monocultural environment dominated by whites and men.[25] In this alienating context they began their training to become sociologists.

Learning to Be an "American" Sociologist

As graduate students, these women were surrounded by alienating rituals and practices experienced every day through the class organization, required readings, student and faculty interaction, and student interaction. The absence of scholars of color as faculty, speakers, and authors of required readings sent clear messages to the graduate students:

> I mean it was like saying that all the thinking in the world comes from Europe. People in other parts of the world don't have ideas.

> If you're interested in communities or ethnic studies then you're going to be ghettoized and you're going to be perceived in a certain way.

There is still, on an informal basis, this sense that you're sort of being rude if you bring up race, issues of race. You know, you shouldn't be talking about these things.

Competition is a significant organizational characteristic of most graduate programs. Students compete for faculty advisors and mentors, teaching and research assistantships, and ranking in the class. The competitive culture of departments is further emphasized by sanctioning against cooperative learning (Kleinman). The following are a few examples:

They encouraged you to work isolated. They don't like you to talk to other students about papers for exams. They always tell you, "This is an individual paper. Don't talk to anyone about this." . . . Very individualistic—the feeling and the method that they [faculty] use.

The relations [between students] are very stressed. And also students are very competitive in my department because there is this informal ranking system. Because they're allowing more and more students into the program, they have less and less money to give to students. And so students really have to compete for money and that competition takes the form of who gets the highest scores and who impresses a professor more. Things like that. And it can be quite nasty at times but the department sort of encourages that because they rank students on a scale of one to ten. So each student has a rank. So it's just an ugly situation.

The high degree of individualism and competition that the women identified as shaping their experiences is not entirely the same experience reported by Kleinman, Crothers, and others. For students of color, individualism and competition increase the burden of graduate school because they are already "the only one." Moreover, as a result of the scarce resources, students of color frequently experience white graduate students' resentment about affirmative action. In their study of graduate students of color, Anne S. Pruitt and Paul D. Isaac noted that faculty contributed to the hostile environment: "Often the expectations and attitudes of white faculty lead minority students to feel stigmatized. Some students feel that they would not be enrolled except for affirmative action requirements. They feel that they must continue to prove themselves" (534). The following two incidents exemplify the way women of color experience their fellow classmates' resentment:

I remember one guy coming up to me about my second year. He said, "Geez, so you must be the affirmative action case." I said, "What the hell do you mean?" I happen to have seen his transcript from Princeton which was a C- or a C transcript. My transcript was an A transcript. So I just said, "No. As a matter of fact, my transcript is better than some of yours [white students]." One student put a note in a professor's mailbox with an article written in the *New York Times* by a conservative. And the argument was "Well these minority students are just so ill prepared for universities. That's why there's so much racial conflict because the better prepared white students have to deal with these stupid Black students and then they come in and try to ask for equality and then you give them scholarships on top of that—that's what the whole problem is." So this student in our department thought those of us who were sitting around "bitching" for equity fell into this category.

White classmates frequently express their resentment by attributing all the accomplishments of students of color to race rather than merit. Consequently, white students often do not treat women of color as serious students. Actions generated out of this attitude include the reference to women of color as "the affirmation action student," and their exclusion from study groups and informal activities (Romero and Storrs).

Women's accounts of graduate school also contained reference to conflicts they experience maintaining their own values and ideas, especially when they run counter to mainstream sociology. Socialization into the profession included internalizing the hierarchy and its supporting value system. Three aspects of the hierarchy most commented upon were (1) the low status accorded to the study of race and ethnicity; (2) the hierarchy of elite educational institutions and low status of state-funded institutions, particularly community colleges; and (3) the relegation of interest in social justice to a non-research track. Almost all the women interviewed recalled incidents involving faculty placing negative value on the study of race. The advice an advisor gave to one graduate student was not unique: "One of the things the faculty told us is don't get in that field, especially if you're a Chicana scholar. Don't get into issues that deal with gender and the family because you're ghettoizing yourself. You're not going to be marketable."

However, women of color found themselves in a double bind when facing job market expectations. For instance, one graduate student who taught at a community college with a large enrollment of students of color received pressure from her advisor to limit her teaching to the university. The student interpreted the advice as an attempt to change her values:

> They never liked the fact that I was teaching at a community college. It was almost like a step below them that I would even stay at the community college. In fact I had one professor who at the time was the graduate advisor try to give me this line that I could do more for my people if I did go full time and be in this intellectual arena.

If a woman of color wanted to teach in an institution with a high minority enrollment, she frequently had to choose between teaching and research. However, if she selected an institution with a large minority enrollment, she risked being labeled as mediocre and not a serious student. Another student resented her advisor's conclusion that she was not good enough to be hired to teach in a research institution or a graduate program: "Personally she makes a lot of assumptions about me that I find insulting. Like maybe I'm destined to teach at a community college instead of a university."

Students who expressed a research interest in race and involvement in social issues ran the risk of being defined as not serious students. This stigma was also attached to students interested in applied sociology. As one student commented on the lack of status for applied sociology, "Women of color are interested in doing the kinds of research that has some real policy implications and that's really oriented toward problem solving issues and in this program, that is the kind of research that's almost disdained and it is almost looked down upon." Another student also acknowledged the distinctions: "my hunch would be that my work would be much more welcomed in, say ethnic studies or women's studies than sociology."[26]

Socialization was not limited to learning how to rank areas in the discipline and to value research over teaching; students were also socialized to appreciate "correct" theoretical approaches and perspectives. For instance, a student recalled that the approach she selected for her qualifying exam was rejected by the committee. She wanted to study sex workers using labor theory, but the committee would accept only the theories on deviance for this topic. Their insistence that sex work only be analyzed through a deviance lens trained students to ignore political action and self-definition of the situation and to develop a mainstream standpoint.

Learning the hierarchy in the discipline involved accepting several racist and elitist messages: (1) serious graduate students do not have an interest in teaching students of color, particularly not at community colleges; (2) research on race relations is not a scholarly pursuit; (3) serious students and scholars are not involved in political action; (4) non-sociologists, particularly the poor and people of color, are unable to define, analyze, and understand their circumstances in a meaningful way.

While many of the students recognize that most hurdles they face in obtaining a Ph.D. in sociology stem from the traditional and conservative nature of mainstream sociology, statements they made in interviews frequently contradicted their own experiences and political views. Given their isolation and subordinate status in the program, some women internalized the dominant norms and values. A pattern that emerged in the women's descriptions of their graduate education was a socialization process involving a "blaming the victim" approach and a "cooling-out" process. "Blaming the victim" involved teaching students to identify themselves as the problem and to look at the situation from a psychological perspective rather than a sociological perspective. Rather than addressing the patterns of events outlined in their accounts of graduate school, a blaming the victim approach treated each event as unique and particularistic. "Cooling out" involved a process whereby students learn to lower their expectations and identify situations they once protested as "normal" and unchangeable.[27] Both experiences became important in learning to take their place in the discipline.

A major function of the blaming the victim process was to socialize students to accept traditional sociology and the customary structure of graduate programs as right and all others as illegitimate or appropriate for some other department such as ethnic studies or women's studies. This process required students to internalize the norms and values surrounding traditional sociology and the academic structure. For example, in comparing the courses assigned to teaching assistants, one student referred to the nongender courses as "meatier." As graduate students, these women were already internalizing the values of their "white, male and conservative" faculty (Margolis and Romero).

Another function of the "blaming the victim" and "cooling-out" processes was to thwart criticism of the social organization of the

graduate program. While most of the women listed structural problems involved in acquiring a mentor, they frequently concluded with
psychological or individualistic explanations. Structural problems included the absence of faculty interested in similar research areas, or,
when there was a faculty member interested in their area, they were
frequently nontenured and had enormous time pressures. If there
was only one faculty of color or woman in the department, the burden of mentoring fell heavily on her shoulders. While recognizing
these limitations, many students blamed themselves or individual
faculty for personal differences, or identified their own lack of "aggressive behavior" or "the right attitude" as responsible for the lack
of mentoring.[28]

Interestingly enough, the women began with a sociological analysis of the formal and informal structure of the department, but the
"cooling-out" process taught them not to apply sociology to their
everyday life. The following is a typical explanation attributing the
lack of mentoring to personality: "Part of it may just be that I'm not
the kind of person that asks a lot of other people." Students are also
socialized to accept individual responsibility for structural issues.

> Again I don't know if [the lack of mentoring] . . . If that's because I
> didn't ask for it [guidance]. Although the couple times I asked for it
> [advice] the responses I got weren't very good. It was almost like—well
> you're supposed to sort of just inherently know how to do this.

The women listed difficulties finding mentors and obtaining teaching
and research assistantships as the primary obstacles in graduate
school. There is no formal structure to socialize students into the profession, and faculty are not likely to mentor students who are not
seen as self-directed (Roth; Kleinman). However, unlike white graduate students, students of color faced a situation that was further impacted by race—that is, the absence of faculty of color and the white
faculty's difficulty in mentoring students of color. As one student
explained,

> It would be one thing if there were no women of color on the faculty
> and women of color [students] could still get a mentor—that's sort of
> one problem. But neither of these things are happening. One, there's no
> one [white faculty] who is going to mentor us and two, there are no
> women of color on the faculty. So the two sort of compound one
> another.

Each woman cited numerous incidents in which she or other students of color were treated differently or stereotyped by their racial group.[29] Here too, the women attributed the incidents to personality differences or personal interests. For example, a student explained away the discriminatory behavior she observed:

> There's always that kind of thing in the back of my mind for instance when I start hearing critiques or criticisms that I don't agree with. So I start to think well maybe it's because they're not used to seeing someone who's a woman or a minority at this level. And maybe because we see things differently and then they tend to disagree with us.

The following comment shows how students rationalize the faculty's disinterest in the sociology of race and lower their expectations about mentorship: "Some of their [faculty] problems are race based and some of their problems are that they are primarily interested in their own research and don't offer much to anyone." And then some students continue to recognize and name acts of discrimination and racism in the program but learn to blame themselves: "If you took issue with everything that happened you would be filing a grievance every single day. And so I thought well who cares, it's just that I was really taking it personally." The statement reveals that the student has not only taken responsibility for her pain but has also learned to lower her expectations about learning and eventually teaching in a racist-free environment. This type of rationalization was summarized by another student: "I haven't expected very much and I haven't gotten very much. And I have just taken it as that's the way it is."

Cooling out also involves socializing students to be silent about issues of equity, racism, and sexism within the department, the university, and the discipline. Students who speak out against policies and practices are silenced and ostracized in the department. One extreme case involved a student who recalled her advisor getting very upset about her participation on a panel on women of color at a sociology meeting. Her advisor resented the student's comments about the department and felt directly attacked. She refused to work with the student for almost a year, which resulted in a delay in the progress of the student's dissertation. More common incidents involved white graduate students and faculty avoiding women of color graduate students after they had spoken out against racism at a department meeting or during a panel discussion (Margolis and Romero).

Women of color discovered that the socialization process into the profession involved thinking and writing against their own personal experiences, denying their sociological analysis of race, class, and gender dynamics in their education, and replacing a sociological perspective with an individualistic interpretation. Several sociologists have noted the absence of a sociological perspective in the discussion about our departments and the profession. Crothers wrote,

> Although the lives of many professional sociologists are embedded in academic departments,and despite the universal exposure of sociologists to at least the experience of being a graduate student in an academic department, there seems to be a singular and amazing lack of attention to the sociological analysis of academic sociology departments. (333)

Eric Plutzer goes so far as to argue that graduate programs operate on a belief in predestination and simply ignore their own writings in sociology of education in the everyday operations of Ph.D. departments.

However, in addition to the lack of a sociological perspective, the accounts of women of color also point to the violence toward people of color when they are socialized to deny their own experience. Patricia J. Williams's critique of the law's "preference for the impersonal above the personal, the 'objective' above the 'subjective'" also applies to sociology. Ignoring the existence of scholars of color or research published in ethnic studies and assigning only readings by conservative white sociologists "requires students either to indulge the imaginative flowering of their most insidious rationalizations for racial hatred; or it requires them to suppress any sense of social conscience." Emphasis on the impersonal, objectivity, and the conservatism of mainstream sociology goes a long way in explaining the race relations women of color describe in Ph.D. departments in sociology. As Williams explains,

> The result will be students who are cultured to hate; yet who still think of themselves as very very good people; who will be deeply offended, and personally hurt, if anyone tries to tell them otherwise. I think this sort of teaching, rampant throughout the educational system, is why racism and sexism remain so routine, so habitually dismissed, as to be largely invisible. (87)

The socialization process of becoming an American sociologist is aimed at "cooling out" candidates committed to thinking, teaching, writing, or creating social justice. The competitive nature of the learning environment is intensified by the extreme isolation women of color experience as the "lone" voice, rarely having their norms and values validated through interaction with faculty or other graduate students. Students are encouraged to accept responsibility for their exclusion and pressured to accept the dominant paradigms and elite hierarchy of the discipline as legitimate and right. However, the socialization provided by the graduate program is only one part of the women's experience in learning to be sociologists. The other part of their experience involves resistance and strategies to obtain the education to fulfill their own personal goals of making a difference.

Learning to Be a Sociologist Committed to Social Justice

Traditional requirements of theory and method have generally not been revised to incorporate the publications and research on gender and race. Required theory courses rarely if ever include feminist theory and critical race theory. The "founding parents" of American sociology are still identified as "white fathers"; Black sociologists, such as W. E. B. Du Bois, and founding mothers, like Jane Addams, are ignored. Gender and race also remain outside the discussion of methods even though feminists and scholars of color have written extensively on methodology. Graduate students are expected to be familiar with the classic community study of Middletown, the experimental method of Stanley Milgram, or William Foote Whyte's Street Corner Society, but few are introduced to the classic study of the Philadelphia Negro by Du Bois or the survey Lucy Salmon conducted on domestic servants at the turn of the century. Consequently, women of color graduate students are faced with the dilemma of establishing their competency in traditional theory and methods and struggling to prepare themselves to teach an inclusive curriculum and conduct research that places gender and race at the center of the discipline. In order to obtain such an education, they must engage in a double day.

Recognizing the limitations of the education offered in their Ph.D. programs in sociology, women of color sought classes in women's studies, ethnic studies, and international studies in order to develop expertise in the area of race and gender. Students were more likely to have access to faculty of color through these interdisciplinary programs. Obtaining their training in these outside programs allowed students to learn an interdisciplinary approach to race and gender. These students were more likely than other graduate students in sociology to establish social networks outside the department. This exposure assisted the women in understanding the structural constraints established in their own programs and helped them move away from individualistic interpretations of their personal experiences. Involvement with other graduate students interested in learning about race and gender also provided the students in sociology with a larger support group to lobby for advanced courses. Working with other graduate students, particularly other women of color, frequently created new opportunities, such as study groups, information about grants and fellowships, teaching and research assistantships, and networking.[30] Breaking the isolation of the "lone" woman of color graduate student is extremely important in affirming values and norms of social justice and not internalizing elite values.[31]

Several women applied their commitment to learning about race and gender to direct action in the department. They participated in committees to recruit more students of color and struggled to bring scholars of color on campus as tenure-track faculty, visiting faculty, and guest speakers. Most of the women viewed these various activities as survival strategies. As one student stated, "Push for a better offer. Do not just accept a department's offer but try to get what you need to survive in graduate school." The experience they gained through their political activity as graduate students will no doubt be beneficial to them as they begin teaching full-time.

Another important step in their development toward thinking about social injustice was the employment of a sociological analysis to their own experiences and thus moving beyond the personal and individualistic type of interpretations. For example, one student recalled questioning why the white heterosexual male graduate student was treated so much better than students of color and women students. Her account captures the development beyond a blaming the victim approach and toward the development of sociological explanations.

> I'd go home and think, you know, is it just me? Is it just that I'm really competitive? Is it just that maybe I don't have anything to say? And it wasn't until my third year when I was doing a writing seminar where we would evaluate one another's work and actually looked at this person's work and realized, no, I wasn't all wrong. You know, a lot of what

he was saying was really fluff and it wasn't rigorous. But the fact that he'd been given the floor over and over and over again had [validated him]. . . . It really pissed me off because there was this incredible irony of being in sociology and having professors and graduate students there ignore the social dynamics of the classroom and how they were affecting us. And I felt frustrated because people who I thought should have been up in arms about it just sort of, you know, blamed themselves or talked about, you know, their own fears about being in graduate school and they didn't look at the sociological implications of what was going on in the department.

By analyzing their own experiences from a sociological perspective, women of color graduate students learn to think about issues of race and gender.[32] However, C. Wright Mills's call for the development of a sociological imagination that intersects biography and history is not reflected in the formal training. There is strong evidence that graduate school is actually structured to do exactly the opposite for most students (Crothers; Mayrl and Mauksch; Kleinman; Plutzer). Consequently, the conclusion drawn by one student points to the major problem:

I don't think faculty think about the differences in our experiences and what that means in terms of our academics—what makes a viable graduate experience for us. . . . I don't think a lot of thought has been given to how to make it [the program] a more open community. How are we going to make this work for everybody? And on some level of course there's no interest in making it work for everybody because we don't want everybody.

Even in the face of such powerful negative messages, women of color graduate students demand to be heard and struggle to obtain an education geared toward their commitment to social justice. By making the struggle for racial justice central to learning to become a sociologist, women of color are developing an informal structure to graduate education. But the costs are heavy. Creating an informal structure calls for a double day of graduate work in order to accommodate the extra political work to transform the curriculum, hire faculty of color, increase the enrollment of students of color, and lobby for courses on race and other resources required to cover the current deficiencies of graduate education.

NOTES

This essay was originally presented at the Center for Advanced Feminist Studies (CAFS) Rockefeller Conference, "Thinking, Writing, Teaching and Creating Social Justice," April 22-24, 1994. I wish to thank Eric Margolis for his comments and suggestions. I am also grateful to the CAFS editorial collective for their helpful review.

1. In her article on opposition and Chicana/o education, Laura Elisa Perez recounts receiving similar "advice" from the department chair at the University of Chicago when interviewed for graduate school.

2. The Committee on the Status of Women of the American Sociological Association (ASA) had written the following reports: "The Treatment of Gender in Research," "Guidelines for Incorporating Women Faculty into Sociology during the Eighties," "Equity Issues for Women Faculty in Sociology Departments," and "Recommendations on the Recruitment and Retention of Women Sociologists." The Pacific Sociological Association (PSA) also published several reports on the status of women (Nigg and Axelrod; Kulis and Miller; Araji and Ihinger-Tallman).

3. For a more detailed description of the sample, see Romero and Storrs.

4. The sample was primarily shaped by the respondents' willingness to be interviewed. However, we also made selections to include women from various regions, ethnic groups, private and public institutions, and stages of graduate school. Since there are so few women of color graduate students in sociology, in order to assure anonymity, we do not provide a further breakdown of sample characteristics. All names and places have been changed or deleted.

5. Student complaints that Ph.D. programs are traditional and have not kept up with changes in the discipline are supported by an ASA survey of current graduate program directors. Mayrl and Mauksch criticize departments for responding to the state of graduate training with "little indication that anything might be wrong . . . no eagerness . . . to raise questions about the nature of graduate education . . . the operating assumption appears to be that we are moving along with the best (perhaps the only) road to the development of scholars" (17).

6. For a discussion of such efforts in sociology, see Anderson; Reinharz; Stacey and Thorne.

7. For instance, course titles included "Problems in Emerging Countries," "World Historical Study of Stratification," "Poverty, Women and Third World Development," "Latin American Society," "Selected Topics in Sociology of East Asia," "Japanese Society," "Sociology of Latin American Legal Systems," "Development and Underdevelopment," "Social Thought in Latin America,"

"Peasants," "Seminar on Problems of Modernization in Latin America," and "Cuban Revolution" (Romero and Margolis).

8. In their report of the 1986 ASA survey of graduate programs, Mayrl and Mauksch stated, "The most remarkable finding of the American Sociological Association's first survey of graduate departments in sociology was the striking similarity among programs in terms of course requirements, the number of credits, thesis requirements, and other formal procedures that lead to the M.A. and Ph.D." (11).

9. Alfredo Mirande addressed a similar experience:

My interest in sociology was first sparked by a sociology class which I took as a junior in high school, although I was to learn, subsequently, that, like many others, I had entered sociology for all of the "wrong" reasons. My initial conception of the discipline was that it entailed the study of society with the aim of alleviating societal ills, social inequality, and racism. In graduate school, however, I learned that what I thought was sociology was social work and/or political activism, not sociology. Sociology, according to my mentors, was the detached scientific study of society; objective, value neutral, and universal. (356)

10. For instance, the work by Pauline Bart, Jessie Bernard, Alice Rossi and Ann Calderwood, Pamela Roby, Athena Theodore, Harriet F. Adams, and Sandra Acker.

11. For instance, Blackwell and Janowitz; Conyers; Epps; Wilkerson, "Black Sociologists"; and Barnes.

12. Numerous sociologists have pointed out the absence of a sociological analysis in our interpreting our own profession and work environment. See Goulder; Plutzer; Crothers; Van Sickle; and Cuadraz and Pierce.

13. For instance, see Crothers; Egan; Plutzer.

14. For instance, see Finkelstein; and Ladd and Lipset.

15. In a more recent article, Eric Plutzer identified how sociology faculty determine which students are "most likely to succeed" and who are potential failures. His findings suggest that sociologists administer graduate programs in an irrational fashion that counters the established sociological knowledge, and act on a belief in predestination; that is, "some graduate students are members of the elect and predestined for success" (302).

16. Crothers notes that the structure of graduate school acknowledges only academically gained and credentialed knowledge and treats it as superior to practical social knowledge.

17. In his article "I Never Had a Mentor: Reflections of a Chicano Sociologist," Alfredo Mirande states, "I also had to develop verbal aggressiveness, since this was clearly a valued trait in graduate students."

18. Meisenhelder points out that this distribution occurs with a hierarchical structure that ranks faculty in subdivisions (e.g., full, associate, assistant, tenure-track, lecturer). Crothers also calls attention to the fact that the range of inequalities occurs "within a group of people ostensibly carrying out the same sort of activities" (335).

19. For a discussion of barriers that women and minorities face in establishing mentorship relationships, see Fox; Katz; Mirande; Barnes; Redmond; Pruitt and Isaac; Blackwell.

20. Recently two sociological journals have devoted special issues to graduate education, *American Sociologist* (1988) and *Teaching Sociology* (1991).

21. Rendon comments on the devaluation of past experience and knowledge in education.

22. See Rosen and Bates for comment on the contradiction of attempting to train students to be independent in an authoritarian social structure.

23. In Kulis and Miller's national sample of sociology departments, minority women represented only 1.9 percent of faculty members and women of color graduate students represented approximately 10 percent of the total graduate student population.

24. The absence of people of color in the curriculum is not just a problem in sociology. June Jordan speaks for many students of color when she writes about her undergraduate experience at Barnard:

> no one ever presented me with a single Black author, poet, historian, personage, or idea, for that matter. . . . Nothing that I learned, here, lessened my feeling of pain, and confusion and bitterness as related to my origins: my street, my family, my friends. Nothing showed me how I might try to alter the political and economic realities underlying our Black condition in white America. (100)

25. Students of color selected graduate programs on the basis of their expressed interest in diversity, multiculturalism, and specialty in race. However, upon arrival to the program, they discovered otherwise. In an early article, I discuss the ways that departments packaged and sold themselves to recruit women of color to their graduate program (Romero and Storrs).

26. Since Ph.D. programs in ethnic studies and women's studies did not exist in their institutions, the women remained enrolled in sociology programs. They also remained committed to becoming sociologists and transforming the discipline.

27. My use of the concept "cooling out" is different from previous applications. Burton R. Clark's use of the concept refers to a specific function in higher education, in which he claims there is a major problem created in a democratic society involving the "inconsistency between encouragement to

achieve and the realities of limited opportunity." However, embedded in his work is the assumption that the problem is really the nontraditional (e.g., working-class) student who is served by open admissions policy. These students gain access to higher education with goals that they cannot achieve and therefore "cooling out" is an important function of counseling to "sidetrack unpromising students rather than have them fail" and to provide an alternative. I do not begin with the assumption that women of color graduate students are unpromising or in any way unable to do graduate work in sociology. My use of the concept has more in common with T. R. Young's discussion of graduate school. Young also used the concept of "cooling out" to describe the process used in graduate programs in sociology to eliminate or discourage the politically committed and active student. Neither of us starts with the assumption that politically committed students are any less qualified than any other graduate students. Rather than making unsubstantiated assumptions about nontraditional students, Young and I focus our analyses on the formal and informal structure to identify the "cooling-out" process and to understand the way it functions to discourage students from pursuing their original plans. My use of the concept "cooling out" is more like the structuring of choice that Hearn and Olzak analyze in their work on the reproduction of sexual inequality in college departments.

28. Recognizing these structural limitations fits well into the characteristics that Roth identified with faculty's conception of success in graduate school. These women of color graduate students appear to have been "reading" the situation correctly from the faculty's perspective.

29. The problems identified by the women are consistent with the findings of other research on mentoring and students of color. See, for example, Trujillo; Allen; Redmond.

30. Many of these strategies are tactics that T. R. Young recommended to graduate students in resisting the "cooling-off and cooling-out" routine.

31. This is quite similar to characteristics Kleinman identified in her discussion of peer culture.

32. For instance, Mirande traces his biography and contribution to the development of a Chicano sociology:

> Chicano sociology has given focus and direction to my career and enabled me to bridge the gap between my public and private self. I have accomplished what C. Wright Mills advocated so strongly in *The Sociological Imagination*, developing a scholarship that effectively links personal troubles and public issues. Ironically, by advocating a sociology that is proactive, value committed, and seeks to merge truth and feeling, I have, in a sense, come full circle. These were the reasons why I had first entered the discipline. (361)

WORKS CITED

Acker, Sandra, "Women, the Other Academics." *Women Studies International Forum* 6 (1983): 191–201.

Adams, Harriet F. "Work in the Interstices: Women in Academe." *Women's Studies International Forum* 6 (1983): 135–41.

Allen, W. R. *Study of Black Undergraduate Students Attending Predominantly White, State-Supported Universities: Preliminary Report.* Ann Arbor: University of Michigan Center for AfroAmerican and African Studies, 1981.

American Sociological Association. "Equity Issues for Women Faculty in Sociology Departments." Washington, DC: American Sociological Association, 1985.

———. "Guidelines for Incorporating Women Faculty into Sociology during the Eighties." Washington, DC: American Sociological Association, 1984.

———. "Recommendations on the Recruitment and Retention of Women Sociologists." Washington, DC: American Sociological Association, 1986.

———. "The Treatment of Gender in Research." Washington, DC: American Sociological Association, 1985.

Anderson, Margaret L. "Moving Our Minds: Studying Women of Color and Reconstructing Sociology." *Teaching Sociology* 16 (1988): 123–32.

Araji, Sharon K., and Marilyn Ihinger-Tallman. "The Status of Women in the Pacific Sociological Association: Report from the Status on Women Committee." Presented at the Pacific Sociological Workshop, Las Vegas, Nevada, 1988.

Barnes, Denise R. "Transitions and Stresses for Black Female Scholars." In *Career Guide for Women Scholars,* ed. Suzanna Rose, 66–77. New York: Springer, 1986.

Bart, Pauline, and Diana Scully. "A Funny Thing Happened on the Way to the Orifice." *American Journal of Sociology* 78.4 (1973): 1045–50.

Becker, Howard S. *Art Worlds.* Berkeley: University of California Press, 1982.

Bernard, Jessie. *Academic Women.* University Park: Pennsylvania State University Press, 1964.

Blackwell, James E. *Networking and Mentoring: A Study of Cross-Generational Experiences of Blacks in Graduate and Professional Schools.* Atlanta: Southern Education Foundation, 1983.

Blackwell, James E., and Morris Janowitz, eds. *Black Sociologists: Historical and Contemporary Perspectives.* Chicago: University of Chicago Press, 1974.

Clark, Burton R. "The 'Cooling-Out' Function in Higher Education." In *Sociology of Education.* Itasca, IL: Peacock Publishers, 1968.

Conyers, James E. "Negro Doctorates in Sociology in America: A Social Portrait." *Phylon* (1968): 209–23.

Crothers, Charles. "The Internal Structure of Sociology Departments: The

Role of Graduate Students and Other Groups," *Teaching Sociology* 19 (1991): 333–43.

Cuadraz, Gloria H., and Jennifer L. Pierce. "From Scholarship Girls to Scholarship Women: Surviving the Contradictions of Class and Race in Academe." *Explorations in Ethnic Studies* 10.1 (1994): 77–101.

Egan, Janet Malenchek. "Graduate School and the Self: A Theoretical View of Some Negative Effects of Professional Socialization." *Teaching Sociology* 17 (1989): 200–208.

Eitzen, D. Stanley. "The Introduction of Graduate Students to the Profession of Sociology." *Teaching Sociology* 16 (1989): 279–83.

Epps, Edgar G. "A Profile of Black Sociologists." In *Black Sociologists: Historical and Contemporary Perspectives,* ed. J. E. Blackwell and M. Janowitz, 231–52. Chicago: University of Chicago Press, 1974.

Finkelstein, Martin J. *The American Academic Professorate.* Columbus: Ohio State University Press, 1984.

Fox, Mary F. "Women and Higher Education: Sex Differentials in the Status of Students and Scholars." In *Women: A Feminist Perspective,* ed. Jo Freeman, 238–55. Palo Alto, CA: Mayfield, 1984.

Goulder, Alvin. *The Coming Crisis in Western Sociology.* New York: Avon, 1970.

Gurin, Patricia, and Edgar G. Epps. *Black Consciousness, Identity, and Achievement: A Study of Students in Historically Black Colleges.* New York: Wiley, 1975.

Hearn, James C., and Susan Olzak. "The Role of College Major Departments in the Reproduction of Sexual Inequality." *Sociology of Education* 54 (1981): 195–205.

Hood, Jane. "The Lone Scholar Myth." In *Scholarly Writing and Publishing: Issues, Problems and Solutions,* ed. Mary Frank Fox. Boulder: Westview Press, 1985.

Jones-Johnson, Gloria. "The Victim-Bind Dilemma of Black Female Sociologists in Academe." *American Sociologist* 19.4 (1988): 312–22.

Jordan, June. "Note of a Barnard Dropout." In *Civil Wars,* 96–102. Boston: Beacon Press, 1981.

Katz, Joseph. "White Faculty Struggling with the Effects of Racism." In *Teaching Minority Students: New Directions for Teaching and Learning,* ed. J. H. Cones, J. F. Noonan, and D. Janna, 33–42. San Francisco: Jossey-Bass, 1983.

Kleinman, Sherryl. "Collective Matters as Individual Concerns, Peer Culture among Graduate Students." *Urban Life* 12.2 (1983): 203–25.

Kulis, Stephen, and Karen A. Miller. "Are Minority Women Sociologists in Double Jeopardy?" *American Sociologist* 29 (Winter 1988): 323–39.

Ladd, E. C., and S. M. Lipset. *The Divided Academy.* New York: McGraw-Hill, 1975.

Margolis, Eric, and Mary Romero. "'The Department Is Very Male, Very White, Very Old, and Very Conservative': The Functioning of the Hidden

Curriculum in Graduate Sociology Departments." *Harvard Educational Review* 68.1 (1998): 1–21.

Mayrl, William W., and Hans O. Mauksch. "The ASA Survey of Graduate Programs: Some Problems with Unproblematic Responses." *American Sociologist* 18.1 (1987): 11–18.

Meisenhelder, Tom. "The Class Position of College and University Faculty." *Social Science Journal* 23.4 (1986): 375–89.

Mirande, Alfredo. "I Never Had a Mentor: Reflections of a Chicano Sociologist." *American Sociologist* 19.4 (1988): 335–62.

Nigg, Joanne M. and Morris Axelrod. "Women and Minorities in the PSA Region: Results of the 1979 Survey." *Pacific Sociological Review* 24.1 (1981): 107–28.

Pavalko, Ronald M., and John Holley. "Determinants of a Professional Self-Concept among Graduate Students." *Social Science Quarterly* 55.2 (1974): 462–77.

Perez, Laura Elisa. "Opposition and the Education of Chicana/os," *Race Identity and Representation in Education,* ed. Cameron McCarthy and Warren Crichlow. New York: Routledge, 1993.

Plutzer, Eric. "The Protestant Ethic and the Spirit of Academia: An Essay on Graduate Education." *Teaching Sociology* 19 (1991): 302–307.

Pruitt, Anne S., and Paul D. Isaac. "Discrimination in Recruitment, Admission, and Retention of Minority Graduate Students." *Journal of Negro Education* 54.4 (1985): 526–36.

Redmond, Sonjia Parker. "Mentoring and Cultural Diversity in Academic Settings." *American Behavioral Scientist* 34.2 (1990): 188–200.

Reinharz, Shulamit. "Teaching the History of Women in Sociology: Or Dorothy Swaine Thomas, Wasn't She the Woman Married to William I.?" *American Sociologist* 20.1 (1989): 87–94.

Rendon, Laura. "From the Barrio to the Academy: Revelations of a Mexican American 'Scholarship Girl.'" *New Directions for Community Colleges* 80 (1992): 55–64.

Roby, Pamela. "Women and the ASA: Degendering Organizational Structures and Processes, 1964–1975." *American Sociologist* 23 (1988): 18–48.

Romero, Mary, and Eric Margolis. "Integrating the Department: Observations on Race and Gender Relations in Sociology Graduate Programs." *Race and Society* (in press).

Romero, Mary, and Debbie Storrs. "'Is That Sociology?' The Accounts of Women of Color Graduate Students." In *Women's Leadership in Education: An Agenda for a New Century,* ed. Diane M. Dunlap and Patricia Schmuck, 72–86. Albany: State University of New York Press, 1994.

Rosen, Bernard C., and Alan P. Bates. "The Structure of Socialization in Graduate School." *Sociological Inquiry* 37 (1967): 71–84.

Rossi, Alice K., and Ann Calderwood. *Academic Women on the Move*. New York: Russell Sage Foundation Press, 1973.

Roth, Julius A. "A Faculty Conception of Success in Graduate Study." *Journal of Higher Education* 26.7 (1955): 350–56, 398.

Sherlock, Basil J., and Richard T. Morris. "The Evolution of the Professional: A Paradigm." *Sociological Inquiry* 37 (1967): 27–46.

Stacey, Judith, and Barrie Thorne. "The Missing Feminist Revolution in Sociology." *Social Problems* 32 (1985): 301–16.

Stanfield, John. "Racial Diversity in Becoming a Sociologist." *American Sociologist* 19.3 (1988): 291–300.

Theodore, Athena. *The Professional Woman*. Cambridge, MA: Schenkman, 1971.

Trujillo, C. M. "A Comparative Examination of Classroom Interactions between Professors and Minority and Non-Minority Students." *American Educational Research Journal* 23 (1986): 629–42.

Van Sickle, Larry. "Review Essay: Education and the Radical Critique." *Mid-American Review of Sociology* 2 (1977): 89–101.

Weiss, Carin S. "The Development of Professional Role Commitment among Graduate Students." *Human Relations* 34 (1981): 13–31.

Wilkerson, Doris. "Black Sociologists: Historical and Contemporary Perspectives." *American Journal of Sociology* 81 (1975): 461–62.

———. "A Report during the UN Decade of Women." In *Slipping through the Cracks: The Status of Black Women*, ed. Margaret Sims and Julianne Malveaux, 83–96. New Brunswick, NJ: Transaction Books, 1986.

Williams, Patricia J. *The Alchemy of Race and Rights: Diary of a Law Professor*. Cambridge: Harvard University Press, 1991.

Young, T. R. "Transforming Sociology: The Graduate Student." *American Sociologist* 9 (1974): 135–39.

Chapter 12

Anger, Resentment, and the Place of Mind in Academia

Diana L. Vélez

When we speak of social justice we tend to envision changing "out there" into a better place that we and others can inhabit, but I have learned that effective change must begin in one's own mind and move outward. Both happiness and suffering are mental states, and by changing one's own mind one can transform one's environment and become an agent for positive change in the world. People whose minds are clear and free of obsessions with the self and its desires can operate in society and improve it. One way to say this is that one must *be* peace to bring it about in the world.

I believe that in these difficult times it is essential that progressive faculty members have mental clarity and a willingness to act responsibly, wisely, and ethically in the social space that we inhabit, academia. Those actions, I believe, can best be taken if our ethos is one of service and responsibility. Angry people do not bring about positive change because the mind of anger is clouded. Anger and resentment are impediments that must be overcome if we are to be effective.

"On what do you base an ethics?" one of my students asked me several years ago. I am grateful to her for that question, for in it lies the most important issue facing us as women, as scholars, and as human beings. What is our ethical position in academia? We used to think that our various feminisms held the answer. Do we still think so? What first drew us to feminism? Was it not the vision of a just society? Isn't this still what we want? How can we bring it about? As teachers and scholars we manifest our values in our interaction with others. What values do we embody? Have we been transforming academia as we thought we would? Has our presence made a difference?

Several years ago I used a sabbatical leave to study and practice at a Tibetan Buddhist retreat center in the Santa Cruz hills of northern California and to learn how to meditate at a Tibetan Buddhist monastery in Kathmandhu, Nepal. The decision to do these things came about after I noticed a pattern in my life that frightened me. Every spring, around March or April, sometimes earlier, I would develop difficulty breathing. Each year the ailment became more serious: from walking pneumonia to bronchitis, to a mystery ailment that behaved very much like pneumonia. The spring before my sabbatical leave I had such a bad case of this mystery ailment that there were moments when I felt I could not breathe. At night there were sandbags on my chest. There was one specific moment I remember that I can only compare to the "clicks" of feminist recognition during the earliest consciousness-raising era. I had climbed the stairs to use the bathroom and when I reached the landing my heart was pounding from the effort. I was frightened. I thought, "This time it's going to kill me." I became keenly aware of my own mortality.

The pulmonary specialist at our state-of-the-art university teaching hospital was stumped. My illness was not responding to drugs. The Western doctors I saw didn't seem to know what was wrong with me. No one could help me.

When I confided to a female colleague that I was having trouble breathing, she said, "It's this place. It doesn't let you breathe." I wondered whether her metaphor was accurate. Was I somatizing the disorder and dysfunction around me? Perhaps what had been making me ill all these years *was* my workplace. I remembered then that during the five years before I was tenured, I had suffered from chronic sore throats. I had wanted to speak out, I had wanted to scream.

Now the malady was an inability to take in air. I took a good look around me. What I saw was a noxious environment in which infighting, posturing, grandiosity, and self-enhancement seemed to be the norm, especially—but by no means exclusively—among my male colleagues. What a contentious place! Daily I witnessed aggression, meanness of spirit, and a lack of generosity that I found intolerable. What could possibly be the cause of this inhumane behavior?

What I was witnessing daily began to make sense to me when I read Alice Miller's description of the narcissistic disorder; it corresponded closely to a personality type I saw all around me: the "gifted child" who struggles desperately for the parental gaze—of the institution—the scholar who is "making a name for him/herself" not necessarily out of genuine intellectual curiosity or even a will to knowledge, but because of a longing for acknowledgment.[1]

Alice Miller's "gifted child" does well in everything he or she undertakes: admired and envied, successful,

> but all to no avail. Behind all this lurks depression, the feeling of emptiness and self-alienation and a sense that their life has no meaning. These dark feelings will come to the fore as soon as the drug of grandiosity fails, as soon as they are not "on top," not definitely the "superstar," or whenever they suddenly get the feeling they failed to live up to some ideal image and measure they feel they must adhere to. Then they are plagued by anxiety or deep feelings of guilt and shame. What are the reasons for such narcissistic disturbances in these gifted people? (6)

While the gifted child syndrome doesn't explain all of the disorder found in academia, it goes some way toward explaining some of the personality disorders commonly found there and the resulting behaviors that are so damaging to the people whom we are supposed to be serving—the students. Everyone at an institution doesn't have to suffer from this malady in order for the environment to suffer, to become poisoned with anger and resentment. When I read these passages of Miller, I began to understand some of the deeply troubled people I saw daily in academia and how they were charging the environment with their illness. I asked myself, how many of my colleagues missed getting what they had needed as children and were now resentful adults? How does this affect interpersonal relations in academia? Was I myself one of those people described by Miller?

While not all of my colleagues were behaving in the grandiose, self-enhancing way described by Miller—there are indeed many generous, hardworking, altruistic people among them—I did notice a lot of the kind of behavior that suggests a personality disorder. That was bad enough, but more disturbing was the system of rewards used by the institution. It seemed to me then that service and good teaching, the ongoing hard work of our profession, were not deemed as important as one's number of publications. It is hard to avoid internalizing those values. The result is a space of competition, not cooperation.

Recently a colleague from another university told me that one of his colleagues had committed suicide, leaving a note saying that his academic life was drawing to a close due to his impending retirement, so he saw no reason to go on living. If this person's life had been motivated by a healthy love of knowledge or by a keen desire to be of service to others, why would retirement be anything but an opportunity? Why suicide? There are many reasons someone commits suicide, but I thought of two: the strict identification of the self with the label "professor" and the depression underlying the grandiosity so poignantly depicted by Alice Miller.

Miller is describing a personality disorder, so it cannot be used as a model for all that is wrong with academia. Moreover, mere recognition of the problem doesn't solve it. In my own case, for example, my awareness that academia often rewards narcissism did nothing to improve my own health. It just added to my resentment. For a radically different approach—and perhaps a cure for my ailment—I knew I would have to seek elsewhere.

When my husband was offered a job helping to build retreat cabins at Vajrapani Institute—a Tibetan Buddhist retreat center thirty minutes into the woods from Boulder Creek, California—I jumped at the chance to get away. I mailed several boxes of books and bought myself a good fountain pen. I knew there was a desktop publishing business in town where I could use computers whenever I needed them. There was no electricity in the sixteen-by-twelve-foot wooden cabin that was to be our home for nine months. Although I didn't know it at the time, I was going to spend my academic year studying Buddhism, an approach I knew to be a radical challenge to my previous way of being in the world. I moved away from what I then saw as the source of my illness—academia—in order to figure out my relationship to my workplace. If I was going to thrive in academia—or even survive, given the state of my health at the time—something was going to have to change. Intuitively, I knew that I would have to unlearn deeply ingrained patterns of thought and behavior and substitute others if I was to recover. I was going to have to give up wanting that institutional gaze.

Looking back, I realize that the change I began to undergo was not external, but a change in focus: looking inward, beginning to examine my own mind, starting to see how involvement in my own negative thoughts was responsible for my illness. That year away from academia allowed me to begin to look closely at the profound truth that satisfaction and suffering were not and are not to be found in anything external, that they are the product of one's own mind. This challenged some of my most deeply held beliefs about the world.

Desperate for some way to heal my suffering body and unwilling to continue with Western medicine, I went to see a Brazilian healer who had studied traditional Tibetan medicine. He took my pulse and diagnosed my malady as "resentment" and "stress."

Resentment? When I looked for resentment in my mind, the conversation went something like this: "How is it that I, who had shown so much promise, etc. etc., was now *here* among these people who had thus and such drawbacks, etc. etc., and how was it that despite my hard work I still did not find satisfaction in my work, etc. etc.?" This line of thinking always brought me to the same conclusion: I had been dealt an unfair hand. I deserved better. This is what I now call the "poor little me" attitude—self-pity and resentment. This train of thought is what my Buddhist teachers call "the self-cherishing mind." It is simply the thought that my own happiness is all-important, that of others is secondary. This mind of resentment is the one that always wants *more* and sees others as those who should provide it. It is childish, really, and leads to an internal narrative that leads nowhere but to unhappiness and dissatisfaction. It also leads to anger.

Needless to say, the recognition of this thought pattern was unpleasant. Who wants to acknowledge her selfishness? But fortunately the books I was reading and the teachings I was receiving from the Tibetan lamas stressed that selfishness is what they call an obscuration of the mind and not an inseparable part of it. In other words, the mind can be freed of selfishness and the resentment it produces. The mind is not one with these negativities.

Then I began to think about stress. One way I define stress is that mental and physical suffering of feeling rushed, thinking there is not enough time for everything. Moving inexorably onto the next task, not savoring the completion of the last one—a driven feeling that is exhausting. This drive catapults me forward, makes it impossible for me to take joy in the present moment. It is a way of not being fully alive. From conversations I have had with friends and colleagues, I know this to be a common problem in academia.

If resentment and stress were the cause of my illness, what were the antidotes, the mental states that would counteract them? According to the lamas, the antidote to resentment or anger is patience, and the antidote to the stress of being scattered is mindfulness.

Mindfulness

The mental habit of constantly projecting ourselves into the future is itself a source of suffering. The Spanish essayist Carmen Martín Gaite goes so far as to define it as a kind of death. She states that if a person who misses the bus spends the ten-minute wait cursing fate, the time will be truly wasted, for the person will have been "outside" him or herself. During that ten minutes, the person can be said to not have been truly alive (Gaite 101–2). And the Theravadin nun Ayya Khema says,

> Those who are young think of the future because they've got more of it. Those who are older think more about the past because for them there is more of that. But in order to experience life, we have to live each moment. Life has not been happening in the past. That's memory. Life is not going to happen in the future. That's planning. The only time we can live is now, this moment, and as absurd as it may seem, we've got to learn that. When we have learned (that) we will have eliminated a great many of our problems. (Khema 9)

Similarly, the Vietnamese monk and political activist Thich Nhat Hanh, in his guidebook to meditation, *The Miracle of Mindfulness,* writes of watching his friend eating a tangerine.

> He popped a section of tangerine in his mouth and, before he had begun chewing it, had another slice ready to pop into his mouth again. He was hardly aware he was eating a tangerine. All I had to say was, "You ought to eat the tangerine section you've already taken." Jim was startled into realizing what he was doing. It was as if he hadn't been eating the tangerine at all. If he had been eating anything, he was "eating" his future plans. (Hanh 5-6)

All three are addressing what Buddhists call mindfulness: being aware of the moment in all its fullness, bringing the mind back to now. I believe this ongoing process of bringing the mind back to now has a direct impact on the quality of our work. Thich Nhat Hanh's primer speaks to me every time I read it because I find that when I'm mentally in two places at once I lose clarity and don't perform either task well. Moreover, the stress involved in trying, if it becomes habitual, often results in illness.

By watching what happens to me throughout the day I have discovered that if I am to be in the moment—to be mindful—I need to concentrate fully on the task at hand, whether it be reading, leading a class discussion, attending a faculty meeting, talking with a student in my office, or any of the other tasks I perform daily in my role as a university professor.

This sounds easy but it is not. More often than not, I find my mind wandering to future events—an upcoming deadline, a faculty meeting that afternoon. When that happens the person or the task before me gets shortchanged because I am, in Thich Nhat Hanh's words, "eating" my deadline or my meeting. Carmen Martin Gaite would say I wasn't fully alive at that moment.

The dualistic thought "I am here but would rather be there," "I'm doing this now, but would prefer to be doing that" stems from a pervasive sense of dissatisfaction. I have found that the stress disappears if I stop breaking up time into "my" time and the time I devote to others. One colleague told me that if it weren't for the demands of teaching, she would get her work done. Work here is defined as one thing: research. The system of rewards of which I spoke earlier is partly to blame for this, but it is also due to an approach to time that breaks it up into mine and not-mine, a dualism that undermines our pleasure in our work.

The Faults of Anger

It is difficult to talk about anger in our culture—and feminist circles are no exception. When it is addressed at all it is seen as an energy boost. And no doubt it *is* that. Anger can provide a "high" that is addictive. For years I blamed my angry response on many rational-sounding "causes" of anger: the racism and class oppression of America, being female in the two gynophobic cultures I straddle—Puerto Rican and North American—the injustices I saw all around me. They all made me angry, resentful. And I saw them as the causes of my anger.

I don't want to underplay these realities, which must be addressed and changed; we must create a humane world. But I have come to the conclusion that anger is a habitual response, a mental habit, and not a very skillful one. I believe that if one's goal is to be an agent for positive change in the world, anger is an impediment, not a tool.

Women, especially women who have learned to suppress their anger, are expressing it openly now. But it is not only women who are expressing their anger. The media inform us almost daily that there are many angry white males in our midst. The number of angry people in the United States seems to be growing. There is a downright celebration of anger in our culture right now. And it is often coupled with violent action.

But is this useful? If we analyze it we have to admit that when we're angry we are out of control. How do we feel when we're angry? Anger clouds the mind; the body becomes tense; we lose sleep; we lose our appetite. Anger actually renders us useless. Moreover, who wants to be around an angry person?

Actually, women often maintain the status quo through anger. By establishing our positions in a complex interplay of egos, we often guarantee that change does not take place. Harriet Lerner, in her book *The Dance of Anger,* has studied the phenomenon by which women often express anger but fail to do anything to bring about true structural change. By calmly doing what she knows is best, a woman can bring about more change than she can by getting angry and guaranteeing that nothing structurally changes.

Before anger comes expectation. It begins with the thought that "I and my needs come first." When one's expectation is thwarted, anger rises. This can build up with other, similar thoughts to the point where one is enraged. This kind of thinking can also be done in groups, as in, for example, the popular academic group sport of narrating the collective pain.

If, instead of engaging in this self-defeating behavior we work on developing patience and cutting down on the expectations we have of others, taking responsibility for our own role in any interaction, we reduce anger. It is a fact of life that we will face rudeness, racism, anger on the part of others, but by trying to free our own minds of anger, we are taking responsibility for our own response. We do not have to respond in kind because it is possible to exercise control over our own minds. This way we can shorten our periods of anger. Eventually we can eliminate that response altogether. We can become more patient. As one lama put it, we can cover the earth with leather or we can clad our own feet in it—which is feasible?

But *shouldn't* we have expectations of others, expectations about how they should treat us? In fact we have no control over the actions of others. The only thing we can ever hope to control is our own mind.

But how do we deal with problematic colleagues, those uncooperative, competitive, annoying ones? There are so many potential objects of anger. Say you're in a faculty meeting and one of your colleagues makes a provocative or rude remark to you. One way is to respond in kind, thereby contributing to creating an unpleasant, contentious environment painful for the whole group and especially demoralizing for junior faculty. Another is to allow the rude remark to remain suspended in the air, for all to hear. Other colleagues are then free to see the rudeness for what it is. Often the negative energy passes away if one doesn't feed it with one's own anger. At other times one must speak forcefully to such a person, because it is not good for them to think such behavior is acceptable. But these interventions are best made not with a mind of anger but with a thought not to allow that person to hurt himself, oneself, or others. The space we occupy as faculty belongs to all of us and no one person should be allowed to spoil it for all. But this person who is "acting out" is just the same as oneself in wanting happiness. They are merely unskillful. If anger enters one's mind, the resulting response loses credibility and one becomes no better than the person with whom one is engaged in an angry exchange.

This is not something I have mastered. That's why it's called practice. It is not easy to bring the mind back to a peaceful state once one lets it get angry. This practice of being peaceful and calm is tested daily in the academic workplace. There are plenty of opportunities to work on developing patience. But we can look upon these difficult times as challenges, opportunities to practice patience, to become better human beings.

The very process of trying to manage anger, to keep it from growing, creates a space in the mind, and one is better able to watch one's response and analyze it. If I can feel the anger beginning to rise within my mind I can sometimes stop it. The reason I try to do this is that I have found that one angry thought feeds another and another until I have been rendered useless, torturing myself with dark thoughts of more anger, more resentment, more useless ruminating. I clearly have a choice: either give in to anger and watch it grow, watch it control my mind little by little, or exercise some control and cut that mind before it has taken hold.

If, instead of thinking, the minute I see Professor X, "Oh, here (s)he comes again. (S)he did this and such in the past and will likely do it again," I think, "Here is someone who is just like me in wanting happiness and never quite achieving it. Here is someone who also has this vague feeling of dissatisfaction. This is someone just like me. Perhaps (s)he has old psychic injuries and is trying to achieve happiness but is not achieving it." At that moment, the mind has some space from which to generate a feeling of compassion for that person, a strong feeling that, like me, they are a suffering human being and should be an object of compassion, not anger. Then the actual image of the person changes in my mind.

Thubten Chodron suggests that a good way to fight anger is to begin to question our own interpretations of the situations that give rise to it:

> The pain [of anger] comes from our thinking: "She is talking to me! How dare she talk to ME like this?" "I" and "me" get bigger the more we think about what happened. We look at the situation from one side—MY side—and think that's how it exists in reality. We believe our biased views are objective. (Chodron 48–49)

She goes on to point out that any situation has more than one perspective and that it would be hard to prove that the views of our self-centered minds are the only correct ones. We tend to see people as solid, immutable entities. But everyone is a combination of their histories, their fears, their desires, their goals. All of us have positive and negative aspects of our personalities and makeup. We are all in a state of flux, not solid, but constantly changing. If the object of our anger were inherently one way, the way we see and label them right now— say "that in-my-face colleague"—everyone without exception would agree that that is who this person is, inherently. But it is never the case that all agree as to what constitutes person x.

In an article entitled "The Uses of Anger: Women Responding to Racism" Audre Lorde states, "Every woman has a well-stocked arsenal of anger potentially useful against those oppressions, personal and institutional, which brought that anger into being. Focused with precision it can become a powerful source of energy serving progress and change" (Lorde 127).

She begins by relating some interactions she has had with white women and the way those interactions gave rise to her own anger. Originally a talk at a National Women's Studies Association conference, the paper articulates resentment toward white (feminist) women's often unexamined expectations that Black women should protect, educate, and nurture them. This expectation is often manifest in white women's demand that Black women express their positions, but not in anger. An example: "I speak out of direct and particular anger at an academic conference, and a white woman says, 'Tell me how you feel but don't say it too harshly or I cannot hear you.' But is it my manner that keeps her from hearing, or the threat of a message that her life may change?" (Lorde 125).

It is condescending, and counterproductive, to tell someone when they are angry, "Can you please say that to me, but politely?" That form of infantilization—all too familiar to women of color in this country—is guaranteed to push buttons.

I read this piece as a poignant statement of the painful injuries of race in North America. Lorde examines barriers to real communication between white and Black women in the United States, asking how we as women of color can build alliances with white women who have not seriously examined their own racism. White women need to recognize their own insensitivity, their own ingrained racism, as a structural barrier that must be addressed and overcome if alliances are to be made. The article is painful to read because it shows how white women who want to be the allies of Black women in their struggle for justice are prevented from being so by their unexamined racism. It is a wake-up call to white women to stop hiding, to own up to their skin and class privileges in a spirit of solidarity. But the article is anything but a coherent defense of anger as the title implies.

How does Audre Lorde actually address the issue of anger's uses? She states, "Anger is loaded with information and energy" (127). But when she elaborates, she gives an example that actually *undermines* her argument that anger is useful. She describes an interaction with a member of a group with whom she wants to communicate—other women of color—and demonstrates how anger is an *impediment* to communication:

> The woman of Color who is not Black and who charges me with rendering her invisible by assuming that her struggles with racism are identical with my own has something to tell me that I had better learn from, lest we both waste ourselves fighting the truths between us. If I participate, knowingly or otherwise, in my sister's oppression and she calls me on it, to answer her anger with my own only blankets the substance of our exchange with reaction. (127–28)

So Lorde is actually saying it is necessary to subdue one's anger if one is to listen to the other party, to hear them, to get valuable information. This listening does not happen if the listening party is herself angry. She is actually arguing that anger is just a reaction that "blankets" the substance of the exchange.

Audre Lorde urges her audience not to become blinded to "the size and complexities of the forces mounting against us and all that is most human within our environment" (128). These words, spoken in 1981, could not be more appropriate now. Congressional Republicans gleefully dismantle affirmative action and the welfare state and undo civil society's responsibility to the disenfranchised. Welfare mothers are made scapegoats of the Right. If ever there was a time to build alliances and try to work with like-minded people for a just society, it is now.

So what role does anger have to play here? Shall we see it as an energy-packed information giver or as an impediment to clarity, to communication? I see it as the latter. I agree with Thubten Chodron's observation:

> We often get angry when something we consider undesirable happens. But what use is this anger? If we can change the situation, then let's go ahead and do it. There's no need to be angry. It's very useful to think like this when confronted with social problems and injustice. They can be changed, so rather than be angry, it's wiser to work calmly to improve the society. (Chodron 49–50)

As long as we inhabit academia, we will meet all the social ills of the larger society and more: discrimination, sexism, racism, grandiose posturing, unethical behavior, and injustices of all kinds. Only if we are prepared to walk through that ground with a prepared, calm, and patient mind can we survive the minefields we will find there and become agents for change. Only if we can speak forcefully and clearly with a mind unclouded by anger can we bring about the changes we all want.

But being patient does not mean we become doormats. When faced with unethical behavior we should name it. When colleagues act irresponsibly we should speak openly about it. It would be a mistake to confuse a patient, reasoned approach with passivity. Sometimes forceful speech and action *are* called for, but that is not the same thing as speaking with anger and aggression. The internal state, the mind, is very different in each case. It is a matter of using the most skillful action, the one that will meet with success in that particular situation. Sometimes that will mean speaking forcefully to a colleague who is "trashing" another, other times it will mean holding one's tongue so as to dissipate the charged atmosphere of conflict. We must develop skill and wisdom in the means we use in our work environment. Otherwise our work can become a source of suffering for ourselves and others.

Even if we think only in terms of short-term goals such as staying healthy, it is desirable to generate equanimity. But even if we do decide that we want to eliminate anger in our minds it is not easy; we must train our minds when we are in a calm and peaceful state, not when we are angry. The antidote to anger is patience and this must be cultivated when we are in a calm mental state. When we are angry, it's already too late.

While we in the West have developed materially to a point that is truly impressive, we have not done so mentally or spiritually. In fact, the problem is so severe that parents often do not know how to teach their children what is right and what is wrong. The result is a violence-ridden, alienated, consumerist society. People's inner lives are often so empty that they go shopping for entertainment.

Does our society suffer from a lack of ethical discipline? It comes back to my student's question: on what do you base an ethics? The university—as a subset of the larger culture—suffers from some of the same problems. On what can we base an ethics as academics? I would argue that if, when faced with a decision, the mind that values selfless service can be substituted for the mind that seeks rewards, we will have a very different relationship to our work. This is our challenge as educators. It is all too easy to fall into habitual patterns of responding with anger and impatience in the face of ignorance in all its forms: classism, racism, sexism, homophobia. But in the best interests of our students, our coworkers, and all with whom we interact, we might spend some time observing our own minds, trying to determine when we are acting responsibly and when we are acting out of self-cherishing. It's a matter of being honest, of watching our minds closely, and gradually training in the direction of patience and equanimity.

Our world is becoming very small. E-mail and other elements of the communications revolution make our interdependence inescapable. The concrete impact of people who have mental peace, minds controlled by ethics and patience, is enormous. Wars take place because the humans who fight them are subject to delusionary thinking. One of my teachers, Lama Zopa Rimpoche, uses the example of Hitler to illustrate the importance of mind. Hitler's was definitely out of control; as a result, he had an enormously devastating impact on the human beings around him. His Holiness the Dalai Lama of Tibet is an example of someone who has an equally powerful impact on millions of people, but in this case it is due to having a mind free of anger. Even with regard to the Chinese communists who engineered the destruction of his country, he is unwilling to countenance violent struggle as a means of social change. The difference between these two human beings who have impacted our modern world is apparent: if hatred and anger prevail, we will be fashioning a world fit for big and little Hitlers; if loving kindness, a good heart, and a clear mind prevail, peace will follow. Our different cultures, our religious and ethical traditions do provide us with ethical codes by which we can live healthy, productive lives. We can heal ourselves by contacting those traditions that have the potential to feed our human need for working for the common good.

Seeking happiness in external things—status, power, recognition—does not lead to satisfaction. It is only by working with the mind that we can begin to experience its clarity. Disturbing mental states can be changed. Afflictive emotional responses such as anger can be unlearned. By learning other states of mind, other motivations, we can bring the mind to peace. And when we practice this regularly we cannot help but be peaceful and therefore be available to others.

I believe that we are here to serve the needs of our students, which requires that we cultivate in ourselves a basic sanity, that we reduce our anger and begin to develop a calm and patient mind.

This does not mean we allow insane, deluded behavior that harms our students while we sit in meditation. But it does mean that we attend to our own subjective state *first*—checking our motivation—before we take action. Academia does not have to be a spiritually barren place where all suffer from a driven, stressed-out mentality. We can transform it into a humane environment. Indeed, it is our duty to do so.

It has been my experience that my ego-grasping, resentful mind only brought illness. My search for satisfaction "out there" led me nowhere; I realized that I could not get satisfaction that way, that I needed to find it in my own mind.

Being calm does not mean being passive in the face of institutional injustice. On the contrary, it makes us *effective* oppositional forces. One is ineffectual even for oneself—let alone others—with an angry, grasping mind. A mind that seeks the institutional nod cannot radically question and struggle against social injustice. It is too invested in the rewards. If one instead begins to loosen or eventually even give up that search for the institutional gaze, then one can be an agent of change. If, instead of endlessly narrating our own suffering—such a widespread habit in academia—we take action, not with anger, but with patience, from a centered place, we can bring about positive change and social justice in our institutions.

NOTES

1. Poignantly, for Miller, the narcissistically disturbed patient

begins to make progress in their therapy when he (or she) comes to the emotional insight that all the love he has captured with so much effort and self-denial was not meant for him as he really was, that the admiration for his beauty and achievements was aimed at his beauty and achievements, and not at the child himself. In analysis, the small and lonely child that is hidden behind his achievements wakes up and asks: "What would have happened if I had appeared before you, bad, ugly, angry, jealous, lazy, dirty, smelly? Where would your love have been then? And I was all these things as well. Does this mean that it was not really me whom you loved, but only what I pretended to be? The well-behaved, reliable, empathic, understanding, and convenient child, who in fact was never a child at all?" (Miller 15)

WORKS CITED

Chodron, Thubten. *Open Heart, Clear Mind*. Ithaca: Snow Lion, 1990.

Gaite, Carmen Martin. "Recetas contra la prisa." In *La busqueda de interlocutor y otros ensayos*. Barcelona: Ediciones Destino, 1982.

Hanh, Thich Nhat. *The Miracle of Mindfulness: A Manual on Meditation*. Boston: Beacon Press, 1987.

Khema, Ayya. *Being Nobody, Going Nowhere: Meditations on the Buddhist Path*. Boston: Wisdom Publications, 1987.

Lerner, Harriet Goldhor. *The Dance of Anger: A Woman's Guide to Changing the Patterns of Intimate Relationships*. New York: Harper and Row, 1985.

Lorde, Audre. "The Uses of Anger." In *Sister Outsider*. Trumansburg, NY: Crossing Press, 1984.

Miller, Alice. *The Drama of the Gifted Child*. New York: Basic Books, 1981.

Wallace, B. Alan. *Tibetan Buddhism from the Ground Up*. Boston: Wisdom Publications, 1993.

Chapter 13

Stupidity "Deconstructed"

Joanna Kadi

Introduction

Dozens of workers move deliberately around the site where a new University of Minnesota building is going up. They drive huge machines, handle dangerous equipment, carry heavy loads. Over the noise of the machinery they can barely talk to each other, but it is obvious they are communicating well and working together. They have to communicate well and work together because a wrongly interpreted nod, a misunderstood word, a petty quarrel could mean a hand cut off, a back irreparably harmed, a life lost. That's not the only reason for cooperative efforts; they're a common working-class practice.

The workers are mostly men and mostly white. I am not a man and I am not white, but I feel a gut connection to these men. I know what it's like to work with them—the jokes, the camaraderie, the easy flow of conversation, the precise directions, the sweat, the dirty hands, the missing teeth, the lined faces. I know who they are and where they come from. I feel at home with them. The familiar sweat, dirty hands, missing teeth, and lined faces reassure me.

We are working-class. We've built every university that has ever existed. But far from receiving any acknowledgment of this, let alone praise, we've been shunned and despised at each university we've created. We've been taught our place in these hallowed halls of academia so thoroughly and so well and so fully that few of us have even *considered* crossing those well-drawn lines.

I used to think that we don't belong at the university. Now I understand that there is a clearly defined place for our hands and feet—but not our minds—in these sacred halls. We build the university, maintain it, clean it, repair it, cook the available food, serve the available food, deliver supplies, unload supplies.

We are always welcome here, within our proper place. We know the monster lurking close to the surface that presents itself if we dare step out of our place. *Stupid. We are too stupid to study, learn, think, analyze, critique. We are working-class and that means we are stupid.* So much energy goes into the social lie that poor people are stupid; capitalism needs a basic rationalization to explain why things happen the way they do. So we hear, over and over, that our lousy jobs and living situations result from our lack of smarts. And I internalized this lie.

I want to examine these dynamics in this essay. I titled this essay "Stupidity 'Deconstructed'" in order to connect my writing with my construction worker brothers and sisters *and* to express the sarcasm and irritation I feel toward postmodernists who consistently use the term. In putting forth these ideas, I want to make it clear that I'm speaking for myself, and not assuming there is one monolithic working-class experience. I do believe that there are common themes linking working-class lives, one having to do with stupidity, and I'm trying to talk about this particular theme in ways that allow room for differences among us.

This essay is part of a larger movement by working-class people who are working-class–identified and strongly committed to writing theory about our experiences, whether in universities or factories. I'm thrilled about this because I believe it's imperative that we write the theory about our lives. No one else. If middle- and upper-middle-class people want to write about how they got indoctrinated into class privilege and how they're unlearning it, great. But we'll create the theory about our lives and experiences.

A sordid history lurks here. There's a tradition of middle- and upper-middle-class academics seeking out the experiences and stories of working-class/working-poor people, for use in shaping theory. That is, we provide the raw material of bare facts and touching stories; they transform these rough elements into theory. Sound familiar? I've had academics come up to me after I've given presentations on class and tell me, "The stories about your family are so *interesting. (Oh, thank you so much.)* Don't you think they'd be stronger if you let them stand on their own?" Translation: I'll take your stories and write the theory. Leave it to the experts. *Well, kids, it's time to forget that shit.*

Yes, I'm a Worthy Person, I Have Two University Degrees

I know a lot about universities and how they work. I learned most of what I know from the time I spent earning degrees at University of Toronto and the Episcopal Divinity School in Cambridge, Massachusetts. I've spent time hanging around other campuses, including the University of Minnesota, and I've heard stories about universities all over the country. Levels of elitism and arrogance vary with regional difference, size, prestige, and how many misfits end up on the campus, but the core system remains: privileged people belong here.

I wish I had known all of this years ago, so that during the time that I was earning my university degrees I would have felt angry instead of crazy. Instead of stupid. *Don't get me started. Even hearing that word makes my blood boil. Even hearing the word "smart" makes my blood boil. I want to wring your neck.*

From a young age I loved to read and write and learn. But my future in that general motors town had been mapped out, and books didn't appear anywhere. I didn't like the map; nor did I like being surrounded by people who treated me like a handy repository for muddy boots and unmitigated rage. The university offered a good solution (or so I thought). I started working paid jobs at age ten and saved every penny for university.

I remember sitting in Mr. Smythe's math class on the third floor of my ancient high school, sun streaming through the windows onto our old wooden desks, our test results read out loud, no one surprised at the results. My name stood with the Johnson twins, Brian Kingsley, Jonathon Woodley, Amanda Britian. All of us in the nineties. Their label: brain. Mine: jock and partyer. Their parents: doctor, lawyer, psychiatrist, executive. Mine: line worker. Mr. Banks advised the Johnson twins to apply to universities in Waterloo or Toronto but not in Hamilton; our guidance counselor pored over pamphlets and reference books with Brian once a week; Mr. and Mrs. Woodley took Jonathon on weekend trips to universities across the province. I got wrecked every Friday and Saturday night and drove around in cars driven by boys as stoned and drunk as me.

Despite my partyer status, despite the lack of help in choosing the "right" school, despite my total cluelessness, I applied to three universities and was accepted. Fresh out of high school, naive but steadfast, I carried my cheap vinyl suitcase up those marble steps of Queen's University. Four months. I had enough money for two years but not enough class privilege. My throat locked, my tongue twisted, I sat in the back row with my arms wrapped around my chest and stomach. To say I felt like a fish out of water hardly begins to touch on the overwhelming feelings of confusion, depression, inadequacy, and shame. People actually asked me when my grandparents had graduated from university. Not just my parents, my *grandparents*. I thought everyone's grandparents were poor. I thought everyone in that generation experienced poverty. I knew everyone's parents weren't poor, and that this marked a big difference between people, but I assumed everyone's grandparents had grown up poor. Now here I was, being asked by rich white girls with straight teeth, "When did your grandparents graduate?" Four months. I'm surprised I lasted that long.

Years later I returned to those hallowed halls. Not through any formal, reasonable plan—more because I was pissed off. Today the whole thing strikes me as a big joke. During a bitter separation, a lawyer told me I could get more money from my ex-husband if I enrolled in university. During our marriage I had worked and supported him while he earned a university degree. I had the legal right to an equivalent education. It sounded good to me. We got the money and I went back to school.

Women's studies, University of Toronto. Middle-class and upper-middle-class women. *I am so stupid.* I sat surrounded by women years younger than I, women who were poised, confident, discussing graduate school options and Karl Marx. (Marx. Oh, yeah, that guy all those other rich people I worked with at CBC Radio used to spout off about.)[1] *What am I doing in this place?* I talked to the janitors and I talked to Kim. Kim. The last holdout for cigarettes in the whole department. We sat in the smoking lounge so she could indulge and I didn't care that the smoke gave me a headache. Better a headache than crazy. Kim anchored me. A white girl, working-class, smart as a whip, skinny and tough. We sat in the back rows together, whispered comments to each other, chewed gum. What would I have done without her?

Graduate school. Another bizarre turn of events got me there. A professor at the University of Toronto actually took an interest in me. My brain didn't know what to do. "You should go on to graduate school," she told me earnestly. "You're very smart. And you have such good study habits. You would do so well." Smart? No, stupid. Graduate school? No, janitor. What is graduate school? What do you do there? What is an M.A.? What is a Ph.D.? How are they different from each other, from a B.A.? I asked none of these things out loud; that would reveal my stupidity. A friend told me about a university where you could get an M.A. in feminist ethics. I didn't know about any other graduate programs. I didn't know how to find them. *I can't believe I am writing this down. Now people will know just how stupid I really am.* I didn't know jackshit.

I applied for the feminist ethics program. I laid out stringent conditions so I wouldn't have to go. *If* I got accepted, *if* I got a scholarship covering tuition, *if* I got work on campus, *if* my lover and I got campus housing. Then, and only then, would I go. My divorce money had run out and I would never, never in a million years, take out a loan to go to school. I knew all about loans and debts. Every working-class person I grew up with had been clear on that: Never take out a loan for anything except a mortgage on a house. Loans are bad. Debts are bad. They are a burden you will never be able to get rid of. I'd fly to the moon before taking out a loan for graduate school. *Graduate school. What the hell is that?*

The school met my stringent conditions. Uh-oh. But this time there were more of us than me and Kim. Joann and Sheri and Meck and I laughed until we cried and cried until we laughed about academia and how stupid we felt. We didn't have Aristotle and Socrates as reference points, couldn't even spell the names right. We hadn't grown up with parents and family friends telling stories about university days and thus easing our entry into this world. We didn't know how to use the library system.

Then, something truly amazing. A professor, a working-class professor. I took class after class with one of the most brilliant minds in this country, Dr. Katie Geneva Cannon, a working-class, African American woman from the South, who pushed me and pushed me and pushed me to think critically about class. Take it apart, figure it out, analyze it, *it's just like my brother used to do when he started building stereo equipment at age ten,* pull and pull and pull, you are smart, she said, write all of it down. I would sit in class, sweating, tongue-tied, scared shitless, and look at her, teaching away, her brilliance shining like a star. *She was supposed to end up cooking and cleaning for white people, that is, if she was lucky and didn't get something worse; my destination was the general motors secretarial pool, if I was lucky and didn't get something worse. If she can do it, maybe I can too.*

Universities. Those buildings on the Cambridge campus, fine stone, beautiful wood, my hands ache with the remembering, we created this. The maintenance men I worked with: Tony, shy and sweet with a faint Portuguese accent; Al's tough hide covering a heart like worn flannel; Tom, too big and too angry, I think he probably did beat his wife; Eddy, booze on his breath, twisted grin, broken front tooth. I spent a summer working with them and felt so comfortable in our little lounge, drinking coffee and smoking, smoking, always smoking, rich people have given it up, but we're still puffing away. *I feel so at home.* I did not feel this way in the classroom or in meetings or in offices. In those places my stomach clenched and people gave me quizzical sideways glances. Who is she? Laughs too loud, skin too yellow, legs and arms too hairy. *None of the janitors cared about those things.*[2]

Looking back now, I know I'm one of the lucky ones. I got through with my self more intact than when I went in. I got through by learning just how stupid I am not. I sat in the back of the class, first with Kim, then with Sheri and Joann, I sat and sweated, my jaw locked up on me, I wanted to curl up and die, I fought and fought, people said to me over and over and over again *You are not stupid.* The system is set up to make you feel stupid. We figured out our own analysis: the university system is intricately linked with the capitalist system. People with power at the university will do their part to reinforce and promote the capitalist explanation for class difference—smart rich people, stupid poor people—in return for continued benefits and privileges. They don't want any upstart working-class urchins figuring this out and refusing to sit in quiet shame.

They don't want graduates of their system to end up like me: class identity and loyalties stronger than ever, angry about the others who never had a chance, who still believe they're stupid, who always will, some already in their graves. Yes, I'm angry.

Constructing/Deconstructing: Building/Hiring

For the capitalist system to continue grinding on in its ruthless way (or for the capitalist system to "succeed," as you would say), those of us bred to do the stupid and/or dangerous necessary work must believe certain things. One key belief we have to maintain is that we aren't as smart as the people who boss us around. We have to believe that; it's absolutely critical. I grew up learning that not just I, not just my family, not just my neighborhood, but the bulk of the population in our general motors town was stupid. Dumb, brutish, idiotic, boring, close to animals. Very close. I learned it from a young age and yet when I set foot in academia I was hit harder than ever with this belief system, a belief system propagated and carefully tended and reinforced by the ruling class. *Who knows what will happen if we realize that we're not so stupid and you're not so smart?*

Of course, I didn't feel stupid at university only because of constructions concerning stupid workers. That coupled with an unfamiliar upper-middle-class world made me feel stupid. I didn't know any of the middle-class/upper-middle-class reference points and contexts. I didn't know what GREs or LSATs were. I couldn't swish around with the entitlement and privilege most other students showed; I tended to creep. I liked the janitors but not my professors; more to the point, I identified with the janitors and not the professors.

Language proved of crucial importance. It first added to my feelings of shame and confusion, and then provided a door into clarity, awareness, and class pride.

I grew up around people who built things—houses, additions on houses, large buildings. They told me they had built it by saying, "I built that." This meant they had planned and designed something, then picked up a hammer, nails, and saw, and constructed it from the ground up.

University professors used this same phrase, often when talking about their summer homes. They said authoritatively, "I built that." I knew what it meant to build something and I thought they meant they had built their home. But they didn't look like they knew the first thing about construction work. I felt confused. Then I felt astounded when I stumbled across the translation. "I built this" really meant "I hired some of you to build this for me."

So. Privileged people misuse language in ways that distort meanings of commonplace, easy-to-understand words like "build." This told me something. Then I read articles focusing on class, usually written by university professors. I looked forward to these, because I needed to develop my class analysis. But again disappointment and shame resulted. I didn't understand most of what I read. Abstract and impersonal, these essays stood three times removed from the concrete reality of working-class life.

After confusion and shame, another door opened. If they misused a simple word like "build," how could I trust them? If their articles used weird words like "proletariat" and showed they didn't know the first thing about us, then maybe they weren't quite so smart. Maybe we weren't quite so stupid.

My hunch solidified after I examined academic attraction to and use of postmodern theory and language. This mix of distorted language and casual appropriation of our ideas allowed me once and for all to dismiss the ideology about stupid workers. As far as I can tell, postmodern theoreticians don't have anything new to say, but their use of inaccessible language makes it appear as though they had. For example, one idea they're particularly fascinated with is that multiple realities exist in society, and this has generated much discussion and writing.

Puh-lease. Everybody in my neighborhood, including the mechanics who sniffed carbon monoxide in tiny, enclosed garages all day long, grasped that idea with no problem. We lived it. We had our reality, the bosses had theirs, and we understood them both. Theorists like W. E. B. Du Bois wrote about double consciousness, whereby African Americans are aware of their own reality as well as that of white people, at the turn of the century. But I've never seen postmodernists attribute these ideas to the people of color and/or the working-class people who've lived and understood them for centuries. Instead, postmodernists steal these ideas and dress them up in language so inaccessible that only a tiny, elite group can discuss them.

It's time we started asking hard, practical questions: Who gets to define smart and stupid, and why? Who misuses language, and for whose benefit? Who gets to write theory, and why? Who gets to go to university, and why? Who does the academy serve? Can universities be transformed into places where all are welcome and all can learn?

Why must working-class people be forced to believe we are stupid and rich people are smart?

In this country, middle- and upper-class white people had the universities to themselves for quite a while. Then the rest of us began banging on the door. Grudgingly, after years and years of hard work, little chinks appeared in those thick, stone doors. *The doors that we built, with our hands. The doors we couldn't walk through.* All the misfits demanded entrance: Africans, Asians, Natives, Arabs, Latinos, women, queers, even welfare mothers. Even the sons and daughters of factory workers and miners and janitors. What's a rich white man to do? The stress must be unbelievable. Poor guys.

Capitalism is a human construct, not a natural or innate system. We've been steeped in lies about its inevitability, and it seems to take on a life of its own as its institutions reinforce each other and the system. But it is a human construct, carefully set up to keep a small number of people stretched out comfortably along the backs of the rest of us. Remember: Human constructs can be destroyed.

Rich Equals Smart, Poor Equals Stupid

I think of the university and a swift hot anger rushes from the pit of my stomach, sweeping over my throat and bursting out of my mouth. The university. I think of stone buildings beautifully carved, wooden rooms beautifully balanced. I think of underpaid exploited workers who built these. I think of my hands/their hands against the hands of the professor at the front of the room "deconstructing" ideas with strings of six-syllable words. *Stupid.* I think of underpaid exploited workers who keep these buildings clean. *Stupid.* I think of myself and every working-class person I have ever known, sitting at the back of the classroom, saying nothing, sweating, fearful that with one word from these stubborn, hurt mouths we will betray who we really are, we will expose our selves/our class, we will be known for what we really are: Stupid.

Many mechanisms exist in this rigidly defined, class-structured society that keep poor people in our place. Our place. We crouch over and the rest of you keep your feet on our necks. You sit complacently, feet resting comfortably, "Could you move just a little bit to the left?" crossing ankles, smiling in our direction, "Very nice." You have constructed several mechanisms for keeping us here. One mechanism for keeping us here is the constant, cross-racial image of the worker as stupid. In our general motors town, where class divisions were easily drawn between workers and executives,[3] I had early on attached "stupid" to workers and "smart" to executives. This was not an arbitrary or personal act of mine. Rather, it came about as a result of force-fed images and words that came through TV and newspapers, and out of the mouths of schoolchildren. Middle-class kids called us stupid, but that particular insult was not hurled back at them. We called them stuck-up, but not stupid. Any TV show that had working-class characters, first *The Honeymooners* and *I Love Lucy,* then *All in the Family,* went out of its way to highlight in overt and covert ways the stupidity of bus drivers, factory workers, and plumbers. Working-class/working-poor kids failed and dropped out of school. Middle-class kids never did. Our town newspaper consistently quoted and wrote about general motors executives as calm, rational types, while union members appeared unthinking, wild, and chaotic.

Oh, you're exaggerating. You've gone too far. Stupid merely refers to someone not terribly intelligent. You've attached all these cultural, class-based meanings. You're way out on a limb. Chill out. People are gonna think you're nuts.

When I look up "stupid" in the dictionary, this is what I find: (1) slow of mind, obtuse, brutish; (2) dulled in feeling or sensation, torpid; (3) marked by or resulting from dullness, senseless; (4) lacking interest or point, vexatious, exasperating.[4] When I look up "stupid" in the dictionary, this is what I feel: (1) recognition; (2) affirmation of what I have felt my whole life and of what I am saying in this essay; (3) fury; (4) disgust.

All those words above fit precisely with what I learned in my bones before I could talk. A very particular set of cultural baggage goes along with stupid. Stupid does not merely describe how well someone thinks. It is a cultural concept that carries with it a particular code and set of signifiers that describe the working class, *as we are understood and formed by the middle and upper classes.* It does not describe the working class as I know it, but it does describe the particular understanding rich people have about us, and to which they hold with a vengeance.

Brutish, dull, senseless. *I grew up believing that all of us were thick-skinned, slow-witted, impervious to pain, boring.* I saw it everywhere I looked. Someone referred to me as sensitive and I stared at her, completely unable to grasp her meaning. *I can't be sensitive, I'm working-class.* Rich people believe we are this way, they brainwash us from the day we are born to make us believe we are this way, we read their newspapers, watch their TV shows, pay money to take in their movies, the only jobs we can get reinforce this, it's a vicious vicious circle.

What's the reality? I do know working-class people who fit the stereotype. Of course, their brains have been fried from decades of drudge work. Like Howie, my partner on the assembly line. Slow, barely able to get a complete sentence out of his mouth, unable to believe I learned his job in two hours. Vacant look, hollow eyes. Couldn't read. *You try working on an assembly line, at the same station, for thirty years. I wonder how interesting you'll be, how much you'll know about world affairs, how creative you'll feel, what art exhibits you'll attend.*

It's painful to acknowledge the fact that some of our brains have been fried. Not fried from birth, as the rich would have us believe. Fried from decades of the most boring, idiotic, repetitive work you can imagine. I've done it. I fought every minute not to let my mind be swept away into the void hovering there. The boredom, lethargy, apathy, and meaninglessness that surrounded that factory, that surround every factory, are a horrible and violating reality of daily life for us.

Stupid. I knew that everyone in my family was marked as stupid, even though this label confused me because I knew what we were capable of. My aunt with her grade-school education, the neighborhood CPA, knew all the deductions and all the answers, did everyone's taxes for free. My brother constructed stereo equipment at age ten. My grandfather, literate in three languages, poor, dying of pneumonia, known through the Lebanese Quarter of Toronto as someone who could help new immigrants deal with lawyers, landlords, bosses. My father and uncles, educated to grade ten, my father doing the daily crossword puzzle in ink, painstakingly planning, calculating, measuring, adding rooms on our small houses, wiring, plumbing, support beams, ceiling, floor tile, never a sixteenth of an inch out, precise and measured. I once helped a friend build a porch; I held the boards in place as she hammered them in and blinked in disbelief because some of the time she was a sixteenth of an inch out. My mother and aunts, balancing budgets, paying bills with money that wasn't there, borrow some from here, beg some from there, adding and subtracting large sums in their heads, the columns will match, I think *Stupid,* I recoil from what has been done.

Class socialization begins early. Material possessions, home environment, and neighborhood provide information about our present situation and our future. Family members' sense of/lack of entitlement and expectation provides more. Social constructions of class, put out by institutions such as media and school, are a third factor. Whether family members resist or unquestioningly take in these social constructions impacts class socialization.[5]

In order to ensure a continuous supply of expendable workers, capitalism needs a particular ideology and a particular set of experiences that match the ideology. The capitalist system has devised many mechanisms to keep a rigid, class-stratified society functioning. Material position and need are two; if you're poor, you'll take whatever job you can, and because you're poor, it's going to be a bad one. Another is the "reward" offered to middle-class lackeys—who don't have much more power than working-class people—but they are kept happy knowing "At least I'm not like them," that is, stupid and poor.

Ideas help reinforce and explain our different class locations. Capitalism relies on various institutions to pass on these pertinent pieces of knowledge, and one of these is the university. Like all institutions under capitalism, they must produce. Universities produce and reproduce certain ideas that shore up capitalism. And so, when I showed up at this institution, I ran full-tilt into an idea I had been taught from birth. Poor people stupid, rich people smart. This is a perfect example of the kind of dualistic thinking that has hindered and weakened Western thought for centuries. The simplistic categorizations of male/female, white/black, heterosexual/homosexual, virgin/whore, good/evil, feeling/thinking also include rich/poor and smart/stupid. And these last two groupings not only exist on their own, they map on to each other to become rich smart/poor stupid.

In the years I spent in women's studies we spent hours and hours analyzing the dangerous and superficial nature of this dualistic thinking, and reflecting on more complicated and realistic views. But we never touched on this smart/stupid, rich/poor breakdown, and no one else I've read has either. I believe that this particular ideological split has done incalculable harm on a daily basis to millions of people. It's time to pay attention.

When I think about rich smart/poor stupid, I realize that one necessary task of analyzing this dichotomy is figuring out what stupidity and intelligence are. The problem with writing an essay like this is that in some ways it plays into the belief that there is only one kind of intelligence, the kind defined and revered by the ruling class in conjunction with academics. Because I'm focusing on the university, the stupid/smart dichotomy, and class oppression, I might end up reinforcing the belief that there is only one kind of intelligence. That is not my intention. In the same way I understand the category of "race" as a myth while I acknowledge the reality of racism and of different physical traits, I want to bring forth the idea of "intelligence" as defined in a limited and narrow way by the ruling class as a myth, while acknowledging a variety of mental capacities across classes and different types of intelligence.[6]

There are many different kinds of intelligence, and these different kinds cross class lines. The type of intelligence revered by universities is connected to the ability to synthesize information rapidly and understand abstract concepts. Other equally valid types of intelligence come through when a child designs and builds a birdhouse, a mother balances a budget with no money, an "uneducated" man keeps everyone enthralled with his stories, a young woman who has not had music lessons composes a piano tune, a girl writes a poem, a homeless person comprehends the poem, a neighborhood devises a plan to stop a company from dumping toxic waste, two young women think of scathing responses to the catcalls and whistles they get on the street. These types of intelligence require one or more of the following qualities: creativity, humor, ability to ask questions, care, a good memory, compassion, belief in solidarity, ability to project an image of something that doesn't exist.

Some manual labor jobs require a great deal of intelligent, creative thinking, such as carpenter, video technician, and groundskeeper/ designer. Most manual labor jobs require little thinking of any sort, and are monotonous and dull. Some executive jobs require intelligence and creative thinking, and most do not. On the whole, the capitalist system has offered its participants little in the way of stimulating, educational, growth-enhancing work experiences.

Can I Really Be Working-Class and Smart?

The sarcasm in this heading is an attempt to get at underlying and often unconscious beliefs about stupidity that popped up constantly after I got my master's degree. People freaked out. Working-class people with university degrees freak out ourselves and our middle-class "sisters and brothers" (more sarcasm). We[7] ask, "Am I still working-class?" Middle-class people inform us, delicately and sensitively, "You're not working-class anymore."

Where do these reactions come from? Let me first examine what working-class people mean when we say, *Am I working-class now? I have a university degree.* A secret subtext, a critical message lurks here.

One day I got the translation. *How can I be working-class? I have a university degree* really means *Am I working-class now that I'm smart?* Let's assume that my theory about dualistic thinking is correct, and the stupid/smart dichotomy is a cornerstone of the academy. This division rests clearly along class lines. That is, rich people are smart, poor people are stupid. The conferring of university degrees onto the middle- and upper-class, then, is not only about knowledge, courses passed, GPAs, degrees, and job security. It is another symbol, another marker, another notation announcing to the world that the owner is part of the middle/upper class. It separates them out from lowly, stupid workers.

What happens, then, when working-class people somehow traverse the minefield of academia and end up with initials after our names? We are confused. We are very confused because we know certain things. We know that those letters are symbols for rich people that they need in part to keep themselves separate from us. They need it to feel smart, they need it to remind themselves they are not us. They are not a lowly janitor sweeping the hall, a lowly cook slopping out lousy food in the university cafeteria. They need these degrees, they guard them, but somehow we end up with them. We are confused. We feel something is askew. We seem to be announcing that we are smart. But if we are working-class, we can't be smart. It's that simple. *If we are working-class, we can't be smart. Therefore, once we have earned a university degree, we are no longer working-class.*

It's been clear to me for a long time that I and my friends, B.A., M.A., whatever silly initials we have after our names, are still working-class.[8] We still talk the same and feel the same and work shit jobs.

We don't float around thinking we're entitled to whatever we want so we can grab things when we feel like it. We don't acquire privilege, entitlement, and arrogance after slogging it out in academia's hallowed halls. No, we're still working-class. The problem is we don't know what to do with this confusing, gut-level knowledge about the university system.

Most of this reasoning and dialogue happens on deep, unconscious levels. On a conscious level, working-class people know that people with university degrees are not necessarily smart. In fact, we know—because we clean their houses and type (code word for rewrite) their incoherent essays—that many of them are not smart.

Last, all of this begs the question: does class location change if one factor governing class location alters? Some people say yes. For them, once working-class people make a good salary they cease being working-class. By the same standard, if working-class people earn university degrees, they leave their class of origin.

I disagree with this, since I believe that class identity comes from many places: education, values, culture, income, dwelling, lifestyle, manners, friends, ancestry, language, expectations, desires, sense of entitlement, religion, neighborhood, amount of privacy. If one of these, such as education, shifts dramatically, class identity doesn't change.

That's what I've come to believe about working-class people asking each other who we are once we graduate. I now want to examine the statement of "fact" by middle-class people saying, "You can't be working-class. You have a university degree." This has happened to me many times, and the remark always comes after I've asserted my working-class identity.

Now there's a great deal of arrogance in that remark, arrogance that goes unnoticed by the speaker *(surprise, surprise)* but not by me *(surprise, surprise)*. When a person with class privilege assumes they can define and articulate the class location of someone from a lower class, that is arrogant. That is offensive.

I believe that class-privileged people are threatened when we working-class people claim our identity. Class is not supposed to be talked about by anyone in this society, let alone some upstart house cleaner or garbage man. A response is needed, preferably a verbal attack that will quickly silence the speaker. Questioning someone's identity usually does the trick.

This action is similar to the one some white people take to try and shut me up when I critique racism. They question my identity as a person of color because of my light skin. Middle-class people have also attempted to shut me up by discrediting me and calling my identity into question; anything to stop me from claiming a working-class identity that might imply some criticism of their class privilege.

Also implicit in this remark by middle-class people is the erroneous, and yet popular, belief that upward mobility is easily achieved and highly desirous. Neither of these is true as far as I can tell. Some small percentage of working-class families have moved into the middle class in one or two generations, but they are the exception rather than the rule. As for upward mobility being highly desirous? I just look at those wildly happy lives of the rich people I've cleaned for, and think, No thanks.

How Do You Spell "Class"?

The university has changed in the last twenty years. Critiques of the system, hard questions, cross-disciplinary dialogues, new programs and departments springing up—women's studies, ethnic studies, queer studies. As a woman, a person of color, a lesbian, I'm happy about these changes and I've benefited from them. But a critical component is missing.

I want to examine what's happening among progressive professors and administrators in terms of class. I don't want to be harsh, because I know the kind of rampant sexism, racism, and heterosexism they deal with as they struggle to carve out some turf at the university. But in other ways, it's harder to deal with classism among this crowd because I expect more. It's ludicrous to me to read the advanced theories these people have to offer when discussing race, gender, or sexuality, and position that with the blank looks that arise when someone says the c-l-a-s-s word.[9]

I've heard progressive professors present information about social change movements, and been excited about studying common people's history and struggles. But I'm angry when pertinent information about participants' class location is completely left out of the discussion. In a lecture about the 1960s Black civil rights movement, a professor carefully delineated racial issues but somehow forgot to mention that most of the people putting their ass on the line were poor. Few people discuss the unfortunate and perhaps not coincidental timing of Martin Luther King's assassination, which happened as he was making the connections between the Vietnam war and poverty at home, not only in Black communities but in white communities as well, as he was beginning to speak for class-based solidarity. Another professor discussing the Stonewall riots talked about "gays" and "lesbians" fighting back. I didn't learn until later that the main instigators were Black and Puerto Rican drag queens and white butches and femmes; I doubt any of these people held executive day jobs.[10]

I want to challenge progressive professors to make class an integral part of discussions and work. Most professors are middle and upper-middle-class, and unfortunately they are as out-to-lunch about class as are the straight white men they criticize. I want these progressive professors to become educated about this issue and devise a curriculum devoted to it.

I want to make a radical proposal here, one that I've never seen in print before. *I must be out of my mind.* I want Working Class Studies set up. I want working-class and working-poor histories, cultures, ideologies, theories, languages studied. I want the many worthy individuals who spent their lives working for social justice studied and examined. I want us teaching each other, want the labor halls and community centers filled with janitors, secretaries, house cleaners, garbage men, line workers, want us in charge of curriculum and reading lists and teaching. I'm not envisioning the "experts" coming in to explain our lives to us, standing behind a lectern and pontificating for two hours on proletarians.

I know what the reaction to my suggestion is. *You've got to be kidding.* Eyes focused on the front of the room, look anywhere else but toward me, silence, shifting bodies, unease, a bright smile from the professor: "Thank you for that interesting suggestion. Shall we move on?" *It's happened to me before. Once I actually told a group of rich, white theology students I thought we should have Class Speak-Outs where only poor people could speak. No one could look at me. My words rolled into a hole in the middle of the floor and disappeared from the face of the earth.* I know what the reaction to this will be: What on earth are you suggesting? *Study a bunch of stupid rednecks?*[11] Chuckle, chuckle.

Conclusion

The construction workers on the University of Minnesota campus are done for the day. It's three o'clock. I hear several smug, privileged rich passersby—the university students—grumble about what an easy job these guys have and how early they're leaving. They have no idea these workers arrived at six or seven in the morning. They don't know how a body feels after eight hours of physical labor. And they don't care.

As for me, I just watch the workers go by. I feel many things. I feel at home, because these men look so familiar to me, from their flannel shirts, jeans, and work boots down to their lunch pails and thermoses, cigarettes and hard hats. I feel comfortable, because I like being around people like this. *These are my people. And we're not stupid.* I feel angry, because I know how these workers are perceived by the students and professors. Because I know that many of these workers believe the lies about who is stupid and who is smart, who has the right to think and study here and who has the right to build and clean here. I feel clear. "If I'm working-class, I can't be smart. So if I have a university degree, I can't be working-class." Absolutely wrong. Dead wrong. *I'm working-class. I'm smart. I have two university degrees.* Working-class people are smart. We know how to screw the system, we know how to take care of ourselves and survive when the odds are against us. We cook tasty meals with one onion, we build our own stereo speakers, we cut precisely fitting pieces of wood for porches, we know how to wire our houses and sew our clothes, we like to read and think and talk to each other. We know how to work cooperatively and we know how to give, generously, both hands open. We make music and art and tell stories. And I can assert without any qualms that we are funnier than rich people.

I've figured out I belong in the university. Not just when they need a janitor, or a cook, or a construction worker, but when I want to go and hone my skills for critical thinking. Working-class people have always thought critically. Our theories about economic systems, the necessity for unions, our plans to destroy the capitalist system have always required critical thinking.

So I'll go to the university to study, if I choose. I won't let anyone make me feel stupid, and I'll know why it's so important that they try to. I won't let them turn me into an assimilationist, a fraud, a middle-class–identified polite girl who's grateful for all the help she gets from these nice rich people. I'll stay true to my roots. I'll use my brains, and my hands, to take this system apart. I'll use my brains, and my hands, to get your feet off my neck.

NOTES

1. In this essay when I use the word "rich" I mean anyone middle-class and up. "Poor" means anyone working-class and down. That is the way the working-class and working-poor people I grew up with use the terms. I find these categories problematic on one hand because they miss a lot of the subtleties of class. For example, they ignore my privilege in being working-class instead of working-poor. On the other hand, I still find them powerful and appropriate categories.

2. By saying this, I'm not implying that all working-class men are comfortable around and supportive of women who don't shave their legs. I've found it's connected to age (younger men don't appreciate it at all) and race (most Arab men—and women—would be aghast at my unshaven legs).

3. See my essay "Catholic School Days: Sketch #1," for a discussion of how these class divisions were and were not easily drawn. (In Kadi, *Thinking Class: Sketches from a Cultural Worker,* Boston: South End Press, 1996, 33–37.)

4. From *Webster's New Collegiate Dictionary,* 1979.

5. I'd love to see middle-class and upper-middle-class allies analyze the process by which they were socialized to believe that they are smart.

6. Thanks to Jeff Nygaard for helping me articulate this point.

7. When I use the word "we" here, I am referring to dozens of working-class friends and acquaintances. I am not referring to every working-class person who has ever gone through the academy.

8. I also know other working-class people who have gotten a university degree and are no longer working-class–identified. These people are intent on passing and assimilating. I'm not sure if they really are middle-class, but they are middle-class–identified.

9. Notable exceptions to the lack of discussion/curriculum around this issue are the courses I took from Dr. Katie Cannon, which consistently dealt with critical questions relating to race, class, sex, ability, and sexuality. Dr. Cannon is continuing this groundbreaking work at Temple University in Philadelphia.

10. I want to mention here the regular inclusion, in women's studies, of the women's campaign to get the vote. I believe that it is an important struggle to study, but I've come to believe that part of its popularity in women's studies is that the social location of that group of activists reflects the social

location of the women teaching in those programs in a way that other struggles usually do not.

11. For the best discussion I have ever read on the offensiveness of rich people using the term "redneck," read Elliott, "Whenever I Tell You the Language We Use Is a Class Issue, You Nod Your Head in Agreement—and Then You Open Your Mouth," in *Out of the Class Closet: Lesbians Speak,* ed. Julia Penelope (Freedom, CA: Crossing Press, 1994). Elliott's article first appeared in *Lesbian Ethics* 4, 2 (spring 1991).

Chapter 14

To Challenge Academic Individualism

Sharon Doherty

The weekend I attended a feminist conference on social justice in academe,[1] a friend of mine was in the same city at a national conference on preventing homelessness.[2] We did not go to each other's meetings, but we did exchange information about ideas and actions at the two events. For a few minutes, we imagined together what it would have been like to merge our conferences, with revolutionary intentions. This didn't last long, as we decided that the participants would have difficulty communicating, and may not even recognize their connections to each other.

Why did the idea of connecting in this way seem unrealistic to us? Why are academics'—even feminist academics'—attempts to put our intellectual talents to work in our communities, to create a more just society, so rare and so difficult? My purpose here is not to criticize the participants in our conference (including myself) for not being at the homelessness conference. Rather, I want to examine cultural forces that pull us away from such work, and consider alternative paths.

Many feminists come into academic life with social justice goals. Once there, we find out that those goals are not rewarded. We are faced with several choices:

(a) *Get out.* Some storm out; some become disempowered and fade out; some leave with regret, to work in more justice-oriented contexts.

(b) *Stay in, ignore or resist the system's dominant values, and do academic work that advances causes of justice in our communities.* In the current system, it is difficult to be clear about this choice. Most disciplines socialize graduate students to see applied and activist scholarship as academically less serious than more distanced work. Institutional reward systems support distanced perspectives. Consequently for

347

many people, selecting option (b) is a ticket to option (a), with the institution making the choice by granting activist scholars limited power—for example, temporary positions with no voting rights—or by denying them tenure because they are not "intellectually serious" enough.

(c) *Stay in and try to change the educational system.* That is what I have done, and what most of the conference participants seemed to be doing. Our work is important, but it is wearing. If we don't pursue it, though, too many people interested in working for justice will continue to (sanely) choose option (a). Their influence, then, will not be present among students, in research agendas, and in other educational activities.

In trying to change the system, we consider the cultural forces driving it. Many of us focus on forces of exclusion, such as institutional sexism, racism, and classism. Through my research and institutional change activities I have become convinced of the destructive power of a related force: individualism. For many in U.S. culture, individualism is integral to their personal and cultural histories, to the framework of their lives. For those whose lives have been framed more communally, the dominant culture's individualistic pressures are coercive, obstructing work for justice in academe and elsewhere. If we come to better understand how this cultural force operates in higher education and face its myriad implications, we will be better prepared to change our institutions and our professional activities, in order to create a more just world.

Individualism is a complex legacy of modern life. To understand this legacy, we need to distinguish individualism's different meanings: as theory of human existence, as perspective or element of a person's worldview, and as strategy. As theory of human existence, individualism is related to Enlightenment ideas about persons existing as separate, atomistic beings. Closely related to this theory is the perspective many people operate from in their day-to-day existence. While not everyone is engaged in academic debate about the nature of the self, each of us does operate from more or less conscious views regarding who we are and how we relate to others. An individualistic perspective leads people to think of themselves independently of others. Strategy is a person or group's conscious approach to living. While perspective is descriptive and interpretative, strategy is prescriptive, related to what a person thinks she should be doing to make a good life. In the sense that individualist strategy does not connect one's own good life to others having good lives, there is a moral component to the question of strategy.

In its positive associations, individualism is linked to ideologies of human rights, privacy, and autonomy. The inherent value of the individual has been a foundation for revolutions overthrowing autocratic rule; for efforts to replace inherited position with meritocracy; for democratic governments in the United States and elsewhere. Individualism is related epistemologically and politically to liberalism, which places a premium on "the ideal of the limited state and the worth of individual human freedom" (Frazer and Lacey 73). Indeed, many gains of Western feminism are embedded in individualism—particularly such liberal measures as antidiscrimination laws.

But social justice gains built on individualism have been limited. As Elizabeth Fox-Genovese points out, as a strategy to create a good life, "[i]ndividualism for women lagged far behind individualism for men, as individualism for the dispossessed of all races lagged far behind that for the propertied" (43).[3] Theories of individualism were built around the idea that propertied men are the relevant individuals in society. This idea has been expressed in societal institutions through limitations regarding who has had access to formal power, indeed through the very definition of citizen. The facts that in the early United States only propertied men were allowed the vote and that women and people of color were excluded from higher education were not coincidental to the U.S. system of individualist democracy, but were integral to its founding vision. (For an eloquent discussion of related political issues, see Iris Marion Young's 1987 article, "Impartiality and the Civic Public.")

In the United States, such formal exclusion for the most part is no longer legal. The liberal emphasis on rights has been used by members of excluded groups and their allies to argue and mobilize for expanded access to full citizenship and educational opportunity. Women now do have a right to vote, and higher education institutions are prohibited from formally excluding women and people of color. Such rights today are established irrespective of property and sex. Those formal rights remain grounded, nonetheless, in the three-part reality of their individualist roots: (1) only propertied men originally were considered citizens; therefore (2) models of citizenship were embedded in private property ownership and male dominance.

At the same time, (3) citizens were considered atomistic beings separate from their social context.

Liberal individualism has never recovered from those origins. (See Weiss for an excellent feminist critique of the liberal legacy.) Now that the formerly excluded have a right to, for example, higher education, the first part of the formula has changed. But individualist theory and values keep many people in denial about the extent to which citizenship is based on being a propertied white man, or being as much like him as possible. People of color, white women, and low-income white men are not formally excluded from participating in higher education, but both structures and values tend to push some of us out or keep us marginal. Cultural analysis can help us understand those structures and values, as we look behind the legal, formal realities to the textures and forces influencing our lives.

Individualism as a dominant cultural force remains compatible with inequality and self-centered actions. To live without consideration of social context, power relations, and ties to other people requires that a person be in error, even if sincere (a problem of theory or perspective); or aware of human connections, power, and social context, but willing to use others to pursue his or her individual goals (a problem of strategy).

Those who benefit from individualism—be they sincere but wrong or aware but exploitative—in practice either directly oppose the well-being of others or manage to place others in their service without recognizing (or admitting) it. Placing others in one's service without acknowledging it is a central element of institutionalized patriarchy. That small group of men with the most power in our society seem to operate as individuals, but they have virtual armies of people keeping them on top—from servants to accountants, factory workers to middle managers to wives. If a person is benefiting from the societal status quo, he may not recognize his connection to other people because he controls so many of them, either directly or indirectly through his resources. In this way, it is possible to maintain a perspective and a strategy of individualism. Women, as well as men of color, white working-class men, and other men who are not in power, have the opportunity for a clearer vision of connections, but the weight of a society's dominant ideologies can be overwhelming. When we yield to individualistic cultural forces—whether or not we are in power—

our priorities often lead us away from accountability to others outside the narrowest of personal circles.

Individualism, then, is a deeply patriarchal perspective that still prevails across U.S. social institutions today. Individual achievement is the guiding principle behind the reward system in most higher education institutions, despite rhetoric in praise of community service. Core elements of individualism in the higher education context include getting ahead by knocking others down; overspecializing, with no concern for linking research to societal needs; and being disconnected from community life. Each of those elements reflects a lack of commitment to shared understanding and purposes of justice, as well as a lack of connection and accountability—to colleagues, students, and communities outside academe.

Getting ahead by knocking others down. Related to this is a pugilistic, warrior mentality regarding intellectual endeavors. A conversation I observed between two men after a university lecture provides an illustration. One of them had asked the speaker a hostile question, and his admiring friend said, "You landed a good clean punch. She was reeling." This is an extreme version of the competitive individualist environment that still prevails in many classrooms. Feminist scholars and others committed to liberation pedagogies have done a great deal to work against this element of individualism, through team projects, small group discussions, and other collaborative practices.

Overspecializing with no concern for tying research to societal needs. This is a particularly insidious characteristic of individualism. I observed a meeting where a Latino administrator-activist asked a high-ranking university official what actions the institution was planning to foster outreach and research relevant to communities of color in our state. The official, who is white, did not seem to understand the question, and focused his answer on the faculty's freedom to choose their research topics. Such behavior is related to a liberal individualist "negative view of freedom" (Frazer and Lacey) in which freedom is seen as a lack of interference from the state (or, in this case, the administration).[4] Form here is valued over substance. The form is that faculty have academic freedom to pursue whatever research topics they consider important. A contextualized, substantive view of the situation reveals a disproportionately white male faculty who are rewarded for research published in conventional (traditionally exclusive according to race and gender) journals. The activist-oriented administrator put his question in terms of community needs, and the official could not answer him in those terms. The concept the official found relevant to the situation was freedom. As Frazer and Lacey argue, "negative freedom is worth little if it is not accompanied by the positive conditions for self-determination" (73). Their discussion of gender neutrality sheds light on the university official's "race-neutral" perspective:

> In a sexually unequal society, gender neutral procedures and gender neutral language do not lead to gender fair results. Instead the position of gender neutrality has served as a cover for what are implicitly male concerns and interests, which are thereby construed as objectively valid. (71)

Liberal individualism leads to an emphasis on form over substance, and thus results in the perpetuation of injustice through values like negative freedom. If the official's perspective were centered on connection and accountability, he would see faculty freedom in its social context. With such a perspective, those in powerful positions would not consider themselves free to think only of themselves, but would think of themselves in relationship to those whose freedom is limited by unjust social conditions. In this way, connections and accountability have the potential to lead academe toward social justice.

Being disconnected from community life. This element is closely related to the lack of engagement with societal needs. It has been discussed most eloquently by scholars of color and working-class scholars. The use of elitist language symbolically reflects this disconnection, as bell hooks explains:

> [T]he use of a language and style of presentation that alienates most folks who are not also academically trained reinforces the notion that the academic world is separate from real life, that everyday world where we constantly adjust our language and behavior to meet diverse needs. (104)

Our language reflects who it is we hope will read, understand, and act on our work. Elitist language is linked to the perspective that knowledge exists for its own sake, its meanings universally, generically important. This promotes the ivory tower idea that there is a small club of people worthy of engaging with these universal, important ideas. Those in the club are people who have the time and training to use this specialized language. If, by contrast, we see our work as applicable to societal needs and if we are engaged with community activists and others who are addressing those needs, we will write accessibly. Similarly, if we consider engagement with community life to be a central educational process, we will structure our programs and curricula to foster community-faculty-student links. In most of academe, this is not happening.

These three elements of individualism are barriers to working for social justice. Through pugilistic competitiveness we lead students to see others as people to beat. Through overspecialization and lack of community ties we produce much scholarship that supports the status quo of societal power, and teach students not to use their talents to strengthen communities.

Attempts to transform the higher education system often also operate from an individualistic perspective. Feminist and antiracist strategies such as grievance systems and the threat or reality of lawsuits have forced campuses to begin to be more open. Those strategies, while important, have not been sufficient to bring us to justice. When we try to transform educational institutions within the context of individualism, we achieve some change but not enough. Grievances, for example, sometimes help to change the behavior of individual staff, faculty, or students, but they are usually mediated or adjudicated one-on-one encounters, with great potential for polarization. While I believe that these enforcement systems are necessary for the foreseeable future, their processes rarely engage groups of people in discussing and carrying out change.

Feminists and other progressive academics who want to work for social justice will strengthen our position if we more systematically challenge individualism.

The Good Society Challenge to Individualism

Those of us who wish to emphasize social justice are not the only academics concerned about the effects of individualism on U.S. education and the wider society. Social theorists' concern over the effects of individualism on U.S. culture is at least as old as Alexis de Tocqueville's work in the early nineteenth century. Recent years have brought renewed attention to the issue by mainstream political scientists, sociologists, and other scholars, who have been trying to speak to and for the society as a whole. The "communitarian" movement, for example, led by such authors as the sociologist Amitai Etzioni, has captured national attention.

With respect to higher education in particular, a prominent mainstream challenge to individualism is that offered by Robert Bellah, Richard Madsen, William M. Sullivan, Ann Swidler, and Steven M. Tipton in *The Good Society*. They focus on individualism in U.S. education as well as in other social institutions, including religion, law, and politics. This approach is a follow-up to their more general discussion of cultural values in *Habits of the Heart: Individualism and Commitment in American Life*. If we want to systematically challenge individualism, why shouldn't we simply join in their critique?

Unfortunately, Bellah and his coauthors' critique of individualism will not move us toward the kind of connections and accountability that can lead to social justice. If we hope for an anti-individualist movement in academe that places justice at its center, we will need to move beyond their perspectives. I will engage in some detail with Bellah and his coauthors' ideas here because I believe they are operating in good faith and with some depth regarding questions of individualism and its harm to our society. Their discussion, however, misses key elements of power and difference.

Bellah et al. argue that the United States has been taken over by radical individualism. "The citizen," they argue in *Habits of the Heart*, "has been swallowed up in 'economic man'" (271). Private life has taken over from public life, and we interact publicly through special interest groups. Bellah et al. believe that economics has become the dominant model for common life in the United States, and that people are increasingly tempted to "put ourselves in the hands of the manager and the expert" (ibid.). We are fragmented, they argue; our culture is one of separation. People are too cynical. We need to re-create common life. In *The Good Society*, the authors shift their focus from "cultural and personal resources" to institutions, exploring structural elements of what they call a "culture of individualism."

Though this work is compelling, several flaws limit its potential for contributing to social justice. First, like other mainstream social theorists who have focused on individualism and their conception of its opposite ("commitment" for Bellah et al., "communitarianism" for

Etzioni and others), the *Good Society* authors are working from an underlying premise that there is a *monolithic* American tension between the two. "Special interest groups," regardless of a particular group's goals, for Bellah et al. are the enemy of "common values". This is oversimplified, and rooted in dualistic thinking. To place organized interest groups and societal commitment at the two poles of a universalized dualism, and then attempt to analyze social problems within that framework, is a limited approach.

The conversation about interest groups and the common good must be made more specific, and thus more complex. Is the tobacco lobby really equivalent to the National Organization for Women, the Navajo Nation, or the NAACP? It is not, and neither, in the academic setting, is an African American cultural center equivalent to a neo-Nazi white student union. To equate all organized groups and assume they are individualistic reflects a failure to recognize issues of power and the legacies of brutal domination in our country. We need to analyze "special interest groups" in their historical and contemporary specificity. If we open the concepts of community and commitment to specifically examine how different contexts and actions work for or against individualism, we will be able to provide such an analysis.

A second, closely related flaw has been identified by the philosopher-theologian Cornel West. West grants that the *Good Society* authors are concerned about people who are "bearing the social cost" of the culture's crisis of individualism; he names "the one-third who are ill-fed and ill-sheltered and ill-housed" as those bearing the primary cost (West 200-201). But West argues that Bellah et al. have not provided a specific or complex enough analysis; the social costs "are not concretely fleshed out. . . . the analysis has to be focused on where in fact those social costs are being borne and what the responses are" (201). Individualism, in its particular forms in the United States today, benefits some people more than others. It is not a neutral practice, any more than it is a neutral ideology. In higher education, the social costs are borne disproportionately by those whose community responsibilities are greatest, those who attempt to apply academic work to community needs, and those who do not subscribe to the competitive pugilist approach, as well as those whose material resources are most limited.

Bellah and his coauthors' dualistic approach and lack of engagement with social costs are related to a fundamental problem: their failure to consider women and other nondominant groups as key sources of cultural knowledge about human connections and accountability. Bellah et al. effectively identify some basic problems of individualism, as they criticize the overspecialized and fragmented condition of universities in the late twentieth century:

> The research university, the cathedral of learning, rather than interpreting and integrating the larger society, came more and more to mirror it. Far from becoming a new community that would bring coherence out of chaos, it became instead a congeries of faculty and students, each pursuing their own ends, integrated not by any shared vision, but only by the bureaucratic procedures of the "administration." (155)

But they seem to have little knowledge of those within academe who have been operating from stronger connections. They give only superficial attention to groups most visibly working for change today: "Educational reform consisting largely in search-and-destroy missions to prove that previously canonical works promote racism, sexism, and class domination will not be of much help to students for whom those canonical works had no meaning in the first place" (174).

Neither do Bellah et al. grant students the attention they deserve regarding their community perspectives, as the authors consider late-twentieth-century undergraduates a rather homogeneously enculturated group: "The operative culture of most of our undergraduates is the monoculture of the tube: 'L.A. Law' or 'Miami Vice'" (174).

This approach blithely dismisses efforts to address issues of diversity, as Bellah and his coauthors seem to consider such efforts both excessively negative and irrelevant to our populations' real concerns. Such an approach also dismisses the texture of real students' lives, overgeneralizing and overemphasizing the cultural influence of television. Even if media influences have become dangerously powerful, it is crucial that we draw our conclusions about students' cultural frameworks from real people's voices and experiences.

In fact, the project of challenging individualism can be deepened and made more effective through engagement with a greater diversity of voices and experiences. Bellah et al. are looking for signs of hope, but their search is unfortunately limited by a narrow set of sources. Eloquently and passionately they call for democratic transformation:

> The spinal cord of democracy, the connection between government and an enlightened public, is broken. A . . . democratic transformation

needs to renew a serious public conversation and to strengthen the institutions that nurture and extend it. Picking up the public conversation . . . is one way to start that renewal. (293)

They then proceed to discuss the thinkers relevant to this task—affluent white men, almost every one. In their chapter on education they cite fifty-one sources: forty-five European and white American men (from Thomas Paine, William James, and Aristotle to Daniel Boorstin and Allan Bloom); Confucius, the only non-Western man; and five others—the *New York Times*; an unnamed child of Vietnamese refugees; the educator and social reformer Jane Addams; the anthropologist Mary Douglas; and the educational sociologist Zelda Gamson. (I did not originally set out to count the sources; I counted them because by the time I finished reading the chapter I was so stunned by its incomplete discussion that I needed a reality check on my reaction.)

As I attempt to avoid a search-and-destroy mission, let me say that I do not think this imbalance of sources stems from bigotry. The situation is more complicated than that. Bellah and his coauthors' choice of sources relates to their acceptance of liberal conceptions of "common good" and citizenship, which erroneously favor the ideas of those who separate the common good from people's identities. Those theorists who are least engaged in questions of how race, gender, and other realms of difference relate to community and common good are therefore most appealing to them. This problem of assumed neutrality is related to another confused dualism, that of public/private, as in public citizen versus private interest. (In a 1987 essay, Nancy Fraser provides an excellent discussion of the gendered character of "public citizen.") Such an idea leads to the perception that all "interest groups" collapse into a mass of individualism, when in fact many such groups are pursuing greater accountability across segments of society.

Questions about how differences relate to the common good involve high stakes indeed. Relationships between communities and the larger society in the United States today are ambiguous and troubled. Within and among communities, oppression is thriving. Differences of culture, region, and especially resources place different groups in a vast range of relationships to each other, and result in divergent views of the "whole" society. Debates about values, resource distribution, and reward systems in education and other institutions are taking place in the context of tremendous gaps in understanding. Those gaps prevent us from successfully addressing the epidemics of violence and poverty afflicting the nation. The United States is currently on a destructive path, as selfish individualism is out of control. It is important to the national debate that we "get specific" about issues of community (see Phelan), and that we never consider questions of commitment separately from questions of justice.

Going against the Individualist Grain

Bellah and his coauthors understand that the stakes are high, but their view of what is happening in our universities is unduly pessimistic, and yields to a monolithic vision of U.S. culture. It is true that individualism is powerful, that many communities are in crisis or decline, and that higher education has not been particularly effective in countering those trends. It also is true that some people, particularly those in oppressed groups, have maintained or created community forms and practices—as political resistance, as cultural persistence, and in some cases for their very survival. (Sara M. Evans and Harry C. Boyte discuss such forms in historical context in *Free Spaces: The Sources of Democratic Change in America*.) We need to look for signs of hope in our time, to explore how some people in higher education are connecting meaningfully and working against individualism.

I have found the most illuminating sources of hope to be the stories of people whose lives are going against the individualistic grain. My main sources are undergraduate students who participated in my dissertation research at the University of Minnesota–Twin Cities. This research addresses issues of connection and accountability as they relate to social justice and higher education. In the early 1990s I conducted in-depth interviews with University of Minnesota–Twin Cities undergraduates from different backgrounds about communities and other connections in their lives, and how their connections relate to their experiences of higher education. By working with a diverse group of students, I engaged with differences within U.S. culture in how community is defined, whether it is a workable concept, and what connections are important to people.

I centered my research on personal narratives because they provide the necessary complexity for better understanding connections and accountability. Life histories and other narratives provide a "vital entry point" for understanding the dynamic interaction between social structure and individual agency (Personal Narratives Group 5). Building social knowledge from personal narratives differs from other kinds of generalization because the methodology fosters close attention to difference, relationships, and process. This approach allows me to address community and other connections without neglecting differences. The interviews covered a range of topics, but here I will focus particularly on four students' discussions of people who influenced their education, placed in context by brief descriptions of the students' activities, plans, and discussions of connections.

Before I turn to the students' stories, allow me to identify several concepts and values that I consider important in avoiding a universalized community/individualist dualism. Key elements to explore as we seek a more complex view of community are substantive connections, accountability, and heterogeneity. I am most interested in those elements as they relate to questions of justice.

Substantive connections and *accountability* are grounded in relational rather than individualistic notions of human life. I use the word "connections" to open our thinking beyond traditional concepts of community. Connection is a fluid concept, calling for concrete examples in order to be meaningful. Substantive connections in which I am interested include those occurring in towns and neighborhoods—commonly recognized sites of community—as well as those occurring in extended families, ethnic groups, voluntary organizations, and other groups. Many potential sites of connection exist in universities: workplaces, student organizations, residence halls, classrooms, and so on. My interest is in what happens as people attempt to connect with each other, and what meanings those connections have for different people. "Accountability" here is similar to commitment, but I use the concept because it implies relationships. One can be committed to many things (including one's grades, one's bank account, etc.); one is accountable to other people.

By emphasizing connections and accountability I am not discarding the term "community"; rather, I am attempting to move toward greater specificity in our understanding of it. As with the concept of culture, dozens of definitions of community exist. Instead of offering another definition here, I am focusing on these related concepts.

What I do reject is the common practice of linking community to homogeneity. I assume heterogeneity in all human connections—that is, people who connect to each other do so across differences. In addition to differences among people, heterogeneity refers to differences within people, given our complex identities. As Marilyn Friedman points out, "The problem is not simply to appreciate community per se but rather to reconcile the conflicting claims, demands, and identity-defining influences of the variety of communities of which one is a part" (194). To place heterogeneity at the center involves consideration of power, conflict, and exclusion, in ways that do not emerge from an assumption of homogeneity. I do not abandon the possibility of common ground or common good; instead I am interested in exploring how people strive to connect across differences.

It is important to realize that not every connection stems from a desire for unity, friendship, or emotional sharing. With an assumption of heterogeneity, we should realize that connections can be based on a realization of interdependence, of needing each other in order to make a good life. In the best of circumstances, the give and take of interdependence will lead to understanding and caring for each other, but not to denial of differences.

Working for *justice* involves pursuing accountability among and within segments of society. I am interested in exploring how justice relates to issues of common good for different people, and what kinds of connections promote social justice. I accept Iris Young's definition of justice as involving fair distribution of resources along with an absence of oppressive domination in social structures, processes, and relationships (Young, *Justice* 241).

With these concepts and values in mind, I now turn to the stories of anti-individualism at the University of Minnesota. The following excerpts are from interviews with students from low-income or working-class backgrounds (I use pseudonyms, based on an agreement with the students). Their ideas and activities provide a contrast to the stories of academic individualism at the beginning of this essay.

Come with Me; Let's Do It

Gloria Chavez came to the University of Minnesota directly after high school from a poor urban neighborhood in another state, and intended to go back after graduating. At the time of our interviews she held a leadership position in La Raza student cultural center and in a Chicana group on campus. She tutored children once a week at an elementary school. Gloria was not sure what her work would be when she returned home, but she knew she wanted to work with other Mexicans in the barrio. When I asked her what gets in the way of important connections, she said,

> I think the competition that people try to build around us. . . . You're special, you, only you—when all our lives we've been taught by our familias that it's everybody, the whole community. But they stick it in your brain at school—it's *you, you're* the one who's special, *you're* different from *them*. You are doing this [college], you know—and a lot of people are gonna believe that, and then just go off on that, (thinking) "If I do this, then you're gonna hold me back from doing what I want," instead of "Come with me, let's do it."

Gloria's critique of her formal education focused on how people are pulled from the contexts of their lives and treated as individuals, rather than as members of groups. Her response to this differed from that of Bellah and his coauthors. She was learning all she could about Chicano history, so that she could work for social justice with the people to whom she considered herself accountable. She was as deeply engaged in issues of power as in issues of connection.

The person at the university who influenced Gloria the most was a fellow student who was about forty.

> She's a Chicana too, she's from Texas. She's older, and I thought all this anger and everything was me, and she's like, "Oh, I've gone through all that." And she gets angry too and we go through a lot of things together. I guess at first . . . she was like my mother figure type of thing. Now I think I see her like more of a friend, more than a mom.

The more experienced student went out of her way to help Gloria, their friendship grew, and together they worked to build connections through the women's group and the cultural center.

Gloria used language of "home" and "La Chicana" to describe her links to people. "Community" for her had limited meaning, she said, in part because of what she considered superficial use of the word at the university. I believe that Gloria's work might make Bellah and his coauthors nervous, as they consider endeavors like ethnic studies to be divisive. In fact, Gloria's work was defined by accountability and meaningful connections. She was angry, and sought to challenge injustice. That goal is not opposed to "community" building and is not individualistic, but rather an important kind of connection.

Gloria did not accept the idea of universalized community. One of the reasons she liked the cultural center was its value as a retreat, a place where she didn't have to "be the expert" about Chicano history, as she felt many white students expected.

> GC: I could go a whole day without even talking to a white person, you
> know. I like that. Not that I'm not gonna see them—yeah, I'll see
> them but I don't have to talk to them.
> SD: Do you know how threatened that makes some white people? . . .
> Some people say you know we all should be together; it doesn't
> matter how we're different.
> GC: Yeah, together on *your* terms, not on mine. And I do have white
> friends and white people coming into La Raza, that I can talk to, and
> I *like* them, and it just comes out at a different level.

Gloria was acutely aware of differences—of gender and economic background among students in the cultural center; of race/ethnicity among women student activists at the university. This awareness did not lead her to reject possibilities of connection, but it did lead her to understand how power-charged and tenuous connections can be.

Knowledge for a Better World

John Wilson considered himself a fortunate "one in a million" because he was an African American from an inner-city Minneapolis neighborhood graduating from the university. A major influence on his university education was a white woman economics professor in General College who taught a class John expected to hate but ended up loving. It was the first time he really liked school; he participated in all the study groups and got to know the professor because she spent extra time working with him.

The class was different from other economics classes he encountered at the university.

> JW: A lot of my economics classes—when I look at the difference be-
> tween a subject like economics and how that's taught, and a subject
> like sociology and how that's taught, it's like they're almost on two

different planes. I think they need to make the student, no matter what their degree is in—they could give them a kind of base. Like in economics, we'd never talk about any *social* aspects of the policy. It was all based on math and lines and curves and graphs, and like you're never gonna *use* this stuff.

SD: And that was not how the economics that you liked so much had been taught?

JW: I believe, yeah, you do need to know, you know, the elasticity of a line, but when it comes to solving problems in this country, that's really irrelevant, you know, when you deal with these social issues. . . . But then you get on the sociology aspect and it was almost the reverse. I mean, a lot of times they would look almost too much into the human issues, at least as an undergraduate. . . .

SD: It is true, the disciplines get off in their own specializations.

JW: Exactly. And it seems like they don't work together.

The economics professor who did integrate social and economic issues hired John as an undergraduate teaching assistant, working for course credit.

I started to work for her as a T.A. in the fall and I was getting credit for it, and I thought that was great. And then, I really liked working with students, and I started forming my own study groups—and I think she was like, wow, this guy really went beyond what he had to do. And so she hired me, and paid me as a T.A., which got me out of being a janitor, which got me more into academics.

John's performance as a T.A. led college staff to ask him to apply to be a peer tutor. After that, he was on his way to a series of roles as a student leader, including orientation group leader and residence hall staff person. During his undergraduate years he occasionally spoke to inner-city school groups about the importance of going to college. John hoped to either go to graduate school or to work in business, and continue his community volunteer work.

Like John, Mark Nelson considered himself fortunate to be graduating from college. Mark grew up poor and white in another inner-city Minneapolis neighborhood. None of his college classes inspired him about learning until he took an African American history class from an African American woman professor.

And that was the first class that I had where the material that we read and that we discussed actually seemed relevant to *life,* and to the life that I was living. And not only was it relevant but it also talked about the need for a better world. And that was the first class that I had that had said *that* too. And so those two combined, you know, really had a big impact on me. And for that reason I became much more interested in Afro-American studies, and not only Afro-American studies but it was at that point that I became interested in *school*.

Mark and several friends from diverse ethnic backgrounds started an antiracism group on campus.

The idea behind the group was . . . if we can just get people from different groups together, you know, and get them talking, they'll realize then that everybody's okay and they'll begin to get along. And that'll be a step, you know, toward political involvement. . . . And we'd see ourselves as bridging that gap. We would advertise social events like dances or discussions, through word of mouth and through the dormitories.

As Bernice Johnson Reagon advises in "Coalition Politics: Turning the Century," new possibilities emerge when people reach out beyond their own identity groups, without denying their identities. John and Mark's professors heeded Reagon's argument that "[i]t must become necessary for all of us to feel that this is our world. . . . And watch that 'our'—make it as big as you can" (Reagon 365). By linking course material to social issues and by taking the time to reach out, they used their power as teachers to inspire John and Mark, young men with racial/ethnic identities different from their own. Both men responded by using their knowledge to claim the world and connect with others to make it more like the world they wanted.

Connecting to Community Life

Gloria, John, and Mark all spoke with certainty about their desires to make community contributions after college. Gloria expected her work to take her back to the barrio, where many people were living in poverty: "You gotta come back. . . . I mean how can you see your people like that and not want to do anything?"

John explained his speaking in schools and other community work as conscious efforts to provide a role model.

I think it's important to go back to North Minneapolis, South Minneapolis, or wherever . . . and give these kids a *positive* role model, 'cause they see the drugs going on, the gangs, all that. And it's like the guys who did—the few of us who did leave to go to college or do whatever—we all move to Minnetonka [a wealthy suburb], and there's no more role models; we disappear. And you gotta let a kid say, well hey, if John can do it, I can do it.

Mark was accepted into a graduate school social science program, where he planned to do research connected to low-income people, the people he considered his own group: "I will always keep the connections to lower-class people."

Community connections on the part of faculty and staff also can help students find their way to college. Grace Tanner is a white single mother and former Aid to Families with Dependent Children (AFDC) recipient who, when we met, was halfway toward her bachelor's degree and working in a civil service position on campus. Her original source of inspiration for college was her father, who had worked the line in a meatpacking plant until he had a heart attack and could no longer work. Because he was not college educated, he had "nothing to fall back on," and the family income plummeted. Grace's father talked to her about his absence of options, and encouraged her to go to college. But when she married young and had two children, Grace lost track of her college aspirations. The marriage ended in divorce and she was dropped into poverty. Grace credited a General College staff member with getting her back on the educational track.

About seven, eight years ago when I was working part-time at the church I belong to—I had started out volunteering there—I was on AFDC, I was working part-time. I heard about . . . "Project Self-Sufficiency." It's a project; . . . they were going to give you a certificate for housing where you'd only pay so much of your income, and they'd pick up the rest, and then they'd help you with school plans, and long-term goals and stuff. I was involved in Head Start at the time. I was a board member. They really encouraged parents who had children in the program to become involved, and I got elected to the board. . . .

So anyway I applied for Project Self-Sufficiency. You had to get all these letters of recommendation, and write stories about yourself, and all kinds of things. So ——— who works in General College also was on the board at that time, and she said she'd do a letter of recommendation. At that time, she encouraged me—she said, "Why don't you take a class through extension at the university? It would give you extra points" on this thing that I was applying for. So I said, "Oh, okay." So she signed me up for a course and helped me to get funded. And that was the start on the road. I liked it and I've been going ever since.

In addition to Head Start, Grace was involved in other volunteer work through church activities and the city's recreation programs. She also was a leader in a project on campus to improve the educational climate for women students.

For Grace, community meant

a sense of belonging, a group of people that you belong to, and because you belong to it you should care about—about the other people in that group. . . . There are some nights that come along and you know that you have maybe a Head Start meeting coming up and you don't want to go. But my sense of duty, I generally always will go just because I've made that commitment.

To successfully build community, Grace stressed the importance of having values beyond individual achievement.

You have to be sincere in your commitment and not in it just for the glory of yourself, like "Oh, look what I've done. . . . Oh look at me, I'm a very important person," but just being involved and saying this is something I'm committed to and it means a lot to me. People can generally discern that within a few months of meeting you . . . if you're really sincere about it, or if you're just out there to put another little mark on your little list of things to do.

These students were struggling to connect, be accountable, and work for justice. Some people within the university—staff, students, faculty—were helping them do it. The university's reward system, however, did not respond to the activities of those who influenced the students. This work is not measured or counted as important, compared to individualistic accomplishments like publishing papers for faculty and taking tests for students. In the U.S. higher education system, tenure, promotions, and grades depend primarily on individualistic measures. Minimal resources are dedicated to rewarding the work of connection and justice. Granted, advising and teaching awards do exist, providing recognition and limited financial rewards. Some universities and colleges also have introduced mentoring and community action programs that work against the individualistic status quo, and departments like women's studies and ethnic studies often attempt to support these alternative educational priorities. In recent years, community based learning programs have gained momentum. On the whole, though, these programs and awards do not disrupt the power of academic individualism, as they are attached to an existing structure rather than altering the structure itself. Their results are important, but often marginalized.

Meanwhile, those who are committed to this transformative work go out of their way to continue it—a staff member leading a Head Start mother toward college, a white professor taking extra time with an African American student, a professor of Afro-American history connecting her subject material to the concerns of a low-income white male student, an older Chicana student serving as mentor and friend to her young colleague.

Perhaps most important, these four students considered themselves accountable to groups in their lives, and they acted on those commitments. Connections important to the students ranged from neighborhood to ethnic group, to people of the same economic class, to families involved in Head Start. Those are contexts in which anti-individualist values can be fostered. Since meaningful connections are not limited to geographically bounded populations, and a person can be a part of more than one community, we can view society as comprising many interrelated groups that have the potential to foster anti-individualist values. The students' important connections involved contexts in which people considered themselves accountable, in which people would go out of their way for each other. Issues of justice emerged in the students' discussions of their values. All four identified their work for justice as being in some way with "their own" people—but each knew that his or her own people were not a homogeneous community. They recognized different kinds of heterogeneity, and struggled for common ground without domination. None had clear answers to the dilemmas of connecting across differences, but all were engaged in the work of building those connections. Based on values of connection, accountability, and justice, the students were preparing themselves for the difficult work of healing and transformation that our society needs. Those who influenced them were doing some of the most important educational work of our time.

Academic Women and Community Values

Those influential staff, students, and faculty were not operating as part of an anti-individualist or communitarian movement in academe. But their separate actions could help build such a movement if people would learn to recognize patterns and reinterpret actions within a context of community building. It is notable, for example, that the university people named as influential by all four students were women. That was a pattern in my interviews. While my study is qualitative and based on a limited number of participants, that apparent trend is worthy of further exploration. Such a pattern supports the view that women often are effective academic citizens, seriously engaged in the missions of teaching and service. If women in higher education are personally influential beyond their numbers, it would be consistent with women's socialization in many segments of U.S. culture to be empathic and connected to others. I believe that women of color and white working-class women in academe can be particularly effective in reaching out, because of the values of accountability and connection embedded in our life experiences. Some have begun the task of clarifying issues related to this work.

Beatrice Medicine, for example, has insightfully examined her commitments as a Lakota anthropologist. Her theories about cultural mediation are rooted in activities: writing letters for elders to government agencies, testifying in a treaty case, disseminating information to Indian activists about private and public funding sources, helping Native people research genealogies, presenting interpretations of her own and other scholars' research on her home reservation (Medicine 282–96). Medicine is accountable because of the structures and expectations of the communities to which she belongs; her life is not framed by individualism, and her perspective is solidly grounded in Lakota traditions.

Many of the authors in the anthologies *Working Class Women in the Academy: Laborers in the Knowledge Factory* (ed. Tokarczyk and Fay) and *Spirit, Space, and Survival: African American Women in (White) Academe* (ed. James and Farmer) also address accountability to their communities of origin. These women realize that maintaining their commitments goes against the grain of the higher education establishment. Joy James describes the conflict for African American scholars trying to live within and contribute to their cultures and communities:

Commercial academic *hougons*[5] know that objectifying the community for print promotes tenure. Theorizing responsive to community is costly in academe. Alienation, a signature of academia, pays. In belonging to a people seeking freedom from colonization, African American academics face issues of responsibility and accountability, unrecognized by White colleagues. (James 42)

Writing and teaching about community ties is one way to change the academy. Lillian S. Robinson communicates to her students a "notion of connectedness," in contrast to the hypocrisy about community she sees among the dominant forces in academe:

There is incredible power in the individualistic ideas of the dominant society, but you can try to communicate that connectedness as a real strength in the lives of working-class women. . . . But the academic world tells us we are playing that game [of individualism], and at the same time, it holds a fundamental myth about itself—that it is a community of scholars. (Ellis and Robinson 44–45)

bell hooks tells working-class academics we have a choice regarding whether or not our education will separate us from our past. The decision to stay connected and committed, she says, requires explicit attention.

Maintaining awareness of class differences, nurturing ties with the poor and working-class people who are our most intimate kin, our comrades in struggle, transforms and enriches our intellectual experience. Education as the practice of freedom becomes not a force that fragments or separates, but one that brings us closer, expanding our definitions of home and community. (hooks 109)

Like the university students' stories, these women's statements demonstrate that modernity did not destroy the practice of operating with a community rather than an individualist framework. Such a framework provides cultural preparation to work against the odds to transform academe. Their ideas can support a movement for accountability and social justice at our colleges and universities.

My Community Influences

It may be useful to provide a glimpse of how my own background has influenced my interest in linking social justice, community values, and education. My approach to education grew out of discussions with and overheard conversations among my mother and aunts, who were one-room school teachers in rural western Minnesota in the 1930s and 1940s. While they worked at the elementary level and their students were relatively homogeneous, their experiences did provide lessons about justice and community. Through stories of teachers trying to control ethnic conflict among students (in my home area during my parents' generation the fights were primarily German American versus Irish American), of debates over rules requiring women teachers to resign their positions when they married, of struggles between our mothers' club and a school district administrator who did not value rural students, I learned that every person is entitled to an education, and that working-class women have a great deal to say about education and community life.

I also learned to think in community terms about almost everything. The dual context of our Irish Catholic heritage and the economic marginalization small farmers have experienced in this country gave me a sense of urgency about working to make things better as a group, and for the group. "We" had opinions about what the British have been doing to Irish Catholics. "We" as an extended family were involved in the National Farmers' Organization in the 1960s, and we measured neighbors according to whether or not they were in that struggle for survival with the rest of the community.

Like many other working-class women, I am suspicious of joining mainstream efforts for societal renewal. I may be less suspicious than some because we were farmers, not urban laborers, so the oppressive classes were not an intimate part of our daily reality. We also (eventually) owned our quarter-section of land. Small as it was, it was ours; we were not sharecroppers or wage laborers. Because we are white and of Irish descent—not African, not Mexican—the United States was a place to which my great-grandparents could flee and be settled by the Catholic church. My awareness of colonialism and land theft did not transfer from the British-Irish context to the white immigrant–American Indian context until I went to college. Like many whites on the margins, I believed in America, sort of—and that belief was based in part on handed-down immigrant gratitude, in part on democratic potential, in part on ignorance of and lack of attention to racism and other wrongs.

In higher education, my background has led me to community-focused work where I could find it: most notably, a community college inner-city outreach program; a Catholic women's college with social justice values; and a university commission on women, which did community organizing within the university in an effort to transform educational and employment practices. My own best experiences of community at the university occurred in a work setting—the office of equal opportunity and affirmative action, the commission on women's administrative home. This was the most diverse group of people with whom I have ever worked—women and men of different ethnicities, economic backgrounds, sexual orientations, and religions—and also the most committed to each other.

Building a Movement to Transform Academe

Many of us know from experience that individualism has not totally taken over this country. We also know the concrete realities—that in the dominant educational, political, and economic systems, individualism can quite directly help a person gain power, obtain or maintain status in the mainstream, and acquire wealth.

We have the contextual knowledge to begin moving academe toward less individualistic cultural paths. Those alternative paths will depend on understanding how our own complex heritages have related to individualism, and where our sources of hope for change reside. As Frazer and Lacey argue, feminism, antiracism, and other academic/political movements for justice are potential correctives to the false dualisms of liberal individualist versus communitarian debates. As we move forward, I believe we should engage with mainstream scholars like Robert Bellah. I know that some feminists would disagree, seeing his work as too firmly caught in a universalizing approach to community and commitments. The possibilities for alliance, nonetheless, are important enough for us to take the risk. Such engagement is likely to be frustrating, as we try to move beyond accusations of exclusive thinking on the one hand, and divisiveness on the other. Frustration and conflict are to be expected as we build both intellectual and political connections across our differences.

Telling the stories linking connections, attention to difference, accountability, and social justice is one step toward transforming academe's cultural expectations. To systematically move beyond scattered

contributions, a movement to challenge individualism in higher education will require pressuring institutions to take such cultural
knowledge seriously as we develop curricula, policies, and job descriptions. It will call for strategizing and political work to change
academic reward systems. Such a movement also will require naming
individualism when we see it, in structures as well as ideologies, and
pointing out the ways it serves unfair domination and bigotry. It will
require moving away from dualistic thinking about the principles of
individual rights and community responsibilities. It will require patience with each other, forgiveness without denying wrongs, and sustained mutual support. Perhaps most important, it will require those
of us who work in higher education to collaboratively take more
risks, as we push our institutions toward accountability and justice.

NOTES

1. The conference I attended was "Thinking, Writing, Teaching, and Creating Social Justice," at the University of Minnesota in April 1994.

2. My friend's conference was "Homelessness: Renewing Our Commitment," sponsored by the National Coalition for the Homeless. It took place in
Minneapolis, Minnesota.

3. In *Feminism without Illusions* Fox-Genovese's approach to the individualism question is somewhat problematic. She engages in dualistic thinking
similar to that of Bellah et al., whose work I criticize later in the essay. She
also seems unduly focused on white middle-class feminism in the United
States, and does not discuss feminist contributions to community. (A book
providing important contrast is *Feminism and Community*, edited by Penny
Weiss and Marilyn Friedman.) But like Bellah and his coauthors, Fox-Genovese nonetheless identifies some key social problems related to individualism, particularly among the dominant classes.

4. Frazer and Lacey provide an extended discussion of the concept "negative view of freedom," which can be traced to the work of Isaiah Berlin.

5. See Berlin, *Against the Current* 152.

WORKS CITED

Bellah, Robert, Richard Madsen, William M. Sullivan, Ann Swidler, and
Steven M. Tipton. *The Good Society*. New York: Knopf, 1991.
———. *Habits of the Heart: Individualism and Commitment in American Life*.
Berkeley: University of California Press, 1985.

Berlin, Isaiah. *Against the Current: Essays in the History of Ideas*. London: Hogarth Press, 1979.

Ellis, Kate, and Lillian S. Robinson. "Class Discussion: A Dialogue between Kate Ellis and Lillian S. Robinson." In *Working Class Women in the Academy: Laborers in the Knowledge Factory,* ed. M. Tokarczyk and E. Fay, 25–46. Boston: University of Massachusetts Press, 1993.

Etzioni, Amitai. *The Spirit of Community: The Reinvention of American Society.* New York: Touchstone, 1993.

———, ed. *The Essential Communitarian Reader*. Lanham, MD: Rowman and Littlefield, 1998.

Evans, Sara M., and Harry C. Boyte. *Free Spaces: The Sources of Democratic Change in America*. New York: Harper and Row, 1986.

Fox-Genovese, Elizabeth. *Feminism without Illusions: A Critique of Individualism*. Chapel Hill: University of North Carolina Press, 1991.

Fraser, Nancy. "What's Critical About Critical Theory?" In *Feminism as Critique: On the Politics of Gender,* ed. Seyla Benhabib and Drucilla Cornell, 31–56. Minneapolis: University of Minnesota Press, 1987.

Frazer, Elizabeth, and Nicola Lacey. *The Politics of Community: A Feminist Critique of the Liberal-Communitarian Debate*. Toronto: University of Toronto Press, 1993.

Friedman, Marilyn. "Feminism and Modern Friendship: Dislocating the Community." In *Feminism and Community,* ed. Penny A. Weiss and Marilyn Friedman. Philadelphia: Temple University Press, 1995.

hooks, bell. "Keeping Close to Home: Class and Education." In *Working Class Women in the Academy: Laborers in the Knowledge Factory,* ed. M. Tokarczyk and E. Fay, 99–111. Boston: University of Massachusetts Press, 1993.

James, Joy. "African Philosophy, Theory, and 'Living Thinkers.'" In *Spirit, Space, and Survival: African American Women in (White) Academe,* ed. Joy James and Ruth Farmer, 31–46. New York: Routledge, 1993.

James, Joy, and Ruth Farmer, eds. *Spirit, Space, and Survival: African American Women in (White) Academe*. New York: Routledge, 1993.

Medicine, Beatrice. "Learning to Be an Anthropologist and Remaining 'Native.'" In *Applied Anthropology in America,* ed. E. M. Eddy and W. L. Partridge, 282–96. New York: Columbia University Press, 1987.

Personal Narratives Group. "Origins." In *Interpreting Women's Lives: Feminist Theory and Personal Narratives,* ed. The Personal Narratives Group, 3–16. Bloomington: Indiana University Press, 1989.

Phelan, Shane. "Getting Specific about Community." In *Getting Specific: Postmodern Lesbian Politics*. Minneapolis: University of Minnesota Press, 1994.

Reagon, Bernice Johnson. "Coalition Politics: Turning the Century." In *Home Girls: A Black Feminist Anthology,* ed. Barbara Smith, 356–68. New York: Kitchen Table, Women of Color Press, 1983.

Tokarczyk, Michelle M., and Elizabeth A. Fay, eds. *Working Class Women in the Academy: Laborers in the Knowledge Factory.* Boston: University of Massachusetts Press, 1993.

Weiss, Penny A. "Feminism and Communitarianism: Exploring the Relationship." In *Gendered Community: Rousseau, Sex, and Politics,* 121–48. New York: New York University Press, 1993.

Weiss, Penny A., and Marilyn Friedman, eds. *Feminism and Community.* Philadelphia: Temple University Press, 1995.

West, Cornel. *Prophetic Thought in Postmodern Times: Beyond Eurocentrism and Multiculturalism.* Vol. 1. Monroe, ME: Common Courage Press, 1993.

Young, Iris Marion. "Impartiality and the Civic Public: Some Implications of Feminist Critiques of Moral and Political Theory." In *Feminism as Critique: On the Politics of Gender,* ed. Seyla Benhabib and Drucilla Cornell, 57–76. Minneapolis: University of Minnesota Press, 1987.

———. *Justice and the Politics of Difference.* Princeton: Princeton University Press, 1990.

Editors and Contributors

Editors

Rose Brewer is the Morse-Alumni Distinguished Teaching Professor and interim chair of Afro-American and African studies at the University of Minnesota. She is the coeditor of *Bridges of Power: Women's Multicultural Alliances* (New Society Publishers). Her current research on adolescent family formation and change is an analysis of the social reproduction of motherhood for young African American women. Her book *Engendering the "Race"* will be published in the Sage Gender Lens Series. She has published widely on Black feminism and race, class, and gender.

Mary Louise Fellows is the Everett Fraser Professor of Law at the University of Minnesota. She writes and teaches in the areas of law and violence against women, women and property, and women and taxes. She was the coeditor of a special issue on law and feminism for *Signs* in 1994. She coauthored *Law and Violence Against Women* (Carolina Academic Press) and coedited *Taxing America* (New York University Press). Her most recent publications are "Rocking the Tax Code (A Case Study of Child-Care Employment-Related Expenses)," *Yale Journal of Law and Feminism*, and a coauthored article, "Becoming Respectable: A Matter of Prostitution," *New York University Law Review*.

Shirley Garner is a professor and chair of English and a former director of the Center for Advanced Feminist Studies at the University of Minnesota. She writes and teaches on Shakespeare, autobiography, and feminist psychoanalytic literary theory and criticism. She is the coeditor of *Antifeminism in the Academy* (Routledge), *Shakespearean Tragedy and Gender* (Indiana University Press), *The (M)other Tongue: Essays in Feminist Psychoanalytic Interpretation* (Cornell University

Press), and *Interpreting Women's Lives: Feminist Theory and Personal Narratives* (Indiana University Press).

Amy Kaminsky is a professor and former chair of the department of women's studies at the University of Minnesota. She is the author of *Reading the Body Politic: Latin American Women Writers and Feminist Criticism* and *After Exile: Writing the Latin American Diaspora,* and the editor of a bilingual anthology, *Waterlilies/Flores del Agua: Spanish Women Writers from the Fourteenth to the Nineteenth Century,* all from the University of Minnesota Press.

Jane Olmsted is the director of women's studies and an assistant professor of English at Western Kentucky University. Her publications include an article on Paule Marshall in *African American Review,* another on Leslie Marmon Silko's *Almanac of the Dead* in *Contemporary Literature,* and a chapter on Langston Hughes in a collection on the Orphic theme in African American literature (Garland Publishers). She is currently collaborating with Elizabeth Oakes on a collection of poetry by Kentucky feminists and activists.

Jennifer L. Pierce is an associate professor of American studies and an affiliate with the Center for Advanced Feminist Studies, Women's Studies and the Law School at the University of Minnesota. Her first book, *Gender Trials: Emotional Lives in Contemporary Law Firms,* was published by the University of California Press and was nominated by the American Sociological Association for the best book on sex and gender. She has also published articles on women and work, feminist theory, and feminist methods. Currently she is doing research on the effects of the backlash against affirmative action on white women and men and women of color in California.

Naomi Scheman is a professor of philosophy and women's studies at the University of Minnesota and a former associate editor of *Signs.* Her collected papers in feminist epistemology, *Engenderings: Constructions of Knowledge, Authority, and Privilege,* were published by Routledge.

Contributors

Alice Adams, a Rockefeller Scholar for 1992-93, is an associate professor of English and women's studies at Miami University of Ohio.

She is the author of *Reproducing the Womb: Images of Childbirth in Science, Feminist Theory, and Literature* (Cornell University Press). Her published articles include "Out of the Womb: The Future of the Uterine Metaphor," *Feminist Studies*; "Remolding the Body: The Surgeon as Sculptor," in *Bodily Discourses: Essaying the Body* (State University of New York Press); and "The American Short Story in the Cybernetic Age" in the *Journal of the Short Story in English*. Her current project is about reproduction and mothering that occur outside nuclear, heterosexual traditions: lesbian mothering, biological male mothering, and interspecies/cybernetic/interracial reproduction.

VèVè A. Clark is an associate professor of African and Caribbean literatures in the department of African American studies at the University of California, Berkeley. Her many published articles include "Katherine Dunham: Method Dancing or the Memory of Difference," in *African American Genius in Modern Dance*; and "When Womb Waters Break: The Emergence of Haitian New Theatre (1953–1987)," *Callaloo*. She coedited and contributed an essay to the *Signs* anthology *Revising the Word and the World*. Her most recent book is an edited collection entitled *Ritual*, forthcoming from the Anthology Film Archives in New York.

Sharon Doherty is an assistant professor of women's studies and anthropology, and the director of the Abigail Quigley McCarthy Center for Women at the College of St. Catherine, in St. Paul, Minnesota. She also works at Hope Community, an organization in south central Minneapolis that builds community through affordable housing, active education, and organizing.

Marilyn Frye, a Rockefeller Scholar in 1990-91, is a professor of philosophy at Michigan State University, where she also teaches feminist theory in the women's studies program. She is the author of *The Politics of Reality: Essays in Feminist Theory* and *Willful Virgin: Essays in Feminism, 1976–1992* both from the Crossing Press. She has also published numerous articles on philosophy and feminist theory, including "The Necessity of Differences—Constructing a Positive Category of Women," *Signs*.

Joanna Kadi is a writer, poet, and musician. She is the author of *Thinking Class: Sketches from a Cultural Worker* (South End Press) and the editor of *Food for Our Grandmothers: Writings by Arab-American and Arab-Canadian Feminists* (South End Press). She studies Arabic, West African, and Afro-Cuban drumming, and regularly performs.

Peggy Pascoe is an associate professor and the Beekman Chair of Pacific and Northwest History at the University of Oregon, where she teaches courses on the history of race, gender, and sexuality. Her published articles include "Miscegenation Law, Court Cases and Ideologies of 'Race' in Twentieth-Century America," *Journal of American History*. She is currently working on a book tentatively titled *What Comes Naturally: Race, Gender, and Marriage Law, 1865 to the Present.*

Cheri Register earned a Ph.D. in Germanic languages and literatures from the University of Chicago in 1973 and taught women's studies courses at the University of Minnesota (1974–80), where she was also employed by the Scandinavian department. She now lives in Minneapolis, where she teaches creative writing and does freelance editing. She has published extensively in the areas of feminist literary criticism and Scandinavian women's literature, in both the United States and Sweden. More recently, she has authored two books: *Living with Chronic Illness: Patience and Passion* (Bantam), which was re-released in 1999 as *The Chronic Illness Experience* (Hazelden Books); and *"Are Those Kids Yours?" American Families with Children Adopted from Other Countries* (Free Press), as well as numerous essays. A documentary memoir of working-class life at midcentury is forthcoming.

Mary Romero is the author of *Maid in the U.S.A.* (Routledge) and the coeditor of *Women's Untold Stories: Breaking Silence, Talking Back, Voicing Complexity* (Routledge), *Challenging Fronteras: Structuring Latina and Latino Lives in the U.S.* (Routledge), and *Women and Work: Exploring Race, Ethnicity and Class* (Sage). Her recent articles have appeared in *Journal of Gender, Social Policy and the Law; Signs: Journal of Women in Culture and Society; University of Miami Law Review; Harvard Educational Review;* and *Race and Society.* She currently teaches in the School of Justice Studies at Arizona State University.

Kathryn Shanley is an associate professor in the Native American studies department at the University of Montana. Born and raised on the Fort Peck Reservation in Montana, she is an enrolled member of the Assiniboine tribe. In addition to university teaching, Shanley has offered seminars in several tribal community colleges. She has written many essays on American Indian writers, Native American literature in general, and autobiography; a book on the poetry and fiction of James Welch (Blackfeet/Gros Ventre), *"Only an Indian": Reading James Welch,* is forthcoming from the University of Oklahoma Press.

Mrinalini Sinha, a Rockefeller Scholar at the University of Minnesota in 1990-91, is an associate professor of history at Southern Illinois University at Carbondale. She is the author of *Colonial Masculinity: The "Manly Englishman" and the "Effeminate Bengali" in the Late Nineteenth Century* (Manchester University Press), and the editor of *Selections from Mother India* (University of Michigan Press). She is the coeditor of the collection *Feminisms and Internationalism* (Blackwell) and serves as the North American coeditor of *Gender and History.* She is currently working on a book on the emergence of a nationalist "Indian" modernity in the interwar period.

Edén E. Torres earned her Ph.D. in American studies at the University of Minnesota, where she is now an assistant professor in Chicana studies and women's studies. Active in both institutional and grassroots organizations serving the needs of groups as diverse as migrant workers and young urban Latinas, Torres struggles daily to balance family, academic, and community responsibilities. While "authentic" teaching and a mutually enriching relationship with her students remain her personal objectives—and publishing scholarly articles a necessary responsibility—Torres hopes to spend more time on the creative writing she had to largely abandon in pursuit of her doctorate.

Diana L. Vélez is an associate professor at the University of Iowa. Her publications include *Reclaiming Medusa: Short Stories by Contemporary Puerto Rican Women* (Aunt Lute Press), now in its second edition, as well as numerous articles on such twentieth-century Puerto Rican writers as Julia de Burgos, Rosario Ferré, Luis Rafael Sánchez, and Ana Lydia Vega.

Kath Weston, a Rockefeller Scholar at the University of Minnesota in 1989–90, is an associate professor of anthropology at Arizona State University West, in Phoenix. She is the author of *Long Slow Burn:*

Sexuality and Social Science (Routledge), *Render Me, Gender Me* (Columbia University Press), and *Families We Choose: Lesbians, Gays, Kinship* (Columbia University Press).

Rhonda M. Williams is a political economist and an associate professor of Afro-American studies at the University of Maryland; she is also an affiliate faculty member in women's studies and in American studies. Her writings have appeared in *Feminist Studies; Review of Black Political Economy; Review of Radical Political Economics; Review of Economics and Statistics;* and numerous edited volumes. She coedited *Race, Markets, and Social Outcomes* with Patrick Mason (Kluwer-Nijhoff), and until recently was an editor for *Feminist Economics.*

Index

Abbott, Sydney, 53
abortion, 6–7, 77. *See also* reproductive rights
academic environment: culture of, 13; described, 267, 283–310, 312–15, 319, 322, 327–46, 261–65; personal relation to, 133
academic persona, 151, 153–54. *See also* identity
academics: reproduction of, 283–310; working-class, 187–203, 327–46, 369
accountability: academic, 351–52, 358–61, 367–69, 371; and academic feminism, 200
Achebe, Chinua, 30
ACLU, and same-sex marriage, 103–4, 108
activism: defined, 211, 227; academic, 347–48, 362
Adams, Alice, 6
Addams, Jane, 300, 357
adoption, and American Indian kinship, 221–22
advocacy, and academics, 200. *See also* accountability
affirmative action, 18, 284, 289, 293–94, 322, 371
Africa, identification with, 274, 276
African American studies, 20, 22–24, 26, 266, 278. *See also* Black studies
Afrocentricity, 20–27
Age of Consent Act (India), 176
agency. *See* sovereignty
AIDS, and racism, 277
Alarcón, Norma, 243, 251
Allen, Paula Gunn, 30, 219
American Indian Freedom of Religion Act, 223

American Indian women's history, 204–32
American Sociological Association, 284, 286–87
"American" sociology, 292–300
Amerindian traditional knowledge, 242
Andrews, Lynn, 220
anger, in academia, 263, 311–26
Anglo-conformity, 9, 11, 27–28, 32, 34–35
anthropologist, virtual, defined, 137–38
anthropology: and American Indian culture, 213; and difference, 157
antiessentialism, 48–49, 56–57
antifeminism, 2; and ERA, 96–97
Anzaldúa, Gloria, 238, 245, 250, 252–54
Aristotle, 357
Armah, Ayi Kwei, 25–26
art, functions of, 244–46
artists, as eccentrics, 244
Asante, Molefi K., 20, 24
assimilation, 13; of American Indians, 215–16; Chicana/o, 249; in education, 35
audience: elite, 239; problematic of, 205
authority, in pedagogy, 22
autonomy: construct of, 66–67; women's, 67, 79–80. *See also* individualism
Aztec culture, 242–43, 250–51

Baehr, Ninia, 104
Baehr v. Lewin, 97, 104, 106, 108–9
Baker, James, 92
Bakhtin, Mikhail, 26
balkanization, cultural, 40
Banton, Michael, 211
Baraka, Amiri, 268
Barsh, Russell, 211–12
Barwick, Paul, 97–99

Bayh, Birch, 100
Bellah, Robert, 354–56, 358, 361, 371
Bellin, Saul, 33
Bengal, and *sati*, 180–81
Bernal, Martin, 24
Berry, Sylvia, 272
Bettelheim, Bruno, 196
Bhabha, Homi, 37
bilingualism, 34
binarism: limits of, 174–75. *See also* dualism
Black studies, 12, 21, 24–25
Blackness: defined, 278; ideology of, 262–63; and queerness, 266–82
"blame the victim," and academics, 296–97, 301
Blank, Robert H., 64–67
Blaut, J. M., 20, 28
Bloom, Allan, 20–22, 25–26, 357
Boorstin, Daniel, 357
borders. *See* boundaries
boundaries: of Blackness, 268, 275–78; and identity, 252; personal/political, 205
Brant, Beth, 204, 225–26
Brathwaite, Edward Kamau, 34–35
Briggs, John V., 101
British Empire. *See* imperialism
Bryant, Anita, 101
Buddhism: and anger, 263; and social justice, 311–26
Bureau of Indian Affairs, 215
Burton, Antoinette, 173
Bush, George, 216

Cade (Bambara), Toni, 53
Callahan, Joan C., 68
Cannon, Dr. Katie Geneva, 331
canon, ethnic, 30
cante ista, 225–27
capitalism: and academics, 332–33, 335, 338; ideology of, 338; and nature of work, 339; and working class, 344
careers, academic, and class, 200
caregiver, woman as. *See* motherhood, discourse of, and reproductive rights
Castillo, Ana, 245
categories: and generalizations, 49–51; racial and sexual, 90, 92–93, 104, 108–9, 141–42, 149–50, 174; resistance to,

252–53; Western, 338, 340. *See also* motherhood, discourse of, and reproductive rights
category, "other" as, 252–53
Catholic Church and culture, 241, 243, 251
center/periphery, academic. *See* marginality, academic
Cerullo, Margaret, 277
Cervantes, Lorna Dee, 245
Chang, Kevin, 107
Charboneau, 219
Chavez, Gloria, 360–61, 364
Chesler, Phyllis, 73–74, 82
Chicana/o culture, 233–59; and community, 134–35, 361
Chicanisma, defined, 240
Chicano Brown Power movement, 235, 240, 245, 251; social issues, 283–84
Chodorow, Nancy, 49, 51, 54–56
Chodron, Thubten, 320, 322
choice: language of, 71–75, 77, 79; and domesticity, 198–99. *See also* individualism; reproductive rights
Christ, Carol, 132
Cisler, Lucina, 63–64
Cisneros, Sandra, 246, 249–50, 253
citizen, defined, 349–50
citizenship, and cultural literacy, 11
civil rights, 195; and foundational narratives, 9; and same-sex marriage, 108. *See also* rights, discourse of
civil rights movement, 12, 16, 20, 32, 342–43; and sex categories, 90
Clark, Alonzo Thomas, 16
Clark, VèVè A., 5
class: and academic environment, 21, 200, 263, 327–46, 369–70; accountability for, 133; and American Indian culture, 209; and Chicana writers, 134–35; and identity, 187–203; and personal/professional life, 234, 253; and work, 207. *See also* constructionism; loyalty
class identity, and Chicana/os, 249
class location, assignment of, 341
class shifting, 243–59. *See also* class
classism, 177–78; and Mexican-Americans, 238; and rights discourse, 63, 76, 78–79. *See also* class; working class
code-switching, 236

cohabitation, legal status of, 91
collective memory. *See* memory, collective, and colonization
collective voice. *See* voice
Collins, Patricia Hill, 155, 261
colonization: culture of, 10; definition of, 10–11; theorists of, 57
color, women of, and postmodern theory, 52–57
Commission on Sexual Orientation and the Law (Hawaii), 106
communitarian movement, 354, 371
community: and academics, 352–53; Chicana/o, 238; definitions of, 358–60, 362, 366; and individualism, 262; Mexican-American, 233–59; and political ideology, 251; and professional life, 254; and public discourse, 252–53; and storytelling, 133–36
competition, academic, 288, 293, 313, 351, 353, 361
computer technology, 12
Confucius, 357
connection. *See* accountability
consciousness, double, 334
Constitution, U.S., 9–10
constructionism: of class, 338; defined, 48; and essentialist critique, 54–55; politics of, 57; and same-sex marriage, 88, 96, 109–10
"cooling out," in academics, 296–99
counterculture, 89
creativity, and social justice, 234, 244, 253
Creolization, 24, 34–35, 37–38
Crothers, Charles, 288, 293, 299
cultural pluralism, 35
culture wars, 22, 25
curriculum: changing, 21; and classism, 343; and liberal individualism, 372; and sociology, 300, 302
Curzon, Lord, 174
custody, lesbian, 73–74
cynicism: and power, 238; and cultural critique, 254

Dahl, Tora, 196
Dalai Lama, 324
Daly, Mary, 53
Davis, Angela, 63, 65, 76
Dearborne, Mary, 219–20

deconstruction, and working class experiences, 328
Defense of Marriage Act (DOMA), 87
Delano, Jamie, 220–21
Delany, Martin, 270
Deloria, Ella Cara, 222–23
Deloria, Vine, Jr., 213–14, 216
democracy, and individualism, 349
Derrida, Jacques, 26
deviance theories, 295. *See also* pathology, as critique
Diaspora, African, 14–15, 17, 19; and legislation, 41; literacy, 41; literature, 11
Diderot, 30
difference: and anthropology, 157; defined, 169–70; and feminism, 168–86; and retrofit, 6
Diop, Cheikh Anta, 25
discourse: public, 245, 253; racial, and sexuality, 266–82; sexual, 103. *See also* power relations
discourses, hostile to women, 61–62
discrimination, and same-sex marriage, 95, 98, 104–5, 109
distinction, sexual. *See* discrimination, and same-sex marriage
diversity: in academics, 278; as buzzword, 29; in curriculum and classroom, 27; in sociology, 291; and tokenism, 174–75. *See* monocultural environment
Dixon, Timothy, 278
Doherty, Sharon, 262, 264
Dolphy, Eric, 17
domestic containment, 89
domestic partnership laws, 103, 106–7
domesticity, and choice, 198–99
Doña Marina. *See* La Malinche
Douglas, Mary, 357
downsizing, corporate, 18
Du Bois, W. E. B., 31, 300, 334
dualism, 317, 357. *See also* binarism, limits of; categories
Dunham, Katherine, 17
Dye, Eva Emery, 219

economics: of American Indian communities, 215; and common life, 354. *See also* reproductive rights, economics of
education, and class, 188–89, 191, 193–95, 198

Egan, Janet Malenchek, 287–88
Eitzen, D. Stanley, 289
El Movimiento, 235
elections of 1977, and same-sex marriage,
    101–2
elitism: academic, 13–14, 236–37, 239,
    254, 294–96, 301, 329, 334, 340, 352–53;
    in feminism, 177–78; masculine, 243.
    See also classism; privilege
emancipation, women's, and British Em-
    pire, 173
Emberley, Julia V., 204, 225
Emerson, Ralph Waldo, 33
Empire, British. *See* imperialism
epistemes, 25
Epps, Edgar G., 286
Equal Rights Amendment, 89–92, 94–95,
    98–101; defeat of, 102
Ervin, Sam, 96–97, 100
Escamill, Edna, 249
essentialism, 47–60; and African-Ameri-
    can consciousness, 275–76; defined,
    48–49, 58n. 4; and postmodernist cri-
    tique, 54–57
ethics, and academics, 311, 323–25
ethnic pluralism, and multiculturalism, 32
ethnic studies, 12, 342, 367; and commu-
    nity, 361; compared to sociology,
    295–96, 299–300
ethnicity: and community, 254; defined,
    212; Mexican-American, 249–51. *See
    also* loyalty, ethnic
ethnocentrism, 47–60; consequences of,
    22; and difference, 6
Etzioni, Amitai, 354
Eurocentricity, 20–27, 29, 33, 132
exclusion, institutional, 19, 348–49
expediency, and rights discourse, 63

family: analysis of Black, 270–71, 276; de-
    cline of, 89; defined, 274
family tropes and nationalism, 270–76
Fanon, Frantz, 26, 30
fascism, 21
Faubus, Orville, 190
feminism: aims of, 5; and British imperi-
    alism, 170–74; critiques of, 133; de-
    fined, 240; historicity of, 133; and na-
    tionalism, in India, 175–78; and peda-
    gogy, 22; Scandinavian, 196; Western,

and individualism, 349; Western and
    non-Western, 168–86
feminist family reformers, 94–96, 98, 109
Feminists for Life of America, 77
Fernández, Roberta, 248
Fiedler, Leslie, 217
Firestone, Shulamith, 49, 51, 55–56, 71
fit, and retrofit, 8–36
Fletcher, Joseph, 67
Foley, Dan, 104
folklore, and intellectualism, 244; urban,
    251
Foucault, Michel, 26, 245
Fox-Genovese, Elizabeth, 349
Franklin, Benjamin, 33–34
Fraser, Nancy, 6, 47, 49, 51–54, 56, 238,
    357
Frazer, Elizabeth, 352, 371
Freeman, Orville, 190, 192
Friedan, Betty, 196
Friedman, Marilyn, 360
Frye, Marilyn, 5–6, 52

Gabbard, Mike, 106
Gaite, Carmen Martin, 316–17
Gallop, Jane, 197, 199
Gamson, Zelda, 357
Ganguly, Kadambini, 175
Gates, Henry Louis, Jr., 20, 22–24, 26, 211,
    239
gay liberation, 89
gaze, institutional, 313–14, 325
gender roles, American Indian tradi-
    tional, 223–24
gender switching, 233, 240, 243
gender and sex. *See* sex and gender
gender neutrality, 352
gender theory, and sociology, 300
genealogy, women's intellectual, 55
Generation X, 12
gifted child syndrome. *See* narcissistic
    disorder, and academia
Gilligan, Carol, 49–51, 54–56, 76–77
Gilroy, Paul, 274
Goldberg, David Theo, 36
Gonzales, Sylvia Alicia, 243–45, 252
Goodman, Andrew, 19
Gould, Stephen Jay, 211
graduate school, and women of color,
    283–310. *See also* academics

graffiti, 251
Green, Rayna, 217
"gringo" history, 251
Gudvangen, Hazel, 192–93, 198, 202
Gurin, Patricia, 286

Hall, Stuart, 12
Hannerz, Ulf, 34–35
Hare, Julia, 268, 274
Hare, Nathan, 268, 274
Harrison, Jim, 216
Hartsock, Nancy C. M., 56
Hauser, Rita, 89
health, and anger, 323
"healthy sexuality." *See* pathology, as
    critique
heterogeneity, and community, 360, 367.
    See also diversity
heterosexism, and Black community, 264
heyoka, 223–24
Highwater, Jamake, 220
Hill, Anita, 272–73
Hilliard, Asa, 24
Hindu culture, 178–81
Hirsch, E. D., 20
Hirsch, Steven, 33
historicizing feminism, 133, 168–86
history: American Indian women's, 134,
    204–32; Canadian Native, 210–11; "tun-
    nel," 28–29
Holiday, Billie, 17
Holley, John, 289
home culture. *See* class; loyalty, ethnic
homosexuality. *See* queerness
hooks, bell, 52–53, 275, 352, 369
households, female-headed, 268, 271
human rights, and individualism, 349
humor: and religion, 223; and representa-
    tions, 213–14; and story, 225
Hunter, Nan, 110
Hurston, Zora Neale, 30
hybridity, 36, 133, 138–40, 142–45, 151,
    153, 157. *See also* categories
Hyde, Lewis, 222
hypermasculinity, 235
hypersexuality, and Blackness, 270, 274

identity: academic, 137–67, 288, 314;
    American, 34; and borders, 252; class,
    332–33; and common good, 357; ethnic,

250; gender, 49; pluralism in, 47, 57;
    and racism, 342; and storytelling,
    131–36. *See also* academic persona;
    class; queerness; sex and gender
identity groups, reaching beyond, 364
imperialism: history of, 170; impact in
    Britain, 171–74; nationalist and El
    Movimiento, 235, 251
India, and British colonialism, 168–86
"Indian," definitions of, 214–16, 221,
    228n. 6
Indian National Congress, 176
Indian Princess. *See* Pocahontas para-
    digm
individual rights: discourse of, 67, 70–72,
    77, 79, 81; economy of, 76; *see also*
    rights
individualism: and academics, 284, 293,
    299, 347–74; costs of, 262, 355; legacy
    of, 348–53; and storytelling, 131
infanticide, and reproductive rights, 65
infants, women as, 79
Ingram, Lawaune, 17
intellectuals: Chicana, 233–59; profes-
    sional and working-class, 239, 187–203,
    327–46; role of, in Latin American cul-
    ture, 244–45
intelligence, defined, 339; location of, 263
interdependence and community, 360
interdisciplinary studies, 287; and peda-
    gogy, 31, 33; and race/gender, 300–301
international issues, and race theory, 285
international studies, and sociology, 300
Internet, 12
intraethnic relations. *See* multiculturalism
invisibility, of race, 291
Isaac, Paul D., 293
isolation, academic, 284, 288, 290–92, 296,
    300–301

James, Joy, 368
James, William, 357
Jayawardena, Kumari, 175
Jemison, Mary, 221–22
Jesus, Carolina de, 33
jobs, competition for, 18. *See also* competi-
    tion, academic
Johnston, Jill, 53
Jones v. Hallahan, 104
Jones, Marjorie, 92–93

Jones-Johnson, Gloria, 291
Joseph, Gloria, 52

Kadi, Joanna, 263–64
Kampf, Louis, 21
Keillor, Garrison, 188
Kennedy, John, 94
Khema, Ayya, 316
Kidwell, Clara Sue, 206
Kincaid, Jamaica, 30
King, Joyce, 29, 40
King, Martin Luther, Jr., 19, 343
King, Rodney, 211, 251
Kingdom, Elizabeth, 61, 65
Kingston, Maxine Hong, 30, 53
kinship: African models of, 274–75;
    American Indian, 134, 212, 221; and
    treaty making, 221. *See also* community
Kleinman, Sherryl, 293
Knight, Tracy, 92–93
knowledge: production of, 264; sources
    of, 234, 242, 244, 356. *See also* oral
    tradition
Kohlberg, Lawrence, 50
Kristeva, Julia, 26
Kwanzaa, 24

labor, exploitation of, 190, 199, 239,
    327–28, 332–33, 335–38
LaCapra, Dominick, 211
Lacey, Nicola, 352, 371
La Llorona, 134, 241–44, 251
La Malinche, 134, 206, 243, 254
language, in academics, 17, 352–53; and
    class, 333–34. *See also* bilingualism
La Raza, 245
Lauter, Paul, 21
law: American Indian, 214–15; and repro-
    ductive rights, 82
Leakey clan, 25
Lerner, Harriet, 318
lesbians: Afro-Caribbean, 278; and
    postmodern theory, 52–53, 57; and
    same-sex marriage, 86–129. *See also*
    queerness
Levine, Lawrence, 34–35
Lewis, Sinclair, 188
liberal individualism. *See* individualism
Limón, José, 241
Lipsitz, George, 254

literary criticism, feminist, 197–98
location, political economy of, 36–38
Lorde, Audre, 52, 237–38, 263; on anger,
    320–22
Losco, Joseph, 68
Love, Barbara, 53
Loving v. Virginia, 90–91, 99
loyalty: class, 188–89, 200–202, 249, 332,
    342–45; ethnic, 240
Lubiano, Wahneema, 272–73, 275
Lugones, María, 1, 52, 56

MacKinnon, Catharine A., 56
Maclean, Norman, 218
Madhubuti, Haki, 268
Madsen, Richard, 354–56, 358, 361
Maher, Frances, 22
Malcolm X, 19
male dominance: in Black community,
    270, 274. *See also* nationalism, mascu-
    line cultural
Mani, Lata, 180–81
manlyhearted women, 223
marginality, academic, 154–56. *See also*
    academic persona; hybridity; identity
marriage: as civil right, 91; definition of,
    86–87, 93–95, 99, 101, 106–8; economics
    of, 103; institution of, 6; interracial, 90,
    92, 97, 106, 108; legal reforms, 94–95;
    and patriarchy, 87–89, 93–94, 109–10;
    same-sex, 86–130. *See also* miscegena-
    tion laws
Martin, Valerie, 271–72
Marxism, and essentialism, 55
material conditions, and difference, 170
maternal imperialism, 173–74, 177
May, Claudia, 34
May, Elaine Tyler, 89
McConnell, Michael, 92
media, and discourse, 61, 63
Medicine, Beatrice, 368
melting pot, 34
memoir, as genre, 187–203
memory, collective, and colonization, 10
Mendoza, Valerie, 35
mentoring, academic, 288, 297–98, 366–67
meritocracy, and individualism, 349
metaphysical arguments, 49; and post-
    modernism, 54
methodology, and social critique, 239, 247

Milgram, Stanley, 300
military, gays in, 276
Miller, Alice, 312–14
Mills, C. Wright, 302
Milner, Lord, 174
mindfulness, 316–17; and academics, 263
Minnesota Historical Society, 192, 202
miscegenation laws, 90–91, 108
mobility, upward, 342
Modak, Ramabai, 175
mode of production/consumption, storytelling and, 132
Modern Language Association, 199
monocultural environment, 290–92, 356
monologic and polylogic, 47, 57
Moore, Pauline Kirton Clark, 17
Moraga, Cherríe, 30, 245, 249–52
moral development, 50
Morgan, Dr. Elizabeth, 74
motherhood, discourse of, and reproductive rights, 64, 67, 74–80
Moynihan report, 262–63
multiculturalism, 9, 27, 32, 34–39; and Chicana/o community, 252; defined, 36; and education, 33, 41, 134, 168; failures of, 247–48; and hybridity, 142; and pedagogy, 5, 11–12, 20, 30, 32; in sociology, 285–86
Murray, Shannon, 267
mythology: of American Indian women, 206; working-class, 195

NAACP, 267, 279, 355
Nair, Janaki, 172
Nandy, Ashis, 179
narcissistic disorder, and academia, 312–13
narratives, foundational, 9–11
Nation of Islam, 25
National Farmers' Organization, 370
National Organization for Women, 355
National Women's Conference (Houston), 102
National Women's Studies Association, 321
nationalism: Black, 24; and heterosexuality, 262–63; in India, 175–77; masculine cultural, 266–82; and Mexican-Americans, 235, 251

native: definition of, 140–41, 144; relation to ethnographer, 141–42
Native American peoples, and terminology, 227n. 1
Native Ethnographer, 137–67; defined, 143–44
Navajo Nation, 355
Nelson, Mark, 363–65
Neruda, Pablo, 245
Nestande, Bruce, 101
networking, academic, 301
Nicholson, Linda, 6, 47, 49, 51–54, 56
Nickel, Sara, 35

O'Barr, Jean, 22
Obenga, Théophile, 25
objectivity: and anthropology, 146–47, 151, 153–54; scientific, 212
O'Brien, Sharon, 214–15
Olsen, Tillie, 53
oral history, 31, 40
oral tradition, 244–45; and text, 243
originality, as value, 287
overspecialization, academic, 351–53

Paine, Thomas, 357
Palmer, Steve, 267–69
paradigms, and essentialism, 50–54
parent/child relationship, in pedagogy, 21–22
Pascoe, Peggy, 6
"passing," and ethnocentrism, 54
pathology, as critique, 248, 262–63, 268, 270–71, 274, 276
patience, 372; and anger, 316, 318–19, 323
patriarchy: and class, 199; critique of Indian nationalist, 176–77; and empire, 174; institutionalized, 350; and marriage, 87–89, 93–94, 109–10; military-style, 13; and racism, 172. *See also* nationalism, masculine cultural
Pavalko, Ronald M., 289
pedagogy, and authority, 22. *See also* multiculturalism
Percy, Walker, 224–25
Peretti, Burton, 34
personal/professional life, in Chicana experience, 234–59; and class, 196–202, 342–45
perspective, individualist, 348, 350

Phelan, Shane, 274
Phillips, Channing, 15
physicians, and individual rights, 72
pluralism, and theory, 47
Pocahontas, 206; and Pocahontas paradigm, 214, 217–18
political ideology, and art, 244–45, 247; and community, 251
polygamy, African model of, 274
polylogic and monologic, 47, 57
Ponce, Mary Helen, 238, 246, 248
Postiglione, Gerald, 27
postmodernism: and ambiguity, 252; canon of, 54; and deconstruction, 328, 335; and essentialist critique, 54, 56–57; and ethnocentrism, 56–57; and racism, 57; and social justice, 264; theory and language, 334
poverty: and education, 330; and individualism, 358; and reproductive rights, 75; and war, 343. *See also* class; reproductive rights, economics of
power relations: with academic peers, 148; in marriage, 110; and media, 61–62
Powhatan, 219
practice, and mindfulness, 319. *See also* theory/practice
Price Herndl, Diane, 205, 210
primitives, and construction of queers, 141
privacy: and individualism, 349; and reproductive rights, 66, 69, 71–72; and same-sex marriage, 103–4. *See also* public/private
privilege: academic, 2, 263, 329–30, 333–34, 341; class, 342; and critique, 2; and education, 224; limited for Mexican-Americans, 238; social, 349; women's limited, 63–64, 73
pro-choice movement, 61–62, 76–77, 81
procreation. *See* reproduction
production of difference, and anthropology, 157
pro-life movement, 61–62, 69, 75; and discourse of motherhood, 66–67
Pruitt, Anne S., 293
public discourse and social justice, 252. *See also* discourse, public
public/private: as dualism, 357; in reproductive rights discourse, 69, 71–73
Puritans, 33

queerness: and anthropology, 141–67; and Blackness, 266–82; coded as white, 276–77; defined, 279n. 1; ideology of, 262–63; and liberal feminism, 102; and queer studies, 342

race: and colonial history, 208, 211, 224; defined, 212–13; and ethnicity, 134, 215, 221, 362; and imperialist feminism, 174; and international issues, 285; and science, 211; sociology and study of, 283–310; theory and sociology, 285, 300
racial representations, described, 269–70
racism: and antiessentialism, 56–57; and Black queerness, 275; and identity, 342; and Mexican-Americans, 238; and patriarchy, 172; and reproductive rights, 75, 79; and rights discourse, 63, 76, 78–79; and sociology, 262. *See also* elitism, academic; race
Ramabai, Pandita, 175
Ramirez, Arnoldo, 108
Ramusack, Barbara, 173
Rao, Dhanvanthi Rama, 177
Rathbone, Eleanore, 177
Reagon, Bernice Johnson, 364
realities, multiple, 334
reflexivity, and anthropology, 147, 151
Register, Cheri, 133
relevance, in academics, 196
reproduction: and definition of marriage, 93, 99, 105–6; and technology, 82–83
reproductive rights, 6–7, 61–85; economics of, 62, 68–70, 75–76, 79; and technology, 82–83
research vs. teaching, 295, 317
resentment, in academia, 311–26
resources, allocation of academic, 288–89
retrofit, 8–46; defined, 5, 8
revolutionary, defined, 241
rewards, in academics, 366
Rhys, Jean, 30
rich smart/poor stupid, 327–46
Rich, Adrienne, 52, 61, 71, 199
right to life. *See* pro-life movement
rights: absolute, and reproduction, 64–67; discourse of, 6–7, 63–85; and liberalism, 349; limits of, 69; mythology, 81; opposite, 61, 80–81; and same-sex marriage, 88, 91; and universalism, 63–64.

See also individual rights, discourse of; individualism
Rimpoche, Lama Zopa, 324
Robinson, Lillian S., 369
Rodríguez, Richard, 30
Romero, Mary, 262–64
Rosaldo, Michelle, 49, 51, 56
Rosenmeier, Jesper, 26, 33
Roth, Julius A., 287
Roth, Philip, 246
Roumain, Jacques, 33
Rushing née Benton, Andrea, 15
Russ, Joanna, 82
Ruykeyser, Muriel, 131

Sacajawea, 206, 219
Sadik, Nafis, 79
same-sex marriage, 6, 86–129; in courts, 92
Sangari, Kumkum, 173
sati, 178–81
satire, in Chicana/o writing, 247
scholarship, legitimacy of queer, 146
schools, and collective memory, 10. *See also* curriculum; education, and class
science: and American Indian culture, 213; and multicultural studies, 32; and race, 211
segregation, distinctions of, 90–91
self-cherishing mind, 315, 324
self-concept and graduate school culture, 287–89
Self-Respect Movement of Madras, 178
separatism, 34
Sertima, Ivan van, 24
sex and gender, 88, 95–96, 100, 109–10, 148–49; and marriage, 91, 93; redefined, 89–90
sexual discourse, racialization of, 266–82
sexual revolution, 89
Shaffer, Lynda, 33
Shanley, Kathryn, 134
Sharp, William, 86
Shepard, Matthew, 279
silence, and academics, 264, 298
silencing, of working class, 343
Silvera, Makeda, 278
Simpson, O. J., 211
Sinclair, Upton, 195
Singer, John, 97–99
Singer v. Hara, 97–98, 100–101, 104

Sinha, Mrinalini, 2, 133
Slapikoff, Saul, 32
social constructionism. *See* constructionism
social justice, 233–59; and academic individualism, 347–74; and academy, 261–65; and American Indian women's history, 210; and Buddhism, 311–26; and pedagogy, 13, 19; and retrofit, 5–7; and sociology, 262, 283–310; and storytelling, 135; and university, 1; and working-class history, 343
social transformation. *See* social justice
Sociologists for Women in Society, 284
sociology: and academic experience, 287, 289, 292, 301; applied, 295; and social justice, 262, 283–310; status of women in, 284
Sollors, Werner, 212–13, 219
Solomon, Howard, 33
sovereignty, personal and tribal, 225
special interest groups, 354–55
Spelman, Elizabeth, 52
Spivak, Gayatri, 20
standpoint, 13, 20, 287, 295
Stanfield, John, 285
state, and reproductive rights, 64–65, 67
stereotypes: of American Indian women, 206; Chicano, 246; classist, 336–37; of queers, 141
sterilization, and reproductive rights, 65
Stoler, Ann, 172
Stonewall riots, 343
storytelling: art of, 248, 250; and identity, 131–36; limits of, 132; and social justice, 135; uses of, 242–43. *See also* un/common stories
strategy, individualist, 348–50
stress, in academia, 315, 317, 325
strike, Albert Lea, Minnesota, 190–93
stupidity: defined, 336; and working-class, 263, 327–46
subjectivity: and American Indian women, 211; conformity of, 13; and sovereignty, 225
Sullivan, William M., 354–56, 358, 361
supremacy, white, 275; and racial categories, 90–91
Supreme Court, and American Indian law, 214–15
Swidler, Ann, 354–56, 358, 361

Takaki, Ronald, 30–32, 34–35, 38
Tanner, Grace, 365–66
teaching vs. research, 295, 317
technology, reproductive, and patriarchy, 82–83
television, influence of, 356
Terry, David, 278
Tetreault, Mary Kay Thompson, 22
texts, and cultural interpretation, 180–81
theories, pluralism in, 47
theory: and essentialism, 47–48; and political concerns, 47–60; and storytelling, 132
theory/practice, 2, 7, 47–60, 134, 209, 211, 287, 334; and Chicana intellectuals, 246; in personal narrative, 264–65
Thich Nhat Hanh, 316–17
Thomas, Clarence, 272, 275
Thompson, Michael, 35, 39
Thoreau, Henry, 33
Tilak, Bal Gangadhar, 176
Tipton, Steven M., 354–56, 358, 361
Tlazolteotl, 239
Tocqueville, Alexis de, 34, 353
tokenism, 30, 174–75
Tom, Terrance, 105
Torres, Edén E., 134–35
Tovar, Inés, 238
tradition. *See* knowledge; oral history; storytelling
Tsing, Anna Lowenhaupt, 78
Twain, Mark, 30

un/common stories, 201
underclass, and race talk, 270
Uniform Marriage and Divorce Act, 95
unions, and working class, 190–92, 201; and Mexican-American community, 236
United Nations Commission of the Status of Women, 94
United Nations Human Rights Commission, 90
United Nations Population Fund, 79
United Packinghouse Workers of America, 190–93
university, and working-class workers and students, 327–46
"university gaze," 261–62
U.S. President's Commission on the Status of Women, 94

U.S. President's Task Force on Women's Rights and Responsibilities, 94

Varady, Carl M., 108
Vélez, Diana, 261, 263–64
violence: and abortion rights, 62; and culture of anger, 318, 323; and individualism, 358. *See also* reproductive rights
Viramontes, Helena, 248
virgin/whore dichotomy, 217–18
virtual reality, 14
Vizenor, Gerald, 30, 205, 208, 213, 226
voice: of American Indian women, 206; Chicana, 244, 248, 252; collective, 189, 202; and community, 133; imperial, 224; and memoir, 189; personal, 2; representativeness of, 205; "woman's voice," 49

Wagner, Sally Roesch, 219
Wampanoack, 33
Warhol, Robyn R., 205, 210
Watkins, Perry, 276–77
Weiss, Carin, 289
Welsing, Frances Cress, 268
West, Cornel, 355
Weston, Kath, 132–33
Wheatley, Phillis, 219
Whitney, Elspeth, 181
Whyte, William Foote, 300
Williams, Patricia, 80–81, 299
Williams, Rhonda, 262–64
Wilson, John, 362, 364
Wilson, William J., 272
winkta, 223
witch hunts, 181–82
women: absence from British India, 171–72; status of, in marriage, 110. *See also* working-class women
women of color, and graduate school, 283–310
women's liberation, 71
women's studies, 338, 342; and community, 367; compared to sociology, 295–96, 300
Woolf, Virginia, 30
work: defined, 317; effects of, 199, 337, 344; gender-specific, 18; need to define, 198
working class: academic assumptions

about, 327–46; and community, 14–17; defined, 340; mythology of, 195; students, 287; and university, 327–46. *See also* class
working-class studies, 343
working-class women, 253; Chicana, 239; interviews with, 202, 235; and mainstream society, 370; and postmodern theory, 52–53, 57, 328, 334–35
World Wide Web, 12

Wright, Gerald, 106
Wright, James W., 68
Wright, Richard, 207
writers and nonwriters, 235
Wyer, Mary, 22
Wynter, Sylvia, 20

Young, Iris, 360

Zamora, Bernice, 253